readings
on
modern
organizations

Amitai Etzioni

Columbia University

prentice-hall, inc. / englewood cliffs, new jersey

prentice-hall readings in modern sociology series
Alex Inkeles, Editor

© 1969 by
PRENTICE-HALL, INC., Englewood Cliffs, N.J.

Library of Congress Catalog Card Number: 69-20157

Printed in the United States of America

Current printing (last digit):
10   9   8   7   6   5   4   3   2   1

readings
on
modern
organizations

prentice-hall international, inc., London

prentice-hall of australia, pty. ltd., Sydney

prentice-hall of canada, ltd., Toronto

prentice-hall of india (private) ltd., New Delhi

prentice-hall of japan, inc., Tokyo

preface

There are several ways in which to view the 28 contributions assembled here. Most basically, they are a mixture of the editor's delight and frustrations; delight—at the fine selections he was able to place before his readers, and frustration—at the many equally fine ones that could not be accommodated. Each selection included here should hence be viewed as representing scores of others.

The second way to view these selections is to note their internal order which roughly follows that of the editor's own work, *Modern Organizations*. Bennis and Waldo introduce us to the field. Weber defines its central concept. Simon represents the later day, sophisticated version, of classical organizational theory. Baumgartel represents the Human Relations approach (see also Homans). Bensman and Rosenberg are "structuralist" (see also Blau and Scott).

Perrow opens the discussion of organizational goals, which is extended by a study of effectiveness by Georgopoulos and Tannenbaum. Zald explores the relationship between goals and structure. "Structure" is also the subject of the next six selections. While Zald studies correctional institutions (a coercive organization), Homan's report concerns a factory (a utilitarian organization). He also represents the essence of one of the most influential research works ever conducted in social science: The Hawthorne Studies. The Human Relations approach to industrial relations drew heavily on it. Dalton deals with the same kind of organization, but extends its analysis from that of the workers to that of higher, executive and staff, ranks. Hagburg's study of a labor union reminds us that the same person may be a member of two or more organizations simultaneously, all of which define demands for the same situation. His study serves to illustrate the qualities of participation in a voluntary organization (a normative one). Coser's study is like that of Dalton, in that it deals with the higher "ranks"—in this case of a normative organization, a hospital. More important, she raises the problems involved in organizations that draw for their work on professionals, which use knowledge on a massive scale. The authority of knowledge and that of rank (the basis of bureaucratic organization) do not readily mesh. Coser illustrates the problem and some modes of adaptation.

These "structural" selections illustrate the full compliance range. It extends from highly alienated members in highly coercive organizations to highly committed members in highly normative organizations, with utilitarian organization, less coercive and less normative ones, "in the middle," respectively. Other selections, included here for purposes other than illustrating the compliance continuum, can be studied with regard to the light they cast on it, including compliance "mixes." For instance, Katz and Eisenstadt deal with a governmental bureaucracy, which is typically utilitarian, but under the special circumstances studied, acquired some normative aspects. Schurmann deals with a political party, which is typically normative, but under the special circumstances studied, acquired some coercive elements.

Blau and Scott close the set dealing with organizational structures with a theoretical selection on two basis dimensions which run through all organizations: formal and informal. The formal represents the findings and insights of the classical tradition; the informal—of Human Relations; their mixture—enriched by Structural analysis—the great convergence toward which contemporary work in this field seems to be moving.

The next five selections, by Bales, Lindblom, Dror, Drew and Selznick (not counting Lindblom's reply to Dror) deal with the ways organizations are guided, with leadership and with decision-making. They all focus on the mixture of rational and the non-rational in guiding organizational efforts. Bales explores the structural and processual bases of leadership and shows the rise of the two main kinds of leadership (one more, one less, "rational") and the relations among them are neither accidental nor determined by their personalities, but much affected by the social situation. Lindblom is critical of the rational approach and offers an alternative way of making decisions. Dror views Lindblom's approach critically, and Lindblom has a chance for a rejoinder. Drew reports the outcome of an attempt to use rational models. Selznick closes this section by tying the sociological analysis of leadership to that of its ethical consequences and hence responsibilities.

Etzioni attempts to bridge the preceding "structural" selections with the following ones, which deal with the relation of organization to society. The question here is: to what extent is society itself manageable by various organizations? Kaysen asks to what degree society is managed by the business corporations, a discussion which needs to be extended to the role of other corporate bodies, from military services to civil rights groups. Michael and Bell represent two divergent views as to the impact automation in organizations will have on society. Katz and Eisenstadt deal with the relation between public administration and its immediate clientele, as distinct from its indirect one, with the society-at-large. Schurmann's study of the Community Party in China introduces both a cross-cultural dimension—and illustrates the universality of the problem of the articulation of political and "knowledge" authority.

Coleman and Barton show how organizations are studied. Coleman draws on his personal experience; Barton adds a review of the measurements used by scores of organizational studies.

AMITAI ETZIONI

table of contents

**readings
on
modern
organizations**

Beyond Bureaucracy

WARREN BENNIS

Most of us spend all of our working day and a great deal of our non-working day in a unique and extremely durable social arrangement called "bureaucracy." I use the term "bureaucracy" descriptively, not as an epithet about those "guys in Washington" or as a metaphor *a la* Kafka's *Castle* which conjures up an image of red tape, or faceless and despairing masses standing in endless lines. Bureaucracy, as I shall use the term here, is a social invention, perfected during the industrial revolution to organize and direct the activities of the business firm.

It is my premise that the bureaucratic form of organization is becoming less and less effective; that it is hopelessly out of joint with contemporary realities; that new shapes, patterns, and models are emerging which promise drastic changes in the conduct of the corporation and of managerial practices in general. In the next 25 to 50 years we should witness, and participate in, the end of bureaucracy and the rise of new social systems better suited to twentieth century demands of industrialization. (Sociological evolutionists substantially agree that 25 to 50 years from now most people in the world will live in industrialized societies.)

Corsica, according to Gibbon, is much easier to deplore than to describe. The same holds true for bureaucracy. Basically, bureaucracy is a social invention which relies exclusively on the power to influence through rules, reason, and law. Max Weber, the German sociologist who developed the theory of bureaucracy around the turn of the century, once described bureaucracy as a social machine.

Bureaucracy is like a modern judge who is a vending machine into which the pleadings are inserted together with the fee and which then disgorges the judgment together with its reasons mechanically derived from the code.

The bureaucratic "machine model" Weber outlined was developed as a reaction against the personal subjugation, nepotism, cruelty, emotional vicissitudes, and capricious judgment which passed for managerial practices in the early days of the industrial revolution. The true hope for man, it was thought, lay in his ability to rationalize, calculate, to use his head as well as his hands and heart. Thus, in the bureaucratic system social roles were institutionalized and reinforced by legal tradition rather than by the "cult of personality"; rationality and predictability were sought for in order to eliminate chaos and unanticipated consequences; emphasis was placed on technical competence rather than arbitrary or "iron whims." These are oversimplifications, to be sure, but contemporary analysts of organizations would tend to agree with them. In fact, there is a general consensus that the anatomy of bureaucracy consists of the following "organs":

A division of labor based on functional specialization.

A well-defined hierarchy of authority.

Warren Bennis, "Beyond Bureaucracy," *Trans-action*, 2 (1965), 31-35.

A system of rules covering the rights and duties of employees.

A system of procedures for dealing with work situations.

Impersonality of interpersonal relations.

Promotion and selection based on technical competence.

It does not take great critical imagination to detect the flaws and problems in the bureaucratic model. We have all *experienced* them:

Bosses without (and underlings with) technical competence.

Arbitrary and zany rules.

An underworld (or informal) organization which subverts or even replaces the formal apparatus.

Confusion and conflict among roles.

Cruel treatment of subordinates based not on rational or legal grounds but upon inhumanity.

The tremendous range of unanticipated consequences provides a gold mine of material for comics like Charlie Chaplin and Jacques Tati who capture with a smile or a shrug the absurdity of authority systems based on pseudologic and inappropriate rules.

Almost everybody, including many observers of organizational behavior, approaches bureaucracy with a chip on his shoulder. It has been attacked for many reasons: for theoretical confusion and contradictions; for moral and ethical reasons; on practical grounds such as its inefficiency; for methodological weaknesses; for containing too many implicit values and for containing too few. I have recently catalogued the criticisms of bureaucracy and they outnumber and outdo the ninety-five theses tacked on the church door at Wittenberg in attacking another bureaucracy. A small sample of these:

(1) Bureaucracy does not adequately allow for personal growth and the development of mature personalities.

(2) It develops conformity and "groupthink."

(3) It does not take into account the "informal organization" and the emergent and unanticipated problems.

(4) Its systems of control and authority are hopelessly outdated.

(5) It has no adequate juridical process.

(6) It does not possess adequate means for resolving differences and conflicts between ranks, and most particularly, between functional groups.

(7) Communication (and innovative ideas) is thwarted or distorted due to hierarchical divisions.

(8) The full human resources of bureaucracy are not being utilized due to mistrust, fear of reprisals, etc.

(9) It cannot assimilate the influx of new technology or scientists entering the organization.

(10) It modifies personality structure so that people become and reflect the dull, gray, conditioned "organization man."

Max Weber, the developer of the theory of bureaucracy, came around to condemn the apparatus he helped immortalize. While he felt that bureaucracy was inescapable, he also thought it might strangle the spirit of capitalism or the entrepreneurial attitude, a theme which Schumpeter later developed. And in a debate on bureaucracy Weber once said, more in sorrow than in anger:

It is horrible to think that the world could one day be filled with nothing but those little cogs, little men clinging to little jobs and striving towards bigger ones—a state of affairs which is to be seen once more, as in the Egyptian records, playing an ever-increasing part in the spirit of our present administrative system, and especially of its offspring, the students. This passion for bureaucracy . . . is enough to drive one to despair It is as if in politics . . . we were deliberately to become men who need 'order' and nothing but order, who become nervous and cowardly if for one moment this order wavers, and helpless if they are torn away from their total incorporation in it. That the world should know no men but these: it is such an evolution that we are already caught up in, and the great question is therefore not how we can promote and hasten it, but what can we oppose to this machinery in order to keep a portion of mankind free from this parcelling-out of the soul, from this supreme mastery of the bureaucratic way of life.

In what ways has bureaucracy been modified over the years in order to cope more successfully with the problems that beset it? Before answering that, we have to say something about the nature of organizations, *all* organizations, from mass production leviathans all the way to service industries such as the university or hospital. Organizations are primarily complex, goal-seeking units. In order to survive they must also accomplish the secondary tasks of (1) maintaining their internal system and co-ordinating the "human side of enterprise"—a process of mutual compliance here called *reciprocity* —and (2) adapting to and shaping the external environment—here called *adaptability*. These two organizational dilemmas can help us to organize the pivotal ways in which the bureaucratic mechanism has been altered— and found wanting.

Reciprocity primarily covers the processes which can mediate conflict between the goals of management and the individual goals of the workers. Over the past several decades a number of interesting theoretical and practical resolutions have been made which truly allow for conflict and mediation of interest. They revise, if not transform, the very nature of the bureaucratic mechanism by explicit recognition of the inescapable tension

between individual and organizational goals. These theories can be called, variously, *exchange, group, value, structural, situational*—depending on what variable of the situation one wishes to modify.

The *exchange* theories postulate that wages, incomes, and services are given to the individual for an equal contribution to the organization in work. If the inducements are not adequate, men may withdraw and work elsewhere. This may be elaborated upon by regarding "payments" to individuals as including motivational units. That is to say, the organization provides a psychological anchor in times of rapid social change and a hedge against personal loss, as well as position, growth and mastery, success experience, and so forth—in exchange for energy, work, commitment.

Management tends to interpret motivation in economic terms. Man is logical; man acts in the manner which serves his self-interest; man is competitive. Elton Mayo and his associates were among the first to see human *affiliation* as a motivating force, to view industrial organization as a *social* system as well as an economic-technical system. A manager, they stated, should be judged in terms of his ability to sustain cooperation. In fact, once a cohesive, primary work group is seen as a motivating force, a managerial élite may become obsolete, and the work group itself becomes the decision maker. This allows decisions to be made at the most relevant point of the organization, where the data are most available.

Before this becomes possible, however, some theorists believe that the impersonal *value* system of bureaucracy must be modified. In this case the manager plays an important role as the instrument of change in interpersonal relations. He must instill values which permit and reinforce the expression of feeling, experimentalism, and norms of individuality, trust, and concern. Management, according to R. R. Blake, is successful insofar as it maximizes a "concern for people" with "concern for production."

Others believe that a new conception of the *structure* of bureaucracy will create more relevant attitudes towards the function of management than formal role specifications now do. If the organization is seen as organic rather than mechanistic, as adapting spontaneously to its needs, then decisions will be made at the critical point and roles and jobs will devolve on the "natural" organizational incumbent. The shift would probably be from the individual level to cooperative group effort, from delegated to shared responsibility, from centralized to decentralized authority, from obedience to confidence, from antagonistic arbitration to problem-solving. Management centered upon problem-solving, that assumes or relaxes authority according to task demands, has most concerned some theorists who are as much interested in an organization's success and productivity as in its social system.

However, on all sides we find a growing belief that the effectiveness of bureaucracy should be evaluated by human *situation* as well as economic criteria. Social satisfaction and personal growth of employees must be considered as well as the productivity and profit of the organization. The criticism and revisions of the bureaucratic organization tend to concentrate on the internal system and its human components. But although it appears on the surface that the case against bureaucracy has to do with its ethical-moral posture and the social fabric, the real *coup de grace* has come from the environment.

Bureaucracy thrives in a highly competitive, undifferentiated and stable environment, such as the climate of its youth, the Industrial Revolution. A pyramidal structure of authority, with power concentrated in the hands of a few with the knowledge and resources to control an entire enterprise was, and is, an eminently suitable social arrangement for routinized tasks.

However, the environment has changed in just those ways which make the mechanism most problematic. Stability has vanished. As Ellis Johnson said, ". . . the once-reliable constants have now become galloping variables."

The factors accelerating change include:

The growth of science, research and development activities, and intellectual technology.

The increase of transactions with social institutions (and their importance in conducting the enterprise) — including government, distributors and consumers, shareholders, competitors, raw material and power suppliers, sources of employees (particularly managers), trade unions, and groups within the firms. There is also more interdependence between the economic and other facets of society, leading to greater complications of legislation and public regulation.

Competition between firms diminishing as their fates intertwine and become positively correlated.

My argument so far, to summarize quickly, is that the first assault on bureaucracy arose from its incapacity to manage the tension between individual and management goals. However, this conflict is somewhat mediated by the growth of a new ethic of productivity which includes personal growth and/or satisfaction. The second and more major shock to bureaucracy is caused by the scientific and technological revolution. It is the requirement of *adaptability* to the environment which leads to the predicted demise of bureaucracy and to the collapse of management as we know it now.

A forecast falls somewhere between a prediction and a prophecy. It lacks the divine guidance of the latter and the empirical foundation of the former. On thin empirical ice, I want to set forth some of the conditions that will dictate organizational life in the next 25 to 50 years.

The Environment

Those factors already mentioned will continue in force and increase. Rapid technological change and diversification will lead to interpenetration of the government—its legal and economic policies—with business. Partnerships between industry and government (like Telstar) will be typical. And because of the immensity and expense of the projects, there will be fewer identical units competing for the same buyers and sellers. Or, in reverse, imperfect competition leads to an oligopolistic and government-business controlled economy. The three main features of the environment will be (1) interdependence rather than competition, (2) turbulence rather than steadiness, and (3) large scale rather than small enterprises.

Population Characteristics

We are living in what Peter Drucker calls the "educated society," and I think this is the most distinctive characteristic of our times. Within fifteen years, two-thirds of our population living in metropolitan areas will have attended college. Adult education programs, especially the management development courses of such universities as M.I.T., Harvard, and Stanford, are expanding and adding intellectual breadth. All this, of course, is not just "nice," but necessary. For as Secretary of Labor Wirtz has pointed out, computers can do the work of most high school graduates—cheaper and more effectively. Fifty years ago education used to be regarded as "nonwork" and intellectuals on the payroll (and many of the staff) were considered "overhead." Today, the survival of the firm depends, more than ever before, on the proper exploitation of brain power.

One other characteristic of the population which will aid our understanding of the future is increasing job mobility. The lowered expense and ease of transportation, coupled with the real needs of a dynamic environment, will change drastically the idea of "owning" a job—or "having roots," for that matter. Participants will be shifted from job to job and even employer to employer with much less fuss than we are accustomed to.

Work Values

The increased level of education and mobility will change the values we hold about work. People will be more intellectually committed to their jobs and will probably require more involvement, participation, and autonomy in their work. (This turn of events is due to a composite of the following factors: (1) positive correlation between a person's education and his need for autonomy; (2) job mobility places the educated in a position of greater influence in the system; (3) job requirements call for more responsibility and discretion.)

Also, people will tend to be more "other-directed" in their dealings with others. David McClelland's studies suggest that as industrialization increases, "other-directedness" increases; so we will tend to rely more heavily on temporary social arrangements, on our immediate and constantly-changing colleagues.

Tasks and Goals

The tasks of the firm will be more technical, complicated, and unprogrammed. They will rely more on the intellect than muscle. And they will be too complicated for one person to handle or for individual supervision. Essentially, they will call for the collaboration of specialists in a project or team form of organization.

Similarly there will be a complication of goals. "Increased profits" and "raised productivity" will sound like over-simplifications and cliches. Business will concern itself increasingly with its adaptive or innovative-creative capacity. In addition, *meta*-goals will have to be articulated and developed; that is, supra-goals which shape and provide the foundation for the goal structure. For example, one *meta*-goal might be a system for detecting new and changing goals; another could be a system for deciding priorities among goals.

Finally, there will be more conflict and contradiction among diverse standards of organizational effectiveness, just as in hospitals and universities today there is conflict between teaching and research. The reason for this is the increased number of professionals involved, who tend to identify as much with the supra-goals of their profession as with those of their immediate employer. University professors can be used as a case in point. More and more of their income comes from outside sources, such as private or public foundations and consultant work. They tend not to make good "company men" because they are divided in their loyalty to professional values and organizational demands.

Organization

The social structure of organizations of the future will have some unique characteristics. The key word will be "temporary;" there will be adaptive, rapidly changing *temporary systems*. These will be "task forces" organized around problems-to-be-solved. The problems will be solved by groups of relative strangers who represent a set of diverse professional skills. The groups will be arranged on organic rather than mechanical models; they will evolve in response to a problem rather than to programmed role expectations. The "executive" thus becomes a coordinator or "linking pin" between various task forces. He must be a man who can speak the diverse languages of research, with skills to relay information and to mediate between groups. *People will be differentiated not vertically, according to rank and role, but flexibly and functionally according to skill and professional training.*

Adaptive, problem-solving, temporary systems of diverse specialists, linked together by co-ordinating and task evaluating specialists in an organic flux—this is the organizational form that will gradually replace bureaucracy as we know it. As no catchy phrase comes to mind, let us call this an *organic-adaptive* structure.

As an aside—what will happen to the rest of society, to the manual laborers, to the less educated, to those who desire to work under conditions of high authority, and so forth? Many such jobs will disappear; other jobs will be automated. However, there will be a corresponding growth in the service-type occupations, such as those in the "war on poverty" and the Peace Corps programs. In times of change, where there is a discrepancy between cultures, when industrialization and especially urbanization proceeds rapidly, the market for men with training and skill in human interaction increases. We might guess that approximately 40 percent of the population would be involved in jobs of this nature, 40 percent in technological jobs, with a 20 percent bureaucratic minority.

Motivation

Our above discussion of "reciprocity" indicated the shortcomings of bureaucracy in maximizing employee effectiveness. The "organic-adaptive" structure should increase motivation, and thereby effectiveness, because it enhances satisfactions intrinsic to the task. There is a harmony between the educated individual's need for meaningful, and creative tasks and a flexible organizational structure.

Of course, where the reciprocity problem is ameliorated, there are corresponding tensions between the individual's involvement in his professional community and his involvement in his employing organization. Professionals are notoriously "disloyal" to organizational demands.

There will, however, also be reduced commitment to work groups, for these groups, as I have already mentioned, will be transient and changing. While skills in human interaction will become more important, due to the growing needs for collaboration in complex tasks, there will be a concomitant reduction in group cohesiveness. I would predict that in the organic-adaptive system people will have to learn to develop quick and intense relationships on the job, and learn to bear the loss of more enduring work relationships.

In general I do not agree with Clark Kerr, Harold Leavitt, and others in their emphasis on a "New Bohemianism" in which leisure—not work—becomes the emotional-creative sphere

of life. They assume a technological slow-down and leveling-off, and a stabilizing of social mobility. This may happen in a society of the distant future. But long before then we will face the challenge of creating the new service-type organizations with an organic-adaptive structure.

Jobs in the next century should become more rather than less involving; man is a problem-solving animal and the tasks of the future guarantee a full agenda of problems. In addition, the adaptive process itself may become captivating to many. At the same time, I think that the future I described is not necessarily a "happy" one. Coping with rapid change, living in the temporary work systems, setting up (in quick-step time) meaningful relations —and then breaking them—all augur social strains and psychological tensions. Learning how to live with ambiguity and to be self-directing will be the task of education and the goal of maturity.

In these new organizations, participants will be called on to use their minds more than at any other time in history. Fantasy, imagination, and creativity will be legitimate in ways that today seem strange. Social structures will no longer be instruments of psychic repression but will increasingly promote play and freedom on behalf of curiosity and thought. I agree with Herbert Marcuse's thesis in *Eros and Civilization* that the necessity of repression and the suffering derived from it, decreases with the maturity of the civilization.

Not only will the problem of adaptability be overcome through the organic-adaptive structure, but the problem we started with, reciprocity, will be resolved. Bureaucracy, with its "surplus repression," was a monumental discovery for harnessing muscle power *via* guilt and instinctual renunciation.

In today's world, it is a lifeless crutch that is no longer useful. For we now require structures of freedom to permit the expression of play and imagination and to exploit the new pleasure of work.

Theory of Organization: Status and Problems

DWIGHT WALDO

. . . Of Maps and Models

There have been a number of attempts to survey Theory of Organization, indeed, to survey all theory of human organization, and to provide guidance to anyone seeking to understand the area. In line with my objective of providing guidance to whoever may be interested but uninformed I wish now to review in summary form some of the schemata that have been set forth as devices for classifying and understanding. I grope for the right word: schemata, maps, models, paradigms—these and others suggest themselves, but the usages are not standardized and clear. However, the usefulness of the presentation will stand or fall on its own, whatever name or names might properly be given to my choices.

In fact, I am here speaking of two types of conceptual patterns, and I shall distinguish between them by the terms *map* and *model*. By *map* I mean a conceptual scheme for organizing and classifying models or theories of organization; map is honestly metaphorical and implies no claim of precision. By *model* I mean a conceptual pattern for defining and organizing the phenomena of organization. While at the extremes the distinction between

Dwight Waldo, "Theory of Organization: Status and Problems." Speech delivered at the Annual Meeting of the American Political Science Association, Commodore Hotel, New York City, 1963.

maps and models is clear, the two tend at some point to overlap and meld. This occurs for various reasons, but centrally because writers consciously interweave their own new theory with their interpretation of past theory. (In the same way *typologies* are clearly distinguishable in definition from either maps or models, but tend to overlap and meld with them.) I shall begin with what to me are clearly maps and proceed to what are to me clearly models without trying to mark a clear separation.

But first let me illustrate the need for maps and models. I present in evidence the paper of a bright graduate student, reflecting on Theory of Organization after a survey course. There is, he says, "a bewildering choice between coexisting theories explaining different phenomena. The central issue is rarely whether X or Y is right, but whether they are talking about the same thing."

The neophyte stands, not before a broad ascending plane of theory punctuated by a series of dichotomous choices, but before an immense binary grid with different types of theory on one axis and different views of organization on the other.

Noting that "theory" itself is subject to at least six different meanings, he continues:

If we multiply these types of theory by the various styles of research design . . . and then by the various possible levels of generality . . . we have, at least potentially, an incredible number of entries on the vertical axis of our grid. . . . But the choice along the horizontal axis is perhaps even more difficult. An organization may be defined in terms of its purpose, its hierarchy of authority or status or expertise, its established or evolving pattern of communication or decision-making, its ideology or style, its historical experience, the congruence or incongruence in the value patterns of its members. It may be considered as a stable structure of formal or informal relationships or as an adaptive social process. It may be treated as a self-contained unit with a relatively discrete boundary between itself and its environment or as an open system in constant interaction over an ill-defined border. Its members may be conceived as whole human beings or analytical parts of human beings. It may be viewed as a communication network, a system of shared values, a set of roles; as a system of cooperation or a system of competition; as a problem in efficiency or a companionable search for Truth and Good.

Anyone reasonably familiar with the literature appreciates the point, and knows that the listings could be extended at length. I am not so foolish as to imagine that the provision of a handful of maps and models will solve all the organizing and methodological problems to which this student points; only that they are a help in understanding what appears as chaos.

Rationalism versus Organicism

The first map presented for understanding Theory of Organization is one that poses polar opposites around which theories cluster, or terminal points of a spectrum on which various models may be ranged. Of all the maps, it has perhaps the most general usefulness, but it has its limitations. In general, it is most valuable for getting the long view and the broad view, and as a sort of crude indicator of philosophical-ideological implications—though, since it is only a

crude indicator, it must be used with great caution. For detailed examination of the most recent period it is of limited value.

Various persons at various times and in differing ways have suggested a two-fold classification of rational model versus natural-system model, rationalism versus organicism. In the rational model, organization is viewed as instrument, as machine. It is presumed that man can consciously construct and manipulate organizations, that he can thus use rational processes to achieve consciously posited goals. On the other hand, in the natural-system model, organization is seen as more or less organic. It is an entity that in some sense has a life of its own, that strives to maintain its internal and external balance, to survive and perhaps to grow. It is extremely complicated, subtle, perhaps mysterious; it poses important limitations on what can be done with it by rule and will, at least quickly and with present limits of understanding.

As much of the history and interpretation of social-political theory has been written using this dichotomy for orientation, explanation, and exhortation, the general ideas need not be labored. For whoever wishes to use it in examining modern Theory of Organization more closely, I suggest two essays in application. One of these is Alvin W. Gouldner's "Organizational Analysis,[1] the other the concluding chapter of Sheldon S. Wolin's *Politics and Vision; Continuity and Innovation in Western Political Thought,* "The Age of Organization and the Sublimation of Politics."[2] Both treat the time-span of the French Revolu-

---

[1] In *Sociology Today; Problems and Prospects,* edited by Robert K. Merton, Leonard Brown and Leonard S. Cottrell, Jr. (New York, 1959), pp. 400-27.
[2] Boston, 1960.

tion to the present. Wolin's presentation is in much greater detail but, as there are many other themes and theses interwoven, not so sharply to the present point.

Classical, Neoclassical, and Modern

There is much agreement on the outlines of a map that shows the development of Theory of Organization during the past generation. This map classifies under three headings, though different names are used for them. There is much agreement on the general nature of the developments during this period of a generation but, of course, differing evaluations and interpretations. Also, though there is general agreement on the fact that we have recently (in the past five to fifteen years) entered into a third phase, there is considerable difference in outlook as to what this means and implies.[3]

By classical (or orthodox, etc.) Theory of Organization is meant the type of theory that "matured" in the thirties and is exemplified in Luther Gulick's essay "Notes on the Theory of Organization"[4] and James D. Mooney's *The Principles of Organization*.[5] It is sufficiently identified by noting that Gulick's essay popularized the mnemonic device, POSDCORB,[6] to indicate the work of the executive, and the fourfold distinction: organization by (1) major purpose, (2) major process, (3) clientele or matèriele, (4) place; and that Mooney's work discusses organization in terms of the coordinative principle, the scalar principle, the functional principle, the staff phase of functionalism, and so forth. This is the style of thinking about organization associated with the familiar organization chart. It is strongly oriented toward the values of economy, efficiency, executive control. In terms of the first map, it is correct and just to say that classical theory is rationalist in general tendency.

The origins of neoclassical theory are customarily associated with the Hawthorne studies of the 'twenties and, in particular, the writings of Elton Mayo. "Human relations" was and is often used to designate the approach or meaning involved. It perhaps is not precise or just to characterize it as organicist, but obviously its general tendency was away from the structural, mechanical, rational patterns of classical theory. It emphasized the affective and the social, and was both caused by and caused increasing attention of psychology, social psychology, and sociology to contemporary administered organizations. It "discovered" the small (or face-to-face) group in large organizations, and in general terms emphasized the notion that formal organizations have a large informal, i.e., social and emotional, component.

Before proceeding to the third or "modern" phase, a point should be made and a question raised. The point is that there is no sharp discontinuity between the three phases, that the

---

[3] A good review, using the classical-neoclassical-modern classification, is William G. Scott's "Organization Theory: An Overview and an Appraisal," 4 *Journal of the Academy of Management* (April, 1961), 7-26. This tells in some detail the story I but suggest.

[4] In *Papers on the Science of Administration*, Luther Gulick and Lyndall Urwick, eds. (New York, 1937), pp. 1-46. This work, generally, epitomizes the classical, but introduces the neoclassical.

[5] New York, 1939. This is the revised edition of a work first titled *Onward Industry*, published in 1931, with both Mooney and Alan C. Reiley as authors.

[6] To the uninitiated: planning, organizing, staffing, directing, coordinating, reporting and budgeting.

new is added to and more or less modifies the old rather than displacing it. Classical theory is still very much alive, is widely used and has its defenders;[7] and while there is now a tendency to regard "human relations" as passé, associated with certain excesses and naivetés of the past, there is a massive carry-over of concepts, attitudes, and research interests into the present period.

The question to be raised is: To what extent did the neoclassical represent a discrediting and repudiation of the classical? In some measure this question has already been answered by the statement that there is much continuity of the "old" in the "new." But the question has special relevancy because the neoclassical writers often wrote to attack or discredit the classical; and in the view of some did so. Others, however, have emphasized the continuity of emphasis upon the values of science, managerialism, and efficiency, and have viewed the grand strategy of neoclassicism as that of bringing the newly discovered non-rational into the area and under the control of the rational.

As we move to the third phase, into the period of the past few years, it becomes more difficult to make confident generalizations. There is wide agreement that the present is "different," quantitatively and qualitatively, from five or ten years ago, but there is far from unanimity as to the nature and implications of this difference, the various writers—naturally—seeing the present and trying to shape the future in the image of their own interests. Therefore, I shall try to indicate some

of the competing perspectives—or models.[8]

Some Contemporary Models: Decision-Making

Organization, by James G. March and Herbert A. Simon, both confirms the acceptance of a ternary view of the theories of the past generation and presents a leading contender among models presently urged: the decision-making model:

Because theorizing involves abstracting, the theorists of organization have focused their attention on the particular, partial aspects of the human organism that seem to them particularly significant for their purposes. Thus, the model of the em-

---

7 See William Scott, *op. cit.*, p. 9. See also Dwight Waldo, "Organization Theory: An Elephantine Problem," **21** *Public Administration Review* (Autumn, 1961), 210-25, 219-20. This essay is in some respects an earlier version of the present one.

8 However, I offer a third "map," of a different type: some writers, including Herbert A. Simon, have presented for consideration the conception that human society can be thought of as "layered," with organizations as a layer sufficiently discrete and important enough empirically to warrant study "in terms of themselves," i.e., not as a mere reflection of the individual, a subsidiary aspect of society as a whole, or what not. The exact "layers" offered vary somewhat, but the following designations, in the approximate sequence used, indicate the concept: individual, primary groups, organizations, institutions, society or social system. In the essay in which Simon develops this theme he states as follows: "In such a nest of Chinese blocks the smallest multiperson units are the primary groups; the largest are institutions (e.g., 'the economic system,' 'the state') and whole societies. We will restrict the term 'organization' to systems that are larger than primary groups, smaller than institutions. "Complexity in any body of phenomena has generally led to the construction of specialized theories, each dealing with the phenomena at a particular 'level.' Levels are defined by specifying certain units as the objects of study and by stating the propositions of theory in terms of intra-unit behavior and inter-unit behavior. (Cf. the sequence of elementary particle-atom-molecule in physics and the sequence: gene-chromosome-nucleus-cell-tissue-organ-organism in biology.)" "Comments on the Theory of Organization," **46** *American Political Science Review* (December, 1952), 1130-39.

ployee as instrument is prominent in the writings of the scientific management movement. In the last several decades the second model, emphasizing attitudes and motivations, has gained the greater prominence in research on bureaucracy, human relations, leadership and supervision, and power phenomena. The third model, emphasizing the rational and intellective aspects of organizational behavior, has been less extensively used than the other two, but is represented particularly by the work of economists and others on the planning process, and by the work of psychologists on organizational communication and problem solving.[9]

They view the three models as complementary rather than contradictory, but it is the third, viewing organization members as "decision makers and problem solvers," that they see as neglected and deserving of special attention.

Much of Simon's astoundingly productive career has been devoted to the development of the model of organization as decision maker, and it is impossible here even to outline the major ideas he has set forth in this connection.[10] Some observations on the decision-making perspective, some remarks in the way of characterization must suffice (satisfice?—anyway, I haven't the wit to maximize).

In the social science of the past two decades, decision making has been so amorphous, so protean a concept (or collection of concepts) that one is hard put to generalize about it— though of course to say this is to generalize about it. Certainly a typology of decision-making schemata that has been advanced would be elaborate, and

I have little notion of where Simon, or others who have consciously advanced or worked with decision making as model, would fit in a typology. I will observe only that, as I view it, Simon has used the term and the perspective in varying senses. These varying senses I do not view as incompatible, but rather as stricter or narrower, whole and partial; and perhaps the connections have not been made as clear as they should be for the ordinary consumer (i.e., me).

If one premises that "administrative processes are decisional processes," (and to be sure they *are*, whatever else they may be), one can of course take decision making as the lens through which all else is viewed. This is essentially the scheme of *Administrative Behavior*. Central philosophical-methodological matters (fact and value, end and means, science, efficiency, etc.) and old and new substantive concerns (specialization, authority, communication, etc.); affective phenomena and rational processes; individual psychology and organizational "thinking"—all are comprehended more or less (certainly by intent) in one schema. But Simon is fascinated, above all else, with logic, cognition, rationality; and later work tends to be more limited in scope, more sharply focused on the logical, cognitive, rational. (Some of it of course is addressed to these subjects, not ostensibly to organization and administration.) The result is that one might get the impression that the decision-making model is relevant (intendedly or in fact) only to a limited area of administrative-organizational phenomena. This would seem to me the plain implication of the introduction and organization of *Organization*. To repeat: I do not allege inconsistency or impropriety. My point is rather that decision making is not a single and precise model; but rather is

---

[9] New York, 1958, p. 7.

[10] In addition to *Organization*, see especially his *Administrative Behavior; A Study of Decision-Making Processes in Administrative Organization*, second edition (New York, 1957).

a term referring to a variety or family of models.[11]

Organization as System

Another current model—or, again, variety or family of models—is indicated by the word *system*. Not surprisingly, the essence of the matter is that it is argued that organizations are, and may best be studied as, systems; and by systems is meant entities that are more or less independent and consist of parts that constitute mutually dependent variables. There is, as we shall note, a fair amount of this outlook in the contemporary sociological approach,[12] but the system model, I should judge, deserves to stand by itself.

The distinctive outlook and flavor is given by the school of thought designated by the terms systems theory, or general systems theory, and finds expression in such terms as systems analysis. The central idea is that systems *qua* systems have generic qualities, and that the scientific enterprise as applied to all fields, from astrophysics to nuclear physics; the physical, the biological, the social, the psychological, can find a common ground and meaning in the concept of system. General systems theory is a unity of science movement, and at core has a group of analysts, advocates and "philosophers."[13] I do not assert, or suggest, that all who wish to view organizational phenomena as "system" have committed themselves to all the tenets of the philosophy (if this be the proper term). But it is a certain fact that persons committed to general systems theory wish to, and are trying to, apply systems theory to the study of organization; and it is my opinion that the ideas of the "movement" have a currency beyond formal adherents and that understanding the movement helps to understand this outlook on human organizations.[14]

The systems model is set forth and exemplified in William G. Scott's "Organizational Theory: An Overview and an Appraisal," referred to above. Scott, who if I interpret him fairly is an adherent to, or at least treads the border of a formal adherence to, systems theory,[15] views the contemporary or "third phase" of Theory of Organization as dominated by (certainly given most hope by) a commitment to the systems perspective and approach. System analysis "treats organization as a system of mutually dependent variables. As a result, modern organization theory asks a range of interrelated questions which are not seriously considered by other theories."

Key among these questions are: (1) What are the strategic parts of the system? (2) What is the nature of their mutual dependency? (3) What are the main proc-

---

11 The Inter-University Case Program also takes decision making as its central, organizing concept, and its interests are certainly different from Simon's.

12 I risk in all this creating the impression of separate and distinct "schools" that do not in fact exist. Certainly there is much overlapping and interweaving of interests and concepts. Simon, presumably, would admit that organizations are systems in the general sense described—but he does not subscribe formally to the "systems approach."

13 See *General Systems* (Yearbook of the Society for General Systems Research), *passim*.

14 Cf. fn. 2, regarding the distinction between Organization Theory and Theory of Organization.

15 "Modern organization theory is on the periphery of general system theory. Both general system theory and modern organization theory study: (1) the parts (individuals) in aggregates, and the movement of individuals into and out of the system; (2) the interaction of individuals with the environment found in the system; (3) the interactions among individuals in the system; (4) general growth and stability problems of systems." *Op. cit.*, p. 20.

esses in the system which link the parts together, and facilitate their adjustment to each other? (4) What are the goals sought by systems?[16]

He adds immediately that "modern organization theory is in no way a unified body of thought." And he cites both March and Simon's *Organizations* and Mason Haire's *Modern Organization Theory*[17] as examples of an attempt to see organization "in its totality."

Suffice it to add that in his discussion of the status of Theory of Organization (or more specifically and in his own terms, modern organization theory), he includes notice of many of the themes and concerns that one finds in *Organizations, Modern Organization Theory*, and other summaries and treatises: communications, balance (equilibrium), and so forth. There is, to repeat, much "content" in common from model to model. But there are also distinctly different emphases. For example, in this case, a treatment of cybernetics, a subject of great interest, and related, to general systems theory.

The Bureaucracy Model

Blau and Scott say of Max Weber's analysis of bureaucracy[18] that it is "undoubtedly the most important general statement on formal organization." I agree. Or perhaps I should state, more carefully, that to me the bureaucratic model is on the whole the most interesting and valuable. Models serve differing purposes, and the word "important" is ambiguous, concealing varied considerations of taste, interest, and objective. The bureaucracy model will not "do" what the classical model does. On the other hand, they complement each other in a remarkable way, the bureaucracy model viewing "from the outside" and putting classical theory in its setting. Except for the matter of legal authority and rules, which Weber stressed and classical theory tends to depreciate or ignore, the "fit" is remarkable.

This fit, the widespread acquaintance with classical theory, can be used as justification for a summary treatment of Weber's delineation of the structural and procedural characteristics of bureaucracy. He described it in terms so familiar to one who lives in a society of large, formal organizations and has, by formal instruction or by normal acculturation, become aware of the formal principles of its nature, that the description seems at first a tedious elaboration of the obvious: bureaucracy is a hierarchical structure of authority, with graded levels; jurisdictional areas are generally set by rule; there is methodical provision for filling positions, and so forth.

What is important about Weber's treatment of bureaucracy is not the simple picture of a familiar scene, but the theses and hypotheses (explicit or implicit) that accompany his description. For example, he asserts that the monocratic form of bureaucracy is *the* most efficient type of organization, that it tends to emerge whenever certain "preconditions" exist in a society, that in essentials it characterizes business as well as governmental organization. He says—or seems to say—that the spread and growth of bureaucracy is parallel with what are ordinarily regarded as the essential features of "civilization." His time perspective is

---

[16] *Ibid.*, pp. 15-16.

[17] Haire, ed., subtitled A *Symposium of the Foundation for Research on Human Behavior* (New York, 1959).

[18] The uninitiated—bearing in mind that the forepart of this essay is addressed to the interested but uninformed—can refer to Chapter VIII, "Bureaucracy," in *From Max Weber: Essays in Sociology*, translated, edited, and with an introduction by H. H. Gerth and C. Wright Mills (New York, 1946).

all of human history, and the formulation is buttressed by an impressive array of data from many societies, many disciplines.

The amount, variety, depth, and usefulness of the research and theorizing that has taken Weber's model as its point of departure is eloquent testimony to its importance. Much of writing that "takes off" from Weber is critical, some may even be fairly described as hostile, as I see it, but the result to date of the whole body of Weberian-bureaucracy scholarship is not so much to refute[19] as to add, to qualify, and to indicate the need for further research on various matters. The criticism and qualification follow these main lines: that Weber tended to overemphasize the strategic importance, the indispensability of existing key bureaucracies in modern society, especially with respect to revolutionary situations and transitions; that he overemphasized the functional and ignored the dysfunctional elements of bureaucracy; that he overemphasized the formal, rational aspects of bureaucracy and was blind to the affective, the whole social-emotional "internal environment" of large, formal organizations; that he failed to realize that there is a conflict, actual or potential, between discipline or authority based on formal position or hierarchy, and discipline or authority based on expertise, technical skill, or scientific knowledge.[20]

---

[19] A tremendous amount of controversy has centered on Weber's "ideal type" methodology, and some would argue that his presentation is such that it cannot be refuted: that is, the epistemology and logic used are not properly scientific, and that hence there are no properly formulated propositions that can be tested by accepted scientific means.

[20] The discussions and citations in Blau and Scott, and in Etzioni, cited above, open the door to Weberian-bureaucracy scholarship. An excellent review in more detail is

The Social-System Model

The bureaucracy model is primarily identified with the discipline of Sociology, but there is another, the social-system model, that is also primarily identified with sociology. Before describing it I feel obliged—lest I be misunderstood—to say still again that the various models are not to be thought of as sharply edged and discrete. They are conceptual frameworks found in varying degrees of clarity and consistency and used with varying levels of consciousness. A writer may opt strongly for one, try to give two "equal but separate" status, try to blend two or more, select one as favorite and try to shape the others to it, and so forth. Those whom I shall cite as exemplifying the social-system model also make some use of the bureaucracy model with no feeling of inconsistency or strain. Obviously, also, the social-system model has much in common with the simple, or general, system model described above.

The qualifying adjective, however, indicates also a much different outlook: organizations are systems, but they are *social* systems, functioning in and related to a total social field. I sketch in broad strokes, following Talcott Parsons: organizations in the sense of large, bureaucratic entities do not exist in primitive societies, but in complex, modern societies they come into existence as an aspect of functional specialization and differentiation. It is *"primacy of orientation to the attainment of a specific goal"* that is the

---

Alfred Diamant, "The Bureaucratic Model: Max Weber Rejected, Rediscovered, Reformed," in *Papers in Comparative Public Administration*, edited by Ferrel Heady and Sybil L. Stokes (Ann Arbor, Mich., 1962), pp. 59-96. Other key names include: Alvin Gouldner, Reinhard Bendix, Philip Selznick, Robert Merton, Talcott Parsons, Morroe Berger, and Robert Presthus.

"defining characteristic of an organization which distinguishes it from other types of social systems."[21] Goal attainment is seen as a product or output, which from one point of view constitutes an input for another organization (or organizations) and from another is conceived as functionally related to the whole society. Organizations are both small societies and part of and interrelated with the total entity, the larger system, society.[22] Those who have given some attention to understanding the Parsonian system of sociology will read much into this sketch, and will be aware of my danger in going further. But the basic ideas are simple, however complicated—and controversial—the implications.

Stripped more or less of its Parsonian complications and implications, this perspective is widely used, especially, but by no means only, by sociologists. As noted above, both Etzioni, and Blau and Scott define organization in Parsonian terms, and in general terms both books adopt the social-system model, and have much in common. They are also, however, sharply differing books in some respects. Etzioni sees three major types of social control, namely, *coercion*, *economic assets* and *normative values*. He takes *compliance* as his core variable; sees three varieties of compliance each corresponding to a type of social control; finds that organizations can be classified according to the predominance of coercive, utilitarian, or normative control. The most distinctive feature of Blau and Scott, however, is their typology of organizations on a *cui bono*—who benefits—basis. They find four basic categories of persons standing in relationship to organizations: "(1) the members or rank-and-file participants; (2) the owners or managers of the organization; (3) the clients or, more generally, the 'public-in-contact' . . . ; (4) the public-at-large. . . ."[23] They propose to, and do, classify organizations on the basis of "prime beneficiary," and believe that each type of organization so classified has distinctive qualities.[24]

Other Models

There are various other models, more or less discrete, well-developed,

[21] Chapter I, "A Sociological Approach to the Theory of Organizations," in Parsons's *Structure and Process in Modern Societies* (Glencoe, Illinois, 1963), pp. 16-58, 17. Italics in original.

[22] Because of the difficulty of paraphrasing Parsons, a rather lengthy quote:

> This article will attempt to analyze both this link [the *goal* link between an organization and society] and the other principal ones, using as a point of departure the treatment of the organization as a social system. First, it will be treated as a system which is characterized by all the properties which are essential to any social system. Secondly, it will be treated as a functionally differentiated subsystem of a larger social system. Hence it will be the other subsystems of the larger one which constitute the situation or environment in which the organization operates. An organization, then, will have to be analyzed as the special type of social system organized about primacy of interest in the attainment of a particular type of system goal. . . . Finally, the characteristics of the organization will be defined by the situation in which it has to operate, which will consist of the relations obtaining between it and the other specialized subsystems of the larger system of which it is a part. The latter can for most purposes be assumed to be a society. [p. 19]

[23] *Op. cit.*, p. 42.

[24] "Four types of organizations result from the application of our *cui bono* criterion: (1) 'mutual-benefit associations,' where the prime beneficiary is the membership; (2) 'business concerns,' where the owners are the prime beneficiary; (3) 'service organizations,' where the client group is the prime beneficiary; and (4) 'commonweal organizations,' where the prime beneficiary is the public at large," p. 43.

and important. The input-output approach, suggested above, can be taken as central rather than marginal. An equilibrium-cybernetics framework can inform the adoption of hypotheses and collection of data. The field of communications offers the perspective of an information-communication system. Organizations can be—and are—approached with biological metaphors: thus they are seen as "growing" or as interacting "organisms" in an environment. Some, in economics or imbued with its outlook, see organization in terms of an economy of incentives. Political scientists are inclined to insist that organizations exhibit the major features of a polity. Anthropologists may approach them as they would a primitive tribe, seeking in the organizational culture the functional equivalents of yams, raindances, and potlatches. Drama, medicine, and other areas can, and do, contribute perspectives for viewing organizational phenomena.[25] One of my students, coming from psychology, is convinced that organizations are, above all, to be viewed as structures of interacting anxieties; and wrote a thesis to prove it. I often think his truth is the most important one. Most of the questions working organizational analysts ask are less relevant than: Who can make whom anxious about what? How?

. . . The Problem of Comparativeness

By problem of comparativeness is meant the methodological issues raised by such questions as: What, precisely, is being compared and why? On what criteria of similarity and/or difference are two or more organizations chosen for comparison? Is it more sensible and fruitful to try to compare similar organizations from the same ("same"!) context, dissimilar organizations from the same context, similar organizations from dissimilar contexts, dissimilar organizations from dissimilar contexts? What structures or processes, precisely, should be compared? What theoretical apparatus motivates and guides the comparison, and what type of theory and/or practical results are envisaged as the product?

The problem of comparativeness is given point and urgency by the circumstance that at present there are two major scholarly-scientific efforts ostensibly devoted to comparing organization and administration, but rather sharply different in terms of persons involved, disciplinary bases, methods employed, motives, and so forth.

There is, on the one hand, the Comparative Public Administration approach or movement.[26] This has grown out of various historical and intellectual circumstances, among them that scores, indeed hundreds, of students of and experts in public administration have been overseas, typically in non-Western countries, on technical assistance missions during the past two decades; that this engagement of persons is continuing, that the prob-

---

[25] John M. Pfiffner and Frank P. Sherwood, in *Administrative Organization* (Englewood Cliffs, N.J., 1960), offer the intriguing notion of "transparent overlays." That is, upon the formal structure are imposed, for example, the sociometric network, the system of functional contacts, the grid of decision-making centers, the pattern of power, and the channels of communication. See chapter two.

[26] The door to this literature is opened by: Heady and Stokes, *op. cit.*; Ferrel Heady and Sybil L. Stokes, *Comparative Public Administration; A Selective Annotated Bibliography,* Second Edition (Ann Arbor, 1960); Fred W. Riggs, "Trends in the Comparative Study of Public Administration," **28** *International Review of Administrative Sciences* (No. 1, 1962), 9-15; Riggs and Edward W. Weidner, *Models and Priorities in the Comparative Study of Public Administration,* Papers in Comparative Public Administration, Special Series: No. 1, American Society for Public Administration (Chicago, 1963).

lems of institutional change and adaptation raised thereby are formidable, and that the objectives of the enterprise are generally alleged or assumed to be related to the major issues of our day. There is a large and growing literature, a substantial core of persons making this subject their central professional concern, and an organization, the Comparative Administration Group of the American Society for Public Administration, which has achieved the contemporary equivalent of a royal charter, a grant from the Ford Foundation. While the defining word *administration* is used instead of *organization*, administration takes place in administered organizations; and whether organization be defined in its general or its more limited sense, the Comparative Public Administration movement is strongly, centrally, interested in it.

On the other hand, there is the complex of interests and activities identified with and by the term Theory of Organization, and in this complex, while the interest in comparativeness varies, it is generally assumed, and often asserted, that the road to valid theories (of significant breadth, at least) is via the route of comparison. Recall in this connection the titles of the two most recent books that survey the field and advance a conceptual apparatus for dealing with it: Etzioni, *A Comparative Analysis of Complex Organizations,* and Blau and Scott, *Formal Organizations; A Comparative Approach.*

Now these two clusters of interest in organizational comparison are not wholly unknown to each other. To some extent they share models and concepts—those of bureaucracy most notably. But the differences in approach, interests, and "tone" is remarkable. The essence of the matter is that, at this stage in the development of the

two enterprises, comparative public administration is impressed above all else with the importance of the environment (the "ecology"), with national differences, with the dimension of *culture.* It is seeking strenuously to find or develop conceptual tools to enable them to work with such factors. "Comparative" tends to mean, by the route of interests, experience, and orientation, a comparison of some or all aspects of public administration *interculturally.* Theory of Organization, on the other hand, is still deeply rooted in and engaged with the American experience. In some varieties and in some ways it is closely related to the schools of business administration, and it draws heavily upon the many studies of administration and organization in a factory setting; business-industrial administration, almost exclusively in Western settings, is its chief base, and comparisons of American-British patterns in manning merchant ships, or American-German patterns in steel mill operation, represent approximately its empirical, geographical-cultural perimeter.[27] Within this perimeter, however, it is much concerned with comparison of a variety of organizations in terms of purpose or kinds: insurance companies, mines, universities, prisons, armies, and so forth, in addition to factories. In Theory of Organization the comparative method means primarily *intracultural* comparison.

My objective here must be limited primarily to calling attention to a formal paralleling of subject matter characterized however by a divergence in outlook and approach, which I think is

[27] Let me note Morroe Berger's *Bureaucracy and Society in Modern Egypt* (Princeton, N.J., 1957); and J. C. Abegglen's *The Japanese Factory: Aspects of Its Social Organization* (Glencoe, Ill., 1958), lest I be charged with ignorance of them: I said *approximate* geographical-cultural perimeter.

insufficiently noted and reflected upon. Space does not permit extensive treatment of all the matters involved, and in any case demands more penetration than I could bring to the task. I shall merely state what seem to me to be some of the defining circumstances and some of the issues.

First, I do not regard either school as the more—what is the right word?—sophisticated. Certainly if acquaintance with the literature of social science generally, and that part thought "behavioral" in particular, be taken as the measure, I cannot find a significant, over-all difference.[28] And if the Comparative Public Administration group is the more widely traveled, the research roots of the Theory of Organization group are the deeper. Second, it is obvious that somewhat different conceptions of the scientific enterprise are involved. The Theory of Organization group would be inclined to argue that the scientific enterprise necessarily "starts at the bottom" and must proceed step-by-step if not necessarily slowly; and that only wasted effort and confusion can come by trying to master organization at the intercultural level before it is mastered at the intracultural level. The Comparative Public Administration group would be inclined to argue that success in science does not always follow a cautious, Fabian strategy; and that, in any case, it is administration at the intercultural level that is perforce their concern and that they must study as best they can.

Third, it is my impression that Theory of Organization, for all its methodological and theoretical sophistication, is more culture-bound, more Western, than is appreciated. My own foreign experience is limited to Western countries, but I have had also the advantage of working through the literature with able and perceptive students from non-Western cultures; and I have been impressed with their feeling that the formulations are "not right" for their societies, their conviction that more of our history, values, and general social organization than we imagine is absorbed into our models and theories. Often coming from societies in which hunger is ever-present and the extended family is firmly cemented into social structure, they find theory built around such things as "The Decision to Participate" rather irrelevant if not indeed absurd. They have convinced me that they have an important point.[29] For all of my respect for Weber's model of bureaucracy, indicated above, I now suspect that his modern European (and specifically German) background are more relevant to his reading of history than appears on the surface.

Fourth, Blau and Scott call attention to a dilemma that is centrally involved in the comparative study of organizations. If it is conceded both that comparative study is essential to scientific method and that organizations can only be understood in context, then we face heroic difficulties. To "solve" the problem of comparability at one level, merely poses it at another. Whole societies, or cultures, must eventually be compared; and if it is conceived that, in fact or eventually, there is but one world-wide "organization of societies," what is *it* to

28 There are significant differences in heroes adopted, research tools chosen; but I don't know how these differences weigh out. I have explored them at some length in a yet unpublished paper, "Comparative Public Administration: Prologue, Performance, Problems, and Promise."

29 For this reason I think Etzioni's decision to focus attention on power-compliance is a useful step. Or half step, as it is so narrowly focused on the West.

be compared with?[30] While in their opinion the dilemma cannot be resolved "in principle," they feel that "once it is recognized it poses little difficulty for specific empirical studies with limited objectives."[31] I concur that, because the dilemma cannot be solved "in principle," we should not abandon the enterprise of social science in general and the comparative study of organization in particular. But I have been too long concerned with the problems of the Comparative Public Administration group to be content with: "In short, the important practical implication of the dilemma is that the research design must be adapted to the level of organization to be explained,"[32] followed by a treatment limited to the empirical-theoretical terrain of Theory of Organization.

Problems of Identification of Objective, Level of Generalization, and Types of Theory

Despite the great philosophical-methodological sophistication that is represented in Theory of Organization, which in the mass truly awes me, I feel nevertheless that there is much confusion, misunderstanding, and misdirected effort in the movement. I wish to try—I am not sure I can—to express what bothers me. Please give me credit for trying to address these problems at their own level, so to speak. I may be wrong in my assessment. But I am not, at any conscious level, against science.

I begin by noting what to me is a very interesting phenomenon. A generation ago students of public administration made confident, dogmatic statements about universal principles of administration, either existing or, beyond all doubt, awaiting to be discovered. The events of the past two decades have so shaken the confidence and altered the focus of students of Public Administration that if such statements have been made recently I am not aware of them. On the other hand, such confident faith is often expressed in the recent literature of Theory of Organization. James D. Thompson and associates, for example, state: "We firmly believe that there is in the making a rigorous science of administration, which can account for events in particular times and places and for the ethical or normative content of those events without itself incorporating the particular conditions and values of those events.[33] Similarly, Etzioni prefaces his conviction that "eventually, the comparative study of organizations" will "establish the truly universal propositions of organizational theory."[34]

Now perhaps such statements are

---

[30] See pp. 10-15, op. cit. "A fundamental dilemma is posed for the study of organizations by the double requirement of examining the interdependence between elements in a social structure, on the one hand, and of observing many independent cases to substantiate generalizations, on the other . . . even when comparable empirical data on many organizations are available, conceptualizing the organizations as independent cases would involve ignoring their interdependence in the larger society, whereas focusing on their interdependence would leave the investigator, once more, with only one case," pp. 11-12.

[31] Ibid., p. 13.

[32] Ibid.

[33] Comparative Studies in Administration (Pittsburgh, 1959), p. 4.

[34] Op. cit., p. xiv. And another, at random: "Although the dominant emphasis is on commercial and industrial organizations, the reader will appreciate that the principles discussed apply to any type of organization, including governmental, philanthropic, military, educational, voluntary or political." From the Preface of Some Theories of Organization (Homewood, Ill., 1960), edited by Albert H. Rubenstein and Chadwick J. Haberstroh. From the viewpoint of science one might presume the applicability of the "principles" to all these areas might be a matter to be proved, not "appreciated."

not to be taken too seriously. Perhaps their intent or function is heuristic, inspirational (religious, as I define the term): prefatory to the scientific enterprise and not a part of it. But I submit that to posit as the end of the scientific effort the exact nature of the product that will result may be to confuse and skew the search; to keep us from what science is possible in a futile search for what may be impossible. I have no doubt we shall learn more and more about organizations, information properly labeled scientific, as we study them further. I have no doubt that various theories of and relevant to organization will achieve firmer scientific status and that these will have great practical usefulness. But I regard the idea of achieving "a" or "the" Theory of Organization, completely abstract and value-free, as an illusion.[35] My point is that organization in the more restricted sense

identified above—administered, formal, complex, large-scale—does not exist in a state of nature, but only in particular *societies* that have reached a certain *level* and *type* of "development"; that organizations in such societies reflect, are saturated by, the values of the society—values generic to the type as well as specific to the particular time and place; that we may be witnessing (however depressing the thought) the development of a homogenized world—urbanized, industrialized, etc.—that will provide a basis for a world-wide organizational culture; that in such case we may, and indeed certainly will have, achieved considerable scientific knowledge about realizing purposes through these organizations; but that this scientific knowledge will be relevant to the specific types of values that can be achieved by organizations in a certain type of society.

It may be argued that I have given my case away: that I have just admitted a value-free theory that describes this type of society, and that prescribes how purposes in it can be achieved ("efficiently" perhaps), is possible. Perhaps—if it makes anyone happy so to define the term. I am not interested in winning an argument, but rather in promoting a discussion free from the rigidities and absurdities that too often arise when "values" and "science" are mentioned in the same room. I think it is a quite respectable —scientific if you like—enterprise to study how organizations can achieve purposes efficiently. I also specify that the enterprise will advance more swiftly and surely if we specify what particular purposes we are interested in; but that if we *don't* choose to so specify, a certain class and range of purposes is nevertheless necessarily implied in the simple but crucial fact that we are addressing ourselves to *organization*.

---

[35] A British observer recently compared this fixation on a universal science with an attempt to establish a science of ball games—not of cricket or football, but of ball games in general. Without commenting myself to all of *his* reservations, I would say in this language that I confidently expect more science on all the individual ball games, some even on families of related ball games; but never a generalized Science of Ball Games. If I'm ever proved wrong I'll certainly not be around to learn of it.

My friend James C. Davies has convinced me that there is much to be gained in approaching problems of politics by way of the physiological-psychological substructure of man—Man. But I will at least record in a footnote my thought that if and when the search for Universal Laws of organizational behavior conquer the cultural, they *may* find some problems in the biological—a thought that, in remembrance of Dachau, squeamish friends once persuaded me to delete from a manuscript. How can one know in advance of knowing that race (read: geographically differentiated distribution of genes, if squeamish) makes no difference in patterns of human cooperation that are (a) possible or (b) optimal or efficient for specified purposes?

It is my opinion that harmful bi-polarization of attitudes and confusion of thought arises from a style of Manichaeism characterizing current thought that prides itself on its sophistication, from the use of various paired terms that suggest sharp dichotomies when in fact the phenomena involved and the needs of our discourse are much more varied and subtle.[36] I urge, in this connection, a close look at the distinction between pure and applied science;[37] between description and prescription; between normative and non-normative; and of course between fact and value.[38]

In this vein I call attention to the fivefold classification of the "abstractions" of Theory of Organization used by Sherman Krupp in his critique: (1) expository, (2) analytical, (3) empiri-cal, (4) inductive, and (5) normative.[39] This schema may or may not be "best" or "correct," but it strikes me as very useful for the purpose, a great improvement upon the customary dichotomizing of the world. Also, I commend the book heartily to whoever has doubts that putatively value-free Theory of Organization is in fact value-based and value-oriented.

The Problem of Political Science and Public Administration

There is over-all a wide gap between the interests and activities of the scholars identified with Theory of Organization and the interests and activities of scholars trained in and identified with political science and the related or subdiscipline of public administration. Very few persons are identified with both "camps," and the exceptions, such as James March, would appear to be playing two separate professional roles. Consider the following data.

In the three recent book-length general treatments of Theory of Organization, students of political science or public administration—either persons now living or those a part of the "traditions"—are scarcely noted, quoted, or cited. I have just spent the past half hour with the bibliographies and indexes of these books, making a quantitative study—I know a fashionable trend when I see it. Report: March and Simon have both a general index and a numerical index to variables, but not a name index. However, of the approximately 750 names included in their bibliography, I found only 23 (including the authors) who, by a generous construction of the terms, are identified with political science or pub-

---

[36] The cognoscenti of methodology are properly irritated at the distinction made by the man on the street between "theoretical" and "practical"—what is so practical as a good theory? I am suggesting that their dichotomies are also prejudices, which skew and limit.

[37] I think I have finally discovered why Simon's *Administrative Behavior* has baffled and irritated—as well as informed and enlightened —me. In terms of his distinction in the Appendix between theoretical and practical sciences, I had regarded the body of the work as putatively an exercise in theoretical science. This may have been quite unwarranted in terms of his intention. Perhaps he regarded it as treating both, and saw them as joined through his fact-value, ends-means discussion. In any event, as I now see it, the material therein varies widely as between the poles of "pure" and "applied," or "theoretical" and "practical." (In terms of my presentation here, the efficiency criterion is not simply factual, but both fact *and* value.)

[38] We are well along with this one, in some respects. Incidentally, and to clarify my position: I have no doubt that these dichotomies serve, and will continue to serve, in making certain gross and general distinctions. But the distinctions they make must be regarded as just that: gross and general.

[39] *Pattern in Organizational Analysis: A Critical Examination* (Philadelphia and New York, 1961), Chapter 4.

lic administration.[40] Blau and Scott's index of names contains 255 entries, of whom 11 can be identified with political science or public administration. Their extensive bibliography has been set aside for further research, but it would appear to maintain about the same proportion as the Index. In Etzioni's selected bibliography of approximately 850 names, I identify 13 as connected with our disciplines; in his name index of approximately 750 names I identify 19. I believe it is customary in quantitative studies to recognize error may have crept in, and I generously grant a possible miscalculation of 5%. However, figures do not tell the whole story. Some of the persons included in my calculation of persons identified with political science or public administration are marginal in the sense that their identification is through formal training not later identification; or while noted, only in passing; or if listed in a bibliography, not because they were actually relied upon or referred to in the presentation.

How is this gap to be accounted for? What does it signify? Obviously, those identified with and who are taking the lead in identifying Theory of Organization either are (1) unacquainted with the work of political scientists and public administrationists, or (2) if acquainted with it have a low estimate of it, or (3) if they have a high estimate of it do not regard it as part of or relevant to Theory of Organization. The sociologists probably are not well acquainted with the literature of these fields; and are perhaps inclined both to regard government and politics as a minor subdivision of society, and political scientists as obsessed with a nonscientific study of history, values, and such things. March and Simon certainly are acquainted with the disciplines; their conclusion that they are not making a respectable contribution to Theory of Organization is implicit but glaringly obvious.

This discussion is under the heading of *Problems*. If the gap indicated is a problem, as to me it patently is, to whom is the problem relevant? That it is a problem relevant to political science and public administration I am willing both to concede and to argue. We need more awareness of and dissemination of information about the research and theorizing taking place under the heading of Theory of Organization; there are fresh data, new dimensions and directions, relevant to our historic and (or) proper concerns. In public administration we need more research that pays conscious, careful attention to the development and testing of theory—behavioral research, if this be the proper designation.

But I argue also that the gap is at least equally a problem to Theory of Organization: that we are not all that old-fashioned, bad, and irrelevant. Let me be specific: "sharp" perhaps, but not by intent offensive. It does not overstate the matter to say that March and Simon systematically disregard the literature of political science and public administration. But this literature contains much in the way of theorizing and in the way of case studies[41]

[40] One blinks to find Aristotle's *Politics* and Plato's *Meno* adrift in this behavioral sea— I do not recall that they figured in the presentation. A small act of piety?

[41] More than eighty case studies have now been published by the Inter-University Case Program (and its predecessor, C.P.A.C.). These are reports, often in great depth and detail, centering on the making of decisions in organizations, but covering also a wide variety of other organizational phenomena. There is no reference—as I recall—to any of these reports (or to the war histories) in the three summaries we are considering. What-

and clinical observations that bears on the subjects they discuss; and is fully as "respectable" as many of the sources they do acknowledge. For example, they adduce a "Gresham's Law" of planning: "When an individual is faced both with highly programmed and highly unprogrammed tasks, the former tend to take precedence over the latter even in the absence of strong over-all time pressure."[42] This is an idea appearing repeatedly in the literature of public administration. In the federal government twenty years ago it appeared in such maxims of the administrative craft as "Operations drives out staff work."[43]

It was noted with approval above that Etzioni takes the power-compliance relationship as the foundation for his presentation—which would seem to make it highly relevant to the world of political science and public administration. The subtitle is, recall: *On Power, Involvement, and Their Correlates*. But Etzioni, with a thoroughness truly amazing, turns a blind eye and a deaf ear not only toward our disciplines, but toward government. Harold Lasswell rates a footnote citation and Robert Michels (is he ours or theirs?) is given a respectable role; but Paul Appleby and Mary Parker Follett are not mentioned, and Norton Long, who has written at length and incisively on power in organizations, is ignored. Machiavelli, Hobbes, Sorel, Catlin, de Jouvenal, Morgenthau, are not men-

tioned. On pages 66-67 is a summary of classification of organizations, under the categories "Predominantly coercive," "Predominantly utilitarian," and "Predominantly normative"; included in the classification are organizations commonly or possibly governmental, such as prisons and universities, but not government departments, bureaus, etc.—nor government as an entity. Political parties get some attention, as does the military, but one would never guess from studying the table that millions of Americans are publicly employed in complex organizations other than prisons, schools, and mental hospitals.[44] "Government," "Democracy," "decentralization," "delegation," etc. do not appear in the Index. It comes to this: I found Etzioni's book rewarding but I am certain that he could contribute still more to my understanding of political science and public administration if he could be persuaded to give our concerns some attention; and equally certain that some attention to these concerns would in turn enrich his understanding of complex organizations.

The Problem of Critical Examination and Constructive Synthesis

A final problem on which I wish to comment is that of getting a critical examination of Theory of Organization, an examination in depth, in breadth, and continuing; and which will not be merely critical in the sense that it asks sharp questions about premises, directions, conclusions, and implications, but constructive in the sense that it is understanding of the nature of the scientific enterprise and appreciates in a mature way the nature and values of

---

ever the generic or individual shortcomings of the cases, that they should be ignored is incredible, considering some of the sources (including fiction) that are cited.

[42] Page 185. Perhaps my example is not strategic; there *is* a reference to Gaus and Wolcott on this page.

[43] It might be objected that in this form it was folk wisdom. But I do not understand March and Simon to be claiming it is now science because they have discovered it.

[44] Of course, the classification is not represented as inclusive, only as characterizing "subcategories of larger common-sense types." But are government departments small or out of the realm of common-sense?

organizations in the modern world. What I see as desirable, though it centers on Theory of Organization, really goes beyond it and, for that matter, beyond academia. What I speak for, I suppose, is a continuation, a broadening, and a deepening of the now generations-old dialogue about the role of organizations vis-a-vis our total polity and society that Sheldon Wolin reviews in the final chapter of *Vision and Politics*, "The Sublimation of Politics."

As observed above, this is a complex essay, interweaving many themes, but a central thesis is that during recent times there has been an undue emphasis by many writers upon organizations and their alleged political roles in society, or their alleged political attributes if considered as "small" or quasi-polities—a "flight from that general dimension which, in the past, has served as the basis for viable theories of political life."[45] I agree by half with what he says: There is a range of important theoretical and practical problems that embrace the whole society or polity, which we risk obscuring and confusing with various academic-intellectual versions of the philosophy that what is good for General Motors is good for the country. (Something Peter Drucker once in effect accused me of; and in part the criticism was justified.) On the other hand it has long been my opinion that in general those whose official position it is to deal with political and social theory— "the general political dimension"—are not fully sensitive and responsive to the existence and implications of organization and administration in our day; that they are not performing the

function of relating these phenomena to the "general political dimension;"[46] and that in result much of the operative political theory of our day is written perforce by persons who don't know they are writing it, perhaps shouldn't be writing it, and may be writing it badly.[47] In our time the point of view that the "practical details" of government are for clerks to arrange after doctors have decided on principles is not simply inadequate as an approach to administration, it is a guarantee that political theory will be stable, precious, or dangerous.

The problem of getting criticism in and of Theory of Organization is not only broader than Theory of Organization as used here, but of course broader than "political theory" as customarily construed in our circles. My thesis is that any theory of organization, including those putatively simply causal or descriptive, is by implication and on analysis, either an argument for or against something— something social, political, ethical; that

---

[45] *Op. cit.*, p. 432. Speaking of Berle, Drucker, and others, he says: "The error in these theories comes from trying to assimilate political conceptions to non-political situations," p. 433.

[46] A central point is, obviously, that the "general" political dimension, the dimensions of "the political art," are not givens of a natural order, but defined by each historical period and relative to it. City-state, feudalism, nation-state, world-state, whatever has been and may be in the way of the general, each is relevant to the defining technical-cultural-ideological circumstances of its day. No one, I presume, would argue that political theory in our day can *ignore* organizations, which constitute one of the chief defining circumstances and may well be the central one.

[47] Of course, this may be more generally true than we imagine. As I interpret it, most of the writings that are the subject matter of a survey course in political theory were not produced by someone saying to himself as he sat down to his desk: "Now I am going to theorize about politics." Rather: "What are the facts, the problems, the solutions?" One man's facts are another man's theory. And, of course, my position is further that one man's scientific theory is another man's ethical-political theory.

questions of methodology and the particular methodology selected, have inevitable ideological and ethical implications, raising as they do the question, "*Who* looks at *what, why, how, for what purpose?*; that there is no escape from, only blindness to, these facts. I think I understand and appreciate, in a way I once did not, the cause of this blindness: the harsh behavioral rejection, the repugnance against a seeming obscurantism, dilettantism, formalism, of those who appeared only interested in an everlasting scrutiny of the inscrutable, values. I hope we may be reaching not only a *modus vivendi*, but a situation in which the scientific and the normative (those damned false dichotomies, again) mutually inform and direct each other. In this connection I note with satisfaction several recent works by students knowledgeable on "both sides," which seek to explicate the relationships involved between the theory and facts of organization, and problems of personal fulfillment, cultural development, institutional growth, and ideological commitment.[48]

---

[48] Various items cited, such as Krupp and Wolin, may be so construed. I call attention in this connection especially to various works of Chris Argyris, centrally perhaps his *Understanding Organizational Behavior* (Homewood, Ill., 1960); Victor A. Thompson, *Modern Organization; A General Theory* (New York, 1961); Robert Presthus, *The Organizational Society; An Analysis and a Theory* (New York, 1962); Alfred de Grazia, "The Science and Values of Administration," Parts I and II, **5** *Administrative Science Quarterly* (December, 1960; and March, 1961), 362-97 and 556-82; Carl J. Friedrich, "Organization Theory and Political Style," in *Public Policy* (1960), a publication of the Graduate School

The problem that concerns me is, of course, much broader than our own professional concerns, cutting through society and involving the artist as well as the scientist: How to get a balanced view of organization in the organizational society? How to reconcile and balance undoubted goods and undoubted evils, when one comes—inevitably though in varying proportions and mixes—with the other? Are there paths through the thicket of thorns, more goods with fewer evils? Here our literary lights, to whom part of the task should fall, are almost completely useless; they are almost to a man and by definition antiorganizational. If organization is treated by them at all it is as the enemy—gray, brutal, obscene; or at best as neutral terrain, a mere setting for humor, violence, sex, or exploration of the psyche. Similarly most of our essayists, critics, "philosophers"— the intelligentsia as an establishment: organization is an evil. As the literary men, they suffer with K and refresh their souls at Walden Pond; but they live by choice in Manhattan, Princeton, or the Connecticut "country." Of course, organization *is* an evil—gray, brutal, obscene, as charged. It thwarts, deforms, destroys, human beings. It is also a good: it sends royalty checks and honoraria to its critics, provides them with food, clothing, shelter, transportation, education, recreation, protection against many forms of loss and violence, care in sickness, and, on request, sacraments and solace. . . .

---

of Public Administration, Harvard University, pp. 44-61. To say that I approve of the nature of their inquiries is not, of course, to say I agree with all their conclusions.

Bureaucratic Organizations

MAX WEBER

Legal Authority: The Pure Type with Employment of a Bureaucratic Administrative Staff

The effectiveness of legal authority rests on the acceptance of the validity of the following mutually inter-dependent ideas.

1. That any given legal norm may be established by agreement or by imposition, on grounds of expediency or rational values or both, with a claim to obedience at least on the part of the members of the corporate group. This is, however, usually extended to include all persons within the sphere of authority or of power in question—which in the case of territorial bodies is the territorial area—who stand in certain social relationships or carry out forms of social action which in the order governing the corporate group have been declared to be relevant.

2. That every body of law consists essentially in a consistent system of abstract rules which have normally been intentionally established. Furthermore, administration of law is held to consist in the application of these rules to particular cases; the administrative process in the rational pursuit of the interests which are specified in the order governing the corporate group within the limits laid down by legal precepts and following principles which are capable of generalized formulation

and are approved in the order governing the group, or at least not disapproved in it.

3. That thus the typical person in authority occupies an 'office.' In the action associated with his status, including the commands he issues to others, he is subject to an impersonal order to which his actions are oriented. This is true not only for persons exercising legal authority who are in the usual sense 'officials,' but, for instance, for the elected president of a state.

4. That the person who obeys authority does so, as it is usually stated, only in his capacity as a 'member' of the corporate group and what he obeys is only 'the law'. He may in this connexion be the member of an association, of a territorial commune, of a church, or a citizen of a state.

5. In conformity with point 3, it is held that the members of the corporate group, in so far as they obey a person in authority, do not owe this obedience to him as an individual, but to the impersonal order. Hence, it follows that there is an obligation to obedience only within the sphere of the rationally delimited authority which, in terms of the order, has been conferred upon him.

The following may thus be said to be the fundamental categories of rational legal authority:—

(1) A continuous organization of official functions bound by rules.

(2) A specified sphere of competence. This involves (a) a sphere of obligations to perform functions which has been marked off as part of a systematic division of labour. (b) The provision of the incumbent with the

necessary authority to carry out these functions. (c) That the means of compulsion are clearly defined and their use is subject to definite conditions. A unit exercising authority which is organized in this way will be called an 'administrative organ.'[1]

There are administrative organs in this sense in large-scale private organizations, in parties and armies, as well as in the state and the church. An elected president, a cabinet of ministers, or a body of elected representatives also in this sense constitute administrative organs. This is not, however, the place to discuss these concepts. Not every administrative organ is provided with compulsory powers. But this distinction is not important for present purposes.

(3) The organization of offices follows the principle of hierarchy; that is, each lower office is under the control and supervision of a higher one. There is a right of appeal and of statement of grievances from the lower to the higher. Hierarchies differ in respect to whether and in what cases complaints can lead to a ruling from an authority at various points higher in the scale, and as to whether changes are imposed from higher up or the responsibility for such changes is left to the lower office, the conduct of which was the subject of complaint.

(4) The rules which regulate the conduct of an office may be technical rules or norms.[2] In both cases, if their

---

[1] *Behörde.*

[2] Weber does not explain this distinction. By a 'technical rule' he probably means a prescribed course of action which is dictated primarily on grounds touching efficiency of the performance of the immediate functions, while by 'norms' he probably means rules which limit conduct on grounds other than those of efficiency. Of course, in one sense all rules are norms in that they are prescriptions for conduct, conformity with which is problematical.—Orig. Ed.

application is to be fully rational, specialized training is necessary. It is thus normally true that only a person who has demonstrated an adequate technical training is qualified to be a member of the administrative staff of such an organized group, and hence only such persons are eligible for appointment to official positions. The administrative staff of a rational corporate group thus typically consists of 'officials,' whether the organization be devoted to political, religious, economic —in particular, capitalistic—or other ends.

(5) In the rational type it is a matter of principle that the members of the administrative staff should be completely separated from ownership of the means of production or administration. Officials, employees, and workers attached to the administrative staff do not themselves own the non-human means of production and administration. These are rather provided for their use in kind or in money, and the official is obligated to render an accounting of their use. There exists, furthermore, in principle complete separation of the property belonging to the organization, which is controlled within the sphere of office, and the personal property of the official, which is available for his own private uses. There is a corresponding separation of the place in which official functions are carried out, the 'office' in the sense of premises, from living quarters.

(6) In the rational type case, there is also a complete absence of appropriation of his official position by the incumbent. Where 'rights' to an office exist, as in the case of judges, and recently of an increasing proportion of officials and even of workers, they do not normally serve the purpose of appropriation by the official, but of securing the purely objective and independent character of the conduct of the

office so that it is oriented only to the relevant norms.

(7) Administrative acts, decisions, and rules are formulated and recorded in writing, even in cases where oral discussion is the rule or is even mandatory. This applies at least to preliminary discussions and proposals, to final decisions, and to all sorts of orders and rules. The combination of written documents and a continuous organization of official functions constitutes the 'office'[3] which is the central focus of all types of modern corporate action.

(8) Legal authority can be exercised in a wide variety of different forms which will be distinguished and discussed later. The following analysis will be deliberately confined for the most part to the aspect of imperative co-ordination in the structure of the administrative staff. It will consist in an analysis in terms of ideal types of officialdom or 'bureaucracy.'

In the above outline no mention has been made of the kind of supreme head appropriate to a system of legal authority. This is a consequence of certain considerations which can only be made entirely understandable at a later stage in the analysis. There are very important types of rational imperative co-ordination which, with respect to the ultimate source of authority, belong to other categories. This is true of the hereditary charismatic type, as illustrated by hereditary monarchy and of the pure charismatic type of a president chosen by plebiscite. Other cases involve rational elements at important points, but are made up of a combination of bureaucratic and charismatic components, as is true of the cabinet form of government. Still, others are subject to the authority of the chief of other corporate groups, whether their character be charismatic or bureaucratic; thus the formal head of a government department under a parliamentary regime may be a minister who occupies his position because of his authority in a party. The type of rational, legal administrative staff is capable of application in all kinds of situations and contexts. It is the most important mechanism for the administration of everyday profane affairs. For in that sphere, the exercise of authority and, more broadly, imperative co-ordination, consists precisely in administration.

. . .

The purest type of exercise of legal authority is that which employs a bureaucratic administrative staff. Only the supreme chief of the organization occupies his position of authority by virtue of appropriation, of election, or of having been designated for the succession. But even *his* authority consists in a sphere of legal 'competence.' The whole administrative staff under the supreme authority then consists, in the purest type, of individual officials who are appointed and function according to the following criteria.[4]

(1) They are personally free and

---

[3] *Bureau.* It has seemed necessary to use the English word 'office' in three different meanings, which are distinguished in Weber's discussion by at least two terms. The first is *Amt*, which means 'office' in the sense of the institutionally defined status of a person. The second is the 'work premises' as in the expression 'he spent the afternoon in his office.' For this Weber uses *Bureau* as also for the third meaning which he has just defined, the 'organized work process of a group.' In this last sense an office is a particular type of 'organization,' or *Betrieb* in Weber's sense. This use is established in English in such expressions as 'the District Attorney's Office has such and such functions.' Which of the three meanings is involved in a given case will generally be clear from the context.—ORIC. ED.

[4] This characterization applies to the 'monocratic' as opposed to the 'collegial' type, which will be discussed below.

subject to authority only with respect to their impersonal official obligations.

(2) They are organized in a clearly defined hierarchy of offices.

(3) Each office has a clearly defined sphere of competence in the legal sense.

(4) The office is filled by a free contractual relationship. Thus, in principle, there is free selection.

(5) Candidates are selected on the basis of technical qualifications. In the most rational case, this is tested by examination or guaranteed by diplomas certifying technical training, or both. They are *appointed*, not elected.

(6) They are remunerated by fixed salaries in money, for the most part with a right to pensions. Only under certain circumstances does the employing authority, especially in private organizations, have a right to terminate the appointment, but the official is always free to resign. The salary scale is primarily graded according to rank in the hierarchy; but in addition to this criterion, the responsibility of the position and the requirements of the incumbent's social status may be taken into account.

(7) The office is treated as the sole, or at least the primary, occupation of the incumbent.

(8) It constitutes a career. There is a system of 'promotion' according to seniority or to achievement, or both. Promotion is dependent on the judgement of superiors.

(9) The official works entirely separated from ownership of the means of administration and without appropriation of his position.

(10) He is subject to strict and systematic discipline and control in the conduct of the office.

This type of organization is in principle applicable with equal facility to a wide variety of different fields. It may be applied in profit-making business or in charitable organizations, or in any number of other types of private enterprises serving ideal or material ends. It is equally applicable to political and to religious organizations. With varying degrees of approximation to a pure type, its historical existence can be demonstrated in all these fields.

1. For example, this type of bureaucracy is found in private clinics, as well as in endowed hospitals or the hospitals maintained by religious orders. Bureaucratic organization has played a major role in the Catholic Church. It is well illustrated by the administrative role of the priesthood[5] in the modern church, which has expropriated almost all of the old church benefices, which were in former days to a large extent subject to private appropriation. It is also illustrated by the conception of the universal Episcopate, which is thought of as formally constituting a universal legal competence in religious matters. Similarily, the doctrine of Papal infallibility is thought of as in fact involving a universal competence, but only one which functions 'ex cathedra' in the sphere of the office, thus implying the typical distinction between the sphere of office and that of the private affairs of the incumbent. The same phenomena are found in the large-scale capitalistic enterprise; and the larger it is, the greater their role. And this is not less true of political parties, which will be discussed separately. Finally, the modern army is essentially a bureaucratic organization administered by that peculiar type of military functionary, the 'officer.'

2. Bureaucratic authority is carried out in its purest form where it is most clearly dominated by the principle of appointment. There is no such thing as a hierarchy of elected officials in the same sense as there is a hierarchical

---

[5] *Kaplanokratie.*

organization of appointed officials. In the first place, election makes it impossible to attain a stringency of discipline even approaching that in the appointed type. For it is open to a subordinate official to compete for elective honors on the same terms as his superiors, and his prospects are not dependent on the superior's judgment.

3. Appointment by free contract, which makes free selection possible, is essential to modern bureaucracy. Where there is a hierarchical organization with impersonal spheres of competence, but occupied by unfree officials—like slaves or dependents, who, however, function in a formally bureaucratic manner—the term 'patrimonial bureaucracy' will be used.

4. The role of technical qualifications in bureaucratic organizations is continually increasing. Even an official in a party or a trade-union organization is in need of specialized knowledge, though it is usually of an empirical character, developed by experience, rather than by formal training. In the modern state, the only 'offices' for which no technical qualifications are required are those of ministers and presidents. This only goes to prove that they are 'officials' only in a formal sense, and not substantively, as is true of the managing director or president of a large business corporation. There is no question but that the 'position' of the capitalistic entrepreneur is as definitely appropriate as is that of a monarch. Thus at the top of a bureaucratic organization, there is necessarily an element which is at least not purely bureaucratic. The category of bureaucracy is one applying only to the exercise of control by means of a particular kind of administrative staff.

5. The bureaucratic official normally receives a fixed salary. By contrast, sources of income which are privately appropriated will be called 'benefices.'[6] Bureaucratic salaries are also normally paid in money. Though this is not essential to the concept of bureaucracy, it is the arrangement which best fits the pure type. Payments in kind are apt to have the character of benefices, and the receipt of a benefice normally implies the appropriation of opportunities for earnings and of positions. There are, however, gradual transitions in this field with many intermediate types. Appropriation by virtue of leasing or sale of offices or the pledge of income from office are phenomena foreign to the pure type of bureaucracy.

6. 'Offices' which do not constitute the incumbent's principal occupation, in particular 'honorary' offices, belong in other categories, which will be discussed later. The typical 'bureaucratic' official occupies the office as his principal occupation.

7. With respect to the separation of the official from ownership of the means of administration, the situation is essentially the same in the field of public administration and in private bureaucratic organizations, such as the large-scale capitalistic enterprise.

8. Collegial bodies will be discussed separately below. At the present time they are rapidly decreasing in importance in favor of types of organization which are in fact, and for the most part formally as well, subject to the authority of a single head. For instance, the collegial 'governments' in Prussia have long since given way to the monocratic 'district president.'[7] The decisive factor in this development has been the need for rapid, clear decisions, free of the necessity of compromise between different opinions and also free of shifting majorities.

---

[6] *Pfründen.*

[7] *Regierungspräsident.*

9. The modern army officer is a type of appointed official who is clearly marked off by certain class distinctions. This will be discussed elsewhere. In this respect such officers differ radically from elected military leaders, from charismatic condottieri, from the type of officers who recruit and lead mercenary armies as a capitalistic enterprise, and, finally, from the incumbents of commissions which have been purchased. There may be gradual transitions between these types. The patrimonial 'retainer,' who is separated from the means of carrying out his function, and the proprietor of a mercenary army for capitalistic purposes have, along with the private capitalistic entrepreneur, been pioneers in the organization of the modern type of bureaucracy. . . .

The Proverbs of Administration

HERBERT A. SIMON

A fact about proverbs that greatly enhances their quotability is that they almost always occur in mutually contradictory pairs. "Look before you leap!"—but "He who hesitates is lost."

This is both a great convenience and a serious defect—depending on the use to which one wishes to put the proverbs in question. If it is a matter of rationalizing behavior that has already taken place or justifying action that has already been decided upon, proverbs are ideal. Since one is never at a loss to find one that will prove his point—or the precisely contradictory point, for that matter—they are a great help in persuasion, political debate, and all forms of rhetoric.

But when one seeks to use proverbs as the basis of a scientific theory, the situation is less happy. It is not that the propositions expressed by the proverbs are insufficient; it is rather that they prove too much. A scientific theory should tell what is true but also what is false. If Newton had announced to the world that particles of matter exert either an attraction or a repulsion on each other, he would not have added much to scientific knowledge. His contribution consisted in showing that an attraction was exercised and in announcing the precise law governing its operation.

Most of the propositions that make up the body of administrative theory today share, unfortunately, this defect of proverbs. For almost every principle one can find an equally plausible and acceptable contradictory principle. Although the two principles of the pair will lead to exactly opposite organizational recommendations, there is nothing in the theory to indicate which is the proper one to apply.[1]

It is the purpose of this paper to substantiate this sweeping criticism of administrative theory, and to present some suggestions—perhaps less concrete than they should be—as to how the existing dilemma can be solved.

Herbert A. Simon, "The Proverbs of Administration." Reprinted from the *Public Administration Review*, the journal of the American Society for Public Administration, Vol. vi, 1946 by permission of the publisher.

[1] Lest it be thought that this deficiency is peculiar to the science—or "art"—of administration, it should be pointed out that the same trouble is shared by most Freudian psychological theories, as well as by some sociological theories.

Some Accepted Administrative Principles

Among the more common "principles" that occur in the literature of administration are these:

1. Administrative efficiency is increased by a specialization of the task among the group.
2. Administrative efficiency is increased by arranging the members of the group in a determinate hierarchy of authority.
3. Administrative efficiency is increased by limiting the span of control at any point in the hierarchy to a small number.
4. Administrative efficiency is increased by grouping the workers, for purposes of control, according to (*a*) purpose, (*b*) process, (*c*) clientele, or (*d*) place. (This is really an elaboration of the first principle but deserves separate discussion).

Since these principles appear relatively simple and clear, it would seem that their application to concrete problems of administrative organization would be unambiguous and that their validity would be easily submitted to empirical test. Such, however, seems not to be the case. To show why it is not, each of the four principles just listed will be considered in turn.

Specialization

Administrative efficiency is supposed to increase with an increase in specialization. But is this intended to mean that *any* increase in specialization will increase efficiency? If so, which of the following alternatives is the correct application of the principle in a particular case?

1. A plan of nursing should be put into effect by which nurses will be assigned to districts and do all nursing within that district, including school examinations, visits to homes or school children, and tuberculosis nursing.

2. A functional plan of nursing should be put into effect by which different nurses will be assigned to school examinations, visits to homes of school children, and tuberculosis nursing. The present method of generalized nursing by districts impedes the development of specialized skills in the three very diverse programs.

Both of these administrative arrangements satisfy the requirement of specialization—the first provides specialization by place; the second, specialization by function. The principle of specialization is of no help at all in choosing between the two alternatives.

It appears that the simplicity of the principle of specialization is a deceptive simplicity—a simplicity which conceals fundamental ambiguities. For "specialization" is not a condition of efficient administration; it is an inevitable characteristic of all group effort, however efficient or inefficient that effort may be. Specialization merely means that different persons are doing different things—and since it is physically impossible for two persons to be doing the same thing in the same place at the same time, two persons are always doing different things.

The real problem of administration, then, is not to "specialize," but to specialize in that particular manner and along those particular lines which will lead to administrative efficiency. But, in thus rephrasing this "principle" of administration, there has been brought clearly into the open its fundamental ambiguity: "Administrative efficiency is increased by a specialization of the task among the group in the direction which will lead to greater efficiency."

Further discussion of the choice between competing bases of specialization will be undertaken after two other principles of administration have been examined.

Unity of Command

Administrative efficiency is supposed to be enhanced by arranging the members of the organization in a determinate hierarchy of authority in order to preserve "unity of command."

Analysis of this "principle" requires a clear understanding of what is meant by the term "authority." A subordinate may be said to accept authority whenever he permits his behavior to be guided by a decision reached by another, irrespective of his own judgment as to the merits of that decision.

In one sense the principle of unity of command, like the principle of specialization, cannot be violated; for it is physically impossible for a man to obey two contradictory commands—that is what is meant by "contradictory commands." Presumably, if unity of command is a principle of administration, it must assert something more than this physical impossibility. Perhaps it asserts this: that it is undesirable to place a member of an organization in a position where he receives orders from more than one superior. This is evidently the meaning that Gulick attaches to the principle when he says,

The significance of this principle in the process of co-ordination and organization must not be lost sight of. In building a structure of co-ordination, it is often tempting to set up more than one boss for a man who is doing work which has more than one relationship. Even as great a philosopher of management as Taylor fell into this error in setting up separate foremen to deal with machinery, with materials, with speed, etc., each with the power of giving orders directly to the individual workman. The rigid adherence to the principle of unity of command may have its absurdities; these are, however, unimportant in comparison with the certainty of confusion, inefficiency and irresponsibility which arise from the violation of the principle.[2]

Certainly the principle of unity of command thus interpreted, cannot be criticized for any lack of clarity or any ambiguity. The definition of authority given above should provide a clear test whether, in any concrete situation, the principle is observed. The real fault that must be found with this principle is that it is incompatible with the principle of specialization. One of the most important uses to which authority is put in organization is to bring about specialization in the work of making decisions, so that each decision is made at a point in the organization where it can be made most expertly. As a result, the use of authority permits a greater degree of expertness to be achieved in decision-making than would be possible if each operative employee had himself to make all the decisions upon which his activity is predicated. The individual fireman does not decide whether to use a two-inch hose or a fire extinguisher; that is decided for him by his officers, and the decision is communicated to him in the form of a command.

However, if unity of command, in Gulick's sense, is observed, the decisions of a person at any point in the administrative hierarchy are subject to influence through only one channel of authority; and if his decisions are of a kind that require expertise in more than one field of knowledge, then advisory and informational services must be relied upon to supply those premises which lie in a field not recognized by the mode of specialization in the organization. For example, if an account-

---

[2] Luther Gulick, "Notes on the Theory of Organization," in Luther Gulick and L. Urwick (eds.), *Papers on the Science of Administration* (Institute of Public Administration, Columbia University, 1937), p. 9.

ant in a school department is subordinate to an educator, and if unity of command is observed, then the finance department cannot issue direct orders to him regarding the technical, accounting aspects of his work. Similarly, the director of motor vehicles in the public works department will be unable to issue direct orders on care of motor equipment to the fire-truck driver.[3]

Gulick, in the statement quoted above, clearly indicates the difficulties to be faced if unity of command is not observed. A certain amount of irresponsibility and confusion are almost certain to ensue. But perhaps this is not too great a price to pay for the increased expertise that can be applied to decisions. What is needed to decide the issue is a principle of administration that would enable one to weigh the relative advantages of the two courses of action. But neither the principle of unity of command nor the principle of specialization is helpful in adjudicating the controversy. They merely contradict each other without indicating any procedure for resolving the contradiction.

If this were merely an academic controversy—if it were generally agreed and had been generally demonstrated that unity of command must be preserved in all cases, even with a loss in expertise—one could assert that in case of conflict between the two principles, unity of command should prevail. But the issue is far from clear, and experts can be ranged on both sides of the controversy. On the side of unity of command there may be cited the dic-tums of Gulick and others.[4] On the side of specialization there are Taylor's theory of functional supervision, Macmahon and Millett's idea of "dual supervision," and the practice of technical supervision in military organization.[5]

It may be, as Gulick asserts, that the notion of Taylor and these others is an "error." If so, the evidence that it is an error has never been marshalled or published—apart from loose heuristic arguments like that quoted above. One is left with a choice between equally eminent theorists of administration and without any evidential basis for making that choice.

What evidence there is of actual administrative practice would seem to indicate that the need for specialization is to a very large degree given priority over the need for unity of command. As a matter of fact, it does not go too far to say that unity of command, in Gulick's sense, never has existed in any administrative organization. If a line officer accepts the regulations of an accounting department with regard to the procedure for making requisitions, can it be said that, in this sphere, he is not subject to the authority of the accounting department? In any actual administrative situation authority is zoned, and to maintain that this zoning does not contradict the principle of unity of command requires a very different definition of authority from that

---

[3] This point is discussed in Herbert A. Simon "Decision-Making and Administrative Organization," 4 *Public Administration Review*, 20-21 (Winter, 1944).

[4] Gulick, "Notes on the Theory of Organization," p. 9; L. D. White, *Introduction to the Study of Public Administration* (Macmillan Co., 1939), p. 45.

[5] Frederick W. Taylor, *Shop Management* (Harper & Bros., 1911), p. 99; Macmahon, Millett, and Ogden *The Administration of Federal Work Relief* (Public Administration Service, 1941), pp. 265-68; and L. Urwick, who describes British army practice in "Organization as a Technical Problem," Gulick and Urwick (eds.), *op. cit.*, pp. 67-69.

used here. This subjection of the line officer to the accounting department is no different, in principle, from Taylor's recommendation that in the matter of work programming a workman be subject to one foreman, in the matter of machine operation to another.

The principle of unity of command is perhaps more defensible if narrowed down to the following: In case two authoritative commands conflict, there should be a single determinate person whom the subordinate is expected to obey; and the sanctions of authority should be applied against the subordinate only to enforce his obedience to that one person.

If the principle of unity of command is more defensible when stated in this limited form, it also solves fewer problems. In the first place, it no longer requires, except for settling conflicts of authority, a single hierarchy of authority. Consequently, it leaves unsettled the very important question of how authority should be zoned in a particular organization (i.e., the modes of specialization) and through what channels it should be exercised. Finally, even this narrower concept of unity of command conflicts with the principle of specialization, for whenever disagreement does occur and the organization members revert to the formal lines of authority, then only those types of specialization which are represented in the hierarchy of authority can impress themselves on decision. If the training officer of a city exercises only functional supervision over the police training officer, then in case of disagreement with the police chief, specialized knowledge of police problems will determine the outcome while specialized knowledge of training problems will be subordinated or ignored. That this actually occurs is shown by the frustration so commonly expressed by functional supervisors at their lack of authority to apply sanctions.

Span of Control

Administrative efficiency is supposed to be enhanced by limiting the number of subordinates who report directly to any one administrator to a small number—say six. This notion that the "span of control" should be narrow is confidently asserted as a third incontrovertible principle of administration. The usual common-sense arguments for restricting the span of control are familiar and need not be repeated here. What is not so generally recognized is that a contradictory proverb of administration can be stated which, though it is not so familiar as the principle of span of control, can be supported by arguments of equal plausibility. The proverb in question is the following: Administrative efficiency is enhanced by keeping at a minimum the number of organizational levels through which a matter must pass before it is acted upon.

This latter proverb is one of the fundamental criteria that guide administrative analysts in procedures simplification work. Yet in many situations the results to which this principle leads are in direct contradiction to the requirements of the principle of span of control, the principle of unity of command, and the principle of specialization. The present discussion is concerned with the first of these conflicts. To illustrate the difficulty, two alternative proposals for the organization of a small health department will be presented—one based on the restriction of span of control, the other on the limitation of number of organization levels:

1. The present organization of the department places an administrative overload on the health officer by reason of the fact that all eleven employees of the

department report directly to him and the further fact that some of the staff lack adequate technical training. Consequently, venereal disease clinic treatments and other details require an undue amount of the health officer's personal attention.

It has previously been recommended that the proposed medical officer be placed in charge of the venereal disease and chest clinics and all child hygiene work. It is further recommended that one of the inspectors be designated chief inspector and placed in charge of all the department's inspectional activities and that one of the nurses be designated as head nurse. This will relieve the health commissioner of considerable detail and will leave him greater freedom to plan and supervise the health program as a whole, to conduct health education, and to coordinate the work of the department with that of other community agencies. If the department were thus organized, the effectiveness of all employees could be substantially increased.

2. The present organization of the department leads to inefficiency and excessive red tape by reason of the fact that an unnecessary supervisory level intervenes between the health officer and the operative employees, and that those four of the twelve employees who are best trained technically are engaged largely in "overhead" administrative duties. Consequently, unnecessary delays occur in securing the approval of the health officer on matters requiring his attention, and too many matters require review and re-review.

The medical officer should be left in charge of the venereal disease and chest clinics and child hygiene work. It is recommended, however, that the position of chief inspector and head nurse be abolished and that the employees now filling these positions perform regular inspectional and nursing duties. The details of work scheduling now handled by these two employees can be taken care of more economically by the secretary to the health officer, and, since broader matters of policy have, in any event, always required the personal attention of

the health officer, the abolition of these two positions will eliminate a wholly unnecessary step in review, will allow an expansion of inspectional and nursing services, and will permit at least a beginning to be made in the recommended program of health education. The number of persons reporting directly to the health officer will be increased to nine, but since there are few matters requiring the coordination of these employees, other than the work schedules and policy questions referred to above, this change will not materially increase his work load.

The dilemma is this: in a large organization with complex interrelations between members, a restricted span of control inevitably produces excessive red tape, for each contact between organization members must be carried upward until a common superior is found. If the organization is at all large, this will involve carrying all such matters upward through several levels of officials for decision and then downward again in the form of orders and instructions—a cumbersome and time-consuming process.

The alternative is to increase the number of persons who are under the command of each officer, so that the pyramid will come more rapidly to a peak, with fewer intervening levels. But this, too, leads to difficulty, for if an officer is required to supervise too many employees, his control over them is weakened.

If it is granted, then, that both the increase and the decrease in span of control has some undesirable consequences, what is the optimum point? Proponents of a restricted span of control have suggested three, five, even eleven, as suitable numbers, but nowhere have they explained the reasoning which led them to the particular number they selected. The principle as stated casts no light on this very crucial question. One is reminded of cur-

the proverbs of administration   37

rent arguments about the proper size of the national debt.

Organization by Purpose, Process, Clientele, Place

Administrative efficiency is supposed to be increased by grouping workers according to (a) purpose, (b) process, (c) clientele, or (d) place. But from the discussion of specialization it is clear that this principle is internally inconsistent; for purpose, process, clientele, and place are competing bases of organization, and at any given point of division the advantages of three must be sacrificed to secure the advantages of the fourth. If the major departments of a city, for example, are organized on the basis of major purpose, then it follows that all the physicians, all the lawyers, all the engineers, all the statisticians will not be located in a single department exclusively composed of members of their profession but will be distributed among the various city departments needing their services. The advantages of organization by process will thereby be partly lost.

Some of these advantages can be regained by organizing on the basis of process within the major departments. Thus there may be an engineering bureau within the public works department, or the board of education may have a school health service as a major division of its work. Similarly, within smaller units there may be division by area or by clientele: e.g., a fire department will have separate companies located throughout the city, while a welfare department may have intake and case work agencies in various locations. Again, however, these major types of specialization cannot be simultaneously achieved, for at any point in the organization it must be decided whether specialization at the next level will be accomplished by dis-

tinction of major purpose, major process, clientele, or area.

The conflict may be illustrated by showing how the principle of specialization according to purpose would lead to a different result from specialization according to clientele in the organization of a health department.

1. Public health administration consists of the following activities for the prevention of disease and the maintenance of healthful conditions: (1) vital statistics; (2) child hygiene—prenatal, maternity, postnatal, infant, preschool, and school health programs; (3) communicable disease control; (4) inspection of milk, foods, and drugs; (5) sanitary inspection; (6) laboratory service; (7) health education.

One of the handicaps under which the health department labors is the fact that the department has no control over school health, that being an activity of the county board of education, and there is little or no coordination between that highly important part of the community health program and the balance of the program which is conducted by the city-county health unit. It is recommended that the city and county open negotiations with the board of education for the transfer of all school health work and the appropriation therefor to the joint health unit. . . .

2. To the modern school department is entrusted the care of children during almost the entire period that they are absent from the parental home. It has three principal responsibilities toward them: (1) to provide for their education in useful skills and knowledge and in character; (2) to provide them with wholesome play activities outside school hours; (3) to care for their health and to assure the attainment of minimum standards of nutrition.

One of the handicaps under which the school board labors is the fact that, except for school lunches, the board has no control over child health and nutrition, and there is little or no coordination between that highly important part of the child development program and the balance of the program which is conducted by the board of education. It is recommended that the city and county open negotiations for the transfer of all health work for children of school age to the board of education.

Here again is posed the dilemma of choosing between alternative, equally plausible, administrative principles. But this is not the only difficulty in the present case, for a closer study of the situation shows there are fundamental ambiguities in the meanings of the key terms—"purpose," "process," "clientele," and "place."

"Purpose" may be roughly defined as the objective or end for which an activity is carried on; "process" as a means for accomplishing a purpose. Processes, then, are carried on in order to achieve purposes. But purposes themselves may generally be arranged in some sort of hierarchy. A typist moves her fingers in order to type; types in order to reproduce a letter; reproduces a letter in order that an inquiry may be answered. Writing a letter is then the purpose for which the typing is performed; while writing a letter is also the process whereby the purpose of replying to an inquiry is achieved. It follows that the same activity may be described as purpose or as process.

This ambiguity is easily illustrated for the case of an administrative organization. A health department conceived as a unit whose task it is to care for the health of the community is a purpose organization; the same department conceived as a unit which makes use of the medical arts to carry on its work is a process organization. In the same way, an education department may be viewed as a purpose (to educate) organization, or a clientele (children) organization; the forest service as a purpose (forest conservation), process (forest management), clientele (lumbermen and cattlemen utilizing public forests), or area (publicly owned forest lands) organization. When concrete illustrations of this sort are selected, the lines of demarcation between these categories become very hazy and unclear indeed.

"Organization by major purpose," says Gulick, ". . . serves to bring together in a single large department all of those who are at work endeavoring to render a particular service."[6] But what is a particular service? Is fire protection a single purpose, or is it merely a part of the purpose of public safety? —or is it a combination of purposes including fire prevention and fire fighting? It must be concluded that there is no such thing as a purpose, or a unifunctional (single-purpose) organization. What is to be considered a single function depends entirely on language and techniques.[7] If the English language has a comprehensive term which covers both of two subpurposes it is natural to think of the two together as a single purpose. If such a term is lacking, the two subpurposes become purposes in their own right. On the other hand, a single activity may contribute to several objectives, but since they are technically (procedurally) inseparable, the activity is considered a single function or purpose.

The fact, mentioned previously, that purposes form a hierarchy, each subpurpose contributing to some more final and comprehensive end, helps to make clear the relation between purpose and process. "Organization by

---

[6] *Op. cit.*, p. 21.

[7] If this is correct, then any attempt to prove that certain activities belong in a single department because they relate to a single purpose is doomed to fail. See, for example, John M. Gaus and Leon Wolcott, *Public Administration and the U.S. Department of Agriculture* (Public Administration Service, 1940.)

major process," says Gulick, ". . . tends to bring together in a single department all of those who are at work making use of a given special skill or technology, or are members of a given profession."[8] Consider a simple skill of this kind—typing. Typing is a skill which brings about a means-end coordination of muscular movements, but at a very low level in the means-end hierarchy. The content of the typewritten letter is indifferent to the skill that produces it. The skill consists merely in the ability to hit the letter "*t*" quickly whenever the letter "*t*" is required by the content and to hit the letter "*a*" whenever the letter "*a*" is required by the content.

There is, then, no essential difference between a "purpose" and a "process," but only a distinction of degree. A "process" is an activity whose immediate purpose is at a low level in the hierarchy of means and ends, while a "purpose" is a collection of activities whose orienting value or aim is at a high level in the means-end hierarchy.

Next consider "clientele" and "place" as bases of organization. These categories are really not separate from purpose, but a part of it. A complete statement of the purpose of a fire department would have to include the area served by it: "to reduce fire losses on property in the city of X." Objectives of an administrative organization are phrased in terms of a service to be provided and an area for which it is provided. Usually, the term "purpose" is meant to refer only to the first element, but the second is just as legitimately an aspect of purpose. Area of service, of course, may be a specified clientele quite as well as a geographical area. In the case of an agency which works on "shifts," time will be a third dimension of purpose—to provide a

given service in a given area (or to a given clientele) during a given time period.

With this clarification of terminology, the next task is to consider the problem of specializing the work of an organization. It is no longer legitimate to speak of a "purpose" organization, a "process" organization, a clientele organization, or an "area" organization. The same unit might fall into any one of these four categories, depending on the nature of the larger organizational unit of which it was a part. A unit providing public health and medical services for school-age children in Multnomah County might be considered (1) an "area" organization if it were part of a unit providing the same service for the state of Oregon; (2) a "clientele" organization if it were part of a unit providing similar services for children of all ages; (3) a "purpose" or a "process" organization (it would be impossible to say which) if it were part of an education department.

It is incorrect to say that Bureau A is a process bureau; the correct statement is that Bureau A is a process bureau *within* Department X.[9] This latter statement would mean that Bureau A incorporates all the processes of a certain kind in Department X, without reference to any special subpurposes, subareas, or subclientele of Department X. Now it is conceivable that a particular unit might incorporate all processes of a certain kind but that these processes might relate to only certain particular subpurposes of the department purpose. In this case,

---

[8] *Op. cit.*, p. 23.

[9] This distinction is implicit in most of Gulick's analysis of specialization. However, since he cites as examples single departments within a city, and since he usually speaks of "grouping activities" rather than "dividing work," the relative character of these categories is not always apparent in this discussion (*op. cit.*, pp. 15-30).

which corresponds to the health unit in an education department mentioned above, the unit would be specialized by both purpose and process. The health unit would be the only one in the education department using the medical art ('process') and concerned with health (subpurpose).

Even when the problem is solved of proper usage for the terms "purpose," "process," "clientele," and "area," the principles of administration give no guide as to which of these four competing bases of specialization is applicable in any particular situation. The British Machinery of Government Committee had no doubts about the matter. It considered purpose and clientele as the two possible bases of organization and put its faith entirely in the former. Others have had equal assurance in choosing between purpose and process. The reasoning which leads to these unequivocal conclusions leaves something to be desired. The Machinery of Government Committee gives this sole argument for its choice:

> Now the inevitable outcome of this method of organization [by clientele] is a tendency to Lilliputian administration. It is impossible that the specialized service which each Department has to render to the community can be of as high a standard when its work is at the same time limited to a particular class of persons and extended to every variety of provision for them, as when the Department concentrates itself on the provision of the particular service only by whomsoever required and looks beyond the interest of comparatively small classes.[10]

The faults in this analysis are obvious. First, there is no attempt to determine how a service is to be recognized. Second, there is a bald assumption, absolutely without proof, that a

child health unit, for example, in a department of child welfare could not offer services of "as high a standard" as the same unit if it were located in a department of health. Just how the shifting of the unit from one department to another would improve or damage the quality of its work is not explained. Third, no basis is set forth for adjudicating the competing claims of purpose and process—the two are merged in the ambiguous term "service." It is not necessary here to decide whether the committee was right or wrong in its recommendation; the important point is that the recommendation represented a choice, without any apparent logical or empirical grounds, between contradictory principles of administration.

Even more remarkable illustrations of illogic can be found in most discussions of purpose vs. process. They would be too ridiculous to cite if they were not commonly used in serious political and administrative debate.

> For instance, where should agricultural education come: in the Ministry of Education, or of Agriculture? That depends on whether we want to see the best farming taught, though possibly by old methods, or a possibly out-of-date style of farming, taught in the most modern and compelling manner. The question answers itself.[11]

But does the question really answer itself? Suppose a bureau of agricultural education were set up, headed, for example, by a man who had had extensive experience in agricultural research or as administrator of an agricultural school, and staffed by men of similarly appropriate background. What reason is there to believe that if attached to a Ministry of Education

---

[10] *Report of the Machinery of Government Committee* (H. M. Stationery Office, 1918).

[11] Sir Charles Harris, "Decentralization," 3 *Journal of Public Administration*, 117-33 (April, 1925).

they would teach old-fashioned farming by new-fashioned methods, while if attached to a Ministry of Agriculture they would teach new-fashioned farming by old-fashioned methods? The administrative problem of such a bureau would be to teach new-fashioned farming by new-fashioned methods, and it is a little difficult to see how the departmental location of the unit would affect this result. "The question answers itself" only if one has a rather mystical faith in the potency of bureau-shuffling as a means for redirecting the activities of an agency.

These contradictions and competitions have received increasing attention from students of administration during the past few years. For example, Gulick, Wallace, and Benson have stated certain advantages and disadvantages of the several modes of specialization, and have considered the conditions under which one or the other mode might best be adopted.[12] All this analysis has been at a theoretical level—in the sense that data have not been employed to demonstrate the superior effectiveness claimed for the different modes. But though theoretical, the analysis has lacked a theory. Since no comprehensive framework has been constructed within which the discussion could take place, the analysis has tended either to the logical one-sidedness which characterizes the examples quoted above or to inconclusiveness.

The Impasse of Administrative Theory

The four "principles of administration" that were set forth at the be-

ginning of this paper have now been subjected to critical analysis. None of the four survived in very good shape, for in each case there was found, instead of an unequivocal principle, a set of two or more mutually incompatible principles apparently equally applicable to the administrative situation.

Moreover, the reader will see that the very same objections can be urged against the customary discussions of "centralization" vs. "decentralization," which usually conclude, in effect, that "on the one hand, centralization of decision-making functions is desirable; on the other hand, there are definite advantages in decentralization."

Can anything be salvaged which will be useful in the construction of an administrative theory? As a matter of fact, almost everything can be salvaged. The difficulty has arisen from treating as "principles of administration" what are really only criteria for describing and diagnosing administrative situations. Closet space is certainly an important item in the design of a successful house; yet a house designed entirely with a view to securing a maximum of closet space—all other considerations being forgotten—would be considered, to say the least, somewhat unbalanced. Similarly, unity of command, specialization by purpose, decentralization are all items to be considered in the design of an efficient administrative organization. No single one of these items is of sufficient importance to suffice as a guiding principle for the administrative analyst. In the design of administrative organizations, as in their operation, over-all efficiency must be the guiding criterion. Mutually incompatible advantages must be balanced against each other, just as an architect weighs the advantages

<hr>

[12] Gulick, "Notes on the Theory of Organization," pp. 21-30; Schuyler Wallace, *Federal Departmentalization* (Columbia University Press, 1941); George C. S. Benson, "International Administrative Organization," 1 *Public Administration Review*, 473-86 (Autumn, 1941).

of additional closet space against the advantages of a larger living room.

This position, if it is a valid one, constitutes an indictment of much current writing about administrative matters. As the examples cited in this chapter amply demonstrate, much administrative analysis proceeds by selecting a single criterion and applying it to an administrative situation to reach a recommendation; while the fact that equally valid, but contradictory, criteria exist which could be applied with equal reason, but with a different result, is conveniently ignored. A valid approach to the study of administration requires that *all* the relevant diagnostic criteria be identified; that each administrative situation be analyzed in terms of the entire set of criteria; and that research be instituted to determine how weights can be assigned to the several criteria when they are, as they usually will be, mutually incompatible.

An Approach to Administrative Theory

This program needs to be considered step by step. First, what is included in the description of administrative situations for purposes of such an analysis? Second, how can weights be assigned to the various criteria to give them their proper place in the total picture.

The Description of Administrative Situations

Before a science can develop principles, it must possess concepts. Before a law of gravitation could be formulated, it was necessary to have the notions of "acceleration" and "weight." The first task of administrative theory is to develop a set of concepts that will permit the description, in terms relevant to the theory, of administrative situations. These concepts, to be scientifically useful, must be operational; that is, their meanings must correspond to empirically observable facts or situations. The definition of "authority" given earlier in this paper is an example of an operational definition.

What is a scientifically relevant description of an organization? It is a description that, so far as possible, designates for each person in the organization what decisions that person makes and the influences to which he is subject in making each of these decisions. Current descriptions of administrative organizations fall far short of this standard. For the most part, they confine themselves to the allocation of *functions* and the formal structure of *authority*. They give little attention to the other types of organizational influence or to the system of communication.[13]

What does it mean, for example, to say: The department is made up of three bureaus. The first has the function of ———, the second the function of ———, and the third the function of ———?" What can be learned from such a description about the workability of the organizational arrangement? Very little, indeed. For from the description there is obtained no idea of the degree to which decisions are centralized at the bureau level or at the departmental level. No notion is given as to the extent to which the (presumably unlimited) authority of the department over the bureau is actually exercised or by what mechanisms. There is no indica-

13 The monograph by Macmahon, Millett, and Ogden, *op. cit.*, perhaps approaches nearer than any other published administrative study to the sophistication required in administrative description. See, for example, the discussion on pp. 233-36 of headquarters-field relationships.

tion of the extent to which systems of communication assist the coordination of the three bureaus or, for that matter, to what extent coordination is required by the nature of their work. There is no description of the kinds of training the members of the bureau have undergone or of the extent to which this training permits decentralization at the bureau level. In sum, a description of administrative organizations in terms almost exclusively of functions and lines of authority is completely inadequate for purposes of administrative analysis.

Consider the term "centralization." How is it determined whether the operations of a particular organization are "centralized" or "decentralized"? Does the fact that field offices exist prove anything about decentralization? Might not the same decentralization take place in the bureaus of a centrally located office? A realistic analysis of centralization must include a study of the allocation of decisions in the organization and the methods of influence that are employed by the higher levels to affect the decisions at the lower levels. Such an analysis would reveal a much more complex picture of the decision-making process than any enumeration of the geographical locations of organizational units at the different levels.

Administrative description suffers currently from superficiality, oversimplification, lack of realism. It has confined itself too closely to the mechanism of authority and has failed to bring within its orbit the other, equally important, modes of influence on organizational behavior. It has refused to undertake the tiresome task of studying the actual allocation of decision-making functions. It has been satisfied to speak of "authority," "centralization," "span of control," "function," without seeking opera-

tional definitions of these terms. Until administrative description reaches a higher level of sophistication, there is little reason to hope that rapid progress will be made toward the identification and verification of valid administrative principles.

Does this mean that a purely formal description of an administrative organization is impossible—that a relevant description must include an account of the content of the organization's decisions? This is a question that is almost impossible to answer in the present state of knowledge of administrative theory. One thing seems certain: content plays a greater role in the application of administrative principles than is allowed for in the formal administrative theory of the present time. This is a fact that is beginning to be recognized in the literature of administration. If one examines the chain of publications extending from Mooney and Reilley, through Gulick and the President's Committee controversy, to Schuyler, Wallace and Benson, he sees a steady shift of emphasis from the "principles of administration" themselves to a study of the *conditions* under which competing principles are respectively applicable. Recent publications seldom say that "organization should be by purpose," but rather that "under such and such conditions purpose organization is desirable." It is to these conditions which underlie the application of the proverbs of administration that administrative theory and analysis must turn in their search for really valid principles to replace the proverbs.

The Diagnosis of Administrative Situations

Before any positive suggestions can be made, it is necessary to digress a bit and to consider more closely the exact nature of the propositions of administrative theory. The theory of administration is concerned with how an organization should be constructed and operated in order to accomplish its work efficiently. A fundamental principle of administration, which follows almost immediately from the rational character of "good" administration, is that among several alternatives involving the same expenditure that one should always be selected which leads to the greatest accomplishment of administrative objectives; and among several alternatives that lead to the same accomplishment that one should be selected which involves the least expenditure. Since this "principle of efficiency" is characteristic of any activity that attempts rationally to maximize the attainment of certain ends with the use of scarce means, it is as characteristic of economic theory as it is of administrative theory. The "administrative man" takes his place alongside the classical "economic man."[14]

Actually, the "principle" of efficiency should be considered a definition rather than a principle: it is a definition of what is meant by "good" or "correct" administrative behavior. It does not tell *how* accomplishments are to be maximized, but merely states that this maximization is the aim of administrative activity, and that administrative theory must disclose under what conditions the maximization takes place.

Now what are the factors that determine the level of efficiency which is achieved by an administrative or-

---

[14] For an elaboration of the principle of efficiency and its place in administrative theory see Clarence E. Ridley and Herbert A. Simon, *Measuring Municipal Activities* (International City Managers' Association, 2nd ed., 1943), particularly Chapter I and the preface to the second edition.

ganization? It is not possible to make an exhaustive list of these, but the principal categories can be enumerated. Perhaps the simplest method of approach is to consider the single member of the administrative organization and ask what the limits are to the quantity and quality of his output. These limits include (*a*) limits on his ability to perform and (*b*) limits on his ability to make correct decisions. To the extent that these limits are removed, the administrative organization approaches its goal of high efficiency. Two persons, given the same skills, the same objectives and values, the same knowledge and information, can rationally decide only upon the same course of action. Hence, administrative theory must be interested in the factors that will determine with what skills, values, and knowledge the organization member undertakes his work. These are the "limits" to rationality with which the principles of administration must deal.

On one side, the individual is limited by those skills, habits, and reflexes which are no longer in the realm of the conscious. His performance, for example, may be limited by his manual dexterity or his reaction time or his strength. His decision-making processes may be limited by the speed of his mental processes, his skill in elementary arithmetic, and so forth. In this area, the principles of administration must be concerned with the physiology of the human body and with the laws of skill-training and of habit. This is the field that has been most successfully cultivated by the followers of Taylor and in which has been developed time-and-motion study and the therblig.

On a second side, the individual is limited by his values and those conceptions of purpose which influence him in making his decisions. If his loyalty to the organization is high, his decisions may evidence sincere acceptance of the objectives set for the organization; if that loyalty is lacking, personal motives may interfere with his administrative efficiency. If his loyalties are attached to the bureau by which he is employed, he may sometimes make decisions that are inimical to the larger unit of which the bureau is a part. In this area the principles of administration must be concerned with the determinants of loyalty and morale, with leadership and initiative, and with the influences that determine where the individual's organizational loyalties will be attached.

On a third side, the individual is limited by the extent of his knowledge of things relevant to his job. This applies both to the basic knowledge required in decision-making—a bridge designer must know the fundamentals of mechanics—and to the information that is required to make his decisions appropriate to the given situation. In this area, administrative theory is concerned with such fundamental questions as these: What are the limits on the mass of knowledge that human minds can accumulate and apply? How rapidly can knowledge be assimilated? How is specialization in the administrative organization to be related to the specializations of knowledge that are prevalent in the community's occupational structure? How is the system of communication to channel knowledge and information to the appropriate decision-points? What types of knowledge can, and what types cannot, be easily transmitted? How is the need for intercommunication of information affected by the modes of specialization in the organization? This is perhaps the *terra incognita* of admin-

istrative theory, and undoubtedly its careful exploration will cast great light on the proper application of the proverbs of administration.

Perhaps this triangle of limits does not completely bound the area of rationality, and other sides need to be added to the figure. In any case, this enumeration will serve to indicate the kinds of considerations that must go into the construction of valid and noncontradictory principles of administration.

An important fact to be kept in mind is that the limits of rationality are variable limits. Most important of all, consciousness of the limits may in itself alter them. Suppose it were discovered in a particular organization, for example, that organizational loyalties attached to small units had frequently led to a harmful degree of intraorganizational competition. Then, a program which trained members of the organization to be conscious of their loyalties, and to subordinate loyalties to the smaller group to those of the large, might lead to a very considerable alteration of the limits in that organization.[15]

A related point is that the term "rational behavior," as employed here, refers to rationality when that behavior is evaluated in terms of the objectives of the larger organization; for, as just pointed out, the difference in direction of the individual's aims from those of the larger organization is just one of those elements of nonrationality with which the theory must deal.

A final observation is that, since administrative theory is concerned with the nonrational limits of the

---

[15] For an example of the use of such training, see Herbert A. Simon and William Divine, "Controlling Human Factors in an Administrative Experiment," 1 *Public Administration Review* 487-92 (Autumn, 1941).

rational, it follows that the larger the area in which rationality has been achieved the less important is the exact form of the administrative organization. For example, the function of plan preparation, or design, if it results in a written plan that can be communicated interpersonally without difficulty, can be located almost anywhere in the organization without affecting results. All that is needed is a procedure whereby the plan can be given authoritative status, and this can be provided in a number of ways. A discussion, then, of the proper location for a planning or designing unit is apt to be highly inconclusive and is apt to hinge on the personalities in the organization and their relative enthusiasm, or lack of it, toward the planning function rather than upon any abstract principles of good administration.[16]

On the other hand, when factors of communication or faiths or loyalty are crucial to the making of a decision, the location of the decision in the organization is of great importance. The method of allocating decisions in the army, for instance, automatically provides (at least in the period prior to the actual battle) that each decision will be made where the knowledge is available for coordinating it with other decisions.

---

[16] See, for instance, Robert A. Walker, *The Planning Function in Urban Government* (University of Chicago Press, 1941), pp. 166-75. Walker makes out a strong case for attaching the planning agency to the chief executive. But he rests his entire case on the rather slender reed that "as long as the planning agency is outside the governmental structure . . . planning will tend to encounter resistance from public officials as an invasion of their responsibility and jurisdiction." This "resistance" is precisely the type of non-rational loyalty which has been referred to previously, and which is certainly a variable.

Assigning Weights to the Criteria

A first step, then, in the overhauling of the proverbs of administration is to develop a vocabulary along the lines just suggested, for the description of administrative organization. A second step, which has also been outlined, is to study the limits of rationality in order to develop a complete and comprehensive enumeration of the criteria that must be weighed in evaluating an administrative organization. The current proverbs represent only a fragmentary and unsystematized portion of these criteria.

When these two tasks have been carried out, it remains to assign weights to the criteria. Since the criteria, or "proverbs," are often mutually competitive or contradictory, it is not sufficient merely to identify them. Merely to know, for example, that a specified change in organization will reduce the span of control is not enough to justify the change. This gain must be balanced against the possible resulting loss of contact between the higher and lower ranks of the hierarchy.

Hence, administrative theory must also be concerned with the question of the weights that are to be applied to these criteria—to the problems of their relative importance in any concrete situation. This question is not one that can be solved in a vacuum. Arm-chair philosophizing about administration—of which the present paper is an example—has gone about as far as it can profitably go in this particular direction. What is needed now is empirical research and experimentation to determine the relative desirability of alternative administrative arrangements.

The methodological framework for this research is already at hand in the principle of efficiency. If an administrative organization whose activities are susceptible to objective evaluation be subjected to study, then the actual change in accomplishment that results from modifying administrative arrangements in these organizations can be observed and analyzed.

There are two indispensable conditions to successful research along these lines. First, it is necessary that the objectives of the administrative organization under study be defined in concrete terms so that results, expressed in terms of these objectives, can be accurately measured. Second, it is necessary that sufficient experimental control be exercised to make possible the isolation of the particular effect under study from other disturbing factors that might be operating on the organization at the same time.

These two conditions have seldom been even partially fulfilled in so-called "administrative experiments." The mere fact that a legislature passes a law creating an administrative agency, that the agency operates for five years, that the agency is finally abolished, and that a historical study is then made of the agency's operations is not sufficient to make of that agency's history an "administrative experiment." Modern American legislation is full of such "experiments" which furnish orators in neighboring states with abundant ammunition when similar issues arise in their bailiwicks, but which provide the scientific investigator with little or nothing in the way of objective evidence, one way or the other.

In the literature of administration, there are only a handful of research studies that satisfy those fundamental conditions of methodology—and these are, for the most part, on the periphery of the problem of organization. There are, first of all, the studies of the Taylor group which sought to determine the technological conditions of efficiency. Perhaps none of these is a better example of the painstaking methods of science than Taylor's own studies of the cutting of metals.[17]

Studies dealing with the human and social aspects of administration are even rarer than the technological studies. Among the more important are the whole series of studies on fatigue, starting in Great Britain during World War I and culminating in the Westinghouse experiments.[18]

In the field of public administration, almost the sole example of such experimentation is the series of studies that have been conducted in the public welfare field to determine the proper case loads for social workers.[19]

Because, apart from these scattered examples, studies of administrative agencies have been carried out without benefit of control or of objective measurements of results, they have had to depend for their recommendations and conclusions upon *a priori* reasoning proceeding from "principles

---

[17] F. W. Taylor, *On the Art of Cutting Metals* (American Society of Mechanical Engineers, 1907).

[18] Great Britain, Ministry of Munitions, Health of Munitions Workers Committee, *Final Report* (H.M. Stationery Office, 1918); F. J. Roethlisberger and William J. Dickson, *Management and the Worker* (Harvard University Press, 1939).

[19] Ellery F. Reed, *An Experiment in Reducing the Cost of Relief* (American Public Welfare Administration, 1937); Rebecca Staman, "What Is the Most Economical Case Load in Public Relief Administration?" 4 *Social Work Technique*, 117-21 (May-June, 1938); Chicago Relief Administration, *Adequate Staff Brings Economy* (American Public Welfare Association, 1939); Constance Hastings and Saya S. Schwartz, *Size of Visitor's Caseload as a Factor in Efficient Administration of Public Assistance* (Philadelphia County Board of Assistance, 1939); Simon et al., *Determining Work Loads for Professional Staff in a Public Welfare Agency* (Bureau of Public Administration, University of California, 1941).

of administration." The reasons have already been stated why the "principles" derived in this way cannot be more than "proverbs."

Perhaps the program outlined here will appear an ambitious or even a quixotic one. There should certainly be no illusions, in undertaking it, as to the length and deviousness of the path. It is hard to see, however, what alternative remains open. Certainly neither the practitioner of administration nor the theoretician can be satisfied with the poor analytic tools that the proverbs provide him. Nor is there any reason to believe that a less

drastic reconversion than that outlined here will rebuild those tools to usefulness.

It may be objected that administration cannot aspire to be a "science"; that by the nature of its subject it cannot be more than an "art." Whether true or false, this objection is irrelevant to the present discussion. The question of how "exact" the principles of administration can be made is one that only experience can answer. But as to whether they should be logical or illogical there can be no debate. Even an "art" cannot be founded on proverbs.

Too Much Concern with Human Relations?

HOWARD BAUMGARTEL

William H. Whyte in his book, *The Organization Man*, expresses strong criticism of the application of social science and group dynamics to industrial management and to human life generally. He feels that discussion groups and staff conferences thwart the individual's freedom and prevent him from being creative. Professor Malcolm P. McNair of the Harvard Business School has prepared a widely publicized attack on human relations in an article in *Look* magazine entitled "Too Much Human Relations." He feels that there is too much worry about people's feelings and that there should be more concern about "getting the job done," that is, for the businessman making a high profit and for the school administrator having an "efficient" organization. He

Howard Baumgartel, "Too Much Concern with Human Relations?" *Adult Leadership* (March, 1963).

fears that people are becoming "soft." Some of the critics of modern educational practices in the public schools would certainly apply their comments to the courses in human relations at the universities and to group-centered learning experiences in management and other kinds of adult training programs, if they knew of the existence of such courses and experiences.

Many people feel that we should have higher standards of academic excellence, that we should emphasize traditional and classic educational content, and that we should use strict disciplinary methods to accomplish such objectives. They feel that we should not spoon-feed or mollycoddle. No one can really object to these aims *per se*. Even negative critics would probably agree that more permissive and ego-involving discussion methods accomplish desirable educational goals more adequately in many areas, particularly where attitude change is essential. These critics are particularly bitter about courses that are aimed at social adjustment. They seem to dislike almost any course that is applied science in nature. Where, then, do we in the field of human relations stand in relation to these and other issues raised by these critics?

Too Concerned with Feelings

Some people identify human relations with being nice to people, and being nice to people is seen as leading to a neglect of getting the job done. Such critics are often fearful that human relations will lead to softness and to a neurotic overconcern with the feelings of others. To answer this criticism, it is necessary to identify two separate aspects of the problem. On the one hand, there is the often repeated research finding that considerate treatment of nonsupervisory employees leads to higher productivity. Certainly, human relations skills are doubly important in organizations that depend on volunteer workers. Whether one agrees or disagrees, or whether one likes or dislikes the research is immaterial; most people do better work under considerate and democratic bosses.

The second aspect of the problem lies in the efforts of teachers, trainers, and administrators to apply these and other research findings to the improvement of work relationships in particular work organizations— schools, businesses, government agencies. The research findings in themselves are neither good nor bad; they exist. Only when such findings are translated into social action are questions of value involved. The goals of sound human relations teaching programs go beyond being nice to people. These goals are oriented toward developing a deeper understanding of how human factors are involved in creating situations where people can achieve optimum productivity and a sense of personal fulfillment. Actually, research indicates that simple considerateness such as the old "pat on the back" is not enough. We are really thinking about much more positive and dynamic approaches.

Naïve and sentimental concerns with others can be a problem, however. In our teaching, we may come upon students whose overconcern with the feelings of others is a block to building creative work relationships, just as we find students whose lack of concern for others or manipulative attitudes toward others stand in their way to becoming more effective leaders. The human relations approach is firmly wedded to the findings of empirical research. Hence, it has a built-in, self-correction device as does all activity closely linked with scientific attitudes—"truth" is what the data reveal and not what any traditional belief or the authorities deem is true. As new research findings become available, we can and do modify the goals and methods of the learning experience. There should be no orthodoxy here.

Too Groupy

Similarly, some critics identify conformity to group pressure with human relations and applied group dynamics. Human relations is seen as setting the goal of group agreement above all others and, hence, putting mediocrity above the goal of the validity, excellence, correctness, and creativity in the solution of problems. Again there are two factors involved in this issue. On the one hand, there are well-founded social science findings that the significant groups in a person's life have a relatively greater influence on his actions and opinions than almost any other force. The importance of the group discussion in adult education programs stems from this fact. Experiments have shown that even intelligent college students will go against their own sense perceptions to stay close to group judgments. Social surveys have demonstrated the overwhelming influence of the primary group on adult voting behavior. These observations are, again, neither good nor bad, nor is learning that this is the nature of social reality either good or bad. The pressures for conformity in contemporary society do not come from human relations teachers and writers; the pressure has been and is there all the time in the very nature of social relationships. As a matter of fact it often seems that the real pressures for conformity come from some individualistic top level leaders. It appears to some of us that people with the above-mentioned criticisms are often merely expressing their own resentments of having to deal with other people's feelings as a part of their own reality. Actually, most human relations teachers are hopeful that their students can become more free of defensive needs for overconformity and become more autonomous and less dependent on the opinions of authority figures for guiding their own lives. Furthermore, the extensive use of discussion group methods in adult education presumes a commitment to democratic values, that consensus *is* important for social progress, that the people themselves know what is best for them. It is true, however, that the human relations field is concerned with groups, what makes them tick, what leads to their effectiveness, and what leads to sterile ineffectiveness—the destiny of all too many groups. True enough, membership in many such groups can be a stifling experience for the individual,

but this is not the creation of human relations.

The second aspect of the second issue deals with the relative effectiveness of the group *versus* the individual in creative problem-solving. We know, of course, that certain kinds of intellectual creativity such as writing and composing are inherently an individual effort. There is no argument here. However, the difficulty often arises that, particularly in work organizations, the problem is not only to obtain an elegant solution to the problem but also to obtain the agreement, commitment, and collaboration of many different people in putting the idea into practice. Clever solutions to many problems are only so much Monday morning quarterbacking until they are translated into effective action *through other people*. There is, furthermore, considerable evidence that in certain circumstances groups do come up with more creative solutions to problems than do individuals working alone, particularly when such groups have leaders skilled in applying group dynamics. In any event, the answer lies in empirical investigation and not, we would say, in opinions and argument. This commitment to empiricism leads to some of the problems that the *pros* and the *cons* have in communicating with each other. People more highly involved in philosophic and rationalistic approaches don't think the same way as do the empiricists.

Too Soft and Easy

Another criticism of human relations is that it teaches lax methods of leadership, supervision, and parenthood when stricter methods are the more desirable. This judgmental dimension of strict to lenient seems firmly embedded in most people's minds. However, such thinking results in a gross oversimplification of the complexities of superior-subordinate relationships or human relationships generally. Thomas Gordon in his book, *Group-Centered Leadership*, and Douglas McGregor in his *The Human Side of Enterprise* both comment cogently on the assumptions about human nature implied in authoritarian approaches. Actually, the results of human relations research on leadership (and, hence, their application in the objectives of many teaching programs) do emphasize the value of democratic methods. However, democratic supervisory methods are the most difficult of all to perform, and they are in sharp contrast to what is sometimes called laissez-faire leadership, which is essentially the absence of any leadership at all. Democratic leadership involves a high degree of joint involvement in the decision process and requires great skill and effort. The effective application of democratic leadership often results in a dramatic decrease in apathy, resentment, and conflict and in increase in motivation, performance, and morale. Trust in others, that is, a belief in man's capacity to solve problems and to act in constructive ways, is perhaps the basic ingredient in building such work relationships.

No Conflict

Some people see human relations as directed toward establishing a conflictless, contented social world with everything as one big, happy family. Naturally, human relations research as well as many adult education programs have been greatly concerned with the problems of conflict and co-operation. The absence of conflict would, of course, be as undesirable a situation as it is unlikely. Certain kinds of conflict are, however, destructive of highly valued social and personal goals. Studying the nature and sources of such destructive conflicts in personal, group, and social life seems to be an important objective for responsible scientific and educational groups. A desire to spread this knowledge and encourage its use in social practice characterizes the personnel in the field of human relations. The whole enterprise of adult education derives its "social movement" character from like concerns— to do something about the problems of our era. To deny such activities is to discourage the use of reason in human affairs. However, as certain psychiatrists, such as Lawrence Kubie, have pointed out, many of the best-educated young men of the upper middle-class are defective in their ability to face the fight and conflict necessary to the achievement of important social objectives. Wallace Donham in his original book proposing educational reform, *Education for Responsible Living*, saw the educator's problem as that of creating men and women who want to *do something* about the state of affairs, not merely to acquire passive knowledge.

In some human relations courses, students are encouraged to learn how to get mad and to fight for their own rights and beliefs. It is our opinion that out of effective interpersonal relationships grows the ability and freedom to contend more aggressively for one's beliefs and to be able to plan and execute the strategy and tactics of effectively introducing desired changes. A well-trained student in human relations should know something about the kind of world he wants to help create, and he should have more than ordinarily insightful ideas of how to translate his ideas into action.

Manipulative

Perhaps these last comments suggest a final major criticism of human relations training: that it is manipulative and that it teaches some people how to exploit others, such as getting more work out of employees or changing students' attitudes indirectly. What is there to say on this subject? Human relations teachers have often commented that the most manipulative people are sometimes the ones who are most antagonistic to the manipulative aspects of human relations. A behavioral science view of social life sees human interaction as a continual process of mutual influence—in a sense everybody is already spending a lot of time attempting to influence the attitudes, behavior, and beliefs of others. From one point of view, society is a network of influence attempts. Why then should some people get so upset by courses aimed at helping people use some intelligence in this process?

Perhaps many people deny their own manipulative attitudes. Perhaps some people see society in terms of class conflict, and any action aimed at reducing the conflict is, hence, seen as detrimental to the ultimate benefit of one's own class. Perhaps some individuals do not like to recognize the authority problems in their personal and social lives. They may think that to allow oneself to be influenced by another is to lose one's self-esteem. On the other hand, some people may feel that it is bad for one to attempt to influence or control the people for whom he is responsible or over whom he has authority—a kind of fear of responsibility for others. Suffice it to say that from the human relations point of view every person is an agent of social influence; he is affecting others—his children, his wife, his friends, his superiors, and his subordinates. He is, in Jean-Paul Sartre's concept, participating in the creation of the social world; *he is responsible* whether he accepts it or not. At the same time, he is being influenced and molded by others, his very self is a social product. Whether he likes it or not, he is not completely free. Human relations research and training is very much interested in studying the processes of social influence and in helping individuals use such knowledge in building fuller and richer lives for themselves and their associates. It is equally interested in helping people develop skills in building more effective groups and organizations. The very nature of effective human relations, however, militates against exploitation and subtle manipulation. As more people share in decisions, and as decisions get made on a more empirical basis, the "operator" has less of a chance. . . .

The Meaning of Work in Bureaucratic Society

JOSEPH BENSMAN   BERNARD ROSENBERG

Conflicts between Bureaucratic Roles and the Personal Needs of the Official

Bureaucracy is designed only as a technical system of administration. In practice it is much more than that. This difficulty constitutes an inherent cause of organizational problems, such as those that are bound to plague bureaucrats everywhere. To the official himself, the bureaucracy is a whole way of life, no less exacting than other ways of life. It makes sharp demands, it imposes rigid codes and stringent standards, and it places a special kind of stress upon him as a *total* individual.

To play his role as a bureaucrat at all adequately is to pay a heavy social and psychological price. The official has to repress certain prebureaucratic sentiments that may have been instilled in him as a youth, and he will invariably be forced to reject or neglect nonoccupational roles that are more continuous with his self than with his profession. When those sentiments and roles having no connection with his job are very meaningful to him, the official becomes less of a bureaucrat; on the other hand, if his bureaucratic role has been deeply internalized, he will be anxious and unhappy about subordinating it to other things. He can attempt to stabilize

"The Meaning of Work in Bureaucratic Society" by Joseph Bensman and Bernard Rosenberg.

Reprinted with permission of The Macmillan Company from *Identity and Anxiety* by Maurice Stein, Arthur Vidich, and David Manning White, eds. © by The Free Press, a Corporation, 1960.

the conflicting values and roles within himself, or deliberately pick and choose among them. When this occurs, bureaucracy may be said to have changed the personality of its officials, and when a large number of officials are affected, it also modifies the dominant character-structure of the society.

We will discuss briefly some conflicts generated by the fulfillment of bureaucratic roles, as well as their impact upon the bureaucrat and bureaucracy.

Compulsive Sociability in Bureaucracy

A large number of bureaucrats (scientists, accountants, and other pure technicians) are pure "pencil pushers," men more oriented to abstract symbols than to colleagues or clients. However, by far the majority of bureaucrats are "people-pushing" white collar employees, for whom association with others is a constant requirement. The ordinary bureaucrat is situated in a fixed and highly structured relationship to the public and to other officials, whether they are superiors or subordinates. Satisfactory performance of his tasks is grounded in his ability to secure their co-operation, good will, and support. Furthermore, his chances for advancement depend as much upon whether higher officials like him, trust him, and feel at ease with him, as they do upon his objective qualifications and his technical ability.

With respect to subordinates, the

bureaucrat's success will hinge, to a great extent, on getting them to "produce" for him. Likewise, he must take care not to let other sides of his personality, especially those revealing his real preferences, his personal likes and dislikes, intrude upon any negotiation with either his equals or with outsiders. Up and down the line, large-scale organization puts a high premium on muted discord and surface harmony, as it does on everyone's being likeable and pleasant.

The emphasis is a recurrent, not a constant, one. To a degree, it matches behavior prescribed for the courtier in handbooks like Castiglione's *The Courtier* and Lord Chesterfield's *Letters to His Son*. Surly behavior was appropriate in aristocratic societies among noblemen close to princes and kings. The courtier had, however, only to please those above him. Bureaucracy, which is so much a matter of "teamwork" and "co-operation," constrains the individual to please all his associates: those equal to and below him, as well as those above him. The English yeoman, the independent farmer, and the frontiersman achieved historical fame for their possession of traits directly opposite to those that shape contemporary officials. The sense that poverty or prosperity depended mostly upon their own efforts gave them a feeling of independence, confidence, and even cockiness. It allowed them to be unpleasant without running any great risk of economic loss. Niceness had not yet become compulsory—or compulsive.

Self-rationalization in Bureaucracy

In an employee society, "personality" becomes a market commodity, one that has measurable cash value in terms of present and future income to its possessor. Once the alert bureau-

crat recognizes this, he sets out to acquire his magic key to success. That quest Karl Mannheim has brilliantly analyzed as a "self-rationalization." In Mannheim's words:

By self-rationalization we understand the individual's systematic control of his impulses—a control which is always the first step to be taken if an individual wants to plan his life so that every action is guided by principle and is directed towards the goal he has in mind. . . . Modern society attains perhaps its highest stage of functional rationalization in its administrative staff, in which the individuals who take part not only have their specific actions prescribed . . . but in addition have their life-plan to a large extent imposed in the form of a "career," in which the individual stages are specified in advance. Concern with a career requires a maximum of self-mastery since it involves not only the actual processes of work but also the prescriptive regulation both of ideas and feelings that one is permitted to have and of one's leisure time.

Self-rationalization appears when the official begins to view himself as a merchandisable product which he must market and package like any other merchandisable product. First an inventory is necessary. He must ask: what are my assets and liabilities in the personality market? What defects must be banished before I can sell myself? Do I have the right background? If not, how can I acquire it? With such questions, the inventory is converted into a market-research project. The answers give him findings with which to remodel his personality. The bureaucratic personality is molded out of available raw materials, shaped to meet fluctuating demands of the market.

Old habits are discarded and new habits are nurtured. The would-be success learns when to stimulate enthusiasm, compassion, interest, concern, modesty, confidence, and mastery; when to smile, with whom to laugh, and how intimate or friendly he can be with other people. He selects his home and its residential area with care; he buys his clothes and chooses styles with an eye to their probable reception in his office. He reads or pretends to have read the right books, the right magazines, and the right newspapers. All this will be reflected in "the right line of conversation" which he adopts as his own, thereafter sustaining it with proper inflections. His tone is by turns disdainful, respectful, reverential, and choleric, but always well attuned to others. He joins the right party and espouses the political ideology of his fellows. If he starts early and has vision, he marries the right girl, or if he has been guilty of an indiscretion, he may disembarrass himself of the wrong girl. Every one of these procedures is a marketing operation—with its own imponderable hazards. If the operation succeeds, our official will have fabricated a personality totally in harmony with his environment; in a great many ways it will resemble the personality of his co-workers. The drive for self-rationalization implies nothing less than adult socialization, or, in the majority of cases, radical re-socialization.

The Organization Man

The pressure in bureaucratic organization which forces an individual to make himself amiable, sweet-tempered, and bland, results in conspicuous conformity, but the standards of conformity vary from organization to organization. Standards for a military officer, an academician, a businessman, a journalist, a medical technician, and a civil servant are obviously not the same. Yet, for all their differences, they have in common a deeply assimilated in-

clination to search for *external* standards, by which their interests, activities, and thoughts can be consciously directed. Each man takes on the special tincture of his organizational environment. Each tends to focus his projected self on those qualities which will be most pleasing to others. Since the others are similarly occupied, everyone's personality is fractionated. Part of it can be seen; the rest is subdued and hidden. Bureaucratic organizations sweeten and soften the visible personality.

The sweetening process, however, requires denying other portions of the self. Officials strive to develop those aspects of their personality which fit the bureaucratic milieu. This makes it difficult for them to develop aspects that are "out-of-phase." Hypertrophy in one direction spells atrophy in another. One consequence of self-rationalization as a technique to control personality is that, after some time has passed, the poseur may find that he is a different person. With much practice, "control" becomes unnecessary; the bureaucratic mask becomes the normal face, and refractory impulses get buried beyond reactivation. Functionaries are then, in the fullest sense, Organization Men.

Special Bureaucratic Stresses

The bureaucratic atmosphere may seem to be warm and friendly; officials are encouraged to call each other by their first names, and except in the armed forces, "pulling rank" clumsily tends to be offensive. There is an outward show of civility, politeness and decency. Conspicuous harassment of subordinates is condemned by every efficiency expert and human engineer in America, usually on the ground that it reduces efficiency. Yet tensions are aroused even in the smoothest bureaucracy, and there they cannot be publicly aired. This may make them harder to contain. These stresses can cause officials to violate the norms of their organization and nullify its purposes. The stresses we have in mind are related to impersonality, isolation, and powerlessness.

Let us recall that the principle of uniform administration is based upon specific rules, carried out by those whose duties are rigorously prescribed. Bureaucratic officials are placed in relationship to each other by the rules, and deal with each other—as they do with the outside world—according to fixed regulations. They are not supposed to be influenced by personal preference, affinity, taste, or choice. They deal with and see each other because the situation obliges them to do so. Office contacts of a particular kind are required, and each party to them knows that they are required. Every intraoffice relationship is covered by formal specifications, which, because of their official nature, cannot easily be executed or accepted with spontaneity, or empathy, or a sense of personal identification. But without some degree of warmth no durable human interaction has ever been observed to take place. If dehumanization is the objective, it is never wholly attainable. On the other hand, human spontaneity knows no bounds; it cannot be safely restrained by offices and rules, and is therefore likely to cause trouble. A common compromise occurs in the form of controlled warmth or planned spontaneity; synthetic emotion is meant to pass for real warmth and spontaneity, but it does not actually commit officials beyond the point of involvement formally demanded of them. They act out their parts, performing or discarding them as necessity and convenience require. Such roles are never really internalized.

In the bureaucratic milieu, which is a vortex of togetherness, other-directedness, teamwork, and co-operation, the individual finds it exceedingly difficult to relate or commit himself to his associates. He learns that they respond as shallowly or as deceptively as he does to them. This awareness makes him wary of the apparent camaraderie others offer in their official capacity. Thus, in the midst of endless interaction with clients and other officials, the individual feels isolated, unbreakably tied to, and hopelessly cut off from, those others he will see every working day of his life. Ironically, the greatest measure of social and psychological isolation may be traced to two very different, if not opposite, structures: the city with its extremely loose organization, and the bureaucracy with its extremely tight organization.

The Quest for Identification in Informal Groups

Bureaucratic impersonality bemuses the official at precisely that point where he feels a deep personal need to identify with and relate to people as people. Like almost every other human being, the official has acquired his basic orientation to social life in the family and in other primary groups, where deeper, more intimate, and unpremeditated responses are provided. His formative environment generates expectations that formal bureaucratic organization is not capable of satisfying. Consequently, the bureaucrat improvises patterns of response, calculated to satisfy extra-occupational needs by means that go beyond—and outside of—the prescriptions of his official role.

The quest for personal identification often leads one official to seek out others. In defiance of all the proprieties and all the rules, he may make attachments that have no organizational sanction. As this process spreads, the office comes to be reorganized into informal and unofficial friendship-groups, cliques whose existence is unrecognized in the table of organization. Such cliques form as the result of physical propinquity, or they sprout from common interests, common ambition, common resentment, or common ethnic origin. Each clique evolves a common core of standards from the initial consensus of its members, and again, they may clash with those of the organization. Such separate standards include the restriction of output and systematic violation of office procedure (so that the clique punishes what the highest officials reward). Clique control is perhaps most serious when it is informally responsible for promoting policies which lack official authority to back them up. The clique is hospitable to personnel, from different departments and at different levels of authority, who establish their own channels of communication. They have little regard for preconceived blueprints, reaching each other and selected segments of the public without "clearance" from above. In this way, gossip circulates, secrets are revealed, information is leaked—and official policy has been unofficially nullified.

The informal group has its informal leaders. These leaders are men who, through their network of personal friendship and influence, bring other persons into continuous unofficial interaction. A clique leader is not necessarily an official of the highest rank. The situation which then presents itself—in extreme cases—is such that the nominal bosses exert less influence than those without title to authority. There is no other way to gain intimate knowledge of cliques than by joining them—which those on top and those outside are often precluded from doing. When men vested with official authority try to get things done by using the formal administrative machinery, they may find that machinery inadequate and obsolescent. At the same time, those who manipulate the informal network of clique communications do get things done—by breaking all the rules.

The many cliques in a large office are often at odds with each other. Individual bureaucrats compete for raises, promotions, niches, and prestige symbols. To that competition they bring not only their own rivalries, but also such support as can be mustered from friends, partisans, and cliques. Not just separate individuals, but whole cliques choose sides, lining up on a host of issues that pertain to office politics. They reward their friends on the basis of personal loyalty rather than performance, and they hinder or penalize even those enemies who completely fulfill legitimate functions.

In these circumstances, the bureaucratic regime is turned upside down. Despite its outward quiescence, the office becomes a battleground in which "politics" is a potent weapon, and one in which mines and traps are common dangers. An official may unsuspectingly befriend one of his colleagues who belongs to the wrong camp, and thereby consign himself to oblivion. Or he may hitch his wagon to a floundering team; he may be identified with an unstable clique on its way down—and suffer personally for all the failures of that clique.

In sum: the formation of cliques tends to alter operational bureaucracy to something quite different from its ideal type. The uniformity, predictability, and precision built into it are processed out of it by intervening social and emotional factors. For this reason alone, bureaucracy can never be perfectly smooth or absolutely efficient.

Disidentification with the Bureaucracy

The search for personal identity in social relationships that are not wholly purposive and functional is one of several tendencies. Some bureaucrats, overwhelmed by the impersonality of their work, give up the idea that it is meaningful or that it is a suitable medium for self-realization. They turn to, and enlarge upon, other aspects of life, while doing as little work as possible in offices that are distasteful to them. The major locus of meaning lies in the family, a hobby, a satisfying style of consumption, contact with people from other spheres, in philandering, in romantic dalliance, in suburban and exurban affairs, in the affectations of "Upper Bohemia" or in any of several idiosyncratic activities.

By denying the meaningfulness of their work, they become less devoted and less efficient. They minimize their duties and perform them in a routinely competent way, giving no more thought to the office than is irreducibly necessary. They systematically avoid decisions, pass the buck, and take no action whenever possible. In his analysis of the United States Navy Officers Corps, Arthur K. Davis found "avoiding responsibility: the philosophy of do-the-least," or "shunting responsibility upward" both common and complex; it was surrounded by social, personal, and technical conditions, and it could be disastrous. At the lower and middle levels of bureaucracy, officials are strongly tempted "to slide (problems) into their superior's lap by asking advice, requesting instructions, securing approval in advance." But, Davis says, "For the

man at the top there is no such escape from the strains of decision except by a do-nothing policy." Timid or indifferent bureaucrats who pass the buck and who, when on top, avoid decisions are the bureaucrats whose public imagery has fixed itself upon the popular imagination. Here the man corresponds to the prototype. He has abandoned his initial hope of upward mobility, and looks elsewhere for satisfaction.

To achieve positive action and speedy disposition of business, a bureaucracy needs *esprit de corps*, high morale and enthusiastic dedication. If an organization is staffed with apathetic bureaucrats, its purposes are less and less likely to be achieved.

Over-identification

The very same sense of isolation that leads one bureaucrat out of the organization to seek his "self" will lead another to "over-identify" with the organization. In this case the organization as a whole is substituted for other identifications and for various social relationships. A clear and familiar case (not without pathos) occurs when the lowly clerk employed by a large, powerful, and well-known agency, reaches for the halo of his organization to cover his anonymity and powerlessness in it. He speaks knowingly of policies and practices which circulate through the office grapevine, but are many times removed from himself. He implies by use of the pronouns "we" and "our" that the organization's policies and practices are his policies and practices, that he somehow had a hand in making them. Since he must conceal his actual position in order to exploit it among strangers, his life is sharply divided between office and home. With a fictitious title and some histrionic ability, an elevator man employed by one of the large communications companies, who is domiciled in a fashionable suburb, and who looks, dresses and talks like a Madison Avenue hotshot can effectively exploit his connection. This is what the Captain from Koepnig did in Kaiser Wilhelm's Germany, when he pretended to be an officer and was accepted as such. The assumption of a false identity is increasingly possible in societies that give higher prestige to the organization than they do to the innumerable individuals who must make it work.

Identification with "The Rules"

Another kind of over-identification manifests itself in inordinate and inflexible adherence to rules. To the outsider such rigidity looks like senseless obstructionism, and he finds it maddening enough to have changed the word "bureaucracy" from a label into an epithet. To the functionary whose personal identity has been swallowed up by the organization, rules that are precise, orderly, fixed, and certain, may represent a source of psychological security not otherwise available to him.

In the grip of his passion for legalism, a bureaucrat virtuoso follows the letter of every rule, never deviating, never counting the consequences or considering what possible harm he does to others. Javert, the police official of Victor Hugo's *Les Miserables*, is a perfect example of the legalist. Far beyond the call of duty, Javert remorselessly pursues a man of whose excellent character and good deeds he is fully aware, putting aside his own knowledge and disregarding the sympathy that wells up in him. When confronted with the ineluctable choice between rampant legalism and personal conviction, he takes his life.

Nazi documents, captured after World War II, indicate that on the day Adolf Hitler committed suicide and Russian troops were marching through the streets of Berlin, officials of the Reichschancellery were too busy to look out of their windows. They were engaged in estimating and ordering paper clips for the next fiscal year!

Legalism, which Davis has called the psychology of affirm-and-conform, and for which he lays down a golden rule, "Follow the book or pass the buck," is perhaps the most dangerous and pathological outgrowth of bureaucratic organization. Davis deals with the seriousness of overemphasis upon instrumental devices, among naval officers in time of war. He cites two striking examples:

In one large air unit, even the most trivial correspondence was routed up to the Chief of Staff and often to the Admiral, then down to the appropriate department for action. Here the reply was drafted, typed, routed back to the top for approval and signature (often refused, pending minor changes) and finally routed down to the despatching office. Mail which a clerk should have handled in and out in 24 hours was thus sent to the top and back two or three times, drawing attention from 8 to 12 persons over a ten-day period.

We cite next the behavior of certain heavy-bomber crews on anti-submarine patrols. Because of their short tour of duty, the infrequency of submarine sightings, and the complexity of anti-submarine tactics, these air crews usually made several errors in the course of an attack. For this they would be sharply criticized by their superiors. Hence arose a serious morale problem. At least three flight crews in one flight squadron began going out for "quiet patrols" by their own admission. Observing the letter of their instructions legalistically, they flew their patrols exactly as charted. If a suspicious object appeared a few miles abeam, their course lay straight ahead.

The use of forms and of standard procedures, the transmutation of mechanics into a Sacred Cow, and the reduction of a task to many phases in which only a few persons (or no one at all) can understand the whole flow of a single operation: these are among the factors that contribute most heavily to legalism. And legalism is widely, subtly, and grossly converted into a means of self-identification. . . .

Powerlessness

The feeling of powerlessness often experienced by modern administrators is fundamentally related to the structure of bureaucracy. That structure is notable for its strict hierarchy and the marked differences—in authority, rank, income, and prerogatives—between men at various levels. Such differences exist in any form of social organization, but they are greatly sharpened in a bureaucracy where each job is as systematically defined as all duties and privileges are clearly delineated.

Structurally, every bureaucrat knows where he stands, who is above him and who is below him. He knows this by direct perception or by informed guesswork. It is possible for him to compare his salary, his benefits, and his chances of promotion with those of others, to notice how others get along with each other and whether they are on the "outs" with key figures. It does not take an unusually perceptive actor to realize that he may be one of those functionaries who actually has little power and no real leverage in the organization.

A second form of structurally determined powerlessness issues from the bureaucracy's segmented and special-ized nature. As individuals and departments divide and subdivide the performance of a single operation, there are times when no one person can envisage the total task. More often, it seems chaotic to everyone except the co-ordinator and those few persons taken into his confidence. The first atomic bomb was produced at Los Alamos in just such an atmosphere; most of those engaged in the Manhattan Project had no knowledge of its real purpose. The everyday conduct of bureaucratic affairs which do not involve top secrets may be quite as mystifying to those who are responsible for them. In the case of almost every bureaucrat, his assignments originate in another department, they are passed on to him, and finally completed in still other departments. He works only on one phase of a job, in accordance with directives from above, which, from his worm's eye view, may not make sense. To a detailed specialist, facets of the job other than his own are seldom clear, and he may do no more than conjecture uncertainly about them. He sees what look to him like avoidable mistakes made by bosses who do not have his special competence, and who are therefore viewed with some disdain. This is stylized into the wry and half-serious belief that the men in charge got there by making mistakes so repeatedly that they had to be kicked upstairs. More serious is the belief that luck, marriage, apple-polishing, and bootlicking made for success.

In almost every bureaucracy there is a myth of incompetence which lower officials cherish about higher officials. It is assumed that somehow incompetence mixed with smooth talking and aided by "connections" is what it takes to come out on top. The existence of this myth is a rough gauge of the resentment that powerless people feel for their ostensibly powerful superiors. Resentment—that peculiar emotion which begins with striving and is heightened by impotence—is most especially evoked among lower- and middle-ranking officials who cannot realistically expect to attain power. It leads to disidentification from the bureaucracy.

White-Collar Sabotage

This disidentification is concretely expressed by the bureaucrat who gossips, complains, and searches for errors. In a more advanced stage, it includes passive resistance and subtle sabotage. One's duty is performed in ways that are procedurally correct and yet make the task impossible to accomplish. With no show of malice whatsoever, one's superiors may be deliberately exposed to the probability of error and ridicule. The claim that messages are unclear, that directives are ambiguous, and that therefore misunderstanding cannot be avoided, is a technique instantly familiar to modern readers as Schweikism—after *The Good Soldier Schweik*, by Jaroslav Hasek. Schweik is an obedient Yes Man and an effective saboteur in the Austro-Hungarian army; he does at once everything the officers tell him to do and nothing they tell him to do. Schweik is prototypic. His methods are still widely employed by enlisted men in armies everywhere. Government bureaus are still subject to Schweikism, as they are to the disloyalty of men who reveal office secrets, leak embarrassing data to the press, or otherwise put higher-ups "on the spot." Private business zealously guards its secrets; for a functionary to betray them would be unpardonable; this is true even when everybody in the industry knows what everybody else knows.

According to Raymond Loewy there is no more significant difference among American automobiles than there is among cake mixes. Loewy, an industrial engineer who designed the postwar Studebaker, explains that this sameness has come about because every company produces "imitative, over-decorated chariots, with something for everyone laid over a basic formula design that is a copy of someone else's formula design." With that, Loewy divorces himself from the automotive industry and, hence, never identified with it, is free to report that:

Detroit spends an annual fortune to insure its lack of originality. . . . To protect its styling, Ford has a force of 20 security guards commanded by an ex-FBI agent. Different-colored passes admit different people to specific different rooms and to those rooms only. Unused sketches and clay models are destroyed. Ford's studio locks can be changed within an hour if somebody loses a key. To pierce such a wall of secrecy, each company employs spies and counter-spies, rumorists and counter-rumorists. Rival helicopters flutter over high-walled test tracks. Ford guards peer at an adjacent water tower with a 60-power telescope to make sure no long-range camera is mounted on it by a rival concern. One automotive company installed a microphone in a blond's brassiere and sent her off to seduce a secret. . . . All secrets are discovered! The shape of a Ford hubcap! The number of square inches of chromium on the new Buick! The final result is that all companies know all the secrets of all the other companies, and everyone brings out the same car.

To reveal known or unknown secrets is a form of *lese majesté* practiced only by the disaffected and the dis-identified. Frontline officials in this condition do not remain unidentified. They re-identify—usually with clients, taking their side, waiving rules, and forgetting standard forms. Into this category fall the relief investigator who grants an applicant's claim without carefully checking it; the insurance adjuster who okays the obviously excessive claim of a policy-holder; the foreman who sides with workers in his plant rather than with management; and the supervisor who, instead of correcting his subordinates' mistakes, covers them up. In all such cases, the official who feels powerless in relation to his superiors, stretches, bends, or breaks the regulations so that he can give a better break to persons still less powerful than himself. And in all such cases, personal interaction is substituted for impersonal procedure. Powerlessness and impersonality are negated—at the organization's expense. Such behavior frequently elicits sympathy; it is viewed as human-all-too-human kindness.

Authoritarianism

The public has much less patience with another response to powerlessness, which motivates the bureaucrat who is hedged in on one side to break out in search of power on another side. A lowly clerk, squelched by his superiors, may redirect the resentment that comes over him. He can do this by abusing his clients. So can the case worker who uses legal and extralegal methods to humiliate or otherwise punish those in need of his help. To them, he represents the awful power of a large agency. The official who has no other source of power, who regards himself as an insignificant part of the organization, is very powerful indeed when he faces outsiders who are dependent upon him. Similarly, a middle-level boss may exult in tyrannizing without mercy over his subordinates precisely because he has so little over-all discretion. He may be compulsive and petty

about minor matters for the reason that his area of jurisdiction is petty and unimportant. James Jones's novel, *From Here to Eternity*, is an extended illustration of the fact that such abuse can be torture to its victim.

Every office holder knows that the petty tyrant who overpowers his underlings is simultaneously capable of meekness and sycophancy to those who out-rank him. Such conduct is all of a piece. It may properly be called authoritarian, for it is based upon the premise that authority as such, any and every kind of authority, must be respected. The relation of that authority to wisdom or purpose—or even sanity—goes unquestioned, as Herman Wouk argues in his postwar best seller, *The Caine Mutiny*. That novel placed the onus of scorn on a naval officer who disobeyed his deranged captain, thereby evincing illegitimate disrespect for authority, even insane authority.

In the presence of a superior, the authoritarian bureaucrat is eager to please, musters all the charm in his possession, snaps to attention, fawns, and generally acts with extravagant deference. No matter how much he privately resents his debasement, he gives his all to it. Away from his superiors, despite the humiliation rankling within him, he finds it necessary to humiliate others. He demonstrates his own authority, if only to prove to himself that he is not a rabbit after all.

This pattern of behavior, familiar to psychologists as dominance and submission, is especially common in any bureaucracy. It is no doubt embedded in the individual personality as a trait that makes bureaucratic employment attractive in the first place, but that employment in its objective form accentuates the trait. It produces individual suffering, and, when widespread, it can produce a fundamental weakening of the organization. . . .

. . .

A cautionary word must be added. All of our descriptions distort the appearance of bureaucracy as it visibly operates. These conditions exist, but within a context of overwhelmingly routine work, often neither pleasant nor unpleasant. Moreover, there is nothing so psychically burdensome or intolerably harsh about bureaucracy that it cannot be softened by ordinary social activities or sweetened by "seeing the better side of things." If there are economists (in this case, Kenneth Boulding) who warn that "Beyond a certain point increase in the scale of organization results in a breakdown of communication, in a lack of flexibility, in bureaucratic stagnation and insensitivity," who liken the bureaucratic monster to a dinosaur leaving free men breathing space only in the interstices of its path, there are cheerful academicians (in this case, Harlan Cleveland, Dean of the Maxwell Graduate School of Citizenship and Public Affairs at Syracuse University) to offer consolation.

My impression is that "large-scale" organization generally implies loose organization. Precisely because big organizations make most of the vital decisions affecting our destiny, more people are participating in those decisions than ever before. . . .

In a household managed by people who can walk and talk, a baby begins to experience a sense of personal freedom when it masters the techniques of walking and talking. Just so, in a world dominated by large-scaleness, it is those individuals who learn to work with and in large-scale organizations who have a rational basis for feeling free. There are, of course, plenty of free men who work—for giant corporations or government agencies—but they aren't those who are so afraid of them that they scurry into the "interstices" of smallness. I have no doubt that a large number of middle-grade bureaucrats in the Soviet Union have so mastered the system that they are, in a sense, experiencing within its limits a significant measure of personal freedom. The reason is that the Soviet is not, as Mr. Boulding protests, a "one-firm state," but a myriad collection of manageable size bound together by leadership and a sense of destiny in ways not so fundamentally different from other nations as they (and we) like to assume.

Real bureaucracy is neither as efficient as its ideal type suggests, nor as cruel and inefficient as our treatment of its pathologies suggests. Not all people are frustrated by bureaucracy—towards which they may have gravitated by predisposition. No bureaucracy is exclusively staffed with pathological types. The negative tendencies we have sketched are, however, as much a reality as the positive ones. These tendencies pose typical problems and present typical difficulties which most white-collar workers encounter at one time or another in the course of their careers.

To a certain extent they are inescapable, simply because bureaucracy is here to stay. As society is more and more dominated by largeness, bureaucracy's share of our total life cannot but grow with it. The future, if there is to be one, points to ever greater degrees of hugeness. Beyond that, Boulding is correct in saying, "The electric calculator, the punched card, operations research and decision theory all point to a still further revolution in the making . . ." toward still more bureaucracy.

The Analysis of Goals in Complex Organizations

CHARLES PERROW

Social scientists have produced a rich body of knowledge about many aspects of large-scale organizations, yet there are comparatively few studies of the goals of these organizations. For a full understanding of organizations and the behavior of their personnel, analysis of organizational goals would seem to be critical. Two things have impeded such analysis. Studies of morale, turnover, informal organization, communication, supervisory practices, etc., have been guided by an over-rationalistic point of view wherein goals are taken for granted, and the most effective ordering of resources and personnel is seen as the only problematical issue. Fostering this view is the lack of an adequate distinction between types of goals. Without such clarification it is difficult to determine what the goals are and what would be acceptable evidence for the existence of a particular goal and for a change in goals.

It will be argued here, first, that the type of goals most relevant to understanding organizational behavior are not the official goals, but those that are embedded in major operating policies and the daily decisions of the personnel. Second, these goals will be shaped by the particular problems or tasks an organization must emphasize, since these tasks determine the characteristics of those who will dominate the organization. In illustrating the lat-

ter argument, we will not be concerned with the specific goals of organizations, but only with the range within which goals are likely to vary. Though general hospitals will be used as the main illustration, three types of organizations will be discussed: voluntary service organizations, non-voluntary service organizations and profit-making organizations.

The Over-Rationalistic View

Most studies of the internal operation of complex organizations, if they mention goals at all, have taken official statements of goals at face value. This may be justified if only a limited problem is being investigated, but even then it contributes to the view that goals are not problematical. In this view, goals have no effect upon activities other than in the grossest terms; or it can be taken for granted that the only problem is to adjust means to given and stable ends. This reflects a distinctive "model" of organizational behavior, which Gouldner has characterized as the rational model.[1] Its proponents see the managerial elite as using rational and logical means to pursue clear and discrete ends set forth in official statements of goals, while the worker is seen as governed by non-rationalistic, traditionalistic orientations. If goals are unambiguous and achievement evaluated by cost-accounting procedures, the only turmoil of or-

---

Charles Perrow, "The Analysis of Goals in Complex Organizations," **26** (1961), 854-865, with minor omissions.

[1] Alvin Gouldner, "Organizational Analysis," in Robert Merton, Leonard Broom and Leonard S. Cottrell, Jr., editors, *Sociology Today* (New York: Basic Books, 1959), p. 407.

ganizational life lies below the surface with workers or, at best, with middle management maneuvering for status and power. Actually, however, non-rational orientations exist at all levels, including the elite who are responsible for setting goals[2] and assessing the degree to which they are achieved.

One reason for treating goals as static fixtures of organizational life is that goals have not been given adequate conceptualization, though the elements of this are in easy reach. If making a profit or serving customers is to be taken as a sufficient statement of goals, then all means to this end might appear to be based on rational decisions because the analyst is not alerted to the countless policy decisions involved. If goals are given a more elaborate conceptualization, we are forced to see many more things as problematic.

Official and Operative Goals

Two major categories of goals will be discussed here, official and "operative" goals.[3] Official goals are the general purposes of the organization as put forth in the charter, annual reports, public statements by key executives and other authoritative pronouncements. For example, the goal of an employment agency may be to place job seekers in contact with firms seeking workers. The official goal of a hospital may be to promote the health of the community through curing the

ill, and sometimes through preventing illness, teaching, and conducting research. Similar organizations may emphasize different publically acceptable goals. A business corporation, for example, may state that its goal is to make a profit or adequate return on investment, or provide a customer service, or produce goods.

This level of analysis is inadequate in itself for a full understanding of organizational behavior. Official goals are purposely vague and general and do not indicate two major factors which influence organizational behavior: the host of decisions that must be made among alternative ways of achieving official goals and the priority of multiple goals, and the many unofficial goals pursued by groups within the organization. The concept of "operative goals"[4] will be used to cover these aspects. Operative goals designate the ends sought through the actual operating policies of the organization; they tell us what the organization actually is trying to do, regardless of what the official goals say are the aims.

Where operative goals provide the specific content of official goals they reflect choices among competing values. They may be justified on the basis of an official goal, even though they may subvert another official goal. In one sense they are means to official goals, but since the latter are vague or of high abstraction, the "means" become ends in themselves when the organization is the object of analysis. For example, where profit-making is the announced goal, operative goals will specify whether quality or quantity is

---

[2] A strong argument for considering changes in goals is made by James D. Thompson and William J. McEwen, "Organizational Goals and Environment: Goal-Setting as an Interaction Process," *American Sociological Review*, **23** (February, 1958), 23-31.

[3] A third may be distinguished: social system goals, which refers to those contributions an organization makes to the functioning of a social system in which it is nested. . . .

[4] The concept of "operational goals" or "sub-goals" put forth by March and Simon bears a resemblance to this but does not include certain complexities which we will discuss, nor is it defined systematically. See J. G. March and H. A. Simon, *Organizations* (New York: Wiley, 1958), pp. 156-57.

to be emphasized, whether profits are to be short run and risky or long run and stable, and will indicate the relative priority of diverse and somewhat conflicting ends of customer service, employee morale, competitive pricing, diversification, or liquidity. Decisions on all these factors influence the nature of the organization, and distinguish it from another with an identical official goal. An employment agency must decide whom to serve, what characteristics they favor among clients, and whether a high turnover of clients or a long run relationship is desired. In the voluntary general hospital, where the official goals are patient care, teaching, and research, the relative priority of these must be decided, as well as which group in the community is to be given priority in service, and are these services to emphasize, say, technical excellence or warmth and "handholding."

Unofficial operative goals, on the other hand, are tied more directly to group interests and while they may support, be irrelevant to, or subvert official goals, they bear no necessary connection with them. An interest in a major supplier may dictate the policies of a corporation executive. The prestige that attaches to utilizing elaborate high speed computers may dictate the reorganization of inventory and accounting departments. Racial prejudice may influence the selection procedures of an employment agency. The personal ambition of a hospital administrator may lead to community alliances and activities which bind the organization without enhancing its goal achievement. On the other hand, while the use of interns and residents as "cheap labor" may subvert the official goal of medical education, it may substantially further the official goal of providing a high quality of patient care.

The discernment of operative goals is, of course, difficult and subject to error. The researcher may have to determine from analysis of a series of apparently minor decisions regarding the lack of competitive bidding and quality control that an unofficial goal of a group of key executives is to maximize their individual investments in a major supplier. This unofficial goal may affect profits, quality, market position, and morale of key skill groups. The executive of a correctional institution may argue that the goal of the organization is treatment, and only the lack of resources creates an apparent emphasis upon custody or deprivation. The researcher may find, however, that decisions in many areas establish the priority of custody or punishment as a goal. For example, few efforts may be made to obtain more treatment personnel; those hired are misused and mistrusted; and clients are viewed as responding only to deprivations. The president of a junior college may deny the function of the institution is to deal with the latent terminal student, but careful analysis such as Clark has made of operating policies, personnel practices, recruitment procedures, organizational alliances and personal characteristics of elites will demonstrate this to be the operative goal.[5]

The Task—Authority—Goal Sequence

While operative goals will only be established through intensive analysis of decisions, personnel practices, alliance and elite characteristics in each organization, it is possible to indicate the range within which they will vary and the occasion for general shifts in goals. We will argue that if we know something about the major tasks of an organization and the characteristics of

[5] Burton Clark, *The Open Door College* (New York: McGraw-Hill), 1960.

its controlling elite, we can predict its goals in general terms. The theory presented and illustrated in the rest of this paper is a first approximation and very general, but it may guide and stimulate research on this problem.

Every organization must accomplish four tasks: (1) secure inputs in the form of capital sufficient to establish itself, operate, and expand as the need arises; (2) secure acceptance in the form of basic legitimization of activity; (3) marshal the necessary skills; and (4) coordinate the activities of its members, and the relations of the organization with other organizations and with clients or consumers. All four are not likely to be equally important at any point in time. Each of these task areas provides a presumptive basis for control or domination by the group equipped to meet the problems involved. (The use of the terms control or dominance signifies a more pervasive, thorough and all-embracing phenomenon than authority or power.) The operative goals will be shaped by the dominant group, reflecting the imperatives of the particular task area that is most critical, their own background characteristics (distinctive perspectives based upon their training, career lines, and areas of competence) and the unofficial uses to which they put the organization for their own ends.

The relative emphasis upon one or another of the four tasks will vary with the nature of the work the organization does and the technology appropriate to it,[6] and with the stage of devel-

opment within the organization.[7] An organization engaged in manufacturing in an industry where skills are routinized and the market position secure, may emphasize coordination, giving control to the experienced administrator. An extractive industry, with a low skill level in its basic tasks and a simple product, will probably emphasize the importance of capital tied up in land, specialized and expensive machinery, and transportation facilities. The chairman of the board of directors or a group within the board will probably dominate such an organization. An organization engaged in research and development, or the production of goods or services which cannot be carried out in a routinized fashion, will probably be most concerned with skills. Thus engineers or other relevant professionals will dominate. It is also possible that all three groups—trustees, representatives of critical skills, and administrators—may share power equally. This "multiple leadership" will be discussed in detail later. Of course, trustees are likely to dominate in the early history of any organization, particularly those requiring elaborate capital and facilities, or unusual legitimization. But once these requisites are secured, the nature of the tasks will determine whether trustees or others dominate. The transfer of authority, especially from trustees to another group, may be protracted, constituting a lag in adaptation.

Where major task areas do not change over time, the utility of the

---

[6] For an illuminating discussion of organizations which emphasizes technological differences, see James D. Thompson and Frederick L. Bates, "Technology, Organizations, and Administration," *Administrative Science Quarterly*, 2 (December, 1957), 325-43.

[7] Many other factors are also important, such as the legal framework, official and unofficial regulatory bodies, state of the industry, etc. These will not be considered here. In general, their influences are felt through the task areas, and thus are reflected here.

scheme presented here is limited to suggesting possible relations between task areas, authority structure, and operative goals. The more interesting problems, which we deal with in our illustrations below, involve organizations which experience changes in major task areas over time. If the technology or type of work changes, or if new requirements for capital or legitimization arise, control will shift from one group to another. One sequence is believed to be typical.

Voluntary General Hospitals

We will discuss four types of hospitals, those dominated by trustees, by the medical staff (an organized group of those doctors who bring in private patients plus the few doctors who receive salaries or commissions from the hospital), by the administration, and by some form of multiple leadership. There has been a general development among hospitals from trustee domination, based on capital and legitimization, to domination by the medical staff, based upon the increasing importance of their technical skills, and, at present, a tendency towards administrative dominance based on internal and external coordination. (The administrator may or may not be a doctor himself.) Not all hospitals go through these stages, or go through them in this sequence. Each type of authority structure shapes, or sets limits to, the type of operative goals that are likely to prevail, though there will be much variation within each type.[8]

_____
[8] The following discussion is based upon the author's study of one hospital which, in fact, passed through these stages; upon examination of published and unpublished studies of hospitals; and upon numerous conversations with administrators, doctors, and trustees in

Trustee Domination

Voluntary general hospitals depend upon community funds for an important part of their capital and operating budget. Lacking precise indicators of efficiency or goal achievement, yet using donated funds, they must involve community representatives—trustees—in their authority structure. Trustees legitimate the non-profit status of the organization, assure that funds are not misused, and see that community needs are being met. Officially, they are the ultimate authority in voluntary hospitals. They do not necessarily exercise the legal powers they have, but where they do, there is no question that they are in control.

The functional basis for this control is primarily financial. They have access to those who make donations, are expected to contribute heavily themselves, and control the machinery and sanctions for fund raising drives. Financial control allows them to withhold resources from recalcitrant groups in the organization, medical or nonmedical. They also, of course, control all appointments and promotions, medical and non-medical.

Where these extensive powers are exercised, operative goals are likely to reflect the role of trustees as community representatives and contributors to community health. Because of their responsibility to the sponsoring community, trustees may favor conservative financial policies, opposing large financial outlays for equipment, research, and education so necessary for

_____
the United States. Sophisticated practitioners in the hospital field recognize and describe these types in their own fashion. See Charles Perrow, "Authority, Goals and Prestige in a General Hospital," unpublished Ph.D. dissertation, University of California, Berkeley, 1960, for fuller documentation and discussion.

high medical standards.[9] High standards also require more delegation of authority to the medical staff than trustee domination can easily allow.[10] As representatives drawn from distinctive social groups in the community, they may be oriented towards service for a religious, ethnic, economic, or age group in the community. Such an orientation may conflict with selection procedures favored by the medical staff or administration. Trustees may also promote policies which demonstrate a contribution to community welfare on the part of an elite group, perhaps seeking to maintain a position of prominence and power within the community. The hospital may be used as a vehicle for furthering a social philosophy of philanthropy and good works; social class values regarding personal worth, economic independence and responsibility; the assimilation of a minority group;[11] or even to further resistance to government control and socialized medicine.

Such orientations will shape operative goals in many respects, affecting standards and techniques of care, priority of services, access to care, relations with other organizations, and directions and rate of development. The administrator in such a hospital— usually called a "superintendent" under the circumstances—will have little power, prestige or responsibility. For example, trustees have been known to question the brand of grape juice

the dietician orders, or insist that they approve the color of paint the administrator selects for a room.[12] Physicians may disapprove of patient selection criteria, chafe under financial restrictions which limit the resources they have to work with, and resent active control over appointments and promotions in the medical staff.

Medical Domination

Trustee domination was probably most common in the late nineteenth and early twentieth century. Medical technology made extraordinary advances in the twentieth century, and doctors possessed the skills capable of utilizing the advances. They demanded new resources and were potentially in a position to control their allocation and use. Increasingly, major decisions had to be based upon a technical competence trustees did not possess. Trustees had a continuing basis for control because of the costs of new equipment and personnel, but in many hospitals the skill factor became decisive. Some trustees felt that the technology required increased control by doctors; others lost a struggle for power with the medical staff; in some cases trustees were forced to bring in and give power to an outstanding doctor in order to increase the reputation of the hospital.[13] Under such conditions trustees are likely to find that their legal power becomes nominal and they can only intervene in crisis situations; even financial requirements come to be set by conditions outside their control.[14] They

---

[9] Exceptions to conservative financial policies appear to occur most frequently in crisis situations where accreditation is threatened or sound business principles are violated by run down facilities, or inefficient management. See Temple Burling, Edith M. Lentz, and Robert N. Wilson, *The Give and Take in Hospitals* (New York: G. P. Putnam, 1956), chapters 4, 5, 6.

[10] Burling *et al.* (*ibid.*, p. 43), note that active trustees find delegation difficult.

[11] Perrow, *op. cit.*, chapter 5.

[12] Edith Lentz, "Changing Concepts of Hospital Administration," *Industrial and Labor Relations Research*, 3 (Summer, 1957), p. 2; Perrow, *op. cit.*, p. 86.

[13] Berthram Bernhein, *The Story of Johns Hopkins* (New York: McGraw-Hill), 1948, pp. 142-48.

[14] For a detailed analysis of such a shift of power, see Perrow, *op. cit.*, pp. 43-50.

continue to provide the mantle of community representation and non-profit status, and become "staff" members whose major task is to secure funds.

It is sometimes hard to see why all hospitals are not controlled by the medical staff, in view of the increasing complexity and specialization of the doctor's skills, their common professional background, the power of organized medicine, and the prestige accorded the doctor in society. Furthermore, they are organized for dominance, despite their nominal status as "guests" in the house.[15] The medical staff constitutes a "shadow" organization in hospitals, providing a ready potential for control. It is organized on bureaucratic principles with admission requirements, rewards and sanctions, and a committee structure which often duplicates the key committees of the board of directors and administrative staff. Nor are doctors in an advisory position as are "staff" groups in other organizations. Doctors perform both staff and line functions, and their presumptive right to control rests on both. Doctors also have a basic economic interest in the hospital, since it is essential to most private medical practice and career advancement. They seek extensive facilities, low hospital charges, a high quality of coordinated services, and elaborate time and energy-conserving conveniences.

Thus there is sufficient means for control by doctors, elaborated far beyond the mere provision of essential skills, and sufficient interest in control. Where doctors fully exercise their potential power the administrator functions as a superintendent or, as his co-professionals are wont to put it, as a "housekeeper." The importance of administrative skills is likely to be minimized, the administrative viewpoint on operative goals neglected, and the quality of personnel may suffer. A former nurse often serves as superintendent in this type of hospital. Policy matters are defined as medical in nature by the doctors,[16] and neither trustees nor administrators, by definition, are qualified to have an equal voice in policy formation.

The operative goals of such a hospital are likely to be defined in strictly medical terms and the organization may achieve high technical standards of care, promote exemplary research, and provide sound training. However, there is a danger that resources will be used primarily for private (paying) patients with little attention to other community needs such as caring for the medically indigent (unless they happen to be good teaching cases), developing preventive medicine, or pioneering new organizational forms of care. Furthermore, high technical standards increasingly require efficient coordination of services and doctors may be unwilling to delegate authority to qualified administrators.

Various unofficial goals may be achieved at the expense of medical ones, or, in some cases, in conjunction with them. There are many cases of personal aggrandizement on the part of departmental chiefs and the chief of staff. The informal referral and consultation system in conjunction with promotions, bed quotas, and "privileges" to operate or treat certain types of cases, affords many occasions for the

---

[15] There is a small group of doctors on the medical staff, who may or may not bring in private patients, who receive money from the hospital, either through salary or commissions —pathologists, anesthetists, roentgenologists, paid directors of the out-patient department, etc. These are members of the organization in a direct sense.

[16] Oswald Hall, "Some Problems in the Provision of Medical Services," *Canadian Journal of Economics*, **20** (November, 1954), 461.

misuse of power. Interns and residents are particularly vulnerable to exploitation at the expense of teaching goals. Furthermore, as a professional, the doctor has undergone intensive socialization in his training and is called upon to exercise extraordinary judgment and skill with drastic consequences for good or ill. Thus he demands unusual deference and obedience and is invested with "charismatic" authority.[17] He may extend this authority to the entrepreneurial aspects of his role, with the result that his "service" orientation, so taken for granted in much of the literature, sometimes means service to the doctor at the expense of personnel, other patients, or even his own patient.[18]

Administrative Dominance

Administrative dominance is based first on the need for coordinating the increasingly complex, non-routinizable functions hospitals have undertaken. There is an increasing number of personnel that the doctor can no longer direct. The mounting concern of trustees, doctors themselves, patients and pre-payment groups with more efficient and economical operation also gives the administrator more power. A second, related basis for control stems from the fact that health services in general have become increasingly interdependent and specialized. The hospital must cooperate more with other hospitals and community agencies. It must also take on more services itself, and in doing so its contacts with other agencies and professional groups outside the hospital multiply. The administrator is equipped to handle these

matters because of his specialized training, often received in a professional school of hospital administration, accumulated experience and available time. These services impinge upon the doctor at many points, providing a further basis for administrative control over doctors, and they lead to commitments in which trustees find they have to acquiesce.

The administrator is also in a position to control matters which affect the doctor's demands for status, deference, and time-saving conveniences. By maintaining close supervision over employees or promoting their own independent basis for competence, and by supporting them in conflicts with doctors, the administrator can, to some degree, overcome the high functional authority that doctors command. In addition, by carefully controlling communication between trustees and key medical staff officials, he can prevent an alliance of these two groups against him.

If administrative dominance is based primarily on the complexity of basic hospital activities, rather than the organization's medical-social role in the community, the operative orientation may be toward financial solvency, careful budget controls, efficiency, and minimal development of services. For example, preventive medicine, research, and training may be minimized; a cautious approach may prevail towards new forms of care such as intensive therapy units or home care programs. Such orientations could be especially true of hospitals dominated by administrators whose background and training were as bookkeepers, comptrollers, business managers, purchasing agents, and the like. This is probably the most common form of administrative dominance.

However, increasing professionalization of hospital administrators has,

---

[17] Albert F. Wessen, "The Social Structure of a Modern Hospital," unpublished Ph.D. dissertation, Yale University, 1951, p. 43.

[18] Wessen notes that the doctor "sees ministering to the needs of doctors as a major function of the hospitals." (*Ibid.*, p. 328.)

on the one hand, equipped them to handle narrower administrative matters easily, and, on the other hand, alerted them to the broader medical-social role of hospitals involving organizational and financial innovations in the forms of care. Even medical standards can come under administrative control. For example, the informal system among doctors of sponsorship, referral, and consultation serves to protect informal work norms, shield members from criticism and exclude noncooperative members. The administrator is in a position to insist that medical policing be performed by a salaried doctor who stands outside the informal system.

There is, of course, a possibility of less "progressive" consequences. Interference with medical practices in the name of either high standards or treating the "whole" person may be misguided or have latent consequences which impair therapy. Publicity-seeking innovations may be at the expense of more humdrum but crucial services such as the out-patient department, or may alienate doctors or other personnel, or may deflect administrative efforts from essential but unglamorous administrative tasks.[19] Using the organization for career advancement, they may seek to expand and publicize their hospital regardless of community needs and ability to pay. Like trustees they may favor a distinctive and medically irrelevant community relations policy, perhaps with a view towards moving upward in the community power structure. Regardless of these dangers, the number of administration dominated hospitals oriented towards broad medical-social goals will probably grow.

[19] Charles Perrow, "Organizational Prestige: Some Functions and Dysfunctions," *American Journal of Sociology*, 66 (January, 1961), 335-41.

Multiple Leadership

So far we have been considering situations where one group clearly dominates. It is possible, however, for power to be shared by two or three groups to the extent that no one is able to control all or most of the actions of the others. This we call multiple leadership: a division of labor regarding the determination of goals and the power to achieve them.[20] This is not the same as fractionated power where several groups have small amounts of power in an unstable situation. With multiple leadership, there are two or three stable, known centers of power. Nor is it the same as decentralized power, where specialized units of the organization have considerable autonomy. In the latter case, units are free to operate as they choose only up to a point, when it becomes quite clear that there is a centralized authority. In multiple leadership there is no single ultimate power.

Multiple leadership is most likely to appear in organizations where there are multiple goals which lack precise criteria of achievement and admit of considerable tolerance with regard to achievement. Multiple goals focus interests, and achievement tolerance provides the necessary leeway for accommodation of interest and vitiation of responsibility. Many service organizations fit these criteria, but so might

[20] As in small group analysis, there is an increasing though belated tendency to recognize the possibility that there may be more than one leader in an organization. For a recent discussion of the problem in connection with army groups, see Hanan Selvin, *The Effects of Leadership* (Glencoe, Ill.: The Free Press, 1960), Chapters 1, 7. Amitai Etzioni goes even further in discussing "professional organizations." For a provocative discussion of goals and authority structure, see his "Authority Structure and Organizational Effectiveness," *Administrative Science Quarterly*, 4 (June, 1959), 43-67.

large, public relations-conscious business or industrial organizations where a variety of goals can be elevated to such importance that power must be shared by the representatives of each.

In one hospital where this was studied[21] it was found that multiple leadership insured that crucial group interests could be met and protected, and encouraged a high level of creative (though selective) involvement by trustees, doctors, and the administration. However, the problems of goal setting, assessment of achievement, and assignment of responsibility seemed abnormally high. While the three groups pursued separate and unconflicting operative goals in some cases, and were in agreement on still other goals, in areas where interests conflicted the goal conflicts were submerged in the interests of harmony. In the absence of a single authority, repetitive conflicts threatened to erode morale and waste energies. A showdown and clear solution of a conflict, furthermore, might signal defeat for one party, forcing them to abandon their interests. Thus a premium was placed on the ability of some elites to smooth over conflicts and exercise interpersonal skills. Intentions were sometimes masked and ends achieved through covert manipulation. Assessment of achievement in some areas was prevented either by the submergence of conflict or the preoccupation with segmental interests. Opportunism was encouraged: events in the environment or within the hospital were exploited without attention to the interests of the other groups or the long range development of the hospital. This left the organization open to vagrant pressures and to the operation of unintended consequences. Indeed, with conflict submerged and groups pursuing independent goals, long range planning was difficult.

This summary statement exaggerates the impact of multiple leadership in this hospital and neglects the areas of convergence on goals. Actually, the hospital prospered and led its region in progressive innovations and responsible medical-social policies despite some subversion of the official goals of patient care, teaching, research, and preventive medicine. The organization could tolerate considerable ambiguity of goals and achievements as long as standards remained high in most areas, occupancy was sufficient to operate with a minimum deficit, and a favorable public image was maintained. It remains to be seen if the costs and consequences are similar for other organizations where multiple leadership exists.

Application to Other Organizations[22]

Voluntary Service Organizations

Other voluntary service organizations, such as private universities, social service agencies, privately sponsored correctional institutions for juveniles, and fund raising agencies resemble hospitals in many respects. They have trustees representing the community, may have professionals playing prominent roles, and with increasing size and complexity of operation, require skilled coordination of activities. Initially at least, trustees are likely to provide a character defining function which emphasizes community goals and goals filtered through their own social position. Examples are religious schools, or those emphasizing one field of knowledge or training;

---

21 Perrow, Authority, Goals and Prestige . . . , *op. cit.*, chapters 4, 10.

22 The dogmatic tone of this concluding section is, unfortunately, the consequence of an attempt to be brief.

agencies caring for specialized groups such as ethnic or religious minorities, unwed mothers, and dependent and neglected children; and groups raising money for special causes. Funds of skill and knowledge accumulate around these activities, and the activities increasingly grow in complexity, requiring still more skill on the part of those performing the tasks. As the professional staff expands and professional identification grows, they may challenge the narrower orientations of trustees on the basis of their own special competence and professional ideology and seek to broaden the scope of services and the clientele. They may be supported in this by changing values in the community. Coordination of activities usually rests with professionals promoted from the staff during this second character defining phase, and these administrators retain, for a while at least, their professional identity. Trustees gradually lose the competence to interfere.

However, professionals have interests of their own which shape the organization. They may develop an identity and ethic which cuts them off from the needs of the community and favors specialized, narrow and—to critics—self-serving goals. Current criticisms of the emphasis upon research and over-specialization in graduate training at the expense of the basic task of educating undergraduates is a case in point in the universities.[23] There is also criticism of the tendency of professionals in correctional institutions to focus upon case work techniques applicable to middle-class "neurotic" delinquents at the expense of techniques for resocializing the so-called "socialized" delinquent from culturally deprived areas.[24] The latter account for most of the delinquents, but professional identity and techniques favor methods applicable to the former. Something similar may be found in social agencies. Social workers, especially the "elite" doing therapy in psychiatric and child guidance clinics and private family agencies, may become preoccupied with securing recognition, equitable financial remuneration, and status that would approach that of psychiatrists. Their attitudes may become more conservative; the social order more readily accepted and the deviant adapted to it; "worthy" clients and "interesting cases" receive priority.

It is possible that with increasing complexity and growth in many of these voluntary service organizations, administrators will lose their professional identity or be recruited from outside the organization on the basis of organizational skills. In either case they will be in a position to alter the direction fostered by selective professional interests. Of course, the problem of coordinating both internal and external activities need not generate leadership seeking broadly social rather than narrowly professional goals, any more than it necessarily does in the hospital. Administrative dominance may stunt professional services and neglect social policy in the interest of economy, efficiency, or conservative policies.

[23] Earl J. McGrath, *The Graduate School and the Doctrine of Liberal Education* (New York: Bureau of Publication, Teachers College, Columbia University, 1960).

[24] Robert Vinter and Morris Janowitz, "Effective Institutions for Juvenile Delinquents: A Research Statement," *Social Service Review*, 33 (June, 1957), 118-22; Donald Cressey, "Changing Criminals: The Application of the Theory of Differential Association," *American Journal of Sociology*, 56 (September, 1955), 166; Lloyd Ohlin and W. C. Lawrence, "Social Interaction Among Clients as a Treatment Problem," *Social Work*, 4 (April, 1959), 3-14.

Non-Voluntary Service Organizations

A different picture is presented by non-voluntary service organizations—those sponsored by government agencies such as county or military hospitals, city or county welfare agencies, juvenile and adult correctional agencies.[25] Authority for goal setting, regulation, and provision of capital and operating expenses does not rest with voluntary trustees, but with governmental officials appointed to commissions. In contrast to volunteers on the board of a private service organization, commissioners are not likely to be highly identified with the organization, nor do they derive much social status from it. The organizations themselves often are tolerated only as holding operations or as "necessary evils." Commission dominance is sporadic and brief, associated with public clamor or political expediency. On the other hand, the large size of these organizations and the complex procedures for reporting to the parent body gives considerable importance to the administrative function from the outset, which is enhanced by the tenuous relationship with the commissioners. Consistent with this and reinforcing it is the low level of professionalization found in many of these agencies. The key skills are often non-professional custodial skills or their equivalent in the case of public welfare agencies (and schools). Administrators are often at the mercy of the custodial staff if, indeed, they have not themselves risen to their administrative position because of their ability to maintain order and custody.

Nevertheless, professional influence is mounting in these organizations, and professional groups outside of them have exercised considerable influence.[26] Professionals may assume control of the organization, or administrators may be brought in whose commitment is to the positive purposes of the organization, such as rehabilitation of the clients, rather than the negative custodial functions. This appears to have happened in the case of a few federal penal institutions, a few state juvenile correctional institutions, and several Veterans Administration mental hospitals. Even where this happens, one must be alert to the influence of unofficial goals. The organizations are particularly vulnerable to exploitation by the political career interests of administrators or to irresponsible fads or cure-alls of marginal professionals. In summary, the sequence of tasks, power structure, and goals may be different in non-voluntary service organizations. The importance of administrative skills with system maintenance as the overriding operative goal does not encourage a shift in power structure; but where new technologies are introduced we are alerted to such shifts along with changes in goals.

Profit-Making Organizations

Our analysis may appear less applicable to profit-making organizations for two reasons. First, it could be argued, they are not characterized by multiple goals, but relate all operations to profit-making. Second, skill groups are not likely to dominate these organizations; owners control the smaller firms, and professional executives the larger ones.

---

[25] Public schools are excluded here because of the elective status of school boards; however, with some revisions, the following analysis would be applicable.

[26] Thompson and McEwen note that the "importance of new objectives may be more readily seen by specialized segments (professionals) than by the general society" and argue that public clamor for change has not been the initiating force. *Op. cit.*, p. 29.

Thus power structure and possibly goals may merely be a function of size. We will discuss each of these points in turn.

If profit-making is an overriding goal of an organization, many operative decisions must still be made which will shape its character. Even where technology remains constant, organizations will vary with regard to personnel practices, customer services, growth, liquidity, an emphasis upon quality or quantity, or long or short run gains. An adequate understanding of the organization will require attention to alternatives in these and other areas.

Furthermore, it has often been asserted that the importance of profits, *per se*, has declined with the increased power of professional management, especially in large organizations. The argument runs that since management does not have a personal stake in profits, they consider them less important than stability, growth, solvency, and liquidity.[27] The impressionistic evidence of those who assert this is not supported by a study of James Dent.[28] When asked, "What are the aims of top management in your company?,"

the response of executives of 145 business firms showed no greater mention of "to make profits, money or a living" among large than small firms, nor among those with professional managers than owner-managers. Because goals stated in this form may not reflect actual policies and because of other limitations, one is somewhat reluctant to take this as a fair test of the hypothesis.

Even though his sample was not representative, and the question asked does not get at what we have called operative goals, his study provides good evidence of variations of stated goals in profit-making organizations. Responses coded under the category "to make money, profits, or a living" were mentioned as the first aim by 36 per cent of the executives; "to provide a good product; public service" by 21 per cent, and "to grow" was third with 12 per cent. When the first three aims spontaneously mentioned were added together, profits led; employee welfare tied with "good products or public service" for second place. Dent found that the variables most associated with goals were size of company and "proportion of employees who are white-collar, professional or supervisory."[29] While goals no doubt are influenced by size, this accounted for only some of the variance. Holding size constant, one might discover the effects of major task areas. The association of goals with the "proportion of employees who are white-collar . . ." supports this argument.

R. A. Gordon and others have asserted that in large corporations it is the executive group, rather than stockholders or the board of trustees, that

---

[27] Robert A. Gordon was perhaps the first to deal at length with this proposition, and many have subsequently argued along the same lines. See Robert A. Gordon, *Business Leadership in the Large Corporation* (Washington, D.C.: Brookings Institution, 1954), pp. 308-12, 322, 327-29, 336, 340. For similar assertations see C. E. Griffin, *Enterprise in a Free Society* (Chicago: Irwin, 1949), pp. 96-104; H. Maurer, *Great Enterprise* (New York: Macmillan Co., 1955), pp. 77-8; and F. X. Sutton, *et al.*, *The American Business Creed* (Cambridge: Harvard University Press), 1956, pp. 57-8. For a contrary view see G. Katona, *Psychological Analysis of Economic Behavior* (New York: McGraw-Hill, 1951), p. 197.

[28] James K. Dent, "Organizational Correlates of the Goals of Business Managements," *Journal of Personnel Psychology*, **12** (Autumn, 1959), 375-76.

[29] *Ibid.*, pp. 378, 380, 383. Data on types of business, unfortunately, are not presented, except as reflected in the variable "proportion of employees who are white collar . . ."

generally dominates.[30] A study of the role of trustees, frankly in favor of their exercising leadership and control, actually shows through its many case studies that trustees exercise leadership mainly in times of crisis.[31] The generalization of Gordon, almost a commonplace today, appears to be sound: he asserts that the common pattern of evolution is for active leadership by owners in the early years of the firm, then it is passed on to new generations of the families concerned, and gradually responsibility for decision-making passes to professional executives who frequently have been trained by the original leaders.[32] Goals likewise shift from rapid development and a concern with profits to more conservative policies emphasizing coordination, stability and security of employment.[33]

But does this mean that for large, old, and stable firms that operative goals are substantially similar, reflecting professional administration? Does it also mean that for profit-making organizations in general there are only two alternative sources of domination, trustees (including owners) and professional administrators? Our theoretical scheme suggests that neither may be true, but the evidence is scanty.

Certainly within the organizations dominated by professional managers there is ample opportunity for a variety of operational goals less general than, say, stability and security of employment. Even these are likely to vary and to shape the nature of the firm. (We exclude, of course, the failure to achieve these broad goals because of poor management or environmental factors over which the organization has no control; we are dealing with operating policies which may not be achieved.) Gordon notes that the "historical background" of a company (he does not elaborate this phrase) and especially the training received by its leading executives may be a powerful factor in shaping management decisions. "It is the 'Rockefeller tradition' rather than the present Rockefeller holdings which actively conditions the management decisions of the Standard Oil companies. This tradition is largely responsible for present methods of management organization and internal control, use of the committee system and the domination of boards of directors by [company executives]."[34] Historical factors will certainly shape decisions, but the nature of technology in the oil industry and the trustees' awareness of the prime importance of coordination may have been decisive in that historical experience.

Domination by skill groups is possible in two ways. On the one hand, a department—for example, sales, engineering, research and development, or finance—may, because of the technology and stage of growth, effectively exercise a veto on the executive's decisions and substantially shape decisions in other departments. Second, lines of promotion may be such that top executives are drawn from one

---

[30] Gordon, *op. cit.*, pp. 114, 131-32, 145-46, 180, 347.

[31] M. T. Copeland and A. Towl, *The Board of Directors and Business Management* (Boston: Harvard University, 1947). For a similar conclusion and excellent discussion of these matters see R. H. Dahl, "Business and Politics," *American Political Science Review*, **53** (March, 1959), 6. The argument for increasing managerial control was, of course, also put forth by Burnham in 1941, but he was only faintly interested in the effects upon organizations, his thesis being that managers would supplant capitalists in the national and world power elite. See *The Managerial Revolution* (New York: John Day, 1941).

[32] Gordon, *op. cit.*, p. 180.

[33] *Ibid.*, pp. 327, 339. See his illustrations from General Motors and U.S. Rubber Company in chapter 7.

[34] *Ibid.*, p. 188.

powerful department, and retain their identification with the parochial goals of that department. Gordon asserts that chief executives with a legal background are conservative in making price changes and find 'order in the industry' more appealing than aggressive price competition.[35] It is possible that engineers, sales executives, and financial executives all have distinctive views on what the operating policies should be.

Thus, goals may vary widely in profit-making organizations, and power may rest not only with trustees or professional administrators, but with skill groups or administrators influenced by their skill background. Of course, one task area may so dominate a firm that there will be no shifts in power, and operative goals will remain fairly stable within the limits of the changing values of society. But where basic tasks shift, either because of growth or changing technology, the scheme presented here at least alerts us to potential goal changes and their consequences. An ideal-typical sequence would be as follows: trustee domination in initial stages of financing, setting direction for development and recruitment of technical or professional skills; then dominance by the skill group during product or service development and research, only to have subsequent control pass to coordination of fairly routinized activities. As the market and technology change, this cycle could be repeated. During the course of this sequence, operative goals may shift from quantity production and short-run profits as emphasized by trustees, to the engineer's preoccupation with quality at the expense of quantity or styling, with this succeeded by a priority upon styling and unessential innovations demanded by the sales force, and finally with an emphasis upon the long-run market position, conservative attitude towards innovation, and considerable investment in employee-centered policies and programs by management. It is important to note that the formal authority structure may not vary during this sequence, but recruitment into managerial positions and the actual power of management, trustees or skill groups would shift with each new problem focus. Multiple leadership is also possible, as noted in an earlier section.

There are many critical variables influencing the selection of key problem areas and thus the characteristics of the controlling elite and operative goals. They will be applicable to the analysis of any complex organization, whether business, governmental, or voluntary. Among those that should be considered are capital needs and legitimization, the amount of routinization possible, adaptability of technology to market shifts and consumer behavior, possible or required professionalization, and the nature of the work force. Our analysis of profit-making organizations suggests that we should be alert to the possibility of a natural history of changes in task areas, authority, and goals which parallels that of hospitals and other voluntary service organizations. Non-voluntary service organizations may systematically deviate from this sequence because of the source of capital (government) which influences the commitments of appointive trustees (commissioners), and the character of the administrative tasks. The scheme presented here, when used in conjunction with the concept of operative goals, may provide a tool for analyzing the dynamics of goal setting and goal changing in all complex organizations.

---

[35] *Ibid.*, p. 264.

A Study of Organizational Effectiveness

BASIL S. GEORGOPOULOS

ARNOLD S. TANNENBAUM

Organizational effectiveness is one of the most complex and least tackled problems in the study of social organizations. Many difficulties arise with attempts to define the concept of effectiveness adequately. Some stem from the closeness with which the concept becomes associated with the question of values (e.g., "management" versus "labor" orientations). Other problems arise when researchers choose *a priori* criteria of effectiveness that seem intuitively right, without trying systematically to place them within a consistent and broader framework. In effect, specific criteria that might be proper in one case may be entirely inappropriate to other organizations. The question arises whether it is possible to develop a definition of effectiveness and to derive criteria that are applicable across organizations and can be meaningfully placed within a general conceptual framework.

The present paper has three objectives: (a) to examine the concept of effectiveness and to provide a definition deriving from the nature of organizations; (b) to develop operational criteria and to measure the concept in a specific industrial setting; and (c) to evaluate these criteria and operations in terms of their organizational character, i.e., the extent to which they represent an organizational-level phe-

nomenon, their reliability, and their agreement with independent expert judgment.

The Concept

The concept of organizational effectiveness (sometimes called organizational "success" or organizational "worth") is ordinarily used to refer to goal-attainment. In this sense, it is a functional rather than a structural concept. Furthermore, it is probably most useful in comparative organizational research, i.e., in relation rather than absolute terms, but the concept could also be used developmentally to study the effectiveness of the same organization over time.

Traditionally, in the study of industrial organizations, effectiveness has been viewed and operationalized mainly in terms of productivity. In this connection, Thorndike has noted a general tendency on the part of personnel and industrial psychologists to accept as "ultimate criteria" of organizational success the following: organizational productivity, net profit, the extent to which the organization accomplishes its various missions, and the success of the organization in maintaining or expanding itself.[1] Other variables that have been used in various contexts as criteria of effectiveness include "morale," commitment to the organization, personnel turnover and

Basil S. Georgopoulos and Arnold S. Tannenbaum, "A Study of Organizational Effectiveness," *American Sociological Review*, **22** (1957), 534-40.

---

[1] R. L. Thorndike, *Personnel Selection: Test and Measurement Techniques* (New York: Wiley, 1949), pp. 121-24.

absenteeism, and member satisfactions.[2]

With the exception of organizational productivity, however, practically all variables used as criteria of organizational effectiveness have been found inadequate and unsatisfactory. For example, previous findings regarding "morale" and member satisfaction in relation to effectiveness (effectiveness measured on the basis of productivity) have frequently been inconsistent, nonsignificant, or difficult to evaluate and interpret. The case of turnover and absenteeism is similar. A major problem in using these two variables as criteria of effectiveness is their differential sensitivity to such "third" considerations as the nature and volume of work to be processed, organizational level affected, and season of occurrence apart from the degree of such occurrence. Net profit is likewise a poor criterion in view of many unanticipated fluctuations external to the system, e.g., fluctuations in the general economy, markets, sales, and prices.

In view of these and related inadequacies, the role of other potential criteria of organizational effectiveness should be studied. On this point, and in addition to productivity, Kahn and Morse have suggested the variables of organizational flexibility and maximization of member potential,[3] but no work has been done in this direction. Elsewhere, Bass has proposed as criteria the extent to which an organization is of value to its members, and the extent to which the organization and its members are of value to society.[4] For theoretical reasons, however, it is preferable to look at the concept of organizational effectiveness from the point of view of the system itself—of the total organization in question rather than from the standpoint of some of its parts or of the larger society. Furthermore, proposed criteria should be system-relevant as well as applicable across organizations. It is most satisfactory, moreover, if such criteria are derived from a common framework to which the concept of organizational effectiveness can be meaningfully related.

General Criteria of Effectiveness

A distinguishing characteristic of nearly all variables which have been used as criteria of effectiveness is that, whether directly or indirectly, they tie in with organizational objectives. This relationship, however, is only a necessary condition. Not all criteria that fulfill this requirement are appropriate. Many cannot be applied across organizations (e.g., some organizations have no problems of turnover and absenteeism or may even be overstaffed), and many do not logically conform to a generally accepted conception of organizations.

It is our assumption that all organ-

[2] See, for example, R. L. Kahn, "The Prediction of Productivity," *Journal of Social Issues*, **12** (No. 2, 1956), 41-9; R. L. Kahn and N. C. Morse, "The Relationship of Productivity to Morale," *Journal of Social Issues*, **7** (No. 3, 1951), 8-17; Daniel Katz and R. L. Kahn, "Human Organization and Worker Motivation," in L. R. Tripp (Ed.), *Industrial Productivity* (Madison: Industrial Relations Research Association, 1951). See also the following, published at the Institute for Social Research, University of Michigan, Ann Arbor: Daniel Katz, N. Maccoby, and N. C. Morse, *Productivity, Supervision, and Morale in an Office Situation*, 1950; Daniel Katz, N. Maccoby, G. Gurin, and L. G. Floor, *Productivity, Supervision, and Morale Among Railroad Workers*, 1951; N. C. Morse, *Satisfaction in the White-Collar Job*, 1953; S. E. Seashore, *Group Cohesiveness in the Industrial Work Group*, 1955.

[3] R. L. Kahn and N. C. Morse, *op. cit.*, p. 16.
[4] B. M. Bass, "Ultimate Criteria of Organizational Worth," *Personnel Psychology*, **5** (Autumn, 1952), 157-73.

izations attempt to achieve certain objectives and to develop group products through the manipulation of given animate and inanimate facilities. Accordingly, definitions of organizational effectiveness must take into consideration these two aspects: the objectives of organizations and the means through which they sustain themselves and attain their objectives, particularly those means that usually become functionally autonomous (i.e., that come to assume the character of and function as organizational goals). In short, the study of organizational effectiveness must contend with the question of organizational means and ends.

Assuming that the organizational system maintains itself, the most general and most important common objectives of organizations are: (a) high output in the sense of achieving the end results for which the organization is designed, whether quantitatively or qualitatively; (b) ability to absorb and assimilate relevant endogenous and exogenous changes, or the ability of the organization to keep up with the times without jeopardizing its integrity; and (c) the preservation of organizational resources, of human and material facilities.[5] It should be both feasible and fruitful to study organizational effectiveness by gearing our criterion variables to these general aspects of organization.

We define organizational effectiveness as the extent to which an organization as a social system, given certain resources and means, fulfills its objec-

tives without incapacitating its means and resources and without placing undue strain upon its members. This conception of effectiveness subsumes the following general criteria: (1) organizational productivity; (2) organizational flexibility in the form of successful adjustment to internal organizational changes and successful adaptation to externally induced change; and (3) absence of intraorganizational strain, or tension, and of conflict between organizational subgroups. These three criteria both relate to the means-ends dimension of organizations and, potentially, apply to nearly all organizations. The first relates to the movement of the organization toward its goals (locomotion); the others relate to the requirements of organizational survival in the face of external and internal variability, and to the dimension of preservation (or incapacitation) of organizational means. In an attempt to evaluate the present approach, we have used these criteria in the study of a large-scale organization, which we feel is particularly suitable to our investigation because of the simplicity of its structure.

Method, Operations, and Measures

The organization studied is an industrial service specializing in the delivery of retail merchandise. It is unionized and operates in several metropolitan areas, on a contract basis with department stores. In each area there is a company plant, under a plant manager, which is divided into a number of divisions, each division encompassing a number of smaller organizational units called stations. These constitute the basic operating units of the company.

The plant structure is replicated in every case, i.e. the stations are structurally homogeneous and organizationally

---

[5] Satisfaction of member needs beyond some minimum critical level, and the maintenance of sufficient member motivation and of an effort-reward balance constitute important problems for all organizations. And, it is under this concept of preservation (or incapacitation) of resources that such variables as turnover, absenteeism, morale, and satisfaction could be viewed as "criteria" or correlates of effectiveness.

parallel. They all perform the same kind of activity, employ uniform-standard equipment, draw upon the same type of resources, and function on the basis of uniformly established work-standards. A typical station has a station manager, a day supervisor, a night supervisor, and about 35 workers. Approximately three-fourths of the workers are truck drivers who transport and deliver packages to private residences; the remaining workers sort and load the merchandise prior to delivery. Thirty-two such stations, representing five company plants, are included in the study.

In each case data were collected from all station members, supervisory as well as non-supervisory.[6] The average questionnaire return rate for supervisory personnel was 97 per cent and for non-supervisory 87 per cent (the questionnaires were administered on location). No station having a return rate lower than 75 per cent of its non-supervisory members is represented in the sample. The operations and measures for the concept of organizational effectiveness and for the three criteria are based on this sample.

Independent judgments were obtained from a group of experts concerning the relative overall effectiveness

of the various stations in the five plants. It was on this basis that the 32 stations were selected for study. The expert raters had first-hand knowledge of the stations they rated but were not directly involved in station operations. Included among the raters were the plant manager, the assistant plant manager, some division managers, and other key plant personnel, comprising a total of six to nine experts in each of the five company plants.

Special forms and instructions, developed in consultation with the top management of the company, were sent to the various raters separately. These requested the rater to list all stations in the plant, to cross out those stations he was not able to evaluate, and to judge the remaining stations by placing them into five categories of overall effectiveness, ranging from "best" to "poorest." The raters were asked to use as a time basis the six-month period preceding the evaluation. The following excerpts from the instructions indicate the frame of reference for the concept of effectiveness as presented to the raters:

You are to rank *the performance of the station as a whole* as distinct from the performance of any of the people in it. . . . You may want to take into consideration such things as: how satisfied you are personally with the *total* situation in the station, how well it is measuring up to the expectations and goals of (the company) considering the particular difficulties it faces, also recent progress and development, the way problems are handled, communications, costs, efficiency, morale, performance in relation to standards, etc. The important thing is that all these things taken together and considered as a whole will be the basis for the ranking. . . . Fill the form without checking your opinions with anyone and then send it directly to (the research staff). Your individual rankings will be

6 The major background characteristics of the nonsupervisory station personnel, as of July, 1955, were as follows: all workers are male; nearly all workers are unionized (95 per cent); 81 per cent are between 26 and 49 years old; 82 per cent are married; 77 per cent have gone beyond grade school; 85 per cent have been on the same job for at least one year, 84 per cent have been working in the same station for at least one year, and 73 per cent have been with the company for three years or more. Three-fourths of the workers express "fair" or better than fair satisfaction with their wages, but 42 per cent are "very little" or not at all satisfied with their chances for advancement in the company (probably due to the fact that upward mobility is extremely limited because of the structure of this organization).

treated as confidential and only the summary findings will be used for the purposes of the study.

Additional instructions were given about the mechanics of placing the stations in five effectiveness categories.

All raters submitted their independent evaluations of the stations under their jurisdiction, and their judgments were analyzed. All stations about which there was consistent agreement among raters (i.e., cases clearly falling at either of the two extremes or the middle of the five effectiveness categories), as judged by three members of the research staff, were retained as candidates for inclusion in the sample. A list of these stations was then submitted to each of the two regional managers of the organization. Each manager and one more expert classified the performance of the listed stations as "above average," "average," or "below average," using a procedure similar to that of the first group of raters. After eliminating a few units of ambiguous effectiveness standing, a representative sample of 32 stations resulted.

The effectiveness score for each station was computed by combining and averaging the judgments of all raters.[7] The range on effectiveness was from 1.0, signifying units of highest possible effectiveness, to 4.8, with 5.0 being the lowest possible score. It should be noted that the distribution of the sample on effectiveness was later found to be positively related with the mean responses of non-supervisory station personnel to the question: "How do you feel your station compares with other similar stations in getting

the job done?" Apparently those directly involved with the operations of the organization can make judgments about the performance of their respective units and they seem to use similar frames of reference. A similar finding has been reported by Comrey, Pfiffner, and Beem.[8]

Station productivity, the first of the three criterion variables of organizational effectiveness, was measured on the basis of standard, company-wide records of performance vis-à-vis established work-standards. This measure is expressed in units of time consumed by the worker below or above what is "allowed" according to the standard. The average productivity of all drivers[9] during the month preceding the field study[10] was taken to represent the organizational productivity of that station. (Incidentally, it should be noted that no problems of quality of output are involved.) On the basis of a standard of 2.00, the range of the obtained distribution of the sample on productivity was from 0.81, signifying the highest producing station, to 2.93 signifying the lowest producing station. An interval of .30 in the present scale is equivalent to 18 minutes of de-

---

[7] Stations judged as "above average" by the second group of raters were assigned a scale value of 1, "average" stations 3, and "below average" stations 5 to achieve equivalence of scales for the two rater groups.

[8] A. L. Comrey, J. M. Pfiffner, and H. P. Beem, "Factors Influencing Organizational Effectiveness," *Personnel Psychology*, 5 (Winter, 1952), 307-28.

[9] Drivers constitute three-fourths of all members and operate under uniformly established work standards. The remaining workers operate either under no work-standards or under a group-standard that may vary from station to station. However, their productivity is reflected in that of the drivers since these workers process exactly the same work volume that the drivers deliver.

[10] This particular month was chosen because it was the most recent month for which data could be made available to the researchers, and because it was a "normal" month in terms of work volume. All months, except December, are considered "normal."

viation from the established work-standard.

Intraorganizational strain was conceptualized as the incidence of tension or conflict existing between organizational subgroups. This criterion was operationalized and measured in terms of responses by non-supervisory station personnel to the following question: "On the whole, would you say that in your station there is any tension or conflict between employees and supervisors?" The respondent could choose, on a five-point scale, one of five alternatives ranging from there is "a great deal of tension" to "no tension at all." The average non-response rate to this question was 6.6 per cent. The mean of the responses in each station represents the score of intraorganizational strain characterizing that station. The range of these scores for the sample was from 2.46, signifying the highest strain station, to 4.50 signifying the lowest strain station. It is interesting to note that station supervisors generally agree with the consensus of their subordinates about the degree of strain characteristic of their station.

Organizational flexibility, the third and last criterion, was conceptualized as the extent to which the organization is able to adjust to internally induced change and to adapt to externally induced change. Two measures were used, one for each of these two aspects of flexibility, and the results were then combined into a single measure.[11] The first was based on the following question: "From time to time changes in methods, equipment, procedures, practices, and layout are introduced by the management. In general,

do you think these changes lead to better ways of doing things?" The response alternatives, forming a five-point scale, ranged from "they are always an improvement" to "they never improve things" with an additional "I can't judge" category. The average non-response rate, including "I can't judge" responses, was 7.3 per cent. The second measure was based on the question: "In general, how well do you think your station handles sharp changes in volume during peak periods?" The response alternatives here ranged from "excellent" to "very poor," also forming a five-point scale. The non-response rate to this question was 3 per cent.

The flexibility score assigned to a given station was obtained by computing the mean of the responses of non-supervisory station personnel for each of the two questions, and by adding the two means and dividing the result by two. The obtained sample distribution on flexibility ranges from a score of 1.78, signifying high flexibility, to a score of 2.99, signifying the least flexible station on a five-point scale. Again, as in the case of strain, station supervisors generally agree with their respective subordinates about the flexibility of their station.

Empirical Evaluation

The operations and measures used are evaluated in terms of three major considerations. Since effectiveness is viewed in terms of three criteria, the question arises (1) whether in fact each criterion is significantly related to the appraisal of effectiveness by experts, i.e. whether our operations correspond to such an independent standard; (2) whether the criteria are significantly interrelated and if so, what their joint reliability is. Since the concept of organizational effectiveness is

---

[11] The rank-order correlation between these two flexibility measures was found to be .71 for the study sample of 32 stations, suggesting a strong association between the two aspects of organizational flexibility represented by the two measures.

by definition as well as logically and theoretically a group concept, the question arises (3) whether our criterion measures represent group phenomena.

The results of our study are presented in Table 1. Based on an N of 32 stations, these rank-order correlations are significant at the .05 level or better. In short, as was expected, each of the three criteria is found to be related to an independent assessment of organizational effectiveness by experts. These results lend support to the validity of the three criteria.

TABLE 1   Rank-Order Correlations Among Criterion Variables and Organizational Effectiveness*

| | CRITERION VARIABLES | | |
	Station Productivity	Station Inter-group Strain	Station Flexibility
Station effectiveness	.73	—.49	.39
Station productivity	...	—.48	.35
Station inter-group strain	...	...	—.70

* All correlation coefficients are statistically significant at the .05 level or better, based on an N of 32 organizational units (stations).

Table 1 also shows that the three criteria are significantly interrelated. Based on the reported relationships, the overall reliability[12] of the three criteria is found to be .77. These findings provide support for the statistical reliability of the criteria, theoretically considered in combination. The prediction of the independently obtained measure of organizational effectiveness was attempted by combining the three

---

[12] This reliability was computed on the basis of the relationships appearing in Table 1. For the formula used to compute the reliability coefficient, see J. P. Guilford, *Fundamental Statistics in Psychology and Education* (New York: McGraw-Hill, 1942), p. 282.

criterion measures into a single index.

To construct this index, the station productivity scores were transformed into five-point scale scores, with 1.00 signifying the highest and 5.00 the lowest theoretically possible productivity.[13] With the inversion of the intraorganizational strain scale, this operation resulted in station productivity scores on a scale equivalent to the scales used for the measurement of strain and flexibility. Thus, for each of the 32 sample units, three different scale scores became available, each representing one effectiveness criterion. These scores were averaged resulting in a criterion index score for each station in the sample.

This index score indicates the extent to which a given organizational unit is effective, or the extent to which it is productive, flexible, and devoid of internal strain. The range of criterion index scores for the sample was found to be from 1.69, the most favorable score, to 3.11, least favorable, on a five-point scale. The sample distribution on this criterion index was then related to the distribution of the sample on station effectiveness, and a correlation coefficient of .68 was obtained between the two distributions. When corrected for attenuation (This can be done since we know the reliability of the criterion index), this coefficient becomes .77. This suggests that, by means of the present criterion index, one could predict to organizational effectiveness, as judged by experts, explaining about 46 per cent (or, theoretically, when corrected for attenuation, about 59 per

---

[13] The theoretical scale limits in this transformation were set so as to correspond to the productivity scores of the highest and lowest producing individual worker in the sample. It was assumed that no station can have a higher productivity than the highest producing individual worker in the sample, nor a lower productivity than the lowest producing worker.

cent) of the existing variance.[14] In short, this is the part of variance on station effectiveness that could be accounted for in terms of the employed criterion index.

Finally, to answer the question of whether our three criteria of effectiveness represent organizational rather than individual phenomena, the productivity criterion was chosen for further study. This was done because productivity in the present study contributes more to the explained variance in effectiveness than either strain or flexibility, and because the station productivity measure was derived by averaging the productivity of individuals. Unlike the flexibility and strain measures, which were derived from responses to questions that explicitly referred to organizational aspects, the

station productivity criterion had as its initial referent the individual worker. Therefore, the criterion of productivity is the most doubtful from the standpoint of whether or not it represents an organizational phenomenon.

The productivity criterion was further studied by analysis of variance to determine whether the stations or the individuals in them constitute the primary source of productivity variance. Twenty-seven stations, distributed among four company plants and encompassing a total of 685 individual workers whose productivity had been ascertained, were used. Suitable productivity scores were not available in the case of the remaining five stations, which belong to the fifth company plant studied.

Table 2 presents the results of this

TABLE 2   Analysis of Variance on Productivity for
Twenty-seven Ungrouped Stations*

Source of Variance	Sum of Squares	d.f.	Mean Square (variance)	F-ratio
Between-Stations	10,142	26	390	$F = 5.82$ $p < .001$ $F_{.99(26,658)} = 1.90$
Within-Stations	40,438	658	67	
Total	50,580	684		

* These stations are similar organizational units distributed among four, larger company plants.

analysis. These results indicate that the between-station variance on productivity is far greater than the within-stations variance. The obtained F-ratio

[14] A less satisfactory way to answer the same question empirically would have been to compute the multiple-correlation coefficient between the three criteria and effectiveness on the basis of the obtained correlational findings, without constructing an index. This was computed and found to be .75, suggesting that, in the present study, about 56 per cent of the variance in effectiveness can be accounted for in terms of the joint contribution of the three criteria—productivity, strain, and flexibility. This finding is similar to that obtained by using the criterion index.

of 5.82 is statistically significant beyond the .001 level. This confirms our initial expectation that the productivity criterion measure represents an organizational (station) rather than individual level phenomenon. This evidence, however, is not adequate for it is conceivable that the results might vary from plant to plant. To test this possibility, similar analyses of variance were also performed separately for each of the four company plants represented in the sample of 27 stations. In each case the between-stations variance on productivity was found to be significantly greater than the within-stations variance; i.e., grouping the stations into plants makes no difference in this respect. Therefore, we are reasonably assured that the productivity criterion measure represents an organizational rather than an individual phenomenon. . . .

Organizational Control Structures in Five Correctional Institutions

MAYER N. ZALD

Like universities and mental hospitals, most correctional institutions are organizations that have multiple goals. One can characterize the goals of any given correctional institution in terms of the relative importance of custodial or treatment purposes; some institutions have almost purely custodial goals, some have "mixed goals," and some have almost purely treatment goals.

Custodial goals are operative when an organization devotes a large part of its energies and resources to the control and containment of inmates; treatment goals are operative when a large part of organizational resources and energies are devoted to the rehabilitation and positive social change of inmates.

Organizational goals are conceptualized as the analytic independent variable; action necessary to implement custodial or treatment goals leads to, or requires, differences in organizational control structures.

Two institutions whose goals are approximately the same might differ sharply in structure and practice, however, if they employ different methods. A mental hospital, for example, which utilizes mainly electroconvulsive and other neurological

Mayer N. Zald, "Organizational Control Structures in Five Correctional Institutions," *American Journal of Sociology*, **68** (1962), 335-345.

therapies has different staff-patient relationships and practices than one using primarily psychotherapy. In treatment institutions for delinquents there are important differences in structure required by individual treatment (psychotherapy, casework, or counseling) as contrasted with milieu treatment (interpreting behavior and changing the individual through his relationship with others).

Here we concentrate on the relationship between custodial and treatment goals and aspects of organizational control structures—the pattern of departmentalization and the distribution and balance of power among executives and employees of five institutions for delinquents.[1] My central assumption is that implementation of custodial or treatment goals requires different relationships between insti-

---

[1] There have been few studies from a sociological point of view of institutions for delinquents. For a case study see Robert D. Vinter and Roger Lind, *Staff Relationships and Attitudes in a Juvenile Correctional Institution* (Ann Arbor: School of Social Work, The University of Michigan, 1958). For current approaches to the study of prisons and mental hospitals, see George Grosser (ed.), *Theoretical Studies in Social Organization of the Prison* ("SSRC" Pamphlet, No. 15 [New York: Social Science Research Council, 1960]); Donald Cressey (ed.), *The Prison: Studies in Institutional Organization and Change* (New York: Holt, Rinehart & Winston, 1961); and Milton Greenblatt, Daniel J. Levinson, and Richard H. Williams (eds.), *The Patient and the Mental Hospital* (Glencoe, Ill.: Free Press, 1957).

tutions and the local community, between various groups of employees, and between employees and inmates. These differences directly affect the control structure of the institution.[2]

The control structure of an organization can be described in terms of the distribution of power and the channels for utilizing power.[3] The pattern and amount of departmentalization and interdepartmental relationships are part of the structure of control because they reflect the way in which responsibility (and control) is delegated. The balance of power among executive and staff groups reflects both the formal delegation of control and the informal seizure of control by some executives and groups. My general thesis is that institutions with dominant treatment goals differ in their control structure from those with dominant custodial goals; the more complex departmental structure and tasks require a wider dis-

tribution of power among the executives and a different allocation of power among both executives and staff groups.

Two major hypotheses are examined: Hypothesis 1: *In mixed-goal and treatment institutions power is distributed among executives; whereas in more custodial institutions power is not distributed, only the superintendent possesses power.* Internal practices required in treatment institutions are more complex, less routinized, and more individualized than those in custodial institutions. Similarly, because he must obtain a larger amount of resources per inmate than his counterpart in custodial institutions, and because he must defend the relatively open quality of his program, the superintendent of an institution with treatment goals must concern himself more with external affairs than his counterpart in a custodial institution.

Differences in the relative dominance of custodial and treatment goals among institutions lead to differences in the substantive bases of decisions and imply differences in the importance attached to various activities (e.g., containment, counseling, etc.). Therefore, aside from the extent to which executive power is shared, difference in goals between institutions leads to the allocation of power to executives who differ in their values and goal commitments, that is, to a difference in the balance of power. In a mixed-goal institution, the executive responsible for internal activities is likely to pursue custodial goals and the executive concerned with external affairs ostensibly will pursue treatment goals. Such an arrangement placates the demands of specialized publics for a rehabilitative program at the same time that it insures attainment of basic custodial goals. In a treatment institution, however, the executive responsible

[2] Goals also have more indirect consequences for the attitudes of employees toward inmates, the amount and pattern of conflict, and the role problems of employees. On the patterns of conflict in correctional institutions see my "Power Balance and Organizational Conflict in Correctional Institutions for Delinquents," *Administrative Science Quarterly,* VII (June, 1962), 22-49. On the role problems of employees see Cressey, "Contradictory Directives in Complex Organizations: The Case of the Prisons," *Administrative Science Quarterly,* IV (June, 1959), 1-19.

[3] The concept of organizational control structure used here is more inclusive than that used by Arnold Tannenbaum and his associates. They include only the distribution of influence among groups in their definition of the control structure, in effect assuming or ignoring the patterned channels through which influence is utilized. See Arnold S. Tannenbaum and Robert L. Kahn, "Organizational Control Structure: A General Descriptive Technique as Applied to Four Local Unions," *Human Relations,* X (May, 1957), 127-40; and Tannenbaum and Basil Georgopoulos, "The Distribution of Control in Formal Organizations," *Social Forces,* XXXVIII (October, 1957), 44-50.

for internal control must be fully committed to treatment goals.

Differences in the basic goals of the institution lead not only to differences in the criteria on which decisions are based but also to differences in the amount of power held by various groups within the institution, because custodial and treatment goals require different staff groups to be in control of decisions about discipline and activities for inmates.

Hypothesis 2: *In custodial institutions the influence and authority of the cottage parent is likely to be relatively high and that of a social service worker relatively low. The reverse will tend to hold true in individual treatment institutions; since milieu treatment attempts to involve more of the staff in the decision-making process, a "team" concept results and a general sharing of power is likely. In all institutions teachers are relatively isolated from the major operating problems of the organization and are likely to have little influence.*

Although social service workers have power in both the individual- and milieu-treatment institutions, they differ in their relationship to the other staff members. In a milieu institution the social service staff can make its influence felt only through other staff members; in individual-treatment institutions social service workers may function relatively independently of the rest of the staff. I will explore both the power of staff groups and the kinds of relationships existing among staff groups.

Before the data pertaining to these hypotheses are presented, the sample institutions must be briefly described.

The Sample Institutions

From a large number of institutions whose goals were known on a reputational basis by experts, five were selected for intensive study.[4] In Table 1 the goals, number of inmates and employees, and type of control (public or private) of each institution are shown.

TABLE 1	Five Sample Institutions, by Goals, Size, and Control, Public or Private

	SIZE	
Goals	Small	Large
Custodial		Dick Industrial School 260 inmates 65 staff members Public
Mixed	Regis Home 56 inmates 13 staff members Private	Mixter Training School 400 inmates 177 staff members Public
Treatment	Inland School 60 inmates 40 staff members Private	Milton School for Boys 200 inmates 117 staff members Public

Each of these institutions, particularly those with treatment goals, had been subject to processes of change and conflict in recent times. All of

---

[4] The selection of institutions met four requirements: (1) an array of institutions among the custodial-treatment dimension; (2) institutions of different sizes as a control measure; (3) both public and private institutions; and (4) institutional goals related to the action program of the organization.

I did not attempt to select a representative sample but aimed instead of maximizing comparison of the effects of goals. Comparison of the five institutions to the universe of institutions in the United States indicates that, in fact, they are not representative of the universe of institutions. Institutions with low inmate-staff ratios and high per capita costs are overrepresented, indicating most likely an overrepresentation of treatment institutions (*ibid.*, pp. 51-54). But the institutions selected do fulfil the requirements of my comparative design.

them formally stressed some form of rehabilitation goals (as has been true historically for institutions for delinquents). But institutions with such older or traditional concepts of rehabilitation as "training" also stressed custodial aims. The description of each institution which follows locates the goals with reference to the relative dominance of custody and treatment and highlights important features of each institution's operation.

Dick Industrial School stressed discipline, training, and containment in its goal statements. Operating its own farm, Dick was an isolated, custodial institution.

Regis Home, the smallest institution in the study, was run by a Catholic religious order. Although some boys received individual counseling, Regis aimed primarily at educating and training the boys. The Home was located in an urban community and sent its boys to twenty schools in the community.[5] Discipline was firm, although less punitive than at Dick, and all counseling, especially in regard to sexual practices, had to conform to the tenets of the governing religious order.

*Mix*ter, a *mix*ed-goal institution, was the largest in the study. Mixter represents a benign custodial type which minimizes repressive sanctions while not fully developing a treatment program.

*Mil*ton, which stressed a *mil*ieu approach and *In*land, which stressed *in*dividual treatment, were the two institutions in the sample with relatively dominant treatment goals. They differed from each other in that Milton was a large public institution while Inland was a small private institution. Milton had changed to a milieu approach after a decade and a half of growth and conflict. Its milieu approach was intended to eliminate tensions between professional and lay personnel by having them consult often with each other as well as to implement treatment philosophy.

Because Milton was a public institution and had to accept all delinquents sent to it, it was not able to dispense with custodial goals as completely as Inland. Inland defined itself as a "residential treatment center" and its personnel placed a great deal of stress on the delinquent's progress in counseling.

To summarize, I consider Dick to have had the most custodial goals of the institutions in the sample, followed by Regis and Mixter. Although Inland was able to dispense with custodial emphases to a greater extent than Milton, both Milton and Inland were clearly institutions with dominant treatment goals. With this array of institutions it is possible to compare smaller institutions with larger; public institutions with private; and institutions with custodial, mixed, and treatment goals.[6]

Departmental Structure and Administrative Power Balance

The hypothesis that power is more widely distributed among executives

---

[5] Since there was no attempt to contain delinquents at Regis, its inclusion in the study might be questioned. To fill the required cells of the design of my study a small institution emphasizing containment was sought. Since none was available, excluding Regis would have left an important gap in the comparisons. Its small size permits comparisons with Inland School, and its emphasis on education and respect reflects a parallel with older concepts of rehabilitation.

[6] The absence from the sample of large private or small public institutions means that comparisons for the variables of size and control are confounded. My primary comparisons, however, deal with the custodial-treatment dimension, and I believe these missing data do not seriously affect the basic analysis of the effects of custodial and treatment goals.

in treatment institutions than in custodial ones rests on the greater complexity of organization tasks and on the greater external demands on the superintendent in the former. Without delegating authority, the superintendent would have an overextended span of control. Formal delegation of authority often takes place through the creation of departmental structures, and institutions with different basic goals and methods set up different types of departmental patterns. Since departmental structures also affect the relations among staff groups, before presenting data which bears directly on the first hypothesis, I will discuss the departmental structures of the five institutions as they relate to correctional institutions in general.

Such custodial institutions as Dick and, to a lesser extent, Regis operate on a routine and repetitive basis and require little departmentalization.[7] When containment and control of inmates are achieved, organizational goals are fulfilled. Thus, the coordination of the staff is required primarily for physical movement of inmates and for rotation of personnel shifts. The executive can easily maintain an extended span of control.

Both Dick and Regis had simple formal structures. Of course, Regis' small size as well as its basically routine operation accounted for its lack of departmentalization. Dick was partially departmentalized; only the academic school and the farm had effective departmental heads. Even though each of the five cottages had a nominal

leader, all cottage parents often reported directly to the superintendent. No attempt was made to delegate control of the cottages to a department head, and there was little supervision of cottage parent activity. Furthermore, the departmentalization of the farm did not stem from a desire to implement more complex programs for the boys or to control employee relations with inmates; it occurred only after Dick's farm production was criticized by a citizen's committee and was an attempt to insure an adequate variety of food. Although Dick was larger than Inland, it had less departmentalization, suggesting that size alone does not account for the degree of departmentalization. Moreover, the superintendent and assistant superintendent at Dick had little difficulty in meeting role demands, indicating that under prevailing conditions further departmentalization was not required.

In contrast to custodial institutions, such mixed-goal and treatment institutions as Mixter, Milton, and Inland cannot operate as routinely, and more complex combinations of personnel must be co-ordinated. Both Mixter and Inland had multiple department structures, a form which is most likely to occur when each of the diverse tasks of the institution is relatively autonomous. In an institution with mixed goals, for instance, cottage life, education, treatment, recreation, and maintenance might each be in a separate and unintegrated department. Such an institution as Inland, operating under individual treatment philosophy, also allows departments to function independently, since the relevance of activity in the school or cottage to the rehabilitative process is not stressed, and high integration of departments thus is not required.

Although the larger size of Mixter resulted in more subsystem divisions

[7] A department is defined as a relatively self-contained subsystem of an organization. A group of workers can be considered members of a department when there is a designated liaison or responsible supervisor for the group. Workers performing similar tasks but relating individually to the superintendent, assistant superintendent, or another executive are not considered members of a department.

than at Inland, the basic structure in both institutions was similar. Social service, training and education, cottage life, and business and maintenance each comprised separate departments, no one of which had control over the others. At Mixter the superintendent took responsibility for integrating the activities of the various departments, while at Inland the assistant director performed this function.

The departmental structure at Mixter permitted the superintendent to have a reasonable span of control, while at Inland the assistant superintendent was not so fortunate. The emphasis on individual relations to inmates, inmate voluntarism, and non-routinized programs, as well as his role as chief disciplinarian, overextended the range of control of the assistant superintendent. Although Inland had less than one-fourth the number of employees of Mixter and two-thirds as many as Dick, and although its overall departmental structure was similar to that of Mixter's, the lack of a highly routinized program led to continuous operating pressures on the assistant superintendent.

Milieu-treatment institutions operate on criteria that are more consistently applied throughout the institution than in either mixed-goal or individual-treatment institutions, in this respect resembling custodial institutions. But the milieu institution differs from the custodial institution in its attempt to rationalize greater areas of organizational activity, in the complex combination of personnel, and in the substantive bases of the decisions it makes.

Milton was divided into two major divisions, the business and maintenance division and the clinical division. Under the direction of a psychiatrist, the clinical division had responsibility for all activity with the inmates. The social service staff, which in multiple departmental structures usually gives direct service to clients but only consultant service to the rest of the staff, assumed responsibility for the supervision of the cottage staff. The social service staff and the cottage parents worked together on cottage committees to make decisions about the boys. The basic therapeutic role was not defined as a one-to-one relationship between a clinical staff member and a delinquent but was, theoretically, the relationship between the boy and all staff members with whom he had contact. But, although the school and vocational training areas were under the direction of the clinical director, they were not as fully incorporated into the unitary authority structure as the cottage area. The "dual-division" structure that operated at Milton permitted to a greater extent than a multiple-department structure the centralized control over all activity in which inmates are involved. Personnel dealing with treatment were placed directly in control of the day-to-day operating staff of the institution.[8]

These patterns of departmentalization established the official range of hierarchical positions in an institution, but they do not reveal the actual amount of power or influence that a group or individual may exercise. My first proposition deals with the distribution of power among executives.

In my analysis I was able to compare the staff members' perceptions of the distribution of power among executives within an institution as well as to compare the power of executives in

_____
[8] In "The Reduction of Role Conflict in Institutional Staff," *Children*, **V** (1958), 65-69, Lloyd Ohlin has described a similar structural development in a girls' training institution; caseworkers were given administrative responsibility for the management of the cottages. One result of such a change is to partially shift conflict from an interrole to an intrarole level.

similar positions in different institutions.[9] Employees of the institutions were asked to rate the amount of influence possessed by each of the members of the executive core.[10] Table 2 presents the proportion of staff attributing "high influence" to each of them.[11]

In Dick and Regis, the more custodial institutions, a large proportion of the staff thought only the superintendent had "a great deal of say," while in

TABLE 2   Distribution of Perceived Executive Power: Staff Perception of High Influence of Various Members of Executive Core

Executives Rated	PER CENT OF HIGH INFLUENCE*				
	Dick	Regis	Mixter	Milton	Inland
Superintendent	79	100	59	52	62
Assistant director	34	11	23	65	81
Head of social service	11	0	19	12†	19
Head of cottage parents	10‡	§	52	26	3
Principal of school	15	§	8	7	5
Total no.	(62)	(9)	(155)	(108)	(37)

* Percentages are given for the highest point of a five-point scale ("A great deal of say").
† Business manager substituted for head of social service at *Milton*.
‡ Farm manager substituted for head of cottage parents at *Dick*.
§ No head of cottage parents or school principal at *Regis*.

Mixter, Milton, and Inland, the staff believed that the superintendent and at least one other member of the executive core had a great deal of influence. In fact, the data in Table 2 indicate that at Inland and Milton a larger proportion of the staff regarded the assistant superintendent rather than the superintendent as having "a great

deal of influence." These data add credibility to our first hypothesis. It may be noted that both the school principals and social service directors were consistently perceived as having little power.

One might ask, however, if these findings necessarily related to the goals and departmental structures of these institutions or were merely accidentally

---

[9] Several kinds of data were collected in all five institutions: (1) historical records and institutional publications were examined; (2) loosely structured observations of organizational practices and conferences were carried out over a two-week period in each institution; (3) extended interviews with members of the executive core (the superintendent, assistant superintendent, and heads of major departments) were conducted; (4) questionnaires were distributed to all staff members, yielding a response rate of 85 per cent or more in each of the institutions. The interrelationship of measures and observations is stressed. In no case was a datum accepted as veridical when it did not jibe with other data.

[10] Respondents were asked: "In general, how much say or influence in the way——is run would you say each of the following individuals or groups has? (Put one check on each line.)" Respondents checked a five-point scale.

[11] To the extent that "real power" is overtly expressed, employee ratings of the power of executives is a legitimate reflection of the amount of power wielded. To the extent that power relations are masked or indirect, we would expect employee perception of power to be based on the actual amount of influence of the executive core, and power to be conceived of as a "whole"—as a general attribute. Herbert Simon ("Introduction to the Theory and Measurement of Influence," *American Political Science Review*, XLIX [1955], 431-51) and Nelson Polsby (Community Power: Three Problems," *American Sociological Review*, XXIV [1959], 796-803) have both argued that a general influence rating may conceal the differentiated power wielded in different contexts. Nevertheless, a general measure of attributed power has some validity and has the merit of methodological simplicity.

associated in these institutions. The personalities of the superintendents, the size of the institutions, and—in the case of Regis—the structure of the religious order were variables which might have contributed to the great amount of power attributed to superintendents at Dick and Regis and to the smaller amount of power attributed to them at Mixter, Milton, and Inland.

In accounting for the magnitude of difference between the treatment and custodial superintendents one cannot ignore these factors. The small size of Regis minimized the need for delegation and decentralization of decision-making, while the particular personality of the superintendent at Dick contributed to the staff perception of his role as highly concentrated in power.

While the personality attributes of the superintendents of custodial institutions contributed to the image of their high power, the converse seemed to be true in the treatment institutions. The superintendent at Milton felt that his training did not qualify him to make decisions about the treatment of children, leading him to defer often in judgment to the professionals on his staff. On the other hand, although Inland's director had training that might be considered appropriate, his interpersonal relations were characteristically very tense, and the assistant director instead gained the allegiance and loyalty of the staff.

To say that such factors minimize the magnitude of the difference in patterns of power between custodial and treatment institutions is not to vitiate the over-all pattern. The creation of more than one office with authority in treatment institutions necessitates a wider distribution of power. To act effectively each department must have the right to make some decisions, and professional treatment personnel in particular must be given more power.

Furthermore, the superintendents may have to spend a good deal of time on matters not directly concerned with the internal operation of the institution, such as the relationship of the institution to the community, etc.

If executive power is shared in mixed-goal or treatment institutions, among whom is it shared? The clinical director and assistant director at Milton and Inland, respectively, were attributed high power by the staff, while at Mixter the head of the cottage-life department was perceived as the second in command. The attribution of high power to the clinical director at Milton and to the assistant director at Inland was in line with their official status, and both attempted to implement treatment goals. But the division of power between the superintendent and the head of cottage life at Mixter did not correspond to their official status, and might appear to have indicated a bifurcation of power between rehabilitational and custodial goals, the superintendent representing rehabilitative programs and the head of cottage life custodial programs. But this separation was more apparent than real: although the superintendent claimed to be committed to rehabilitational goals, in practice he concentrated his attention on benign custodial aims. Moreover, the head of cottage life, though custodially oriented, was opposed to using means which he considered overly repressive. In fact, there was little conflict between the superintendent and the head of cottage life; the superintendent felt that the head of cottage life was doing a much better job than two social workers who had previously held the position and "couldn't stand the pressure." Contrary to my expectations, the two men's approaches were not so far apart—I underestimated the pressures for consensus among major executives.

The attribution of high power to the head of cottage life at Mixter was due to his official position inasmuch as the training director was officially the second in command (52 per cent attributed "a great deal of say" to the head of cottage life, whereas only 23 per cent attributed "a great deal of say" to the training director). Power was given to the head of cottage life because he guaranteed control and containment in a situation in which repressive sanctions were banned. The head of cottage life and his assistants acted as roving police, backing up the cottage parents in their decisions and controlling situations beyond the scope of cottage parent power. Of course, the director of cottage life also had to coordinate a staff of approximately seventy men. But the problems of coordination were relatively routine and were partly delegated to the assistant cottage-life supervisors. By itself, the role of coordinator would not have called for granting a high degree of power to the head of cottage life.

I have argued that the clinical director at Milton, the assistant director at Inland, and the head of cottage life at Mixter were in particularly central positions for organizational control; but except for discussing the position of the training director at Mixter, I have not analyzed why other executives were not attributed high power. In all of the institutions the school principal and the director of social service influenced the over-all operation of the institution only by their consultant relationship to the superintendent or assistant superintendent. Although they could influence considerably the operation of their own departments, their influence on the rest of the institution was indirect.

TABLE 3   Distribution of Perceived Group Power: Staff Perception of High Influence of Social Service Workers, Cottage Parents, and Teachers

| | PER CENT OF HIGH INFLUENCE | | | | |
Groups Rated	Dick	Regis	Mixter	Milton	Inland
Social service	39	22	49	76	76
Cottage parents	50	33	34	70	8
Teachers	23	*	11	17	19
Total no.	(62)	(9)	(155)	(108)	(37)

* No teachers at Regis.

It would be a mistake, however, to conclude that the principals or the social service directors were powerless or that their positions did not vary somewhat from institution to institution. Approximately 50 percent of the staff at Mixter and Inland perceived the heads of social service to have "a great deal of say" or "considerable say," the highest two categories in our list of alternatives. Field observations indicated that the assistant director at Inland relied on the head of social service for many clinical decisions, while the superintendent at Mixter consulted more with the head of social service than he did with the training director. The influence of the social service director, especially at Inland, was related to the importance of his position for pursuing treatment aims.

The Balance of Power of Staff Groups

The balance of power among cottage parents, social service workers, and teachers, like the balance of power among executives, is a function of the goals of the organization. I hypothesized that the influence of social service personnel is likely to be higher in treatment institutions than in custodial institutions, while the power of cottage parents is likely to be higher in custodial than in individual treatment institutions. Since the milieu institution requires a team organization, a more general sharing of power is likely.

To measure the power of the various groups in making decisions about clients, I asked the staff of each institution to judge the amount of influence cottage parents, social service workers, and teachers had in making judgments about how the boys should be handled (Table 3).[12]

The statistical differences clearly indicate that a larger proportion of the staff attributes high influence to social service workers in treatment institutions than in custodial institutions. The smallest proportion attributes high influence to social service workers at Dick and Regis, a larger proportion attributes high influence to them at Mixter, and the largest proportion attributes high influence to social service workers at Inland and Milton. Cottage parent power tends to decline as we move from custodial to individual-treatment institutions; however, the cottage-committee structure at Milton, where cottage parents shared in decision-making, led to the cottage parents there being thought of as having high influence by a larger proportion of the staff than at any of the other institutions.

On the other hand, teachers were at-

tributed a relatively low amount of influence in all the institutions. Data in Table 2 indicate that the school principals also were seen as having little influence in the institutions, suggesting that the academic schools had little over-all authority or control in operating the institutions. The school personnel were not central to the definition of institutional philosophy and were restricted to an unproblematic area of institutional operation.

It was originally anticipated that within custodial institutions a larger proportion of the total staff would believe the cottage parents have high influence. This was not so perceived by the social service staff. As it turned out, only 11 percent more of the staff at Dick perceived the cottage parents to have "a great deal of influence," while at Mixter 15 percent attributed more power to social service than to cottage parents. Two factors may account for my incorrect prediction. First, as low-paid, low-status staff at the bottom of the administrative hierarchy, the cottage parents tended to make decisions within the bounds of discretion set by the administrators. Although cottage parents in custodial institutions had more discretion about discipline and more influence on the discharge of inmates, they did not formulate basic rules and procedures. On the other hand, even in the custodial institutions the higher salaried and more educated social service staff members, although they did not make decisions about individual boys, were able to influence the executives in the formulation of policy.

Second, although in the more custodial institutions cottage parents had high discretion to discipline and grade the boys, this power was shared with other staff members who worked with the boys. At Dick, any person who worked with the boys was allowed to

---

12 Respondents were asked: "How much influence do each of the following groups have in making decisions about *how the boys should be handled?*" Respondents checked a four-point scale.

paddle or punish them. At Mixter, while the cottage parent gave each boy 50 per cent of his monthly grade (which was the basis on which he was discharged), teachers and detail supervisors made up the rest of the grade. By contrast, at Milton the cottage committee meted out serious discipline, and the cottage parent on duty had a range of possible sanctions not available to teachers or supervisors.

It is interesting to note that the over-all amount of power attributed to all staff groups was higher at Milton than at any other institution, and lowest at Dick and Regis. (The question permitted all groups to be ranked high, under the assumption that more or less power may be mobilized, depending on both the number of decisions and the number of people involved in decisions in an organization.) This may indicate that milieu treatment requires more decisions and involves more people than custodial institutions, leading to a higher actualization of potential power within the organization.

The data in Table 3 quite clearly indicate the power of social service workers in treatment institutions. Role definitions, however, vary in different institutions so that power expresses itself or is used in very different ways. In the individual-treatment institution the authority of social service is based to a large extent on the staff perception of the prevailing treatment philosophy and on the social service workers' control over decisions made about individual clients. In the milieu institution, although social service workers can make many decisions, they also are required to work through and with other staff members.

In Table 4 are given the proportions of (a) all staff and (b) cottage parents alone at Milton and Inland who viewed social service advice as help-

ful.[13] The data clearly indicate the utility of social service to other personnel at Milton. The entente that existed between cottage parents and social service workers in the milieu institution was especially strong; over twice the percentage of cottage parents at Milton as compared with cottage parents at Inland found social service guidance to be of help. Although the ratio of clinical personnel to other personnel was approximately the same at Milton and Inland, the constant attempt of clinical personnel at Milton to accomplish their aims through the milieu program led them to be useful resources for others. . . .

Conclusion

(1) As organizational complexity increases and organization-community relations lead to greater external commitments by the superintendent, the chief executive must share power. In a mixed-goal institution it is likely that power is shared with a person with basically custodial aims, while in institutions with dominant treatment goals power must be given to a person concerned with treatment goals. (2) The

TABLE 4   **Percentage of Total Staff and of Cottage Parents at Milton and Inland Perceiving High Degree of "Helpfulness" of Social Service Advice**

Group	Milton	Inland
Total staff:		
Total no.	108	37
Per cent	61	43
Cottage parents:		
Total no.	35	7
Per cent	71	29

[13] Respondents were asked: "How much help are the people in social service in advising how to work with the boys?" Three alternatives were used.

balance of power among groups is also a function of organizational goals: social service personnel acquire great influence in treatment institutions, while cottage parent influence is less, except when the major focus of the institution is on the group-living situation, as in the milieu institution.

This analysis has assumed that the structure of control evolves to solve problems of goal implementation; without an organizational structure to support and control staff behavior, organizational objectives are not met. My analysis has been primarily static, comparing institutions at one point in time. A study of any one institution would show that goals are often in flux as forces internal and external to the organization press for redefinitions or extensions of emphasis. Moreover, in correctional institutions movement toward greater treatment or custodial emphasis brings about opposite pressures from groups with divergent perspectives. Even though the basic pattern of departmentalization may be relatively stable, an ebb and flow of power among groups and among executives is likely to occur as compensating policies and mechanisms are introduced.

The Western Electric Researches

GEORGE C. HOMANS

Perhaps the most important program of research studied by the Committee on Work in Industry of the National Research Council is that which has been carried on at the Hawthorne (Chicago) Works of the Western Electric Company. This program was described by H. A. Wright and M. L. Putnam of the Western Electric Company and by F. J. Roethlisberger, now Professor of Human Relations, Graduate School of Business Administration, Harvard University, particularly at a meeting of the Committee held on March 9, 1938. These men, together with Elton Mayo and G. A. Pennock, both members of the Committee, had been intimately associated with the research.[1]

George C. Homans, "The Western Electric Researches," *Fatigue of Workers*. Reprinted by permission of George C. Homans.

[1] This research has been described in detail in a number of papers and in at least three

A word about the Western Electric Company is a necessary introduction to what follows. This company is engaged in manufacturing equipment for the telephone industry. Besides doing this part of its work, it has always shown concern for the welfare of its employees. In the matter of wages and hours, it has maintained a high standard. It has provided good physical conditions for its employees; and it has tried to make use of every established method of vocational guidance in the effort to suit the worker to his work. The efforts of the company have been rewarded in good industrial relations: there has been no strike or other severe symptom of discontent for over twenty years. In short there is no reason to

books. The books are: Elton Mayo, *The Human Problems of an Industrial Civilization* (New York: The Macmillan Company, 1933); T. N. Whitehead, *The Industrial Worker*, 2 vols. (Cambridge: Harvard University Press, 1938); F. J. Roethlisberger and W. J. Dickson, *Management and the Worker* (Cambridge: Harvard University Press, 1939).

doubt that while these researches were being carried out, the morale of the company was high and that the employees, as a body, had confidence in the abilities and motives of the company management. These facts had an important bearing on the results achieved.

The program of research which will be described grew out of a study conducted at Hawthorne by the Western Electric Company in collaboration with the National Research Council, the aim of which was to determine the relation between intensity of illumination and efficiency of workers, measured in output. One of the experiments made was the following: Two groups of employees doing similar work under similar conditions were chosen, and records of output were kept for each group. The intensity of the light under which one group worked was varied, while that under which the other group worked was held constant. By this method the investigators hoped to isolate from the effect of other variables the effect of changes in the intensity of illumination on the rate of output.

In this hope they were disappointed. The experiment failed to show any simple relation between experimental changes in the intensity of illumination and observed changes in the rate of output. The investigators concluded that this result was obtained, not because such a relation did not exist, but because it was in fact impossible to isolate it from the other variables entering into any determination of productive efficiency. This kind of difficulty, of course, has been encountered in experimental work in many fields. Furthermore, the investigators were in agreement as to the character of some of these other variables. They were convinced that one of the major factors which prevented their securing a satis-

factory result was psychological. The employees being tested were reacting to changes in light intensity in the way in which they assumed that they were expected to react. That is, when light intensity was increased they were expected to produce more; when it was decreased they were expected to produce less. A further experiment was devised to demonstrate this point. The light bulbs were changed, as they had been changed before, and the workers were allowed to assume that as a result there would be more light. They commented favorably on the increased illumination. As a matter of fact, the bulbs had been replaced with others of just the same power. Other experiments of the sort were made, and in each case the results could be explained as a "psychological" reaction rather than as a "physiological" one.

This discovery seemed to be important. It suggested that the relations between other physical conditions and the efficiency of workers might be obscured by similar psychological reactions. Nevertheless, the investigators were determined to continue in their course. They recognized the existence of the psychological factor, but they thought of them only as disturbing influences. They were not yet ready to turn their attention to the psychological factors themselves. Instead, they were concerned with devising a better way of eliminating them from the experiments, and the experiments they wanted to try by no means ended with illumination. For instance, there was the question of what was called "fatigue." Little information existed about the effect on efficiency of changes in the hours of work and the introduction of rest pauses. The investigators finally came to the conclusion that if a small group of workers were isolated in a separate room and asked to cooperate, the psychological reaction would in time disappear, and they would work exactly as they felt. That is, changes in their rate of output would be the direct result of changes in their physical conditions of work and nothing else.

The decision to organize such a group was in fact taken. A small number of workers was to be selected and placed in a separate room, where experiments were to be made with different kinds of working conditions in order to see if more exact information could be secured. Six questions were asked by those setting up the experiment. They were the following:

1. Do employees actually get tired out?

2. Are rest pauses desirable?

3. Is a shorter working day desirable?

4. What is the attitude of employees toward their work and toward the company?

5. What is the effect of changing the type of working equipment?

6. Why does production fall off in the afternoon?

It is obvious that several of these questions could be answered only indirectly by the proposed experiment, and several of them touched upon the "psychological" rather than the "physiological" factors involved. Nevertheless, all of them arose out of the bewilderment of men of experience faced with the problem of dealing with fellow human beings in a large industrial organization. In fact, one of the executives of the company saw the purpose of the experiment in even simpler and more general terms. He said that the experiment grew out of a desire on the part of the management to "know more about our workers." In this way began the experiment which is referred to as the Relay Assembly Test Room. With this experiment and the others that followed, members of the Department of Industrial Research of the Graduate School of Business Administration, Harvard University, came to be closely associated.

In April, 1927, six girls were selected from a large shop department of the Hawthorne Works. They were chosen as average workers, neither inexperienced nor expert, and their work consisted of the assembling of telephone relays. A coil, armature, contact springs, and insulators were put together on a fixture and secured in position by means of four machine screws. The operation at that time was being completed at the rate of about five relays in six minutes. This particular operation was chosen for the experiment because the relays were being assembled often enough so that even slight changes in output rate would show themselves at once on the output record. Five of the girls were to do the actual assembly work; the duty of the sixth was to keep the others supplied with parts.

The test room itself was an area divided from the main department by a wooden partition eight feet high. The girls sat in a row on one side of a long workbench. Their bench and assembly equipment was identical with that used in the regular department, except in one respect. At the right of each girl's place was a hole in the bench, and into this hole she dropped completed relays. It was the entrance to a chute, in which there was a flapper gate opened by the relay in its passage downward. The opening of the gate closed an electrical circuit which controlled a perforating device, and this in turn recorded the completion of the relay by punching a hole in a tape. The tape moved at the rate of one-quarter of an inch a minute and had space for a separate row of holes for each operator. When punched, it thus constituted a complete output record for each girl for each instant of the day. Such records were kept for five years.

In this experiment then, as in the earlier illumination experiments, great emphasis was laid on the rate of output. A word of caution is needed here. The Western Electric Company was not immediately interested in increasing output. The experiments were not designed for that purpose. On the other hand, output is easily measured, i.e., it yields precise quantitative data, and experience suggested that it was sensitive to at least some of the conditions under which the employees worked. Output was treated as an index. In short, the nature of the experimental conditions made the emphasis on output inevitable.

From their experience in the illumination experiments, the investigators were well aware that factors other than those experimentally varied might affect the output rate. Therefore arrangements were made that a number of other records should be kept. Unsuitable parts supplied by the firm were noted down, as were assemblies rejected for any reason upon inspection. In this way the type of defect could be known and related to the time of day at which it occurred. Records were kept of weather conditions in general and of temperature and humidity in the test room. Every six weeks each operator was given a medical examination by the company doctor. Every day she was asked to tell how many hours she had spent in bed the night before and, during a part of the experiment, what food she had eaten. Besides all these records, which concerned the physical condition of the operators, a log was kept in which were recorded the principal events in the test room hour by hour, including among the entries snatches of conversation between the workers. At first these entries related largely to the physical condition of the operators: how they felt as they worked. Later the ground they covered somewhat widened, and the log ultimately became one of the most important of the test room records. Finally, when the so-called Interviewing Program was instituted at Hawthorne, each of the operators was interviewed several times by an experienced interviewer.

The girls had no supervisor in the ordinary sense, such as they would have had in a regular shop department, but a "test room observer" was placed in the room, whose duty it was to maintain the records, arrange the work, and secure a cooperative spirit on the part of the girls. Later, when the complexity of his work increased, several assistants were assigned to help him.

When the arrangements had been made for the test room, the operators who had been chosen to take part were called in for an interview in the office of the superintendent of the Inspection Branch, who was in general charge of the experiment and of the researches which grew out of it. The superintendent described this interview as follows: "The nature of the test was carefully explained to these girls and they readily consented to take part in it, although they were very shy at the first conference. An invitation to six shop girls to come up to a superintendent's office was naturally rather startling. They were assured that the object of the test was to determine the effect of certain changes in working conditions, such as rest periods, midmorning lunches, and shorter working hours. They were expressly cautioned to work at a comfortable pace, and under no circumstances to try to make a race out of the test." This conference was only the first of many. Whenever any experimental change was planned, the girls were called in, the purpose of the change was explained to them, and their comments were requested. Certain suggested changes which did not meet with their approval were abandoned. They were repeatedly asked, as they were asked in the first interview, not to strain but to work "as they felt."

The experiment was now ready to begin. Put in its simplest terms, the idea of those directing the experiment was that if an output curve was studied for a long enough time under various changes in working conditions, it would be possible to determine which conditions were the most satisfactory. Accordingly, a number of so-called "experimental periods" were arranged. For two weeks before the operators were placed in the test room, a record was kept of the production of each one without her knowledge. In this way the investigators secured a measure of her productive ability while working in the regular department under the usual conditions. This constituted the first experimental period. And for five weeks after the girls entered the test room no change was made in working conditions. Hours remained what they had been before. The investigators felt that this period would be long enough to reveal any changes in output incidental merely to the transfer. This constituted the second experimental period.

The third period involved a change in the method of payment. In the regular department, the girls had been paid according to a scheme of group piecework, the group consisting of a hundred or more employees. Under these circumstances, variations in an individual's total output would not be immediately reflected in her pay, since such variations tended to cancel one another in a large group. In the test room, the six operators were made a group by themselves. In this way each girl received an amount more nearly in proportion to her individual effort, and her interests became more closely centered on the experiment. Eight weeks later, the directly experimental changes began. An outline will reveal their general character: Period IV: two rest pauses, each five minutes in length, were established, one occurring in midmorning and the other in the early afternoon. Period V: these rest pauses were lengthened to ten minutes each: Period VI: six five-minute rests were established. Period VII: the company provided each member of the group with a light lunch in the midmorning and another in the midafternoon accompanied by rest pauses. This arrangement became standard for subsequent Periods VIII through XI. Period VIII: work stopped a half-hour earlier every day—at 4:30 P.M. Period IX: work stopped at 4 P.M. Period X: conditions returned to what they were in Period VII. Period XI: a five-day work week was established. Each of these experimental periods lasted several weeks.

Period XI ran through the summer of 1928, a year after the beginning of the experiment. Already the results were not what had been expected. The output curve, which had risen on the whole slowly and steadily throughout the year, was obviously reflecting something other than the responses of the group to the imposed experimental conditions. Even when the total weekly output had fallen off, as it could hardly fail to do in such a period as Period XI, when the group was working only five days a week, daily output continued to rise. Therefore, in accordance with a sound experimental procedure, as a control on what had been done, it was agreed with the consent of the operators that in experimental Period XII a return should be made to the original conditions of work, with no rest pauses, no special lunches, and a full-length working week. This period lasted for twelve weeks. Both daily and weekly output rose to a higher point than ever before: the working day and the working week were both longer. The hourly output rate declined somewhat but it did not approach the level of Period III, when similar conditions were in effect.

The conclusions reached after Period XII may be expressed in terms of another observation. Identical conditions of work were repeated in three different experimental periods: Periods VII, X, and XII. If the assumptions on which the study was based had been correct, that is to say, if the output rate were directly related to the physical conditions of work, the expectation would be that in these three experimental periods there would be some similarity in output. Such was not the case. The only apparent uniformity was that in each experimental period output was higher than in the preceding one. In the Relay Assembly Test Room, as in the previous illumination experiments, something was happening which could not be explained by the experimentally controlled conditions of work.

There is no need here to go into the later history of the test room experiment, which came to an end in 1933. It is enough to say that the output of the group continued to rise until it established itself on a high plateau from which there was no descent until the time of discouragement and deepening economic depression which preceded the end of the test. The rough conclusions reached at the end of experimental Period XII were confirmed and sharpened by later research. T. N. Whitehead, Associate Professor of Business in the Graduate School of Business Administration, Harvard University, has made a careful statistical analysis of the output records. He shows that the changes which took place in the output of the group have no simple correlation with the experimental changes in working conditions. Nor can they be correlated with changes in other physical conditions of which records were kept, such as temperature, humidity, hours of rest, and changes of relay type. Even when the girls themselves complained of mugginess or heat, these conditions were not apparently affecting their output. This statement, of course, does not mean that there is never any relation between output rate and these physical conditions. There is such a thing as heat prostration. It means only that, within the limits in which these conditions were varying in the test room, they apparently did not affect the rate of work.

The question remains: with what facts, if any, can the changes in the output rate of the operators in the test room be correlated? Here the statements of the girls themselves are of first importance. Each girl knew that she was producing more in the test room than she ever had in the regular department, and each said that the increase had come about without any conscious effort on her part. It seemed easier to produce at the faster rate in the test room than at the slower rate in the regular department. When questioned further, each girl stated her reasons in slightly different words, but there was uniformity in the answers in two respects. First, the girls liked to work in the test room; "it was fun." Secondly, the new supervisory relation or, as they put it, the absence of the old supervisory control, made it possible for them to work freely without anxiety.

For instance, there was the matter of conversation. In the regular department, conversation was in principle not allowed. In practice it was tolerated if it was carried on in a low tone and did not interfere with work. In the test room an effort was made in the beginning to discourage conversation, though it was soon abandoned. The observer in charge of the experiment was afraid of losing the cooperation of the girls if he insisted too strongly on this point. Talk became common and was often loud and general. Indeed the conversation of the operators came to occupy an important place in the log. T. N. Whitehead has pointed out that the girls in the test room were far more thoroughly supervised than they ever had been in the regular department. They were watched by an observer of their own, an interested management, and outside experts. The point is that the character and purpose of the supervision were different and were felt to be so.

The operators knew that they were taking part in what was considered an important and interesting experiment. They knew that their work was expected to produce results—they were not sure what results—which would lead to the improvement of the working conditions of their fellow employees. They knew that the eyes of the company were upon them. Whitehead has further pointed out that, although the experimental changes might turn out to have no physical significance, their social significance was always favorable. They showed that the management of the company was still interested, that the girls were still part of a valuable piece of research. In the regular department, the girls, like the other employees, were in the position of responding to changes the source and purpose of which were beyond their knowledge. In the test room, they had frequent interviews with the superintendent, a high officer of the company. The

reasons for the contemplated experimental changes were explained to them. Their views were consulted and in some instances they were allowed to veto what had been proposed. Professor Mayo has argued that it is idle to speak of an experimental period like Period XII as being in any sense what it purported to be—a return to the original conditions of work. In the meantime, the entire industrial situation of the girls had been reconstructed.

Another factor in what occurred can only be spoken of as the social development of the group itself. When the girls went for the first time to be given a physical examination by the company doctor, someone suggested as a joke that ice cream and cake ought to be served. The company provided them at the next examination, and the custom was kept up for the duration of the experiment. When one of the girls had a birthday, each of the others would bring her a present, and she would respond by offering the group a box of chocolates. Often one of the girls would have some good reason for feeling tired. Then the others would "carry" her. That is, they would agree to work especially fast to make up for the low output expected from her. It is doubtful whether this "carrying" did have any effect, but the important point is the existence of the practice, not its effectiveness. The girls made friends in the test room and went together socially after hours. One of the interesting facts which has appeared from Whitehead's analysis of the output records is that there were times when variations in the output rates of two friends were correlated to a high degree. Their rates varied simultaneously and in the same direction—something, of course, which the girls were not aware of and could not have planned. Also, these correlations were destroyed by such apparently trivial events as a change in the order in which the girls sat at the workbench.

Finally, the group developed leadership and a common purpose. The leader, self-appointed, was an ambitious young Italian girl who entered the test room as a replacement after two of the original members had left. She saw in the experiment a chance for personal distinction and advancement. The common purpose was an increase in the output rate. The girls had been told in the beginning and repeatedly thereafter that they were to work without straining, without trying to make a race of the test, and all the evidence shows that they kept this rule. In fact, they felt that they were working under less pressure than in the regular department. Nevertheless, they knew that the output record was considered the most important of the records of the experiment and was always closely scrutinized. Before long they had committed themselves to a continuous increase in production. In the long run, of course, this ideal was an impossible one, and when the girls found out that it was, the realization was an important element of the change of tone which was noticeable in the second half of the experiment. But for a time they felt that they could achieve the impossible. In brief, the increase in the output rate of the girls in the Relay Assembly Test Room could not be related to any changes in their physical conditions of work, whether experimentally induced or not. It could, however, be related to what can only be spoken of as the development of an organized social group in a peculiar and effective relation with its supervisors.

Many of these conclusions were not worked out in detail until long after the investigators at Hawthorne had lost interest in the Relay Assembly Test Room, but the general meaning of the experiment was clear at least as early as Period XII. A continuous increase in productivity had taken place irrespective of changing physical conditions of work. In the words of a company report made in January, 1931, on all the research which had been done up to that date: "Upon analysis, only one thing seemed to show a continuous relationship with this improved output. This was the mental attitude of the operators. From their conversations with each other and their comments to the test observers, it was not only clear that their attitudes were improving but it was evident that this area of employee reactions and feelings was a fruitful field for industrial research." . . .

In order to study this kind of problem further, to make a more detailed investigation of social relations in a working group, and to supplement interview material with direct observation of the behavior of employees, the Division of Industrial Research decided to set up a new test room. But the investigators remembered what happened in the former test room and tried to devise an experiment which would not be radically altered by the process of experimentation itself. They chose a group of men—nine wiremen, three soldermen, and two inspectors—engaged in the assembly of terminal banks for use in telephone exchanges, took them out of their regular department and placed them in a special room. Otherwise no change was made in their conditions of work, except that an investigator was installed in the room, whose duty was simply to observe the behavior of the men. In the Relay Assembly Test Room a log had been kept of the principal events of the test. At the beginning it consisted largely of comments made by the workers in answer to questions about their physical condition. Later it came to include a much wider range of entries, which were found to be extremely useful in interpreting the changes in the output rate of the different workers. The work of the observer in the new test room was in effect an expansion of the work of keeping the log in the old one. Finally an interviewer was assigned to the test room; he was not, however, one of the population of the room but remained outside and interviewed the employees from time to time in the usual manner. No effort was made to get output records other than the ones ordinarily kept in the department from which the group came, since the investigators felt that such a procedure would introduce too large a change from a regular shop situation. In this way the experiment was set up which is referred to as the Bank Wiring Observation Room. It was in existence seven months, from November, 1931, to May, 1932.

The method of payment is the first aspect of this group which must be described. It was a complicated form of group piecework. The department of which the workers in the observation room were a part was credited with a fixed sum for every unit of equipment it assembled. The amount thus earned on paper by the department every week made up the sum of which the wages of all the men in the department were paid. Each individual was then assigned an hourly rate of pay, and he was guaranteed this amount in case he did not make at least as much on a piecework basis. The rate was based on a number of factors, including the nature of the job a worker was doing, his efficiency, and his length of service with the Company. Records of the output of every worker were kept, and every six months there was a rate revision, the purpose

of which was to make the hourly rates of the different workers correspond to their relative efficiency.

The hourly rate of a given employee, multiplied by the number of hours worked by him during the week, was spoken of as the daywork value of the work done by the employee. The daywork values of the work done by all the employees in the department were then added together, and the total thus obtained was subtracted from the total earnings credited to the department for the number of units of equipment assembled. The surplus, divided by the total daywork value, was expressed as a percentage. Each individual's hourly rate was then increased by this percentage, and the resulting hourly earnings figure, multiplied by the number of hours worked, constituted that person's weekly earnings.

Another feature of the system should be mentioned here. Sometimes a stoppage which was beyond the control of the workers took place in the work. For such stoppages the workers were entitled to claim time out, being paid at their regular hourly rates for this time. This was called the "daywork allowance claim." The reason why the employees were paid their hourly rate for such time and not their average hourly wages was a simple one. The system was supposed to prevent stalling. The employees could earn more by working than they could by taking time out. As a matter of fact, there was no good definition of what constituted a stoppage which was beyond the control of the workers. All stoppages were more or less within their control. But this circumstance was supposed to make no difference in the working of the system, since the assumption was that in any case the workers, pursuing their economic interests, would be anxious to keep stoppages at a minimum.

This system of payment was a complicated one, but it is obvious that there was a logical reason for every one of its features. An individual's earnings would be affected by changes in his rate or in his output and by changes in the output of the group as a whole. The only way in which the group as a whole could increase its earnings was by increasing its total output. It is obvious also that the experts who designed the system made certain implicit assumptions about the behavior of human beings, or at least the behavior of workers in a large American factory. They assumed that every employee would pursue his economic interest by trying to increase not only his own output but the output of every other person in the group. The group as a whole would act to prevent slacking by any of its members. One possibility, for instance, was that by a few weeks' hard work an employee could establish a high rate for himself. Then he could slack up and be paid out of all proportion to the amount he actually contributed to the wages of the group. Under these circumstances, the other employees were expected to bring pressure to bear to make him work harder.

Such was the way in which the wage incentive scheme ought to have worked. The next question is how it actually did work. At first the workers were naturally suspicious of the observer but when they got used to him and found that nothing out of the ordinary happened as a result of his presence in the room, they came to take him for granted. The best evidence that the employees were not distrustful of the observer is that they were willing to talk freely to him about what they were doing, even when what they were doing was not in strict accord with what the Company expected. Conversation would die when the group chief entered the room, and when the foreman or the assistant foreman entered everyone became serious. But no embarrassment was felt at the presence of the observer. To avoid misunderstanding, it is important to point out that the observer was in no sense a spy. The employees were deliberately and obviously separated from their regular department. The observer did not, and could not, pass himself off as one of them. And if only from the fact that a special interviewer was assigned to them, the members of the group knew they were under investigation.

The findings reached by the observer were more detailed but in general character the same as those which had emerged from the early interviews of other groups. Among the employees in the observation room there was a notion of a proper day's work. They felt that if they had wired two equipments a day they had done about the right amount. Most of the work was done in the morning. As soon as the employees felt sure of being able to finish what they considered enough for the day, they slacked off. This slacking off was naturally more marked among the faster than among the slower workmen.

As a result, the output graph from week to week tended to be a straight line. The employees resorted to two further practices in order to make sure that it remained so. They reported more or less output than they performed and they claimed more day-work allowances than they were entitled to. At the end of the day, the observer would make an actual count of the number of connections wired—something which was not done by the supervisors—and he found that the men would report to the group chief sometimes more and sometimes less work than they actually had accomplished. At the end of the period of observation, two men had completed more than they ever had reported, but on the whole the error was in the opposite direction. The theory of the employees was that excess work produced on one day should be saved and applied to a deficiency on another day. The other way of keeping the output steady was to claim excessive daywork allowance. The employees saw that the more daywork they were allowed, the less output they would have to maintain in order to keep the average hourly output rate steady. The claims for daywork allowance were reported by the men to their group chief, and he, as will be seen, was in no position to make any check. These practices had two results. In the first place, the departmental efficiency records did not represent true efficiency, and therefore decisions as to grading were subject to errors of considerable importance. In the second place, the group chief was placed in a distinctly awkward position.

The findings of the observer were confirmed by tests which were made as a part of the investigation. Tests of intelligence, finger dexterity, and other skills were given to the workers in the room, and the results of the tests were studied in order to discover whether there was any correlation between output, on the one hand, and earnings, intelligence, or finger dexterity, on the other. The studies showed that there was not. The output was apparently not reflecting the native intelligence or dexterity of the members of the group.

Obviously the wage incentive scheme was not working in the way it was expected to work. The next question is why it was not working. In this connection, the observer reported that the group had developed an informal social organization, such as had been revealed by earlier investigations. The foreman who selected the employees taking part in the Bank Wiring Observation Room was cooperative and had worked with the investigators before. They asked him to produce a normal group. The men he chose all came out of the same regular shop department, but they had not been closely associated in their work there. Nevertheless, as soon as they were thrown together in the observation room, friendships sprang up and soon two well-defined cliques were formed. The division into cliques showed itself in a number of ways: in mutual exclusiveness, in differences in the games played off-hours, and so forth.

What is important here is not what divided the men in the observation room but what they had in common. They shared a common body of sentiments. A person should not turn out too much work. If he did, he was a "rate-buster." The theory was that if an excessive amount of work was turned out, the management would lower the piecework rate so that the employees would be in the position of doing more work for approximately the same pay. On the other hand, a person should not turn out too little work. If he did, he was a "chiseler"; that is, he was getting paid for work he did not do. A person should say nothing which would injure a fellow member of the group. If he did, he was a "squealer." Finally, no member of the group should act officiously.

The working group had also developed methods of enforcing respect for its attitudes. The experts who devised the wage incentive scheme assumed that the group would bring pressure to bear upon the slower workers to make them work faster and so increase the earnings of the group. In point of fact, something like the opposite occurred.

The employees brought pressure to bear not upon the slower workers but upon the faster ones, the very ones who contributed most of the earnings of the group. The pressure was brought to bear in various ways. One of them was "binging." If one of the employees did something which was not considered quite proper, one of his fellow workers had the right to "bing" him. Binging consisted of hitting him a stiff blow on the upper arm. The person who was struck usually took the blow without protest and did not strike back. Obviously the virtue of binging as punishment did not lie in the physical hurt given to the worker but in the mental hurt that came from knowing that the group disapproved of what he had done. Other practices which naturally served the same end were sarcasm and the use of invectives. If a person turned out too much work, he was called names, such as "Speed King" or "The Slave."

It is worth while pointing out that the output of the group was not considered low. If it had been, some action might have been taken, but in point of fact it was perfectly satisfactory to the management. It was simply not so high as it would have been if fatigue and skill had been the only limiting factors.

In the matter of wage incentives, the actual situation was quite different from the assumptions made by the experts. Other activities were out of line in the same way. The wiremen and the soldermen did not stick to their jobs; they frequently traded them. This was forbidden, on the theory that each employee ought to do his own work because he was more skilled in that work. There was also much informal helping of one man by others. In fact, the observation of this practice was one means of determining the cliques into which the group was divided. A great many things, in short, were going on in the observation room which ought not to have been going on. For this reason it was important that no one should "squeal" on the men:

A group chief was in immediate charge of the employees. He had to see that they were supplied with parts and that they conformed to the rules and standards of the work. He could reprimand them for misbehavior or poor performance. He transmitted orders to the men and brought their requests before the proper authorities. He was also responsible for reporting to the foreman all facts which ought to come to his attention. The behavior of the employees put him in an awkward position. He was perfectly well aware of the devices by which they maintained their production at a constant level. But he was able to do very little to bring about a change. For instance, there was the matter of claims for daywork allowance. Such claims were supposed to be based on stoppages beyond the control of the workers, but there was no good definition of what constituted such stoppages. The men had a number of possible excuses for claiming daywork allowance; defective materials, poor and slow work on the part of other employees, and so forth. If the group chief checked up on one type of claim, the workers could shift to another. In order to decide whether or not a particular claim was justified, he would have to stand over the group all day with a stop watch. He did not have time to do that, and in any case refusal to honor employees' claims would imply doubt of their integrity and would arouse their hostility. The group chief was a representative of management and was supposed to look after its interests. He ought to have put a stop to these practices and reported them to the foreman. But if he did so he would, to use the words of a short account of the observation room by Roethlisberger and Dickson, "lose sympathetic control of his men, and his duties as supervisor would become much more difficult."[2] He had to associate with the employees from day to day and from hour to hour. His task would become impossible if he had to fight a running fight with them. Placed in this situation, he chose to side with the men and report unchanged their claims for daywork. In fact there was very little else he could do, even if he wished. Moreover, he was in a position to protect himself in case of trouble. The employees always had to give him reasons for any daywork claims they might make, and he entered the claims in a private record book. If anyone ever asked why so much daywork was being claimed, he could throw the blame wherever he wished. He could assert that materials had been defective or he could blame the inspectors, who are members of an outside organization. In still another respect, then, the Bank Wiring Observation Room group was not behaving as the logic of management assumed that it would behave.

Restriction of output is a common phenomenon of industrial plants. It is usually explained as a highly logical reaction of the workers. They have increased their output, whereupon their wage rates for piecework have been reduced. They are doing more work for the same pay. They restrict their out-

put in order to avoid a repetition of this experience. Perhaps this explanation holds good in some cases, but the findings of the Bank Wiring Observation Room suggest that it is too simple. The workers in the room were obsessed with the idea that they ought to hold their production level "even" from week to week, but they were vague as to what would happen if they did not. They said that "someone" would "get them." If they turned out an unusually high output one week, that record would be taken thereafter as an example of what they could do if they tried, and they would be "bawled out" if they did not keep up to it. As a matter of fact, none of the men in the room had ever experienced a reduction of wage rates. What is more, as Roethlisberger and Dickson point out, "changes in piece rates occur most frequently where there is a change in manufacturing process, and changes in manufacturing process are made by engineers whose chief function is to reduce unit cost wherever the saving will justify the change. In some instances, changes occur irrespective of direct labor cost. Moreover, where labor is a substantial element, reduction of output tends to increase unit costs and instead of warding off a change in the piece rate many actually induce one."

What happened in the observation room could not be described as a logical reaction of the employees to the experience of rate reduction. They had in fact no such experience. On the other hand, the investigators found that it could be described as a conflict between the technical organization of the plant and its social organization. By technical organization the investigators meant the plan, written or unwritten, according to which the Hawthorne plant was supposed to operate, and the agencies which gave effect to

[2] F. J. Roethlisberger and W. J. Dickson, *Management and the Worker* (Boston: Harvard Business School, Division of Research, Business Research Studies No. 9). (All quotations relating to the Western Electric researches are from this study as well as from the book of the same title by the same authors.)

that plan. The plan included explicit rules as to how the men were to be paid, how they were to do their work, what their relations with their supervisors ought to be. It included also implicit assumptions on which the rules were based, one of the assumptions being that men working in the plant would on the whole act so as to further their economic interests. It is worth while pointing out that this assumption was in fact implicit, that the experts who devised the technical organization acted upon the assumption without ever stating it in so many words.

There existed also an actual social situation within the plant: groups of men, who were associated with one another, held common sentiments and had certain relations with other groups and other men. To some extent this social organization was identical with the technical plan and to some extent it was not. For instance, the employees were paid according to group payment plans, but the groups concerned did not behave as the planners expected them to behave.

The investigators considered the relations between the technical organization and the social. A certain type of behavior is expected of the higher levels of management. Their success is dependent on their being able to devise and institute rapid changes. Roethlisberger and Dickson describe what happens in the following terms: "Management is constantly making mechanical improvements and instituting changes designed to reduce costs or improve the quality of the product. It is constantly seeking new ways and new combinations for increasing efficiency, whether in designing a new machine, instituting a new method of control, or logically organizing itself in a new way." The assumption has often been made that these changes are designed to force the employee to do more work for less money. As a matter of fact, many of them have just the opposite purpose: to improve the conditions of work and enable the employee to earn higher wages. The important point here, however, is not the purpose of the changes but the way in which they are carried out and accepted.

Once the responsible officer has decided that a certain change ought to be made, he gives an order, and this order is transmitted "down the line," appropriate action being taken at every level. The question in which the investigators were interested was this: what happens when the order reaches the men who are actually doing the manual work? Roethlisberger and Dickson make the following observations: "The worker occupies a unique position in the social organization. He is at the bottom of a highly stratified organization. He is always in the position of having to accommodate himself to changes which he does not originate. Although he participates least in the technical organization, he bears the brunt of most of its activities." It is he, more than anyone, who is affected by the decisions of management, yet in the nature of things he is unable to share management's preoccupations, and management does little to convince him that what he considers important is being treated as important at the top—a fact which is not surprising, since there is no adequate way of transmitting to management an understanding of the considerations which seem important at the work level. There is something like a failure of communication in both directions—upward and downward.

The worker is not only "asked to accommodate himself to changes which he does not initiate, but also many of the changes deprive him of those very things which give meaning and significance to his work." The modern industrial worker is not the handicraftsman of the medieval guild. Nevertheless, the two have much in common. The industrial worker develops his own ways of doing his job, his own traditions of skill, his own satisfactions in living up to his standards. The spirit in which he adopts his own innovations is quite different from that in which he adopts those of management. Furthermore, he does not do his work as an isolated human being, but always as a member of a group, united either through actual cooperation on the job or through association in friendship. One of the most important general findings of the Western Electric researches is the fact that such groups are continually being formed among industrial workers, and that the groups develop codes and loyalties which govern the relations of the members to one another. Though these codes can be quickly destroyed, they are not formed in a moment. They are the product of continued, routine interaction between men. "Constant interference with such codes is bound to lead to feelings of frustration, to an irrational exasperation with technical change in any form, and ultimately to the formation of a type of employee organization such as we have described —a system of practices and beliefs in opposition to the technical organization."

The Bank Wiring Observation Room seemed to show that action taken in accordance with the technical organization tended to break up, through continual change, the routines and human associations which gave work its value. The behavior of the employees could be described as an effort to protect themselves against such changes, to give management the least possible opportunity of interfering with them.

When they said that if they increased their output, "something" was likely to happen, a process of this sort was going on in their minds. But the process was not a conscious one. It is important to point out that the protective function of informal organization was not a product of deliberate planning. It was more in the nature of an automatic response. The curious thing is that, as Professor Mayo pointed out to the Committee, these informal organizations much resemble formally organized labor unions, although the employees would not have recognized the fact.

Roethlisberger and Dickson summarize as follows the results of the intensive study of small groups of employees: "According to our analysis the uniformity of behavior manifested by these groups was the outcome of a disparity in the rates of change possible in the technical organization, on the one hand, and in the social organization, on the other. The social sentiments and customs of work of the employees were unable to accommodate themselves to the rapid technical innovations introduced. The result was to incite a blind resistance to all innovations and to provoke the formation of a social organization at a lower level in opposition to the technical organization."

It is curious how, at all points, the Relay Assembly Test Room and the Bank Wiring Observation Room form a contrast. In the former, the girls said that they felt free from the pressure of supervision, although as a matter of fact they were far more thoroughly supervised than they ever had been in their regular department. In the latter, the men were afraid of supervision and acted so as to nullify it. The Bank Wiremen were in the position of having to respond to technical changes which they did not originate. The Relay Assemblers had periodic conferences with the superintendent. They were told what experimental changes were contemplated; their views were canvassed; and in some instances they were allowed to vote on what had been proposed. They were part of an experiment which they felt was interesting and important. Both groups developed an informal social organization, but while the Bank Wiremen were organized in opposition to management, the Relay Assemblers were organized in cooperation with management in the pursuit of a common purpose. Finally, the responses of the two groups to their industrial situation were, on the one hand, restriction of output and, on the other, steady and welcome increase of output. These contrasts carry their own lesson.

Formal and Informal Organization

MELVILLE DALTON

Formal and Informal as Terms

Systematic focus on the terms "formal" and "informal" as applied to organizations, began with Barnard's theory in 1938, and was fortified with data the next year by Roethlisberger and Dickson, who talked especially of informal activity among workers. Since then the terms have been in common use by sociologists and others. More recent thought and research have shown, however, that multiple relations, with continuous interaction and change, become too dynamic to be handled entirely inside such conceptual walls as "formal-informal." Students are increasingly aware that this is the same kind of trap as "form versus substance," "individualism versus collectivism," "romanticism versus classicism." The bare scheme of formal-informal is helpful but inadequate for grappling with all aspects of the behavior we have been talking about. Exclusive reliance on this couplet ignores the whole confused middle ground where there are "mixtures," and where new formal and informal action are obscurely initiated. Although this area may be impossible to deal with concretely, we should at least recognize that there can be numerous concurrent interplays, interrelated and not, of varying importance for the organization.

The term *informal* has become especially troublesome in the context of organizations. To some it connotes only conspiracy. And when used as the counter pole of a couplet there is difficulty in saying where the informal ends and the *formal* begins. The term is so broad that embarrassingly often it requires delimitation and redefinition. If "informal" is used as "functionally interrelated to the formal," it implies a complete knowledge of formal expectations by the informal group under focus. These points merit enlargement.

Probably in part from the influence of studies on work restriction as an informal technique implicitly confined to workers, the moral feelings of some people are inflamed by their experience with the term. They think of "work paid for but not done," "failure

Melville Dalton, "Formal and Informal Organization," *Men Who Manage* (New York: John Wiley & Sons, Inc., 1959), pp. 222-32, with omissions.

to fight in the open," and the like. Repeatedly my own students, from various disciplines, have raised questions about the distinctions between informal, on the one hand, and intrigue, plotting, frame-ups, "or any other kind of sneakiness" on the other. They require correction to see that informal action may work for many ends: to change and preserve the organization, to protect weak individuals, punish erring ones, reward others, to recruit new personnel, and to maintain dignity of the formal, as well as, of course, to carry on power struggles, and to work for ends we would all frown on.

On the second point, when a clique is recognized, or when grapevines are known and counted on by all, or when higher management considers such a clique or practice in its policy making, obviously the informal is formal for most purposes. Since it is utilized by all and lacks only official recognition, it is more correctly called *unofficial* than informal.

On the third point, one can think of informal organization as Barnard does, as incidental or accidental association without purpose, but this distinction includes story-telling and small talk of all kinds and confines the term largely to what we earlier called a "random clique." Such incidental association admittedly can give a basis for later cooperative activity, but always intermingled with the socializers are members who calculatingly participate with additional purposes in mind. So for our aim of stressing the *ties* between formal and informal we need to consider more than what supplies a potential for joint activity; we must talk of the activity itself. This largely conscious action is what we primarily mean by "informal."

Finally, when one uses "informal" as a necessary counterpart of "formal,"

the implication is that they somehow match and balance each other, that those participating in the informal activity have full knowledge of formal expectations. This oversimplifies the behavior. As we have seen, it is unrealistic to assume that all the managers of a firm have complete knowledge of formal expectations. Since (1) there are varying and inconstant gaps between official and actual influence of members; and (2) the more fully committed members necessarily have secrets not shared by the fringe members; and since (3) some directives are known only by a minority to be for nothing but the record, obviously formal purpose is not shared by all except in the most general way. That is, knowledge of changing policy is often withheld from some subordinates because of belief that they will react unfavorably to the full picture at *this* moment. Then, too, in firms like Milo and Fruhling, procedures, demands by the customer, etc., may change so rapidly that middle and lower officers have only partial knowledge of the formal expectations. Also there is both ignorant and indifferent action in the organization that falls outside this simple scheme.[1]

These criticisms are not to reject the couplets of "formal-informal," "official-

---

[1] For example, in a large office at Fruhling —apparently typical in terms of nonsupervisory staff skills, interest, and morale—the employees frequently showed fluctuating concern for important procedures. Correction of errors found in the time charged to various departmental accounts required much paper work and checking of all departmental records. Most of this crew, however, merely shuffled the correction cards they received and distributed them equally among members. Each person then divided the total time, on the cards he received, among the accounts *currently* on his desk. To my friendly but unauthorized question about this procedure, they answered, "What difference does it make?"

unofficial," etc., but to note their limitations and point the need to study the intervening action.

Formal and Informal as Aspects of Organization

Specialists variously evaluate these two phases of effort. Brief comment on the merits ascribed to each, or to the one that is stressed, will prepare us to talk of how the two interact.

Dimock thinks of what we usually call the official and unofficial as the engineering versus the psychological approaches. Since the two represent inherent bodies of activity in organizations, he demands more effort to correlate them. Overemphasis on the official, he insists, is likely to engender "psychological quirks" in the individual. When the organization tries to entirely replace discretion with certainty it deserves the popular insult of "bureaucracy." Such "routine is the institutional equivalent of personal introversion."

The sociologist, Tönnies, long ago implicitly denied the possibility of a purely official, or planned, structure, and Urwick ridicules the emphasis placed on "official channels." He admits their necessity but sees them as largely "for the record," except during a change of leaders or the breakdown of "good personal relations." Normally only a simpleton would think that effective collaboration is created simply by setting up formal procedure. The "fiction" that the president "runs" the company, Stryker says in agreement, is built on management's reverence for formally charted relations. Experienced managers know that things get done informally, and that the informal exists in management as its "biggest intangible asset" and "touchiest open secret."

Great emphasis has been placed on the merits of the informal by Donham, Roethlisberger, Mayo, Whitehead, Homans, and others. One executive values the informal because it can be absorbed into the daily routine without official notice. This allows him to win unofficial ends without raising questions.

Like the formal, the informal phases can be overstressed. Some groups are prone to make informal communication an end in itself. Where this occurs, formal procedure may be regarded as not even a necessary evil. The informal takes on such prominence that in-plant luncheons and out-plant socializing become the chief vehicles for communication. Facility in party giving, as the ideal atmosphere for policy making, becomes an informal requirement for acceptance, so that a condition develops comparable to that noted by Willkie.

Some students implicitly stress the formal organization by reluctant admission that "there seems to be a certain minimum amount" of informal activity that remains in organizations whether welcome or not.

Students of bureaucracy as an administrative structure designed scientifically to accelerate movement toward stated goals are, of course, stressing the formal phases. In addition to their evaluations and those of Barnard, Urwick, and Dimock on the subject, the weight of the formal phase in organizational practice is clearly shown by the avoidance of discussion of delegation and by the niceties often attending so-called delegation to authority.

For example, Rees, Milo's Head of Industrial Relations, wished to support first-line foremen by giving them the appearance of being quite independent, while he informally made their decisions. The editors of *Fortune* cite

All two similar idea that the formal org. not realistic

similar cases in large corporations of subtle, "even unconscious" communications between higher and lower executives that enable the latter to make "correct decisions." As the editors see it, the subordinate officers "sustain their egos," by the appearance of authority, while the higherups continue to make the decisions.

The weight of formal organization, even when those in high place seek to share their authority, was shown in an English study. The "Managing Director" of a plant which had long tried to "raise the level of democratic participation" found that subordinate executives were likely to interpret sudden delegation of authority—allowing them to act entirely on their own—as concealed punishment and an attempt by the superior to abdicate his responsibility.

Shartle ironically attributes advantages to excessive formality, as when "red tape" slows action that in the thinking of some department should be delayed, or prevents interference with a fast-moving program.[2]

These conflicting emphases also show awareness of the potential for varying gaps to develop between formal and informal. Emmerich, however, believes that the two phases "are so closely related that the attempt to isolate [them] can be as misleading as the newer tendency to equate them." In diverse terms, others see the problem of a breach between formal and informal and propose *integration* in some way. Urwick, for example, speaks of ceaseless reorganization, or a "continuous evolution," which must be constantly guided by permanent machinery for that purpose. . . .

---

[2] Shartle, *Executive Performance and Leadership* (Prentice-Hall, Englewood Cliffs, New Jersey, 1956), p. 201. . . .

The Interplay of Formal and Informal

These discussions of official and informal action in the dynamics, development, reorganization, and evolution, of the organization do not, to repeat ourselves, deal explicitly with the interplay of formal and informal. However difficult, we need to focus more on the interconnections between formal and unofficial as they draw apart, collide, and/or irregularly perform functions. Though the action is colored at times with economic, individual, and even chance factors, we have already seen many interplays springing from this orderly disorder. For example, rise of the FWD at Milo as a response to the developing conflict between Maintenance and Operation; breakdown of the FWD largely as a result of informal evasions and attacks on it; formal action by the Office which was countered and adapted by Milo chiefs; the blocking of Jessup's proposal at Fruhling and his informal perfection of the process which was later adopted; the circumvention of labor agreements by union-management cliques leading to some modification in later contracts; the rise of sinecures and the use of the assistant-to-office to soften formal rigidities; the use of unofficial criteria in the selection of new officers; the rise and action of specific clique types to meet recurring situations growing out of formal changes; the informal use of materials and services to supplement formal reward; the endless formal-informal exchanges through Reynolds at Attica; the responses in O'Brien's department to the formal ranking of shifts by their production level; and the whole cluster of interplays between safety regulations and accidents. . . .

Some important steps and mechanisms that connect the formal and informal and enable them to maintain ongoing action are (1) official meetings, (2) command from high levels for unofficial action from below, (3) informal requests from below for the right to engage in specific unofficial actions, (4) transitional roles, (5) recourse to prefigured justifications, (6) the use of "two-way funnels," and (7) adoption by the formal—acknowledged or not—of unofficial widespread practices that have proved their worth or have become an accomplished fact.

Meetings

As we all know, conferences may be used for more than official purposes. It should be no surprise that the periodic meetings in business and industry are at times much like those of parliamentary gatherings. Because the internal power struggles of business and industry are largely denied and must be cloaked, it is clear that the ferment of unofficial activities may be more intense at times than the frankly parliamentary action.[3] Right down the hierarchy one finds meetings a stage for exploratory skirmishes; for making authoritative hints to those moving too far in some direction; for study of faces and inflections; for catching slips and checking on premeeting tips, etc. The formal meeting is a gallery of fronts where aimless, deviant, and central currents of action merge for a moment, perfunctorily for some, emotionally for others. All depart with new knowledge to pursue variously altered, but rarely the agreed, courses.

One finds executives called into meetings to solve problems precipi-tated by their own informal activities, which naturally bind their hands. At the meeting they may learn—as Milo staff forces did by turning luncheons into meetings—how much of their problem is known, and they may pick up helpful leads from responses to guarded questions they raise. Pre- and postmeeting confabs with clique members incorporate these findings. Where the gap between formal and informal phases becomes great, some officers seek to settle issues in meetings and escape the commitment of written statements. We saw this concern in Chapter 5. This allows greater expression to the free-wheelers and tacticians, but inspires fear among the rule-bound.[4] The existing "balance" of formal-informal action is partially provoked by variants of these two types, and newcomers are in turn selected to some extent in terms of how they will fit into the balance.

Total time spent in meetings can indicate roughly the rate of change and the intensity of interaction between the formal and informal; and also, of course, lack of assurance in making decisions on the part of those calling the meetings. At Milo and Fruhling there were nine to over a dozen different kinds of periodic meetings. Department heads averaged about six hours daily in conferences. General policy, production planning, staff-line, and cost meetings especially reflected the two-way influence. The osten-

---

[3] Barnard (*Functions of the Executive*), p. 226, notes the limited "overt division on formal issues" that authority can tolerate. Hence the volume of informal activity in both cases.

[4] For example, E. Flandin, a general foreman and a formalist on procedure, refused to participate in meetings. He remarked, "I just set and listen. You know a damn sight better than to say anything. You're licked before you go in a meeting. If you speak up and make a complaint, you'll have to prove it and you'll make a dozen guys sore. If you make a suggestion there'll be a dozen guys against it because it'll bother them some way or show up their dodges. I'd rather just keep my mouth shut and draw my pay."

sibly final reports or agreements they brought forth were often tentative. When subject to disapproval and rejection at higher levels or by "powerful" individuals, the reports were officially unofficial for they were often frankly requested to be in pencil—a forewarning that the play of interests would result in revisions and "graphite analyses."

Ordered Unofficial Action

In various emergencies and unusual situations, higherups demand limited unofficial, and even illegal, action by subordinates. . . . Orders to flunk certain job examinees is a case in point. However, when the demand embraces too many personnel moral disturbances break out. . . . Restricted demand confined to tested personnel is more common and is more likely to accomplish formal ends without damage to its dignity. Organizationally necessary change introduced in this way gradually blends into ongoing action.

Granted Departures

Where camaraderie is high, so that subordinates do not fear unofficial punishment by superiors, they may ask permission to settle some issues informally. [For example,] unofficial blanket instructions to all from above to use containable informal methods. This of course embraced an area of issues crucial to production. In many less important cases formal and informal are similarly bridged without indignities to the formal. For example, the dealing with another department, the rewarding—or even penalizing—of some individual who must be lived with, the handling of some plant-community issue, etc., are all made easier by permission, and sometimes cooperation, from above,

though the superior, as in other cases, prefers to remain officially ignorant.[5]

Both commanded and requested informal actions are likely to be followed by protective official statements, which are "orders for the record." The intent is of course usually known only to the chosen. An order for the record may be a temporary blind to cover movement toward an end; or it may start as a stopgap and become semi-permanent when conditions show that dropping it would bring greater problems. Orders for the record may also be issued at lower levels to placate threatening formalists or to follow established disciplinary procedure. . . .

The Transitional Role

I implied just above that "orders for the record" may induce further complications. Both such orders and the various uses of the office of assistant-to are related to the operation of unofficial transitional roles. Typically the accumulated influence of such roles would be little relative to some of the other factors with which they overlap. Usually these roles arise from defective operations, which may have been induced by other informal action, and start as attempts to get the work done and to make loose ends meet. They may be called out by unofficial orders, or start through the voluntary action of some officer who wants to experiment with something new, speed up something underway, or who draws together functions of operation that others have overlooked—or know about and want to avoid. In any case, some-

---

[5] Here again, industry and business have no monopoly on unofficial action. In at least one community of a state in which it is illegal for public school students to give presents to their teachers, student cliques sometimes obtain permission from their well-loved principal to give gifts with the proviso that "I know nothing about it."

one with an official role carries out "temporary" functions (or as Stein said, "sticks his neck out") that become more important than expected. This person may become so expert with these unofficial functions that he must weaken his official contribution. He becomes identified with the function and may be maintained and protected where he is as he is without official changes. If he clamors for reward, he may or not receive it but the function is formalized and someone takes the role.

While this direct interplay of informal and formal can lead to official change, the formal role may merely be enlarged to incorporate informal functions without an official change, according to the abilities of the person playing the role. . . .

Prefigured Justifications

Meetings steer only a part of the course between the formal and informal. The clashes and schisms, the interests of the part and the whole, the action of the bored and the partially committed—all are interwoven by tentative prearranged defenses that cloak much of the action in and out of meetings.

Since integrity of the formal must be preserved, the gap between it and the informal must be within the tolerance of understood propriety. Where personnel must depart from expectations, they feel obliged to have ready explanations at hand. The executive who stumbles onto irregularities he did not order, and that uninvolved persons know about, must do something for the record and demand an explanation. He cannot tell *everyone*, "I don't care what you do, but don't let me see you." In many cases he must act on what he knows, or, as we have noted repeatedly, feign ignorance. Because he resents having to take action when his

subordinates can easily protect him against action-demanding situations, they typically, as in the vertical symbiotic clique, set up essential appearances. The subordinates of course also have a general interest in protecting the formal phases of organization as well as their superior.

Hence from fear of alienating a touchy superior as well as to protect him, they develop logical explanations to cover essential but irregular actions. This is not necessarily defiance of the system. The action may also conceal the spearhead of an embryonic procedure not yet ready for the light. . . . Defenses may cover a short-cut that saves time, economizes currently limited materials, etc., but one that requires rare judgment in its use and for that reason cannot be adopted as a common practice. Or the justification may screen a forbidden stopgap. In any case, the officer concerned would neither advertise his use of the makeshift nor be disturbed about preparing a justification. If detected and questioned by that kind of chief, his convincing response would save both from embarrassment. Justifications can of course become pretexts to conceal malfeasance.

Defenses may be offered by an individual or a team. Some superiors openly welcome ideas and constructive departures. But where rivalries for individual credit are strong in the group and the superior "wants no complications," the departure, though worthwhile, may be hidden, used privately, and not pushed for development or seriously defended. Where no issue of change or improvement in the firm moves deviants they may instead, as is usually said, "dream up explanations," and "keep a drawerful of right answers." There is comparable behavior when line officers prepare to face the effects of staff reports.

As the area of concern becomes more individual than group, the interplay of formal and informal declines and defenses may become only personal subterfuges, as when the ambitious and demanding subordinate supplies his obliging chief with convincing pretexts to forestall the objections of others to favors he receives. In maintaining harmonious appearances, however, probably all departments and key executives must at times exhaust their justifications and have some recourse to pretexts. Among other things, this arises from the obvious practice in most departments of camouflaging those of their activities running counter to plant logic. Incomplete knowledge of practices behind the screens of other departments forces a given department to maintain a store of pretexts to meet criticisms, and thus enable it to control other departments to a degree and win their aid when necessary. . . .

Correlates of Organizational Participation: An Examination of Factors Affecting Union Membership Activity

EUGENE C. HAGBURG

Studies of union organizations in contemporary U.S. society have revealed that most members of trade unions are inactive with respect to organizational matters. That is, many union members do not vote in organizational elections, attend meetings, run for elective offices, serve on committees, or even keep themselves informed about organizational policy and activity. Some exceptions, of course, do exist for certain unions are more active, i.e., have larger proportions of participating members, than do others,[1] and within the same national organizations, some locals are more active than others.[2] Nevertheless, inactivity among union members is by far the prevalent rule within contemporary unionism.

Despite the body of literature on the subject of organizational participation, at present there is not sufficient clarification of those factors associated with this inactive condition. For example, is membership inactivity a consequence of their lack of interest in the union organization stemming from individual attributes or is it that unions, as relatively complex organizations, do not fully encourage integration into their groups?

Much of the work that has been directed toward this question has been philosophical in nature.[3] Other work,

Eugene C. Hagburg, "Correlates of Organization Participation: An Examination of Factors Affecting Union Membership Activity *Pacific Sociological Review*, 9 (1966), 15–21, with omissions.

[1] See, e.g., Seymour Martin Lipset, Martin Trow, and James Coleman, *Union Democracy* (New York: Anchor Books, Inc., 1962), a study of the International Typographical Union, one of the most active organizations in the U.S. as far as its members are concerned.

[2] See Arnold S. Tannenbaum and Robert L. Kahn, *Participation in Union Locals* (Evanston, Illinois: Row, Peterson and Co., 1953), a study which depended on locating several active local unions for the purpose of contrasting them with inactive locals in order to explain the differences between them.

[3] See, for example, Solomon Barkin, *The Decline of the Labor Movement* (Center for the Study of Democratic Institutions, 1961). See also, *The Annals of the American Academy of Political and Social Science*, November, 1963.

frequently, has been concerned primarily with the structure of the organization and its relationship to participation,[4] or concerned only with psychological and social-psychological aspects of the matter.[5] Few studies have focused on the likelihood that the relationship between the union member and his organization depends heavily upon the relationship between the individual and his primary groups, and between those and the larger organization, the union local.

While this study reaffirms some of the relationships observed in previous work, the data collected contribute to a better understanding of factors affecting the extent of membership participation in union organizations. The research itself centered on the following specific hypotheses:

(1) members who are more active in union activities, as contrasted to the less active, regard the organization or some part of it as a source of primary group satisfactions;

(2) members who are more active in union activities, as contrasted to the less active, receive the support and encouragement for this from other primary groups with which they are affiliated, i.e., the family, social clubs, and recreation groups;

(3) active union members, as contrasted to the less active, derive satisfactions from their activity in the union, in addition to those obtained from accomplishment of organizational goals of the union *per se.*

Conceptual Framework

The framework of this study depends heavily upon the concepts of the primary group and organizational participation. Some of the foremost examples of primary groups are the family, the friendship group, and the play group which are characterized by a feeling of solidarity, the spontaneity of face to face informal expression, and the fulfillment of certain psychic needs in a warm and intimate manner. Primary groups are crucial social units in our social structure in that they are an important source of satisfaction for individuals. Insofar as these groups provide satisfactions for individuals, they also exert influence on behavior patterns, since the individual must make his behavior conform to the group's expectations in order to remain within it. Thus, these primary groups mediate between the individual and the larger organizations and serve as the basic building blocks in the social structure.

In attempting to operationalize this concept, a number of items were developed to provide data on the primary group satisfactions provided by various membership groups. And, although there are serious difficulties in delineating all of the relevant primary groups in which an individual participates, an attempt was made to ascertain the relative importance of the different groups in terms of the so-called primary group satisfactions.

Participation in organizations like labor unions seems to require involvement of individuals on a physical and emotional basis. Since it means performing activities for and with the organization, it depends upon the existence of a common ideology and strong identification with the goals and objectives of the organization. Therefore, participation in union organizations is defined as the expenditure of time on union affairs in addition to possession of a set of values. In an attempt to measure the degree of participation in union organization a participation index was designed and included items

---

[4] Tannenbaum and Kahn, *op. cit.*

[5] Robert Dubin, "Industrial Worker's Worlds," in *Mass Leisure* (Glencoe, Illinois: The Free Press, 1958), pp. 215–28.

relating to attendance at meetings, the holding of union office and committee work, participation in union activities and union related activities as well as others.

In addition to the participation index and the items related to primary group satisfactions, the questionnaire was designed to provide data relating to the relationship or competition among different groups and general background characteristics of the respondents. Questionnaire responses were obtained from 434 union members representing many different unions and each response was scored according to the degree of participation. In addition to the questionnaires, a number of personal interviews were conducted with local union officers and members, primarily to test the accuracy of the participation index. And, in order to determine the extent of differences between the union members, a comparison was made between the highly active and the least active.

Analysis of Data

An examination of the data reveals important distinctions between the actives and the inactives. For example, the evidence presented in Table 1 indicates a difference between active and inactive members as they perceive the union as a source of primary group satisfaction. More of the active members regard the union organization and, more specifically, the local union as providing freedom and spontaneity of expression. Ninety-seven per cent of the actives feel this freedom of informal expression does exist as contrasted to 78.9 per cent of the inactive members.

It was also found that 93.2 per cent of the actives usually or always presented their views in union meetings while only 15.6 per cent of the less active or inactives did so. Either more of the

TABLE 1   **Types of Primary Group Satisfactions, Usually or Always Derived by Members from the Union, in Per Cent**

Types of Satisfactions	Actives N = 132	Inactives N = 128	DIFF SED*
Freedom of expression	97.0	78.9	4.6
Presentation of personal views	93.2	15.6	19.9
Identification with common goals	68.9	46.1	3.8
Discussion of common goals	53.8	36.7	2.9

* Difference between active and inactive divided by standard error of the difference.—Ed.

the inactives did not choose to take advantage of this source of satisfaction or did not view it as such. On the other hand, many more of the active union members utilized the union organization as a means to express themselves, thus obtaining from the union satisfactions of a primary group nature.

Insofar as an awareness of common goals is concerned, 68.9 per cent of the actives reported they held goals in common with other members, while only 46.1 per cent of the inactives did so. This adds further evidence to the proposition that the actives are more conscious of the commonalities provided by participation in the union organization. There is also some evidence to suggest that the actives discuss with other members their commonalities to a greater extent than the inactives, thus reinforcing their feeling of unity.

When asked to indicate which of certain other satisfactions were received from participation in the union (Table 2), the actives stressed those satisfactions which might be described as being social in nature, i.e., feeling part of a group and helping other persons. On the other hand, the inactives indicated receipt of more satisfactions of the items which might be described as being economic, or extrinsic, in nature rather than the type of intrinsic satisfactions usually associated with primary groups.

TABLE 2 **Satisfactions Received from Participation in a Union, in Per Cent**

Types of Satisfactions	Actives N = 132	Inactives N = 128	DIFF SED
No satisfaction	0.0	9.4	3.6
Higher wages and better working conditions	56.1	68.8	2.1
Feeling a part of an important group	62.1	29.7	5.6
Helping other union members	82.6	24.2	10.7
Helping other people in general	76.5	28.9	8.8

It is evident that the most important satisfaction stressed by the inactives was "higher wages and better working conditions" (68.8 per cent). Although the actives also felt this to be important (56.1 per cent), it appears to be a less important source of satisfaction than "feeling a part of an important group" (62.1 per cent), "helping other union members" (82.6 per cent), and "helping other people in general" (76.5 per cent). Clearly, the actives are distinguished from the inactives by their higher percentages reporting these satisfactions.

Thus, it is apparent that the actives and inactives are alike insofar as the economic satisfactions are concerned, but differ greatly with respect to the extent social satisfactions are received. The social satisfactions would appear to be primary group satisfactions related to the fulfillment of certain intrinsic needs. In contrast to the actives, the inactives stress more heavily satisfactions of an economic nature, which is more characteristic of members of secondary groups.

Certainly it is clear that whether the union is more accurately classified as a primary or secondary group, participation depends in part upon the perception of satisfactions as a reward. While none of the actives reported obtaining no satisfactions from the union, 9.4 per cent of the inactives reported this to be the case.

Further evidence to show that the more active member regards the union organization as a source of primary group satisfaction is provided in part by the identification of the groups from which most of the union members' close friends are selected. Table 3 indicates that most of the actives (68.9 per cent) had close friends in union groups, as compared with only 8.6 per cent of the inactives.

Table 3 contains data which indicate other differences between the actives and the inactives insofar as selection of close friends is concerned. For example, only 0.8 per cent of the inactives selected friends from political groups as contrasted with 13.5 per cent of the actives. This may be accounted for, at least in part, by the lack of interest in activities associated with political groups. It appears that the inactives do not choose to get involved with such groups because they do not perceive this as a significant primary group source.

TABLE 3 **Groups from Which Respondents Selected Most of Their Close Friends, in Per Cent**

Groups	Actives N = 132	Inactives N = 128	DIFF SED
Union	68.9	8.6	12.6
Work	62.1	51.6	NS
Recreation	28.8	28.9	NS
Church	23.5	26.6	NS
Political	13.6	0.8	4.1
Education	15.1	14.1	NS
Neighborhood	24.2	32.8	NS

NS = not statistically significant

Another important difference appears in connection with the neighborhood group; more of the inactives draw their close friends from neighborhood groups than do the actives. A similar difference occurs for the church group. These differences indicate, at least in part, that the inactives' primary group needs are more frequently fulfilled by groups other than the union, to the extent they are filled at all. Although the differences are not statistically significant, they are in the predicted direction and support the other findings.

The problem for which no distinct answer exists is whether the inactives' needs for primary group satisfactions were being satisfied by the non-union groups. It is possible that the inactives had less need for primary group satisfactions. Or, the inactives seeking such satisfactions in the union group did not have their needs met and hence turned to other groups.

This evidence, insofar as the sample is representative, supports one hypothesis which has been set forth; the active union members obtain primary group satisfactions from some part of the organization. The satisfactions obtained include freedom and spontaneity of expression, identification with people having common goals, informal face-to-face relationships, and affective satisfactions.

It also was hypothesized that active members receive support and encouragement for participation in the union from other primary groups with which they are affiliated. In other words, active union members are not caught in the competition which might be provided by different groups competing for their loyalty and attention. The data suggest that this hypothesis generally is valid. As was shown in Table 3, the active, far more than inactive, union members tend to select close friends from union groups. Additionally, more of the actives select associates for recreational activities from among union members. These associates certainly are likely to lend support and encouragement for union participation because of their similar attitudes, interests, and expectations. The data supporting this claim is presented in a more detailed manner in Table 4.

The actives are more inclined than the inactives to select recreational associates from among work, union, and political groups, which in many ways are interrelated and interdependent (Table 4). On the other hand, significantly more of the inactives than actives select their recreation associates from neighborhood groups which may be, but probably are not, consistently interrelated with union and work groups. While there are certainly many cases of overlap among the various groups, especially between the union and work groups, the data indicate the most salient groups selected by the individual.

TABLE 4   Groups from Which Respondents Selected Most of Their Close Associates for Recreational Activities, in Per Cent

Groups	Actives N = 132	Inactives N = 128	DIFF SED
Work	55.3	43.8	NS
Church	13.6	17.1	NS
Union	46.2	6.2	8.3
Political	7.6	0.8	2.8
Recreation	13.6	19.5	NS
Education	5.3	4.7	NS
Neighborhood	15.1	32.8	3.4

Further evidence that other primary groups influence participation is provided by examining data about the family, the classic example of a primary group. Seventy-two per cent of the active union members (Table 5) receive encouragement to participate in union activities from their spouse. This is in contrast to twenty-five per cent of the inactives who receive such encouragement.

TABLE 5 **The Extent to Which Respondents Receive Spouse's Encouragement to Participate in Various Activities, in Per Cent**

Activity	Actives N = 132	Inactives N = 128	DIFF SED
Union	72.0	25.0	8.5
Church	64.4	56.3	NS
Community	56.8	31.3	4.3
Recreation	65.2	55.5	NS

Additionally, it should be noted that for all of the activities listed, more of the actives than inactives receive encouragement to participate. This is highly suggestive that the influence of the family is powerful for determining the nature and extent of members' social relationships. This evidence appears to support the hypothesis set forth; it is probable that other primary groups with which the active member is affiliated (e.g., the family and recreation groups) also support and encourage participation.

It also was hypothesized that active union members, as contrasted to the less active, derive satisfactions from their activity in the union in addition to those derived from the accomplishment of organizational goals. This was validated, at least in part, by the data presented in Table 2. For example, fewer actives than inactives emphasized traditional job centered goals of the union organization which include security, higher wages, and better working conditions. Relatively more actives emphasized activities such as participating in a group and helping others. The inactive member, on the other hand, stressed the job centered economic goals.

The differences between actives and inactives in this regard can be illustrated further by direct comments recorded during several interviews. One highly active union member, a steward, stated:

I really enjoy handling grievances for other members, however, I am not too interested in those grievances handled by other stewards.

Another active member, also a steward, commented:

You know when you handle a grievance for a co-worker and happen to win you get sort of a warm feeling inside—you feel real good about it.

It is clear that more of the active union members receive social satisfactions in addition to those satisfactions related to the accomplishment of organizational goals. The inactives, on the other hand, more frequently stress satisfactions received from the organization's formally stated goals. Sociologists are quite familiar with the member who is bound more closely to the local union than the international and of the relative importance of loyalty to the smaller group in contrast to the larger organization. One author has suggested that "preoccupation with immediate social relations may obscure major goals of an organization."[6] This appears to be borne out in these findings.

An interesting finding appears when the active union members are compared to the less active members in terms of their participation in other activities. For example, the data show that 53.0 per cent of the actives as contrasted to 23.4 per cent of the inactives (Table 6) participate in community programs such as United Appeal, Big Brother, and others. In addi-

---

[6] H. C. Cooper, "Perception of Subgroup Power and Intensity of Affiliation with a Large Organization," *American Sociological Review*, **26** (April, 1961), 272–4.

tion, it is apparent that more active union members participate in fraternal organizations than do the inactives. In fact, 35.6 per cent of the actives participate in such groups as the Elks, Moose, Knights of Columbus, Masons, and others, as compared to 10.2 per cent of the inactives participating in these groups.

TABLE 6   Respondents Indicating Participation in Various Activities, in Per Cent

Activity	Actives N = 132	Inactives N = 128	DIFF SED
Fraternal Groups	35.6	10.2	5.1
Community Groups	53.0	23.4	5.2
Education Groups	31.8	23.4	NS

In addition to simply participating in other groups, the data also indicate that active union members derive greater primary group satisfactions from their participation than does the less active person. For example, the active union member receives more satisfaction from the family, in such forms as spontaneity of expression, identification with commonalities, and insofar as affective satisfactions are concerned. It is these kinds of satisfactions which a primary group affords the individual active participant whether the primary group is identified as the family, the work place, or union hall.

Further evidence is available on this same point insofar as the work group is concerned. The active union member receives satisfaction from the work place in that it provides a feeling of security (70.5 per cent actives, 64.1 per cent inactives) and he also feels that work is important and makes him feel as though he is accomplishing something (66.7 per cent actives, 46.9 per cent inactives). At the same time, the inactive appears to respond more frequently to other incentives such as

money 68.8 per cent inactives, 56.8 per cent actives) which clearly is an extrinsic reward as contrasted to the others which are more of an intrinsic nature.[7]

A breakdown of primary group satisfactions received from the work place and associations with co-workers is presented in Table 7. Here again more of the active union members appear to receive satisfaction from these sources than the inactives. For example, the inactive receives much less enjoyment from work (46.9 per cent) than does the active (67.4 per cent). In addition, the inactive receives less satisfaction from associating with co-workers (53.9 per cent) than does the active (75 per cent).

TABLE 7   Types of Primary Group Satisfactions Usually or Always Received from the Work Place, in Per Cent

Types of Satisfactions	Actives N = 132	Inactives N = 128	DIFF SED
Spontaneous expression	68.2	50.0	3.0
Common goal identification	82.6	46.9	6.5
Sense of enjoyment	67.4	46.9	3.4
Participating in other activities together	75.0	53.9	3.6

The same pattern holds with respect to participation in educational groups such as the Parent Teachers Association, adult education classes and other educational activities. As is shown in Table 8, 14.1 per cent of the inactives indicated "no satisfaction" received from such activities. In rather sharp

---

[7] According to Frederick A. Zeller and Eugene C. Hagburg, "Participation: The Key to Union Effectiveness," *The American Teacher Magazine*, February, 1965, the member also may be inactive due to "the lack of skills necessary for participating in a fairly complex organization such as the union."

TABLE 8   Types of Satisfactions Usually or Always Received from Participating in Education Activities

Types of Satisfactions	Actives N = 132	Inactives N = 128	DIFF SED
No satisfaction	2.3	14.1	3.2
An obligation	40.2	37.5	NS
Sense of enjoyment	40.2	17.2	4.3
Participate with friends	36.4	17.2	3.6
Feeling of accomplishment	82.6	31.3	9.9

contrast, 40.2 per cent of the active union members enjoyed participating in such groups as compared to the 17.2 per cent response from the inactives.

When other activities are analyzed, there again appears support for the idea that active members generally derive more satisfaction from participation in different activities. Moreover, the active member more frequently stressed satisfactions which might also be identified as "primary group satisfactions," received from group participation. Table 9 presents further evidence to support this position. Data presented in Table 9 show that more of the active union members are politically oriented and derive satisfaction from participation in groups associated with this kind of activity than the inactive members. For example, 28

TABLE 9   Types of Satisfactions Usually or Always Received from Participating in PoliticalActivities, in Per Cent

Types of Satisfactions	Actives N = 132	Inactives N = 128	DIFF SED
No satisfaction	1.5	25.8	6.1
Obligation	53.8	29.7	4.1
Enjoyment, excitement	28.0	10.9	4.0
Associate with friends	24.0	7.8	3.7
Feeling of accomplishment	60.6	20.3	7.3

per cent of the actives derive "enjoyment" from such participation as compared to 10.9 per cent of the inactives. It is evident that more of the inactives do not perceive political groups as a meaningful source of primary group satisfactions since 25.8 per cent of inactives received no satisfaction at all from political activities. On the other hand, the active union member participates because of intrinsic rewards or primary group satisfactions.

Conclusions and Implications

There is, at present, no general theory which adequately explains the patterns of participation in the larger formal structures which characterize our society. In addition, there are no obvious practical solutions for the problem of the lack of participation which plagues many voluntary and quasi-voluntary organizations. The lack of participation in union organizations is widely recognized, as is evidenced by the volume of literature on the subject. Thus, this study was an attempt to deal with a rather concrete problem in order to contribute toward the development of a special theory within a larger framework.

The study itself has identified some marked differences between active and inactive union members and in general supports the hypotheses set forth. The major difference might be described as a varying conception of or relation to the union organization, for the analysis revealed, more specifically, that members who are more active in union activities, as contrasted to the less active, regard the organization or some part of it as a source of primary group satisfactions. Also, of particular interest is the evidence suggesting that activity in one organization is related to activity in other groups. For example, the active union member is active in many groups, while the inactive member apparently derives satisfactions from the more traditional groups like the family, the church, and the neighborhood.

This analysis illuminates certain factors relating to organizational participation, and suggests that the development of meaningful primary groups within an organization, in many ways, is a necessary requisite for greater individual participation. In other words, the larger the extent to which labor unions develop meaningful primary groups within the organization, the greater the individual participation. In addition, this study suggests the need for further research on this question because organizational participation or activity and inactivity is also of importance for the field of sociological inquiry in that it is part of the broad question of how individuals and groups relate to their organizations, institutions, and hence, society itself. More specifically, the relationship between members and their organizations reveals their conceptions of important cultural values, knowledge of which is instrumental for classifying, analyzing, and understanding present and future social behavior of relatively large sectors of American society.

Authority and Decision-Making in a Hospital: A Comparative Analysis

ROSE LAUB COSER

This paper presents a case analysis of the relationship between role behavior and social structure in two hospital wards. The analysis is based on daily observations made over a three-month period in the medical and surgical wards of a 360-bed research and teaching hospital on the Atlantic seaboard. Informal interviews, as well as a limited number of standardized interviews (10 each with house doctors and nurses), were used for the formulation of cues suggested by participant observation. Since only one hospital was studied, the comparisons to be made here—between the social structure of the medical team and that of the surgical team, and between the behavior of nurses on the two wards—should not be generalized beyond the

Rose Laub Coser, "Authority and Decision-Making in a Hospital: A Comparative Analysis," *American Sociological Review*, **23** (1958), 56–63.

case observed without further research. They are presented, however, with the aim of formulating hypotheses about the effect on role behavior of different types of authority structure in the hospital setting.

The surgical and the medical wards of this hospital were situated on two sides of the same floor, one floor each for men and women. An observer walking from one ward to the other, either on the male or on the female floor, would notice at first a superficial difference: joking as well as swearing, laughing as well as grumbling could be heard at the surgical nurses' station where some house doctors and some nurses gathered periodically. In contrast, on the medical ward the atmosphere can best be described as being more "polite." Joking and swearing were the exception; informal talk between doctors and nurses, if it occurred at all, was rare. Mainly medical students, who were not part of the formal ward organization, talked informally with nurses. On the surgical side, however, banter between doctors and nurses was a regular occurrence, and there one could also overhear from time to time a discussion between a nurse and some house doctor about a patient. Little if any of this occurred in the medical ward.

The behavior of the head nurse differed significantly on these two wards. While the medical nurse went through prescribed channels in her dealings with doctors, addressing herself to the interne whose orders she was expected to fill, the surgical nurse would talk to any doctor who was available, regardless of rank. She would more specifically ask that some decisions be made rather than trying to express her views through hints, which was the nurses' custom in the medical ward.

Moreover, in the surgical ward nurses participated much more fully in rounds than in the medical ward. Descriptions of rounds by medical and surgical nurses differed significantly. We heard in the medical ward, for example, from one of the nurses:

If nurses go on rounds they hold the charts, they pass them to the interne, the interne to the chief resident, and then it comes back down the line and the nurse puts the chart back. All that the nurse is there for, according to them, is to hold the charts.

Another medical nurse explained:

I get very little out of rounds. As nurses we're supposed to get something, and give something, but it never works. We're at the end of the line wheeling the charts, then I'm given orders to get something, I have to run out, when I come in again, there's something else they want me to do. . . .

In contrast, the head nurse in one of the surgical wards had this to say:

During rounds, the nurse gains insight into the condition of the patient, finds out changes in terms of medication and treatment. She can inform the doctor what treatment the patient is on and can suggest to the doctor that the dressing procedure can be changed; she can suggest vitamins by month instead of by injection; she can suggest taking them off anti-biotics and point out necessary medication. . . . Occasionally the doctors would bypass the nurse, so before they forget to tell me anything I would ask; also you find out yourself when you're on rounds and that is very important.

This nurse seemed to take initiative, although she appeared to be shy and withdrawn, unlike the head nurses on the medical wards who happened to have a more outgoing personality.

In attempting to account for the different types of nurse-doctor relationship in the two wards, one could examine such factors as personality, character, and level of aspiration of the individuals. We propose, however, to discuss the phenomenon on the level of our observations, namely in terms of the network of social relations in the wards.

Social Structure of the Wards

Although the relationships in the surgical ward seemed to be easy-going, the social distance between the visiting doctor and the house doctors, and between the chief resident and those under him, was more marked among the surgeons. The contradiction between joviality and social distance was well expressed by a surgical interne: "It is not a very strict and formal atmosphere on our ward," he said, and then added: "Of course, the chief resident has everything; he's the despot, he decides who operates, so he takes the cases that he is interested in. The visiting doctor, of course, may propose to take a case over—he can overrule the chief resident."

To resolve this apparent contradiction, we must compare the formal structure of authority with the *de facto* lines of decision-making. We will see that in the surgical ward the formal line of authority does not coincide with the actual line of decision-making; the process of decision-making, rather than the formal line of authority, apparently has an impact on the role of the nurse.

As Charts 1 and 2 show, the chief of service is responsible for the ward. He does not make any decisions for individual patients, however, but delegates his authority for the care of patients to the chief resident. The latter is re-sponsible to the chief of service. In turn, the chief resident delegates the care of patients to the internes, each of whom is in charge of specific patients under the chief resident's continuous supervision. The internes pass on orders to the head nurse for the patients assigned to them. The assistant resident acts as supervisor and "consultant" to the internes.

The formal authority structure is essentially the same in both medical and surgical wards, with a simple organizational difference: there is no separation of tasks among the doctors for the male and female wards on the surgical

CHART 1. SOCIAL STRUCTURE OF THE MEDICAL WARD:
FORMAL LINE OF AUTHORITY AND DECISION-MAKING

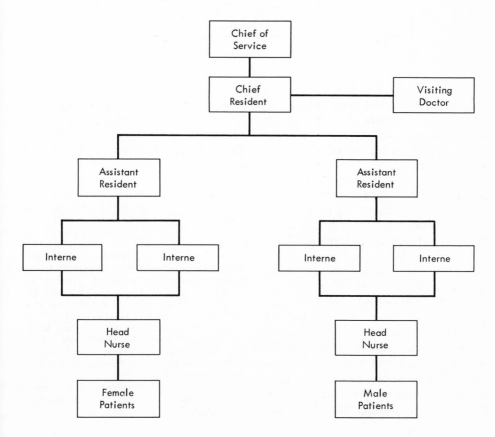

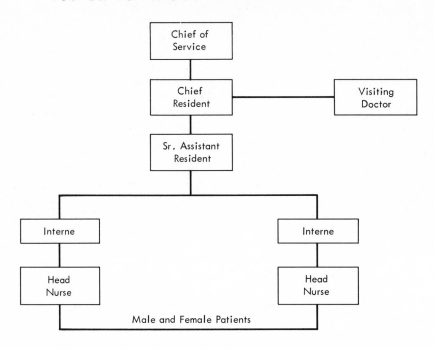

side, as Chart 2 indicates. There, internes and residents walked up and down the steps to take care of their patients who were segregated by sex on two floors.

But the way in which the house doctors made use of the authority attached to their rank differed significantly in the two wards. In the medical ward, there was consistent delegation of authority down the line. The chief resident was heard saying on rounds to one or the other of the internes, "You make the final decision, he's your patient." Such remarks were not part of the pattern on the surgical ward, where the chief resident made the decisions. The medical house officers also based their decisions, to a large extent, on consensus, with the chief resident presiding and leading the discussion while the surgical house doctors received orders from the chief resident.[1] The following incident was typical of the authority relations in the surgical ward:

[1] We have adopted from Alfred H. Stanton and Morris S. Schwartz (*The Mental Hospital*, New York: Basic Books, 1954) the distinction between decisions arrived at through consensus and decisions that are made arbitrarily (p. 258). "When a consensus is reached or assumed, the participants always feel it is completely unforced. There is no element of submissiveness, of defeat in argument. . . . If there is any specific awareness at all it is one of discovery, of clarity, or of understanding" (p. 196). On the other hand, "we define an arbitrary decision as one made by a person higher in the power hierarchy governing a person lower in it, without regard to the agreement of the latter. Most frequently, of course, it is made to override disagreement and without consulting the subordinate. . . ." (pp. 270-71).

An interne and an assistant resident were conversing about an incident that had transpired that morning, when the daughter of an elderly patient had created a scene at the nurses' station about the fact that she had been notified as late as the previous evening at eleven o'clock of her father's operation the next morning. When she came to see her father before the operation, he had already been taken to the operating room and the daughter was extremely upset about not being able to see him. The interne and the assistant resident felt that in the future something should be done to forestall similar reactions from patients' relatives; they thought that the chief resident was too busy to notify relatives in due time and that therefore they would take it upon themselves to notify a patient's relatives if the chief resident would give them sufficient advance notice. They decided to take up the problem with the chief resident at the next occasion, and did so that very afternoon. The chief resident's answer was curt: "I always notify the family on time," he said with an annoyed facial expression, and walked away. He did not wish to delegate authority in the matter, trivial though it may seem.

The chief resident's "despotism," to which the previously quoted interne referred, is part of the surgical ward's culture. Although his decision-making by fiat may seem, at first glance, to be a "bad habit," or due to a lack of knowledge about the advantages of delegation of authority and of agreement by consensus, it has its roots in the specific activity system of the surgical team which differs significantly from that of the medical team.[2] We must

bear in mind that responsibility for an operation, if performed by a house officer, lies with the chief resident or with the attending surgeon. They perform the important operations. As Stanton and Schwartz have pointed out, decision by consensus is time-consuming.[3] An emergency situation, in the operating room as elsewhere, is characterized precisely by the fact that a task must be performed in the minimum possible time. Whether in military operations or surgical operations, there can be no doubt about who makes decisions, that they must be made quickly and carried out unquestioningly and instantly.

The situation is quite different for the medical team. There the problems are those of diagnosis and of different possible avenues of treatment. Such problems require deliberation, and decisions are often tentative; the results of adopted therapeutic procedures are carefully observed and procedures may have to be modified in the process. All this demands careful consultation and deliberation, which are better accomplished through teamwork than through the unquestioned authority of a single person.

In his role as teacher of medical students, moreover, the person in authority teaches different lessons on the two wards: in the medical ward students and house officers are taught to think and reflect, while in the surgical ward the emphasis is on action and punctual performance. If this seems too sharp a distinction, and if it is objected that surgeons should learn to think also and medical doctors should learn to act as well, it must be borne

[2] For a general comparison between surgical and medical floors, see Temple Burling, Edith M. Lentz and Robert N. Wilson, *The Give and Take in Hospitals* (New York: G. P. Putnam's Sons, 1956), Chapter 16. For a dramatic description of work in the operating room, see Robert N. Wilson, "Teamwork in the Operating Room," *Human Organization*, XII (Winter, 1954), 9-14.

[3] *Op. cit.*, pp. 268, 271.

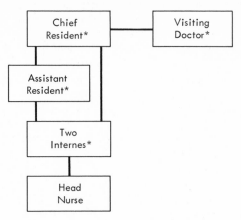

* Participate in decision-making process.

in mind that the latter ideal situation is not always approximated, especially since the physicians themselves seem to have this image of the difference between medical and surgical men. The doctors on the medical ward, asked why they chose their field of specialization rather than surgery, said, for example: "Medicine is more of an intellectual challenge"; "I enjoy the kind of mental operation you go through"; "[Surgeons] want to act and they want results, sometimes they make a mess of it." The physicians on the surgical ward displayed a similar view of the differences between medicine and surgery and differed only concerning the value they gave the same traits. When asked why they chose to be surgeons, they said that they "like working with hands," that they "prefer something that is reasonably decisive," and that "[a medical] man probably doesn't want to work with his hands."

Thus the differences in task orientation and differences in self-images would seem to account in part for the main distinction between the two wards. This distinction can be summarized as follows: On the medical ward there is a scalar delegation of authority in a large area of decision-making,[4] and the important decisions are generally made through consensus under the guidance of the visiting doctor or the chief resident. On the surgical ward there is little delegation of authority as far as decision-making is concerned and decisions about operations and important aspects of treatment of patients are made by fiat. Charts 3 and 4 illustrate this difference.

The Nurse-Doctor Relationship

Under these circumstances surgical assistant residents and internes are

[4] The term "scalar" is here used as defined by Chester I. Barnard in "Functions and Pathology of Status Systems in Formal Organizations" in W. F. Whyte (ed.), *Industry and Society* (New York: McGraw Hill & Co., 1946), pp. 46-83.

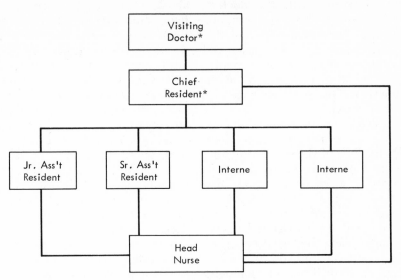

* Participate in decision-making.

more or less on the same level under the authority of the chief resident or the visiting doctor; this makes for a common bond between assistant residents and internes and the strengthening of internal solidarity. The relative absence of actual prestige-grading, notwithstanding the formal rank differences, as they were observed among those who were practically excluded from the decision-making process, tended to eliminate some of the spirit of competition among the junior members. Moreover, with only little authority delegated to them, they could not be consistently superior in position to the nurse. This "negative democratization," as Karl Mannheim has called it,[5] encourages a colleague type of relationship between the nurses and doctors rather than a service rela-

tionship. Hence the banter and joking, which helped further to cancel out status differences,[6] and the relative frequency of interaction to which we referred above.

Since authority was scarcely delegated, all house officers passed on orders to the nurse, who in turn communicated with all of them. Writing orders in the order book was not the task of internes only. This was confirmed by one of the internes who said: "Anyone on surgery writes in the order book," and the head nurse on one of the floors corroborated this situation when asked who gave her orders: "The internes, the residents also give orders, all give orders; we get orders all over the place and then you have to make your own compromise;

[5] Karl Mannheim, *Man and Society in an Age of Reconstruction* (New York: Harcourt, Brace & Co., 1951), esp. pp. 85 ff.

[6] On this function of banter in status systems, see Tom Burns, "Friends, Enemies and Polite Fiction," *American Sociological Review*, **18** (December, 1953), 654-62.

you got to figure out what is most important."

Such a relation with the doctors puts the nurse in a strategic position. In using her own judgment about the importance of orders, she makes decisions about the care of patients, deciding to delay one action rather than another. This gives her a certain amount of power.

The position of the nurse in the surgical ward brings to mind Jules Henry's analysis of the social structure of a mental hospital.[7] Henry discusses two types of social organization: the "pine-tree" type, in which authority is delegated downward step by step, as in the medical ward discussed above (see Chart 3); and the "oak-tree" type, in which orders come down to the same person through several channels, as in the surgical ward described here (see Chart 4). The latter type, Henry says, is a source of stresses and strains because the head nurse must follow orders coming from different directions that may or may not be compatible. This is probably true, to some extent, in the surgical ward described here, but it is accompanied by the fact that such a position gives the nurse more power and more active part in therapy.

The head nurse on the surgical floor, often facing the necessity of compromise, must know a great deal about the conditions of patients; she is constrained to contact patients frequently and to establish a closer relationship with them. This is all the more necessary since during a large part of the day, while surgery is being performed, the surgical staff is confined to the operating room with the exception of one interne on duty in the ward. The

nurse must therefore be "on her toes," checking with the duty interne only if absolutely necessary, since he has his hands full. Her knowledge of the patients is thus greater than that of the nurses on the medical floor. A medical head nurse, although she tried to impress the observer with her own importance, admitted: "The nurse knows more about patients than the doctor on surgical. On the medical floor it's about even. . . ." The doctors, in turn, knowing that the nurse on the surgical floor has more contact with patients than they themselves, rely on her for information and reminders, in this way increasing her influence and decision-making role.

The doctors' expectations of the nurse differ according to ward. Asked to define a good nurse, the doctors on the surgical ward said that she should have foresight, intelligence, or that she must be a good assistant to the doctors, or that she should read. Some even noted that the same criteria apply to her as to a doctor. In contrast, the physicians on the medical ward emphasized her ability to "carry out orders" and "to do her routine work well." Only one of the medical internes declared: "Intellectual curiosity is rare but nice if you see it," thus implying that he wouldn't really expect it. Although our interviews with doctors are too few in number to draw any definite conclusions about expectations that medical doctors and surgeons have of nurses, the differences in their comments support our observations made elsewhere about some degree of autonomy and initiative among surgical nurses.

Moreover, where the rank hierarchy below the top decision-makers is not very strict and the delegation of authority not well-defined, informal relations are built across status lines. House doctors in the surgical ward

[7] Jules Henry, "The Formal Social Structure of a Psychiatric Hospital," *Psychiatry*, **17** (May, 1954), 139-52.

sometimes abdicated their authority if they could rely on the nurses.[8] According to a surgical nurse, "The doctors want to be called in an emergency only, if they know you and they feel you know what you're doing. . . . They let us *do* things first and then call the doctor, as long as we would keep him informed." A third-year student nurse in the surgical ward had this to say: "In this hospital we're not allowed to draw blood or give I.V. I do it occasionally but nobody knows. I do it just to help [the doctors] if there are no medical students around. . . ." Needless to say, such informal arrangements enhance the nurse's prestige and enlarge her realm of power.

The surgical head nurse even made decisions about reference of patients to the social service. One of the head nurses, when asked whether she participated in the social service rounds, replied: "We should have been in on them, but I had close contact with the social worker, and I would ask her what I wanted to know. . . . Anyhow the patients would come to me for reference to the social worker." According to the formal rules, patients are referred to social service by the medical staff, but here, as in previous examples, the nurse by-passed official regulations and maintained considerable control over patients.

Ritualism or Innovation

Nurses on the surgical ward felt less tied to rules and regulations than nurses on the medical floor. This is illustrated by their reactions to the

---

[8] The concept of abdication of authority is here used in the sense defined by Stanton and Schwartz: "By abdiction, we mean the situation in which a person who is supposed to make a decision according to the formal organization does not make it even though circumstances require that it be made." *op. cit.*, p. 274.

following story upon which they were asked to comment:

Interviewer: "I would like to tell you a story that happened in another hospital. An interne was called to the floor during the night to a patient who had a heart attack. He asked the nurse on the floor to get him a tank. She told him to ask an orderly. But there was no orderly around, and she still refused to get it for him. Do you think she had a right to refuse, or do you think he had the right to expect her to get it for him?"

All nurses agreed that the nurse is not supposed to leave the floor if there is no other nurse around. However, while the answers of four of the five medical nurses were unqualified (e.g., "I would never have gotten the tank, the doctor definitely should have gotten it," or "I wouldn't think of leaving the floor for a minute when I'm alone, this is unheard of"), all five surgical nurses made important qualifications (e.g., "she should have called the supervisor," or "she could have said, you keep your ears and eyes open while I get it," or "she could say, if you keep an eye open in the meantime, I'll run and get it"). In spite of the small number of respondents these figures lend support to our observations and other interview material according to which the surgical nurse is more accustomed than the medical nurse to "find a way out," to use her initiative, and is more ready to circumvent rules and regulations.

Nurses are often accused of being "ritualistic," of attaching more importance to routine and rules than to the ends for which they are designed to serve. While the nurses on the medical floor were accused fairly often by the internes of "merely clinging to rules" and "not willing or not able to think," the head nurses on the surgical floor were never the targets of such criticisms. Indeed, the surgical nurses seemed to be capable of innovation and were often relied upon by doctors to use their own judgment and to initiate action, as we have shown.[9]

By relating the attitudes of the surgical nurses to the social structure of the ward, we have tried to confirm Merton's formulation in "Social Structure and Anomie," i.e., that "some social structures exert a definite pressure upon persons in the society to engage in nonconformist rather than conformist conduct."[10] There is reason to

[9] The type of therapy in the surgical ward also makes the surgical nurse's work seem more important than that of the medical nurse. As Burling, Lentz and Wilson have pointed out, on surgical wards "the nurse's skills are tested daily and both her feeling and her prestige rise as she becomes more adept." *op. cit.*, p. 245.

[10] Robert K. Merton, *Social Theory and Social Structure* (Glencoe, Illinois: The Free Press, 1957), pp. 131-60.

believe that in the wards that we observed, "ritualism" or "innovation" is largely a function of the specific social structure rather than merely a "professional" or "character" trait. Nurses are often in a position in which the insistence on rules serves as a means to assert themselves and to display some degree of power. If their professional pride as well as their power and influence are enhanced by breaking through the routine, however, they seem to be ready to use informal means or to act as innovators to reach their goals.

If the relation of the nurse's position —and that of other occupational types, perhaps—to the structure of authority and decision-making is subject to the kinds of influence described in this case, problems of morale might well be considered in the light of their structural context.

Dilemmas of Formal Organization

PETER M. BLAU

W. RICHARD SCOTT

We shall review three dilemmas of formal organization: (1) coordination and communication; (2) bureaucratic discipline and professional expertness; (3) managerial planning and initiative.

Coordination and Communication

The experiments and field studies on communication and performance we have reviewed lead to the conclusion that the free flow of communication contributes to problem-solving. There are three ways in which decisions are

Peter M. Blau and W. Richard Scott, "Dilemmas of Formal Organization," *Formal Organizations: A Comparative Approach* (San Francisco: Chandler Publishing Company, 1961), pp. 242-253.

improved by the unrestricted exchange of ideas, criticisms, and advice. First, social support relieves the anxieties engendered by decision-making. In the discussion of problems with others, their social approval of the first step taken toward a solution mitigates the anxieties that might otherwise create a blocking of associations, and it thus facilitates reaching a solution. Once consultation patterns have become established, moreover, the very knowledge that advice is readily accessible makes it less disturbing to encounter a difficult problem, and the experience of being consulted by others strengthens self-confidence; both factors lessen anxieties that impede decision-making.

Second, communication processes provide an error-correction mechanism. Different persons are guided by different frameworks in their approach to a given problem, and the differences make it easier for them to detect the mistakes and blind spots in the suggestions of one another. Although social support and error correction are in some respect opposite processes, both of them are, nevertheless, important for problem-solving, as indicated by Pelz's finding that optimum research performance is associated with consulting some colleagues whose orientation differs from one's own (who challenge one's ideas) and some who share one's orientation (who support one's ideas).[1]

Third, the competition for respect that occurs in the course of discussing problems furnishes incentives for making good suggestions and for criticizing the apparently poor suggestions of others.

While the free flow of communication improves problem-solving, it impedes coordination. Unrestricted communication creates a battleground of ideas; the battle helps in selecting the only correct or best among several alternative suggestions, but makes it difficult to come to an agreement; and coordination always requires agreeing on *one* master-plan, even though different plans might do equally well. Processes of social communication, consequently, make the performance of groups superior to that of individuals when the task is finding the best solution to a problem but inferior when the task is one of coordination.

Hierarchical differentiation is dysfunctional for decision-making because it interferes with the free flow of communication. Studies of experimental and work groups have shown that status differences restrict the participation of low-status members, channel a disproportionate amount of communication to high-status members, discourage criticism of the suggestions of the highs, encourage rejecting correct suggestions of the lows, and reduce the work satisfaction of the lows and their motivation to make contributions. All these factors are detrimental to effective problem-solving. If hierarchical differentiation does not block but frees the flow of communication, however, it improves decision-making; this observation indicates that the adverse effects that hierarchical differentiation typically has for problem-solving are specifically due to the obstacles to free communication it usually creates. But the very restriction of communication that makes hierarchical differentiation dysfunctional for problem-solving improves performance when the task is essentially one of coordination. Experiments with various communication networks show that differentiation, centralized direction, and restricted communication are necessary for efficient coordination. However, the achievement of such a differentiated organization—itself a problem-solving task—seems to have been easier for groups in which communication flowed freely than for those where it was experimentally restricted.

These conclusions point to a fundamental dilemma in formal organizations. Organizations require, of course, both effective coordination and effective problem-solving to discharge their functions. But the very mechanism through which hierarchical differentiation improves coordination—restricting and directing the flow of communications—is what impedes problem-solving. In peer groups, moreover, the free flow of communication that contrib-

[1] Donald C. Pelz, "Some Social Factors Related to Performance in a Research Organization," *Administrative Science Quarterly*, **1** (1956), 310-25.

utes to problem-solving also creates an informal differentiation of status as some members earn the respect and deference of others, and this differentiation, once established, creates obstacles to communication. This dilemma appears to be inherent in the conflicting requirements of coordination and problem-solving. To be sure, some types of centralized direction are more compatible with work on complex problems than others, but the fundamental dilemma posed by the need for unrestricted and for restricted communication cannot be resolved— it must be endured.

Bureaucratic Discipline and Professional Expertness

Weber's approach to the study of administration fails to distinguish the principles that govern bureaucratic organizations from professional principles, as both Parsons and Gouldner have emphasized.[2] To be sure, these two sets of principles have much in common. Both require that decisions be governed by universalistic standards independent of any personal considerations in the particular cases handled. The orientations of both professionals and bureaucrats are expected to be impersonal and detached, a principle designed to facilitate rational judgment. Both bureaucracy and professionalism are marked by specialized competence based on technical training and limit the official's or professional's authority to a specialized area of jurisdiction. Both professionals and bureaucrats occupy an achieved rather than ascribed status, with the selection of personnel

governed by such performance criteria as competence and training. These are important similarities, but they should not be allowed to obscure the equally important differences between the two.

The first difference between the organizing principles of a profession and those of a bureaucracy is that the professional is bound by a norm of service and a code of ethics to represent the welfare and interests of his clients, whereas the bureaucrat's foremost responsibility is to represent and promote the interests of his organization. Only in the case of service organizations do the ultimate objectives of serving clients and serving the organization coincide, and even here the specific immediate objectives often conflict. For a service organization is oriented to serving the collective interests of its entire clientele, which demands that the interests of some clients may have to be sacrificed to further those of the majority or of future clients, while the distinctive feature of the professional orientation is that each client's interests reign supreme and must not be sacrificed for the sake of the welfare of other clients.

A second basic difference concerns the source of authority. The bureaucratic official's authority rests on a legal contract backed by formal sanctions, but the professional's authority is rooted in his acknowledged technical expertness. Although some technical competence may be required for performing the duties of a customs official, it is not this skill but his legal status that authorizes the customs inspector to decide whether goods can be imported duty-free or not. An individual is legally obligated to submit to the authority of the policeman, whatever he thinks of his decision, but the same person submits to the authority of his doctor because, and only if, he acknowledges that the doctor has the

[2] Talcott Parsons, "Introduction" to Max Weber, *The Theory of Social and Economic Organization,* A. M. Henderson and Talcott Parsons (trans.) and Talcott Parsons (ed.) (Glencoe, Ill.: Free Press and Falcon's Wing Press, 1947), pp. 58–60; and Gouldner, *Patterns of Industrial Bureaucracy,* pp. 22-24.

technical knowledge to determine whether he should have surgery, medicine, or neither.

A third difference, related to the foregoing, is that the bureaucrat's decisions are expected to be governed by disciplined compliance with directives from superiors, whereas the professional's are to be governed by internalized professional standards. To be sure, superiors may be more highly qualified in a field than their subordinates. The crucial problem, however, is that bureaucratic management must base its decisions in part on administrative considerations, which often conflict with purely professional considerations.

Finally, the differences between the two systems are reflected in the locus of the last court of appeal in case of disagreement. When a decision of a bureaucrat is questioned, the final judgment of whether he is right or not is a prerogative of management, but when a decision of a professional is questioned, the right of reviewing its correctness is reserved to his professional colleague group. The actions of the professional expert, therefore, are under the ultimate control of his peers who have the same specialized skills as he, whereas control over the bureaucrat's action is exercised by superiors in the organization whose technical skills tend to differ from his. One complains to the medical society or to the bar association about a physician's or a lawyer's actions, and there his professional colleagues will judge whether or not the complaint is justified; but one complains to a mechanic's boss about a mechanic's actions, and the boss who judges the mechanic is typically not an expert mechanic himself.

With increasing numbers of professionals being employed in bureaucratic settings, much attention has been directed toward examining conflicts between the demands of the adminis-trative organization and those of professional standards. These conflicts usually find expression in contrasting orientations of employees; some adopt management as their major reference group, and others, their professional colleagues. The significance of this difference is indicated by the fact that studies of professionals or semiprofessionals in formal organizations have consistently found that the conflict between bureaucratic and professional orientation is a fundamental issue. Hughes reports conflicts between itinerants and the homeguard in numerous work settings,[3] Francis and Stone emphasize the distinction between a service and a procedure orientation in their study of a public employment agency;[4] and Gouldner focuses on the contrast between cosmopolitan and local orientations in his study of a college faculty.[5] Our research, too, found that semiprofessional workers in a public assistance agency could be differentiated on the basis of whether their orientation was confined to the organization or extended to the profession of social work. Those oriented to their profession tended to be less attached to the welfare agency, more critical of its operations—particularly of service to clients—and less confined by administrative procedure. Although a professional orientation motivates a person to do better work in terms of professional standards, it also gives him a basis for ignoring administrative considerations and thus may lead to poorer performance in terms of the standards

---

[3] Everett C. Hughes, *Men and Their Work* (Glencoe, Ill.: Free Press, 1958), pp. 31, 129-30, 136.

[4] Roy G. Francis and Robert C. Stone, *Service and Procedure in Bureaucracy* (Minneapolis: University of Minnesota Press, 1956).

[5] Alvin W. Gouldner, "Cosmopolitans and Locals," *Administrative Science Quarterly*, **2** (1957), 281-306.

of the organization. Thus, profession-
ally oriented caseworkers were more
apt than others to fail to visit their
clients on schedule.

Research on production organizations in widely different social contexts
indicates that a rational organization
for the collective pursuit of formally
established goals may exist whether or
not the specific mechanism employed
for this purpose is a bureaucratic structure. Stinchcombe presents a comparative analysis of construction and mass-
production industries in our highly
complex and industrialized society.[6]
Udy reports a quantitative investigation of rudimentary production organizations in a large number of simple,
non-Western societies.[7] Despite the
great difference in source materials, the
two studies arrive at essentially the
same conclusion. The findings of both
indicate that a rational formal organization may be but is not necessarily bureaucratic. Specifically, the
fact that an organization is governed
by such rational principles as specialization, rewards for performance, and
contractual agreements is independent
of the existence of a bureaucratic structure, that is, a hierarchy of authority
and an administrative apparatus.
Stinchcombe concludes that the professionalized labor force in the construction industry serves as an alternative to bureaucratization for assuring
rational production, because seasonal
fluctuations in this industry make it
impractical to maintain continuous
bureaucratic organizations. Seasonal
variation, however, is not the only condition that encourages employment of

a professional labor force; another is
the complexity of the services to be
performed. When the over-all responsibility of the organization cannot be
broken down into fairly routine specialized tasks—as exemplified by organizations responsible for research, the care
of the ill, and casework service—expert judgments of professionals rather
than disciplined compliance with the
commands of superiors must govern
operations in the interest of efficiency.

Professional expertness and bureaucratic discipline may be viewed as alternative methods of coping with areas
of uncertainty. Discipline does so by
reducing the scope of uncertainty; expertness, by providing the knowledge
and social support that enable individuals to cope with uncertainty and
thus to assume more responsibility.
The dilemma, however, remains and,
indeed, affects wider and wider circles
as the number of people subject to
both these conflicting control mechanisms grows, since the work of professionals is increasingly carried out in
bureaucratic organizations, and since
operations in bureaucracies seem to become increasingly professionalized,
modern warfare being a conspicuous
example.

Managerial Planning and Initiative

The need for centralized planning
and individual initiative poses a third
dilemma for formal organizations—or,
perhaps more correctly, a third manifestation of the basic dilemma between order and freedom.[8] Notwithstanding the importance of free
communication, freedom to follow
one's best professional judgment, and

[6] Arthur L. Stinchcombe, "Bureaucratic
and Craft Administration of Production,"
Administrative Science Quarterly, 4 (1959),
168-87.

[7] Stanley H. Udy, Jr., " 'Bureaucracy' and
'Rationality' in Weber's Theory," American
Sociological Review, 24 (1959), 791-95.

[8] See the discussion of the dilemma between bureaucracy and enterprise, as he calls
it, by Marshall Dimock, Administrative Vitality (New York: Harper, 1959).

conditions permitting the exercise of initiative, effective coordination in a large organization requires some centralized direction. But the assumption that managerial coordination necessitates control through a hierarchy of authority is questionable, since it can be and often is achieved by other methods, notably through various types of impersonal mechanisms of control designed by management.

The assembly line is such an impersonal mechanism through which managerial planning effects coordination of the production processes without the use of directives that are passed down the hierarchy. As a matter of fact, the impersonal constraints exerted on operators tend to reverse the flow of demand in the hierarchy. Since the moving line makes most of the demands on workers, the role of the foreman is changed from one who primarily makes demands on workers to one who responds to their demands for help and assistance, and similar changes occur on higher levels. There is centralized direction, but it is not attained through commands transmitted down the hierarchy.

Performance records are another impersonal mechanism of control, one suitable for controlling nonmanual as well as manual tasks. The regular evaluation of employee performance on the basis of quantitative records of accomplished results exerts constraints that obviate the need for routine supervisory checking. Performance records, like the assembly line, reverse the flow of demand in the organization and cast the supervisor in the role of adviser and helper to workers rather than in the role of a person who makes continual demands on them. This evaluation system also facilitates coordination, since it centralizes the direction of operations in the hands of the higher managers who design the records.

Both performance records and assembly lines minimize reliance on hierarchical authority and discipline to control operations and, therefore, improve relations between supervisors and subordinates. However, there is an important difference between these two mechanisms. Assembly-line production reduces the discretion workers can exercise and hence lowers their work satisfaction. In contrast, evaluation of performance on the basis of a quantitative record of results achieved increases the discretion employees are allowed to exercise and thus raises their work satisfaction.

We had expected that automation would be an impersonal control mechanism more similar in its consequences to performance records than to the assembly line. We further anticipated that most workers in automated plants, where routine tasks are performed by machines, would be technical experts engaged in maintenance and trouble-shooting, and that they, consequently, would enjoy more discretion and have higher work satisfaction. The surprising findings of studies conducted in automated organizations by Walker, Faunce, and Mann and Williams is that the average level of skill and responsibility of workers was not superior to the level that had existed prior to automation.[9] The discretion permitted workers had not been increased. Indeed, in the automated factory studied by Faunce, supervision was closer than on the assembly line, because foremen were concerned with preventing costly machine breakdowns. Since automation removed some of the

---

[9] William A. Faunce, "Automation in the Automobile Industry," *American Sociological Review*, **23** (1958), 401-07; and Floyd C. Mann and Lawrence K. Williams, "Observations of the Dynamics of a Change to Electronic Data-Processing Equipment," *Administrative Science Quarterly*, **5** (1960), 217-56.

higher positions in the organization as well as some lower ones, it reduced chances for advancement, a situation which was a source of considerable dissatisfaction. It appears that automated plants have not yet reorganized their work processes to take full advantage of the technological innovations. This reorganization would require, in our opinion, the training or recruitment of expert mechanics and the redesigning of the division of labor to include minor machine maintenance in the duties of operators. Under these conditions, machine breakdowns, or the impending danger of them, would not lead to closer supervision as it did in the plants studied, and the highly technical operations would permit the exercise of considerable discretion.

It is conceivable that union pressure to increase wage rates on automated jobs will force management to institute such a reorganization. Higher labor costs constrain management to attempt to improve productivity, and one means for accomplishing this improvement is through further automation that eliminates routine jobs. The remaining highly paid workers could be held responsible for acquiring the skills needed for the maintenance functions now discharged by foremen or specialists. Such changes would give them more discretion, lessen the need for close supervision, and thus probably raise work satisfaction. These predictions are in line with Melman's conclusion that union pressures and high wages have induced management to introduce technological innovations more rapidly than would otherwise have been the case.[10] Such a professionalization of the labor force might

also require a reorganization of the reward system, since piece rates do not furnish incentives suited for professionalized tasks. Even in the semi-automated department studied by Walker, where tasks were far from professionalized, and where workers were quite satisfied with their rate of pay, there was much dissatisfaction with the piece-rate system for failing to take mental work and judgment into account. A reward system that emphasizes advancement chances rather than immediate earnings and evaluation of results rather than sheer productivity would seem to furnish more effective incentives for professionalized tasks.

Managerial planning of the production process and a professionalized labor force that can exercise initiative and is motivated to do so by opportunities for advancement would sharply reduce the need for hierarchical supervision and control through directives passed down the pyramid of authority. Indeed, coordination appears to be achieved frequently through centralized planning and by means of direct communication between responsible managers (as in Simpson's spinning department cited in Chapter VII) rather than through the cumbersome process of passing messages up and down the hierarchy. But our suggestion that managerial planning interferes less with the exercise of initiative than hierarchical authority is not meant to imply that the dilemma between managerial control and initiative is resolved. The best that can be hoped for, as Bendix has suggested, is that

. . . the employees of all ranks in industry and government strike a balance between compliance and initiative, that they temper their adherence to formal rules by a judicious exercise of independent judgment and that they fit their

---

[10] See Seymour Melman, *Decision-making and Productivity* (Oxford, England: Basil Blackwell, 1958), pp. 105-06, 141-43.

initiative into the framework of the formal regulation.[11]

But even this best is too much to expect. For this balance is continually disrupted by the need for more order on the one hand and the need for more freedom on the other.

Dialectical Processes of Change

The conception of dilemma directs attention to the inevitability of conflict and change in organizations. Mary Parker Follett, an astute observer of administrative practice, has noted: "When we think that we have *solved* a problem, well, by the very process of solving, new elements or forces come into the situation and you have a new problem on your hands to be solved."[12] The innovations instituted to solve one problem often create others because effectiveness in an organization depends on many different factors, some of which are incompatible with others; hence, the dilemma. The very improvements in some conditions that further the achievement of the organization's objectives often interfere with other conditions equally important for this purpose. A by now familiar example is that hierarchical differentiation promotes coordination but simultaneously restricts the communication processes that benefit decision-making.

New problems are internally generated in organizations in the process of solving old ones. However, the experience gained in solving earlier prob-

lems is not lost but contributes to the search for solutions to later problems. These facts suggest that the process of organizational development is dialectical—problems appear, and while the process of solving them tends to give rise to new problems, learning has occurred which influences how the new challenges are met.[13] Consequently, effectiveness in an organization improves as a result of accumulated experience. These dialectical processes are illustrated by the introduction of assembly-line production. This new production method raised productivity and effected centralized control and coordination without the need for hierarchical directives. However, by routinizing tasks and lowering work satisfaction, the assembly line created problems of absenteeism and turnover —problems that were particularly serious given the interdependence of operations on the assembly line. Management had succeeded in solving one set of problems, but the mechanism by which they were solved produced new problems which were quite different from those that had existed in earlier stages of mechanization. Contrary to our expectations, the introduction of automation has not yet met the problems created by monotonous tasks and low work satisfaction. But should these problems be solved through a reorganization of the work force that requires operators to assume more responsibility, as we have suggested, management would no doubt again be faced with new difficulties. For example, increased responsibility and discretion in performing complex, interdependent tasks might engender

---

[11] Reinhard Bendix, "Bureaucracy," *American Sociological Review*, **12** (1947), 503.

[12] Mary Parker Follett, "The Process of Control," Luther Gulick and L. Urwick (eds.), *Papers on the Science of Administration* (New York: Institute of Public Administration, 1937), p. 166 (italics in original).

---

[13] If we classify problems into dichotomies or other very broad categories, it inevitably seems as if the same ones recur, simply because all new ones are put into one of the few existing categories.

anxieties over decision-making which would impede effective performance, and these new problems would require management to devote attention to developing mechanisms that reduce such anxieties.

Conflicts of interest between various groups or persons in the organization are another source of dialectical change. What constitutes satisfactory adjustment for one group may be the opposite for another, since different interests serve as the criteria of adjustment. Thus, when the efforts of managers are judged by the results they achieve and they are given freedom to exercise responsibility and initiative in achieving them, conflicts between them are likely to ensue. For each manager will seek to promote the interests and expand the jurisdiction of his department, and his endeavors will bring him into conflict with others who have staked out the same claims. Compromises will be reached and coalitions will be formed, but since the responsibilities and interests of the managers continue to differ, new conflicts are apt to arise as changing conditions produce new challenges. Moreover, as various occupational subgroups in the organization try to improve their economic position, their interests may come into conflict, particularly if the success of one group upsets the existing status hierarchy and motivates the others it has displaced to recoup their advantage. Conflicts of interest are most conspicuous in the relation between union and management. The union is interested in obtaining higher wages and better working conditions, while management is interested in lowering costs and improving productivity. Collective bargaining furnishes mechanisms for resolving issues, but the conflicting interests generate new ones. Thus, management introduces new machines in an attempt to im-

prove efficiency, disturbing the existing adjustment and producing a variety of difficulties with which the union has to deal. Similarly, once workers have attained the right to collective bargaining, they use it to fight for pensions and other fringe benefits, thereby creating new problems for management.

Another source of disruption and change is turnover in personnel. Valuable experience is lost as older workers are replaced by new trainees, and social ties are disrupted by transfers and loss of personnel. As we have seen, the methods available to a new manager in discharging his responsibilities are dependent in part on those of his predecessor. If the latter commanded the loyalty of subordinates, the successor will find it difficult to do so and be constrained to resort to bureaucratic methods, whereas the successor to an authoritarian bureaucrat will find it advantageous to use more informal managerial practices. Again we see that organizational developments alternate in direction in a dialectical pattern. The succession of goals leads to such an alternating pattern of change in the relations between organizations. Once earlier objectives are achieved, management seeks new objectives and by doing so disturbs the existing equilibrium in the network of organizations. The dominance of one organization in a sector restores order as former competitors become exchange partners, but further power struggles are stimulated by a further succession of goals as groups of sellers start to compete with groups of buyers for dominant power over a set of related markets.

In mutual-benefit associations, there is still another source of dialectical change. These organizations are subject to conflicts that arise from the dilemma posed by their twofold formal purpose. One purpose, just as in the case of other organizations, is the effective accomplishment of the specific objectives of the organization—for example, improving employment conditions in the case of unions. But another distinctive purpose of these associations is to provide their members with a mechanism for arriving at agreements on their common objectives. For to serve the interests of its members a mutual-benefit association must furnish mechanisms for ascertaining what their collective objectives are as well as mechanisms for implementing them, and the ascertaining of objectives requires democratic self-government and freedom of dissent. Endeavors to attain one of these purposes frequently impede the attainment of the other. In the interests of effective accomplishment of union objectives, as Michels has pointed out, democratic processes are often set aside. Conversely, preoccupation with democratic self-government and freedom of dissent may interfere with efforts to implement the common ob-

jectives. But the study by Lipset and his colleagues shows that a strong union which has accomplished some of its specific objectives can and sometimes does turn its attention and energy to maintaining internal democracy.

Democratic societies are in this respect organized like mutual-benefit associations. They have the double purpose of remaining strong enough to survive and yet maintaining the freedoms that permit the democratic establishment of common objectives. Under current conditions in the world, the issue of promoting national security and strength versus preserving civil liberties and freedom of dissent poses the dilemma most sharply. No final solution is possible for this dilemma. Indeed, attempts finally to resolve it tend to sacrifice one purpose for the other and thus endanger the very nature of democratic societies. For we surely need to survive in order to preserve our democratic institutions, but we just as surely do not want to survive at the cost of losing our freedom.

In Conference

ROBERT F. BALES

There is a widespread interest in the process of decision making among executives in business, the military, government, research, civic affairs—indeed, in every sort of organization set up to produce anything by cooperation. Technical experts are called in to give advice; management committees must decide on basic policies;

Robert F. Bales, "In Conference," *Harvard Business Review*, 32 (1954), 41-49.

labor teams must plan and regulate their work; staff meetings take place daily at every level. Decision making is the pinpoint focus of the vast social machinery that makes up our democratic society and its economy.

Most decisions are made "in conference." Then they normally require a long series of further conferences for their implementation. Probably no serious estimate has ever been made of the total number of hours American businessmen spend per year "in conference." But the number must be astronomical.

Committee Operation

Yet think how little we know about the actual operation of a committee, and how little we are able to predict or control its success or failure. Many a "good idea" has emerged at the other end of the committee operation as a kind of "bad dream," mangled and amputated in its essentials, patched together with fantasies into a monster that finally dies at the hands of some committee further on down the line. It is no matter for wonder that committee meetings are often viewed with mixed feelings of apprehension and cynical humor.

It is not true, of course, that "nothing good ever comes out of a committee"—not so true, at least, as that nothing good ever reaches practical application without the work of innumerable committees. But the uncertainty whether a particular committee or work group may unexplainably go sour, or simply fail to produce at some critical point, is considerable.

The practical need to reduce this uncertainty and to improve the wisdom of critical decisions is resulting in an increasing amount of scientific research on the underlying problems. Research on decision making is being conducted by groups whose interests range from economics, military and industrial logistics, mathematics and statistics, through formal logic and the theories of information and of communication networks, to conference procedures, the theory of leadership, and social relations.

Direct Experiments

One aspect of this broad front of scientific development is the direct experimental study of committee meetings where decisions are made.

Not many years ago nobody seriously supposed that the subtle aspects of face-to-face human relations could be studied experimentally in the laboratory. All sorts of skeptical objections appeared, even among social scientists, when a few of their more hopeful colleagues began to set up small groups of subjects under laboratory conditions and study social behavior by direct observation. Now a number of such laboratories are in operation, and findings of possible practical importance are beginning to appear.

One of the early installations was set up by the Laboratory of Social Relations at Harvard University in 1947. This laboratory and some of its findings will serve as an illustration of the type of research now going on in a number of centers:

On the third floor of Harvard's Emerson Hall there is a specially designed room for the purpose of observing the operation of committees and similar types of small groups. Containing chairs and a table which can be varied in size, it is well lighted and surfaced in acoustic tile. On one wall is a chalkboard and on another a large mirror. Behind the mirror is an observation room, for in reality the mirror is a one-way glass through which a team of observers on the other side may watch without disturbing the subjects. While the subject group is aware that it is being watched, the illusion is such that any self-consciousness is only brief and the "mirror" is ignored and soon forgotten.

The groups vary in size from two to seven members, depending on the particular problem under discussion. The problem for discussion may be industrial, governmental, military, or educational in character, but in any case it has to do with administration and requires a decision or recommendation of some kind.

During the discussion the observers behind the "mirror" note the action within the group: who speaks, to whom he speaks, and how he speaks. The actual subject matter is not the primary concern, except as it indicates the speaker's feelings.

An ingenious machine, built by the laboratory, makes it easy for the observer to classify each statement as it is made. Observers are trained until they are able to classify within a second or so any remark that is made into one of twelve descriptive categories. (Originally there were 87 categories of response, but gradually the list has been reduced to 12.) In addition, the conversation is sound-recorded for later checking.

Each experimental group takes part in four sessions of 40 minutes each. By the end of this time, an accurate appraisal of the way in which it operates *as a group* is possible, and the relationships between members can be predicted with some confidence should it ever meet again.

Kinds of Behavior

All the behavior that goes on in a committee (or, indeed, in any verbal interchange) can be viewed as a sequence of questions, answers, and positive and negative reactions to the questions and answers. Three types of questions are distinguished: *asking for information, opinion,* and *suggestion.* Corresponding to these three types of questions are three types of answers: *giving information, opinion,* and *suggestion.* These answers are problem-solving attempts, and they call for reactions. Negative reactions include: *showing disagreement, tension,* or *antagonism.* On the positive side the corresponding reactions include: *showing agreement, tension release,* and *friendly solidarity.* These are the 12 categories of remarks used as a basis of analysis in the Harvard experiments.

Successful Decisions

It is interesting to note that, on the average, about 50% of all remarks made in meetings are answers while the remaining 50% consist of questions and reactions. Such a 50-50 balance (or something close to it) may be one characteristic of successful communication. Problem-solving attempts are needed to reach a decision, but that is not all. It may very well be that if enough time is not regularly allowed also for questioning and reaction to occur in the meeting, the members will carry away tensions that will eventually operate to vitiate an apparently successful but actually superficial decision.

Participation of Members

A decision is not a successful decision unless each member who is supposed to have been involved in its making is actually bound by it in such a way that his later behavior conforms to it.

By and large, members do not seem to feel strongly bound by a decision unless they have participated in making it. However, participation does not necessarily mean that each member has to talk an equal amount. As a matter of fact, even approximate equality of actual talking time among members is very rare; and, when it does appear, it is usually associated with a free-for-all conflict. A moderate gradient among members in talking time is the more usual thing.

More significantly, participation means that the meeting operates under the presumption that each member has an equal right to ask questions or voice negative or positive reactions to any proposal made, if he wishes, and a right to expect that, if he makes a proposal, it will receive an appropriate reaction from some other member. Because of time exigencies, most members, most frequently, allow a voiced proposal to represent what they themselves would say, and a voiced reaction to represent what they themselves might respond.

On the other hand, it is difficult to know when a member's feelings and interests are being adequately represented and when they are not. The difference is so subtle that he himself is not always able to tell. He may go away dissatisfied without knowing quite why. Hence there is probably no adequate substitute for *some* actual verbal participation of each member. A few words on his part will serve to express and solidify his involvement, and to avoid his subsequent dissatisfaction.

Optimum Balance

There are about twice as many positive reactions in most meetings as there are negative reactions. One might suppose that the more successful the meeting, the fewer negative reactions and the more positive reactions one would find. But the evidence does not support this view. Rather, there appears to be a kind of optimum balance. Departures too far to either side are indicators of trouble.

Disagreement.—Rates of disagreement and antagonism that are too high are sure indicators of trouble. Apparently, when ill feeling rises above some critical point, a "chain reaction" or "vicious circle" tends to set in. Logic and the practical demands of the task cease to be governing factors. Such an occurrence is an impressive experience when seen from the perspective of the observer behind the one-way glass in the laboratory:

The observer is unseen by the subjects, cannot communicate with them, and so in a basic sense is "not involved." He knows that no action will be taken on the decision of the committee. He may have heard the same case discussed hundreds of times before. Nevertheless, he is "caught in the illusion of reality" as the temperature of the group begins to rise.

Suddenly the credulity of the observer is strained beyond some critical point. The illusion that the group is dealing with some external problem breaks. It becomes perfectly transparent—to the observer—that emotions have taken over, and that what one member is saying does not refer at all to some external situation but to himself and the other members present.

"Facts" are unwittingly invented or are falsified. Other facts drop out of sight entirely. When one member insists that "people in this office should be treated like human beings," it is clear that he refers to himself and how he feels he should be treated in this group. When his opponent insists that "troublemakers should be fired," it is equally clear that he refers to the man who just spoke to him.

The decision, if any, reached by a group in this state has all the characteristics of a "bad dream," indeed.

Agreement.—There can also be too many agreements and too few disagreements. This condition may be an indication either of lack of involvement in the practical demands of the task or of an atmosphere so inhibited and constrained that nobody dares risk disagreement. In the ordinary mill run of opinions and suggestions, there is always a certain percentage so unrealistic, exaggerated, or unsuitable that not to disagree means not to solve the problem.

Closely related to the rate of agreement is the rate of suggestion. Groups in a smoothly operating condition tend to show relatively high rates of suggestion, as well as of agreement. But there is a joker in this finding. This condition is an *outcome* of smooth sailing, *not* a way to attain it.

As most people would suppose, giving facts is fairly safe. The probability of arousing disagreement by reviewing the facts of the case is relatively low. But giving opinions is more risky, for in so doing a man gives his inferences and expresses his feelings and values, including his prejudices. Others are more likely to disagree, and the means of resolving disagreements are much more vague and indirect than in the case of disputed facts.

Indeed, a suggestion can cause a real bottleneck. If a man agrees to the suggestion, he must embrace all it implies, assumes, or involves. He has bound himself to future action. Most people are quite sensitive to this kind of constriction, even though they know that a decision is necessary. That is why, as the rate of giving suggestions goes up, the rate of negative reactions also tends to increase.

Reducing the Risk

Of course suggestions are necessary before a decision is reached. The decision point is inevitably a crisis point. But this is the risk that all decision-making groups have to take. The wise strategist should seek to reduce his risks to a calculated minimum, which is something quite different from trying to escape them entirely.

But how? The laboratory observations suggest a reasonable solution. Most successful groups go through an ordered series of three phases or stages in the solution of a problem:

(1) They attempt to assemble the largest pool of common information about the facts of the case.

(2) They make inferences and evaluations, and try to form common opinions in a general way.

(3) Only in the final phase do they get around to more specific suggestions, after an extensive groundwork has been laid.

Not all groups do this, by any means. Some start the other end to, and some start with an outburst of opinions before they ever look at a fact. Indeed, many of the members are hardly conscious of any difference between a fact and an opinion.

It is probably not any excess of wisdom or extraordinary sensitivity that produces the typical order of stages. It is rather, we may suppose, the "brute logic of natural selection." A suggestion given at a premature stage simply dies for lack of support, or is trampled to death in the general melee. Gradually the discussion is forced back to facts, where agreement can be reached.

In an environment barren of consensus, only a fact can survive; and, where there is hostility, even facts find a slim foothold. But a rich background of common facts lays the groundwork for the development of common inferences and sentiments, and out of these common decisions can grow. No decision rests on "facts" alone, but there is no better starting point. To start the decision-making process at any other point is to multiply the risk of a vicious circle of disagreement—and at no saving of time in the long run.

Dual Leadership

One of the most startling implications of the laboratory research so far is that the concept of "leader," if it is taken too literally, can cause the man who thinks he *is* one to disregard a most important fact—namely, that there is usually *another* leader in the group whom he can overlook only at his peril.

Separate Roles

The laboratory findings, while still tentative, indicate that the man who is judged by the group members to have the "best ideas" contributing to the decision is *not* generally the "best-liked." There are two separate roles—that of task leader and that of social leader. If a man comes into a task-leadership position because he is popular or best liked, he is ordinarily confronted with a choice: (1) If he chooses to try to keep the task leadership of the group, he tends to lose some of his popularity and to collect some dislikes. (2) If he chooses to try to keep his popularity, he tends to lose the task leadership. People differ in the way they solve this dilemma, although most tend to prefer to keep the popularity rather than the task leadership.

The difficulty becomes more acute with time. At the end of the group's first meeting there is 1 chance in 2 that the task leader will be the most liked. At the end of the second meeting the chances are reduced to 1 in 4. At the end of the third they are 1 in 6, and at the end of the fourth they are only 1 in 7.

There are apparently few men who can hold both roles; instead, the tendency is for these positions to be held by two different men. Each is in reality a leader, and each is important to the stability of the group. The task leader helps to keep the group engaged in the work, but the pressure of decision and work tends to provoke irritation and injure the unity of the group. The best-liked man helps to restore this unity and to keep the members of the group aware of their importance as particular individuals, whose special needs and values are respected. These men complement each other, and they are both necessary for smooth operation of a committee.

It is especially important for these two men to recognize each other's roles and in effect to form a coalition. The most stable groups observed have been those in which this coalition has taken place. There are indications that such durable groups as the family and simple small communities are constructed this way, and apparently the coalition also takes place in many administrative staffs, sometimes consciously but more often accidentally.

These findings challenge some very basic concepts of leadership. Millions are spent each year by business, government, and the armed forces in developing means for recognizing leaders, and much has been written about the "characteristics" of leadership. Yet it appears that whatever superior qualities the individual may possess as a simple individual, he may be unable, just because of the way groups work, to maintain a stable leadership position without a co-leader of complementary qualities.

Communication Networks

Significantly, among the half-dozen instances where the observation room and equipment at the Harvard laboratory have been duplicated are several installations by the military:

The Air Force has built a room at Maxwell Field, Alabama, for testing and predicting leadership ability. Other divisions of the armed forces are also engaged in the same kind of experimentation, for one of the most pressing problems they face is the development of leaders and the selection of personnel who have to work in small groups—bomber and submarine crews, intelligence teams, and communications centers—particularly in situations where immediate processing of information and rapid but wise decisions are a tactical necessity.

One of the persistent problems in rapid communications networks such as those found in military defense is how to keep the actual control over critical decisions in the hands of the person or persons who will later bear the formal responsibility for the decision. Practically, the decision-making function on the tactical level tends to gravitate to the person who is at the center of the communication network, where information about the tactical situation is immediately available. But this tactical information center tends not to coincide with the top spot in the chain of command, where formal authority and responsibility are centered.

Here again is an instance where it is unrealistic to operate with a simple notion of a single "leader" in whom all essential leadership functions can be vested. Although this problem appears most clearly in larger organizations, it is essentially a large-scale version of the same tendency toward division of labor in leadership that can be seen in a committee.

Committee Membership

If all this is true, the emphasis should shift from seeking the ideal leader to trying to compose the ideal total group. Accordingly, at Harvard the next few years will be devoted to observing groups for the specific purpose of assessing the personnel, and then attempting actually to compose new committees from them which will function in a predicted way. With the right kind of assessment of each person's action within a group, it may be possible to pick, say, two people who would appear to be complementary leaders, put them with three more "neutral" people, and thus form a committee which would theoretically function at a certain predicted level of effectiveness. This at least is a start in the direction of rational composition of total groups.

Optimum Size

Just to take one of the elementary problems, the question of optimum size of a committee has received many interesting answers, but so far they seem to come mostly from numerology rather than from scientific research. For the particular task and time limits given to subjects in the Harvard laboratory, five seems to be the preferred number. Below that size subjects begin to complain that the group is too small, and above it that the group is too large. The fact that there is a distinct "saddle point" at five suggests that the notion of an optimum size is meaningful, if the task, time, and other circumstances are well enough specified. But the optimum size must surely vary according to conditions.

There seems to be a crucial point at seven. Below seven, for the most part, each person in the group says at least something to each other person. In groups over seven the low participators tend to stop talking to each other and center their communications on the few top men. The tendencies toward centralization of communication seem to increase rather powerfully as size increases.

At the same time, there are certain difficulties inherent in groups of as low as two and three members. In a two-man group no majority short of unanimity can form. Each person can exercise a complete veto over the other. One person can exercise power quite as effectively by simply refusing to react as he can by making suggestions, and this tendency toward withdrawal of one member appears with some frequency.

In a three-man group the tendency of two to form a combination against the third seems fairly strong. If this happens, the would-be task leader may be overcautious because he knows that, if his lieutenant disagrees with him, he may be left in the minority. The lieutenant knows he has this power but that, if he exercises it, the third man may step in to take his place. The third man on the outside of the coalition is left powerless whether he agrees or disagrees, so long as the other two agree, and tends either to withdraw or set up a damaging but unsuccessful protest. It is hard for a three-man group to have a "healthy" amount of disagreement. The structure is too sensitive to disagreement, and therefore it tends to an all-or-none extreme. . . .

The Science of "Muddling Through"

CHARLES E. LINDBLOM

Suppose an administrator is given responsibility for formulating policy with respect to inflation. He might start by trying to list all related values in order of importance, e.g., full employment, reasonable business profit, protection of small savings, prevention of a stock market crash. Then all possible policy outcomes could be rated as more or less efficient in attaining a maximum of these values. This would of course require a prodigious inquiry into values held by members of society and an equally prodigious set of calculations on how much of each value is equal to how much of each other value. He could then proceed to outline all possible policy alternatives. In a third step, he would undertake systematic comparison of his multitude of alternatives to determine which attains the greatest amount of values.

In comparing policies, he would take advantage of any theory available that generalized about classes of policies. In considering inflation, for example, he would compare all policies in the light of the theory of prices.

Charles E. Lindblom, "The Science of 'Muddling Through.'" Reprinted from the *Public Administration Review*, the journal of the American Society for Public Administration, xix, 2 (Spring, 1959), by permission of the publisher.

Since no alternatives are beyond his investigation, he would consider strict central control and the abolition of all prices and markets on the one hand and elimination of all public controls with reliance completely on the free market on the other, both in the light of whatever theoretical generalizations he could find on such hypothetical economies.

Finally, he would try to make the choice that would in fact maximize his values.

An alternative line of attack would be to set as his principal objective, either explicitly or without conscious thought, the relatively simple goal of keeping prices level. This objective might be compromised or complicated by only a few other goals, such as full employment. He would in fact disregard most other social values as beyond his present interest, and he would for the moment not even attempt to rank the few values that he regarded as immediately relevant. Were he pressed, he would quickly admit that he was ignoring many related values and many possible important consequences of his policies.

As a second step, he would outline those relatively few policy alternatives that occurred to him. He would then compare them. In comparing his limited number of alternatives, most of them familiar from past controversies, he would not ordinarily find a body of theory precise enough to carry him through a comparison of their respective consequences. Instead he would rely heavily on the record of past experience with small policy steps to predict the consequences of similar steps extended into the future.

Moreover, he would find that the policy alternatives combined objectives or values in different ways. For example, one policy might offer price level stability at the cost of some risk of unemployment; another might offer less price stability but also less risk of unemployment. Hence, the next step in his approach—the final selection—would combine into one the choice among values and the choice among instruments for reaching values. It would not, as in the first method of policy-making, approximate a more mechanical process of choosing the means that best satisfied goals that were previously clarified and ranked. Because practitioners of the second approach expect to achieve their goals only partially, they would expect to repeat endlessly the sequence just described, as conditions and aspirations changed and as accuracy of prediction improved.

By Root or by Branch

For complex problems, the first of these two approaches is of course impossible. Although such an approach can be described, it cannot be practiced except for relatively simple problems and even then only in a somewhat modified form. It assumes intellectual capacities and sources of information that men simply do not possess, and it is even more absurd as an approach to policy when the time and money that can be allocated to a policy problem is limited, as is always the case. Of particular importance to public administrators is the fact that

public agencies are in effect usually instructed not to practice the first method. That is to say, their prescribed functions and constraints—the politically or legally possible—restrict their attention to relatively few values and relatively few alternative policies among the countless alternatives that might be imagined. It is the second method that is practiced.

Curiously, however, the literatures of decision-making, policy formulation, planning, and public administration formalize the first approach rather than the second, leaving public administrators who handle complex decisions in the position of practicing what few preach. For emphasis I run some risk of overstatement. True enough, the literature is well aware of limits on man's capacities and of the inevitability that policies will be approached in some such style as the second. But attempts to formalize rational policy formulation—to lay out explicitly the necessary steps in the process—usually describe the first approach and not the second.[1]

The common tendency to describe policy formulation even for complex problems as though it followed the first approach has been strengthened by the attention given to, and successes enjoyed by, operations research, statistical decision theory, and systems analysis. The hallmarks of these procedures, typical of the first approach, are clarity of objective, explicitness of evaluation, a high degree of comprehensiveness of overview, and, wherever possible, quantification of values for mathematical analysis. But these advanced procedures remain largely the

[1] James G. March and Herbert A. Simon similarly characterize the literature. They also take some important steps, as have Simon's recent articles, to describe a less heroic model of policy-making. See *Organizations* (John Wiley and Sons, 1958), p. 137.

appropriate techniques of relatively small-scale problem-solving where the total number of variables to be considered is small and value problems restricted. Charles Hitch, head of the Economics Division of RAND Corporation, one of the leading centers for application of these techniques, has written:

I would make the empirical generalization from my experience at RAND and elsewhere that operations research is the art of sub-optimizing, i.e., of solving some lower-level problems, and that difficulties increase and our special competence diminishes by an order of magnitude with every level of decision making we attempt to ascend. The sort of simple explicit model which operations researchers are so proficient in using can certainly reflect most of the significant factors influencing traffic control on the George Washington Bridge, but the proportion of the relevant reality which we can represent by any such model or models in studying, say, a major foreign-policy decision, appears to be almost trivial.[2]

Accordingly, I propose in this paper to clarify and formalize the second method, much neglected in the literature. This might be described as the method of *successive limited comparisons*. I will contrast it with the first approach, which might be called the rational-comprehensive method.[3] More

impressionistically and briefly—and therefore generally used in this article —they could be characterized as the branch method and root method, the former continually building out from the current situation, step-by-step and by small degrees; the latter starting from fundamentals anew each time, building on the past only as experience is embodied in a theory, and always prepared to start completely from the ground up.

Let us put the characteristics of the two methods side by side in simplest terms.

Assuming that the root method is familiar and understandable, we proceed directly to clarification of its alternative by contrast. In explaining the second, we shall be describing how most administrators do in fact approach complex questions, for the root method, the "best" way as a blueprint or model, is in fact not workable for complex policy questions, and administrators are forced to use the method of successive limited comparisons.

Intertwining Evaluation and Empirical Analysis (1b)

The quickest way to understand how values are handled in the method of successive limited comparisons is to see how the root method often breaks down in *its* handling of values or objectives. The idea that values should be clarified, and in advance of the examination of alternative policies, is appealing. But what happens when we attempt it for complex social problems? The first difficulty is that on many critical values or objectives, citizens disagree, congressmen disagree, and public administrators disagree. Even where a fairly specific objective

[2] "Operations Research and National Planning—A Dissent," **5**, *Operations Research*, 718 (October, 1957). Hitch's dissent is from particular points made in the article to which his paper is a reply; his claim that operations research is for low-level problems is widely accepted.

For examples of the kind of problems to which operations research is applied, see C. W. Churchman, R. L. Ackoff and E. L. Arnoff, *Introduction to Operations Research* (John Wiley and Sons, 1957); and J. F. McCloskey and J. M. Coppinger (eds.), *Operations Research for Management*, Vol. II, (The Johns Hopkins Press, 1956).

[3] I am assuming that administrators often make policy and advise in the making of policy and am treating decision-making and policy-making as synonymous for purposes of this paper.

Rational-Comprehensive (Root)	Successive Limited Comparisons (Branch)
1a. Clarification of values or objectives distinct from and usually prerequisite to empirical analysis of alternative policies.	1b. Selection of value goals and empirical analysis of the needed action are not distinct from one another but are closely intertwined.
2a. Policy-formulation is therefore approached through means-end analysis: First the ends are isolated, then the means to achieve them are sought.	2b. Since means and ends are not distinct, means-end analysis is often inappropriate or limited.
3a. The test of a "good" policy is that it can be shown to be the most appropriate means to desired ends.	3b. The test of a "good" policy is typically that various analysts find themselves directly agreeing on a policy (without their agreeing that it is the most appropriate means to an agreed objective).
4a. Analysis is comprehensive; every important relevant factor is taken into account.	4b. Analysis is drastically limited: i) Important possible outcomes are neglected. ii) Important alternative potential policies are neglected. iii) Important affected values are neglected.
5a. Theory is often heavily relied upon.	5b. A succession of comparisons greatly reduces or eliminates reliance on theory.

is prescribed for the administrator, there remains considerable room for disagreement on sub-objectives. Consider, for example, the conflict with respect to locating public housing, described in Meyerson and Banfield's study of the Chicago Housing Authority[4]—disagreement which occurred despite the clear objective of providing a certain number of public housing units in the city. Similarly conflicting are objectives in highway location, traffic control, minimum wage administration, development of tourist facilities in national parks, or insect control.

Administrators cannot escape these conflicts by ascertaining the majority's preference, for preferences have not been registered on most issues; indeed, there often *are* no preferences in the absence of public discussion sufficient to bring an issue to the attention of the electorate. Furthermore, there is a question of whether intensity of feeling should be considered as well as the number of persons preferring each alternative. By the impossibility of doing otherwise, administrators often are reduced to deciding policy without clarifying objectives first.

Even when an administrator resolves to follow his own values as a criterion for decisions, he often will not know how to rank them when they conflict with one another, as they usually do. Suppose, for example, that an administrator must relocate tenants living in tenements scheduled for destruction. One objective is to empty the buildings fairly promptly, another is to find suitable accommodations for persons displaced, another is to avoid friction with residents in other areas in which a large influx would be unwelcome, another is to deal with all concerned through persuasion if possible, and so on.

[4] Martin Meyerson and Edward C. Banfield, *Politics, Planning and the Public Interest* (The Free Press, 1955).

How does one state even to himself the relative importance of these partially conflicting values? A simple ranking of them is not enough; one needs ideally to know how much of one value is worth sacrificing for some of another value. The answer is that typically the administrator chooses—and must choose—directly among policies in which these values are combined in different ways. He cannot first clarify his values and then choose among policies.

A more subtle third point underlies both the first two. Social objectives do not always have the same relative values. One objective may be highly prized in one circumstance, another in another circumstance. If, for example, an administrator values highly both the dispatch with which his agency can carry through its projects *and* good public relations, it matters little which of the two possibly conflicting values he favors in some abstract or general sense. Policy questions arise in forms which put to administrators such a question as: Given the degree to which we are or are not already achieving the values of dispatch and the values of good public relations, is it worth sacrificing a little speed for a happier clientele, or is it better to risk offending the clientele so that we can get on with our work? The answer to such a question varies with circumstances.

The value problem is, as the example shows, always a problem of adjustments at a margin. But there is no practicable way to state marginal objectives or values except in terms of particular policies. That one value is preferred to another in one decision situation does not mean that it will be preferred in another decision situation in which it can be had only at great sacrifice of another value. Attempts to rank or order values in general and

abstract terms so that they do not shift from decision to decision end up by ignoring the relevant marginal preferences. The significance of this third point thus goes very far. Even if all administrators had at hand an agreed set of values, objectives, and constraints, and an agreed ranking of these values, objectives, and constraints, their marginal values in actual choice situations would be impossible to formulate.

Unable consequently to formulate the relevant values first and then choose among policies to achieve them, administrators must choose directly among alternative policies that offer different marginal combinations of values. Somewhat paradoxically, the only practicable way to disclose one's relevant marginal values even to oneself is to describe the policy one chooses to achieve them. Except roughly and vaguely, I know of no way to describe—or even to understand—what my relative evaluations are for, say, freedom and security, speed and accuracy in governmental decisions, or low taxes and better schools than to describe my preferences among specific policy choices that might be made between the alternatives in each of the pairs.

In summary, two aspects of the process by which values are actually handled can be distinguished. The first is clear: evaluation and empirical analysis are intertwined; that is, one chooses among values and among policies at one and the same time. Put a little more elaborately, one simultaneously chooses a policy to attain certain objectives and chooses the objectives themselves. The second aspect is related but distinct: the administrator focuses his attention on marginal or incremental values. Whether he is aware of it or not, he does not find general formulations of objectives very helpful and in fact makes specific marginal or incremental comparisons. Two policies, X and Y, confront him. Both promise the same degree of attainment of objectives *a, b, c, d,* and *e.* But X promises him somewhat more of *f* than does Y, while Y promises him somewhat more of *g* than does X. In choosing between them, he is in fact offered the alternative of a marginal or incremental amount of *f* at the expense of a marginal or incremental amount of *g.* The only values that are relevant to his choice are these increments by which the two policies differ; and, when he finally chooses between the two marginal values, he does so by making a choice between policies.[5]

As to whether the attempt to clarify objectives in advance of policy selection is more or less rational than the close intertwining of marginal evaluation and empirical analysis, the principal difference established is that for complex problems the first is impossible and irrelevant, and the second is both possible and relevant. The second is possible because the administrator need not try to analyze any values except the values by which alternative policies differ and need not be concerned with them except as they differ marginally. His need for information on values or objectives is drastically reduced as compared with the root method; and his capacity for grasping, comprehending, and relating values to one another is not strained beyond the breaking point.

Relations Between Means and Ends (2b)

Decision-making is ordinarily formalized as a means-end relationship:

means are conceived to be evaluated and chosen in the light of ends finally selected independently of and prior to the choice of means. This is the means-ends relationship of the root method. But it follows from all that has just been said that such a means-end relationship is possible only to the extent that values are agreed upon, are reconcilable, and are stable at the margin. Typically, therefore, such a means-ends relationship is absent from the branch method, where means and ends are simultaneously chosen.

Yet any departure from the means-ends relationship of the root method will strike some readers as inconceivable. For it will appear to them that only in such a relationship is it possible to determine whether one policy choice is better or worse than another. How can an administrator know whether he has made a wise or foolish decision if he is without prior values or objectives by which to judge his decisions? The answer to this question calls up the third distinctive difference between root and branch methods: how to decide the best policy.

The Test of "Good" Policy (3b)

In the root method, decision is "correct," "good," or "rational" if it can be shown to attain some specified objective, where the objective can be specified without simply describing the decision itself. Where objectives are defined only through the marginal or incremental approach to values described above, it is still sometimes possible to test whether a policy does in fact attain the desired objectives; but a precise statement of the objectives takes the form of a description of the policy chosen or some alternative to it. To show that a policy is mistaken one cannot offer an abstract argument that important objectives are not achieved;

---

[5] The line of argument is, of course, an extension of the theory of market choice, especially the theory of consumer choice, to public policy choices.

one must instead argue that another policy is more to be preferred.

So far, the departure from customary ways of looking at problem-solving is not troublesome, for many administrators will be quick to agree that the most effective discussion of the correctness of policy does take the form of comparison with other policies that might have been chosen. But what of the situation in which administrators cannot agree on values or objectives, either abstractly or in marginal terms? What then is the test of "good" policy? For the root method, there is no test. Agreement on objectives failing, there is no standard of "correctness." For the method of successive limited comparisons, the test is agreement on policy itself, which remains possible even when agreement on values is not.

It has been suggested that continuing agreement in Congress on the desirability of extending old age insurance stems from liberal desires to strengthen the welfare programs of the federal government and from conservative desires to reduce union demands for private pension plans. If so, this is an excellent demonstration of the ease with which individuals of different ideologies often can agree on concrete policy. Labor mediators report a similar phenomenon: the contestants cannot agree on criteria for settling their disputes but can agree on specific proposals. Similarly, when one administrator's objective turns out to be another's means, they often can agree on policy.

Agreement on policy thus becomes the only practicable test of the policy's correctness. And for one administrator to seek to win the other over to agreement on ends as well would accomplish nothing and create quite unnecessary controversy.

If agreement directly on policy as a test for "best" policy seems a poor substitute for testing the policy against its objectives, it ought to be remembered that objectives themselves have no ultimate validity other than they are agreed upon. Hence agreement is the test of "best" policy in both methods. But where the root method requires agreement on what elements in the decision constitute objectives and on which of these objectives should be sought, the branch method falls back on agreement whenever it can be found.

In an important sense, therefore, it is not irrational for an administrator to defend a policy as good without being able to specify what it is good for.

Non-Comprehensive Analysis (4b)

Ideally, rational-comprehensive analysis leaves out nothing important. But it is impossible to take everything important into consideration unless "important" is so narrowly defined that analysis is in fact quite limited. Limits on human intellectual capacities and on available information set definite limits to man's capacity to be comprehensive. In actual fact, therefore, no one can practice the rational-comprehensive method for really complex problems, and every administrator faced with a sufficiently complex problem must find ways drastically to simplify.

An administrator assisting in the formulation of agricultural economic policy cannot in the first place be competent on all possible policies. He cannot even comprehend one policy entirely. In planning a soil bank program, he cannot successfully anticipate the impact of higher or lower farm income on, say, urbanization—the possible consequent loosening of family ties, possible consequent eventual need for revisions in social security and further implications for tax problems arising out of new federal responsibilities for social security and municipal responsibilities for urban services. Nor, to follow another line of repercussions, can he work through the soil bank program's effects on prices for agricultural products in foreign markets and consequent implications for foreign relations, including those arising out of economic rivalry between the United States and the U.S.S.R.

In the method of successive limited comparisons, simplification is systematically achieved in two principal ways. First, it is achieved through limitation of policy comparisons to those policies that differ in relatively small degree from policies presently in effect. Such a limitation immediately reduces the number of alternatives to be investigated and also drastically simplifies the character of the investigation of each. For it is not necessary to undertake fundamental inquiry into an alternative and its consequences; it is necessary only to study those respects in which the proposed alternative and its consequences differ from the status quo. The empirical comparison of marginal differences among alternative policies that differ only marginally is, of course, a counterpart to the incremental or marginal comparison of values discussed above.[6]

Relevance as Well as Realism

It is a matter of common observation that in Western democracies public administrators and policy analysts in general do largely limit their analyses to incremental or marginal differ-

ences in policies that are chosen to differ only incrementally. They do not do so, however, solely because they desperately need some way to simplify their problems; they also do so in order to be relevant. Democracies change their policies almost entirely through incremental adjustments. Policy does not move in leaps and bounds.

The incremental character of political change in the United States has often been remarked. The two major political parties agree on fundamentals; they offer alternative policies to the voters only on relatively small points of difference. Both parties favor full employment, but they define it somewhat differently; both favor the development of water resources, but in slightly different ways; and both favor unemployment compensation, but not the same level of benefits. Similarly, shifts of policy within a party take place largely through a series of relatively small changes, as can be seen in their only gradual acceptance of the idea of governmental responsibility for support of the unemployed, a change in party positions beginning in the early 30's and culminating in a sense in the Employment Act of 1946.

Party behavior is in turn rooted in public attitudes, and political theorists cannot conceive of democracy's surviving in the United States in the absence of fundamental agreement on potentially disruptive issues, with consequent limitation of policy debates to relatively small differences in policy.

Since the policies ignored by the administrator are politically impossible and so irrelevant, the simplification of analysis achieved by concentrating on policies that differ only incrementally is not a capricious kind of simplification. In addition, it can be argued that, given the limits on knowledge within which policy-makers are confined, simplifying by limiting the focus to small

---

[6] A more precise definition of incremental policies and a discussion of whether a change that appears "small" to one observer might be seen differently by another is to be found in my "Policy Analysis," **48**, *American Economic Review* (June, 1958) p. 298.

variations from present policy makes the most of available knowledge. Because policies being considered are like present and past policies, the administrator can obtain information and claim some insight. Non-incremental policy proposals are therefore typically not only politically irrelevant but also unpredictable in their consequences.

The second method of simplification of analysis is the practice of ignoring important possible consequences of possible policies, as well as the values attached to the neglected consequences. If this appears to disclose a shocking shortcoming of successive limited comparisons, it can be replied that, even if the exclusions are random, policies may nevertheless be more intelligently formulated than through futile attempts to achieve a comprehensiveness beyond human capacity. Actually, however, the exclusions, seeming arbitrary or random from one point of view, need be neither.

Achieving a Degree of Comprehensiveness

Suppose that each value neglected by one policy-making agency were a major concern of at least one other agency. In that case, a helpful division of labor would be achieved, and no agency need find its task beyond its capacities. The shortcomings of such a system would be that one agency might destroy a value either before another agency could be activated to safeguard it or in spite of another agency's efforts. But the possibility that important values may be lost is present in any form of organization, even where agencies attempt to comprehend in planning more than is humanly possible.

The virtue of such a hypothetical division of labor is that every impor-

tant interest or value has its watchdog. And these watchdogs can protect the interests in their jurisdiction in two quite different ways: first, by redressing damages done by other agencies; and, second, by anticipating and heading off injury before it occurs.

In a society like that of the United States in which individuals are free to combine to pursue almost any possible common interest they might have and in which government agencies are sensitive to the pressures of these groups, the system described is approximated. Almost every interest has its watchdog. Without claiming that every interest has a sufficiently powerful watchdog, it can be argued that our system often can assure a more comprehensive regard for the values of the whole society than any attempt at intellectual comprehensiveness.

In the United States, for example, no part of government attempts a comprehensive overview of policy on income distribution. A policy nevertheless evolves, and one responding to a wide variety of interests. A process of mutual adjustment among farm groups, labor unions, municipalities and school boards, tax authorities, and government agencies with responsibilities in the fields of housing, health, highways, national parks, fire, and police accomplishes a distribution of income in which particular income problems neglected at one point in the decision processes become central at another point.

Mutual adjustment is more pervasive than the explicit forms it takes in negotiation between groups; it persists through the mutual impacts of groups upon each other even where they are not in communication. For all the imperfections and latent dangers in this ubiquitous process of mutual adjustment, it will often accomplish an adaptation of policies to a wider range of interests than could be done by one group centrally.

Note, too, how the incremental pattern of policy-making fits with the multiple pressure pattern. For when decisions are only incremental—closely related to known policies, it is easier for one group to anticipate the kind of moves another might make and easier too for it to make correction for injury already accomplished.[7]

Even partisanship and narrowness, to use pejorative terms, will sometimes be assets to rational decision-making, for they can doubly insure that what one agency neglects, another will not; they specialize personnel to distinct points of view. The claim is valid that effective rational coordination of the federal administration, if possible to achieve at all, would require an agreed set of values[8]—if "rational" is defined as the practice of the root method of decision-making. But a high degree of administrative coordination occurs as each agency adjusts its policies to the concerns of the other agencies in the process of fragmented decision-making I have just described.

For all the apparent shortcomings of the incremental approach to policy alternatives with its arbitrary exclusion coupled with fragmentation, when compared to the root method, the branch method often looks far superior. In the root method, the inevitable exclusion of factors is accidental, unsystematic, and not defensible by any argument so far developed, while in the branch method the exclusions

are deliberate, systematic, and defensible. Ideally, of course, the root method does not exclude; in practice it must.

Nor does the branch method necessarily neglect long-run considerations and objectives. It is clear that important values must be omitted in considering policy, and sometimes the only way long-run objectives can be given adequate attention is through the neglect of short-run considerations. But the values omitted can be either long-run or short-run.

Succession of Comparisons (5b)

The final distinctive element in the branch method is that the comparisons, together with the policy choice, proceed in a chronological series. Policy is not made once and for all; it is made and re-made endlessly. Policy-making is a process of successive approximation to some desired objectives in which what is desired itself continues to change under reconsideration.

Making policy is at best a very rough process. Neither social scientists, nor politicians, nor public administrators yet know enough about the social world to avoid repeated error in predicting the consequences of policy moves. A wise policy-maker consequently expects that his policies will achieve only part of what he hopes and at the same time will produce unanticipated consequences he would have preferred to avoid. If he proceeds through a *succession* of incremental changes, he avoids serious lasting mistakes in several ways.

In the first place, past sequences of policy steps have given him knowledge about the probable consequences of further similar steps. Second, he need not attempt big jumps toward his goals that would require predictions beyond

---

[7] The link between the practice of the method of successive limited comparisons and mutual adjustment of interests in a highly fragmented decision-making process adds a new facet to pluralist theories of government and administration.

[8] Herbert Simon, Donald W. Smithburg, and Victor A. Thompson, *Public Administration* (Alfred A. Knopf, 1950), p. 434.

his or anyone else's knowledge, because he never expects his policy to be a final resolution of a problem. His decision is only one step, one that if successful can quickly be followed by another. Third, he is in effect able to test his previous predictions as he moves on to each further step. Lastly, he often can remedy a past error fairly quickly—more quickly than if policy proceeded through more distinct steps widely spaced in time.

Compare this comparative analysis of incremental changes with the aspiration to employ theory in the root method. Man cannot think without classifying, without subsuming one experience under a more general category of experiences. The attempt to push categorization as far as possible and to find general propositions which can be applied to specific situations is what I refer to with the word "theory." Where root analysis often leans heavily on theory in this sense, the branch method does not.

The assumption of root analysts is that theory is the most systematic and economical way to bring relevant knowledge to bear on a specific problem. Granting the assumption, an unhappy fact is that we do not have adequate theory to apply to problems in any policy area, although theory is more adequate in some areas—monetary policy, for example—than in others. Comparative analysis, as in the branch method, is sometimes a systematic alternative to theory.

Suppose an administrator must choose among a small group of policies that differ only incrementally from each other and from present policy. He might aspire to "understand" each of the alternatives—for example, to know all the consequences of each aspect of each policy. If so, he would indeed require theory. In fact, however, he would usually decide that, *for policy-making purposes*, he need know, as explained above, only the consequences of each of those aspects of the policies in which they differed from one another. For this much more modest aspiration, he requires no theory (although it might be helpful, if available), for he can proceed to isolate probable differences by examining the differences in consequences associated with past differences in policies, a feasible program because he can take his observations from a long sequence of incremental changes.

For example, without a more comprehensive social theory about juvenile delinquency than scholars have yet produced, one cannot possibly understand the ways in which a variety of public policies—say on education, housing, recreation, employment, race relations, and policing—might encourage or discourage delinquency. And one needs such an understanding if he undertakes the comprehensive overview of the problem prescribed in the models of the root method. If, however, one merely wants to mobilize knowledge sufficient to assist in a choice among a small group of similar policies—alternative policies on juvenile court procedures, for example—he can do so by comparative analysis of the results of similar past policy moves.

Theorists and Practitioners

This difference explains—in some cases at least—why the administrator often feels that the outside expert or academic problem-solver is sometimes not helpful and why they in turn often urge more theory on him. And it explains why an administrator often feels more confident when "flying by the seat of his pants" than when following the advice of theorists. Theorists often ask the administrator to go the long way round to the solution of his problems, in effect ask him to follow the best canons of the scientific method, when the administrator knows that the best available theory will work less well than more modest incremental comparisons. Theorists do not realize that the administrator is often in fact practicing a systematic method. It would be foolish to push this explanation too far, for sometimes practical decision-makers are pursuing neither a theoretical approach nor successive comparisons, nor any other systematic method.

It may be worth emphasizing that theory is sometimes of extremely limited helpfulness in policy-making for at least two rather different reasons. It is greedy for facts; it can be constructed only through a great collection of observations. And it is typically insufficiently precise for application to a policy process that moves through small changes. In contrast, the comparative method both economizes on the need for facts and directs the analyst's attention to just those facts that are relevant to the fine choices faced by the decision-maker.

With respect to precision of theory, economic theory serves as an example. It predicts that an economy without money or prices would in certain specified ways misallocate resources, but this finding pertains to an alternative far removed from the kind of policies on which administrators need help. On the other hand, it is not precise enough to predict the consequences of policies restricting business mergers, and this is the kind of issue on which the administrators need help. Only in relatively restricted areas does economic theory achieve sufficient precision to go far in resolving policy questions; its helpfulness in policy-making is always so limited that it requires supplementation through comparative analysis.

Successive Comparison as a System

Successive limited comparisons is, then, indeed a method or system; it is not a failure of method for which administrators ought to apologize. None the less, its imperfections, which have not been explored in this paper, are many. For example, the method is without a built-in safeguard for all relevant values, and it also may lead the decision-maker to overlook excellent policies for no other reason than that they are not suggested by the chain of successive policy steps leading up to the present. Hence, it ought to be said that under this method, as well as under some of the most sophisticated variants of the root method— operations research, for example—policies will continue to be as foolish as they are wise.

Why then bother to describe the method in all the above detail? Because it is in fact a common method of policy formulation, and is, for complex problems, the principal reliance of administrators as well as of other policy analysts. And because it will be superior to any other decision-making method available for complex problems in many circumstances, certainly superior to a futile attempt at superhuman comprehensiveness. The reaction of the public administrator to the exposition of method doubtless will be less a discovery of a new method than a better acquaintance with an old. But by becoming more conscious of their practice of this method, administrators might practice it with more skill and know when to extend or constrict its use. (That they sometimes practice it effectively and sometimes not may explain the extremes of opinion on "muddling through," which is both praised as a highly sophisticated form of problem-solving and denounced as no method at all.

For I suspect that in so far as there is a system in what is known as "muddling through," this method is it.)

One of the noteworthy incidental consequences of clarification of the method is the light it throws on the suspicion an administrator sometimes entertains that a consultant or adviser is not speaking relevantly and responsibly when in fact by all ordinary objective evidence he is. The trouble lies in the fact that most of us approach policy problems within a framework given by our view of a chain of successive policy choices made up to the present. One's thinking about appropriate policies with respect, say, to urban traffic control is greatly influenced by one's knowledge of the incremental steps taken up to the present. An administrator enjoys an intimate knowledge of his past sequences that "outsiders" do not share, and his thinking and that of the "outsider" will consequently be different in ways that may puzzle both. Both may appear to be talking intelligently, yet each may find the other unsatisfactory. The relevance of the policy chain of succession is even more clear when an American tries to discuss, say, antitrust policy with a Swiss, for the chains of policy in the two countries are strikingly different and the two individuals consequently have organized their

knowledge in quite different ways.

If this phenomenon is a barrier to communication, an understanding of it promises an enrichment of intellectual interaction in policy formulation. Once the source of difference is understood, it will sometimes be stimulating for an administrator to seek out a policy analyst whose recent experience is with a policy chain different from his own.

This raises again a question only briefly discussed above on the merits of like-mindedness among government administrators. While much of organization theory argues the virtues of common values and agreed organizational objectives, for complex problems in which the root method is inapplicable, agencies will want among their own personnel two types of diversification: administrators whose thinking is organized by reference to policy chains other than those familiar to most members of the organization and, even more commonly, administrators whose professional or personal values or interests create diversity of view (perhaps coming from different specialties, social classes, geographical areas) so that, even within a single agency, decision-making can be fragmented and parts of the agency can serve as watchdogs for other parts.

Muddling Through—"Science" or Inertia?

YEHEZKEL DROR

In a much-quoted article published in the *Public Administration Review* in 1959, Charles E. Lindblom put

forth a brilliant justification of policy and decision making through "muddling through," that is through incremental change aimed at arriving at agreed-upon policies which are closely

Yehezkel Dror, "Muddling Through— 'Science' or Inertia?" Reprinted from the *Public Administration Review*, the journal of the American Society for Public Administration, XXIV, 3 (Sept. 1964) by permission of the publisher.

based on past experience.[1] As developed and expanded in other articles,[2] he presents a well-considered theory fully geared to the actual experience of practicing administrators and well designed to reinforce their actual behavior patterns by giving them the blessings of scientific approval.

Indeed, there can be no doubt that in comparison with the "rational-comprehensive" models of decision making commonly accepted in management sciences and their related disciplines, Lindblom's approach constitutes a very valuable contribution. It is more closely tied to reality, more sophisticated in theory, and more adjusted to human nature. Nevertheless, the question must be asked whether the favorable evaluation of "incremental change" and "muddling through" (in the sense of policy making through successive limited comparisons) does not, in some respects, constitute a dangerous overreaction.

More specifically, it is necessary to reexamine the "Science of 'Muddling Through' " thesis both in respect to its inherent validity and its potential impact on actual policy making and decision making practices. The possibilities for constructing a mixed optimum model of policy making, superior to both the "muddling through" and "rational-comprehensive" ones also requires attention, especially because of the neglect of such a possibility in the professional literature.

Conditions Limiting the Validity of the "Science of 'Muddling Through' " Thesis

Conceding the many penetrating insights in Lindblom's paper, there may nevertheless be a critical examination of two main elements of the "Science of 'Muddling Through' " thesis, namely the incremental nature of desired changes in policy, and agreement on policy as the criterion of its quality.

The basic strategy of incremental change, as stated by Lindblom, is one of maximizing security in making change. All reliable knowledge being based on the past, the only way to proceed without risk is by continuing in the same direction, limiting consideration of alternative policies "to those policies that differ in relatively small effect."[3] This is sound advice, provided certain conditions pertain—a requirement not adequately faced by Lindblom.

Unless three closely interrelated conditions are concurrently met, incremental change by "successive limited comparison" is not an adequate method for policy making. *These three essential conditions are: (1) the results of present policies must be in the main satisfactory (to the policy makers and the social strata on which they depend), so that marginal changes are sufficient for achieving an acceptable*

---

[1] See Charles E. Lindblom, "The Science of 'Muddling Through' " **19**, *Public Administration Review*, 79-88 (Spring, 1959). Unless otherwise noted, quotations from Lindblom included in the present paper are taken from that article.

[2] See especially Charles E. Lindblom, "Policy Analysis," **48**, *American Economic Review*, 298-312 (June 1958), and Albert O. Hirschman and Charles E. Lindblom, "Economic Development, Research and Development, Policy Making: Some Converging Views," **7**, *Behavioral Science*, 211-22 (April 1962). Both these papers are more careful in their conclusions than "The Science of 'Muddling Through'," both recognizing some limitations inherent in the method of "change through incremental comparison" and its locality-bound assumptions. In a recent book Lindblom further develops his ideas, but without changing this basic rationale. See David Braybrooke and Charles E. Lindblom, *A Strategy of Decision* (Free Press of Glencoe, 1963).

[3] Lindblom, "The Science of ' Muddling Through'," p. 84.

rate of improvements in policy-results; (2) there must be a high degree of continuity in the nature of the problems; (3) there must be a high degree of continuity in the available means for dealing with problems.

When the results of past policies are undesirable, it is often preferable to take the risks involved in radical new departures. For instance, in newly developing states aspiring to accelerated socio-economic development, the policies followed by the former colonial policy makers clearly do not constitute an acceptable basis to be followed with only incremental change. Similarly, in modern countries when changes in values make formerly accepted policy-results unacceptable, radical departures in policy are required despite the risk, for instance in respect to the segregation problem in the United States.

When there are no past policies in respect to a discrete policy-issue, incremental change is in fact impossible. For instance, many of the problems faced during the New Deal had novel characteristics making most policies (other than doing nothing) a radical departure from the past.

Changes in knowledge—technological and behavioral—put at the disposal of policy makers new means of action, which, unless ignored, lead to radically new policies. The best illustrations are provided in military technology, where "incremental change" results in the often noted tendency of a nation's armed forces to be excellently prepared for the last war. Similar illustrations can be cited in most spheres of social action where innovations in knowledge take place, such as medicine (policy making in regard to smoking) and education (utilization of programmed teaching-machines).

The three conditions essential to the validity of the "muddling through" thesis are most likely to prevail where there is a high degree of social stability. Under conditions of stability, routine is often the best policy, and, change being at a slow rate, incremental policy-change is often optimal. But, even in the most stable societies, many of today's qualitatively most important problems are tied up with high speed changes in levels of aspirations, the nature of issues, and the available means of action, and require therefore a policy making method different from "muddling through."[4]

A similar conclusion may be reached from examination of the reliance on agreement on policy as the criterion of the policy's quality. Under conditions of stability, when all relevant parties have a more or less clear image of the expected results of a certain policy, with a high correlation of subjective and objective probability, a policy agreed upon will ordinarily involve little risk of catastrophe; also, under such conditions, it is in fact much easier to agree on a discrete policy than on abstract goals. In contrast, under conditions of high-rate change, ignorance can produce agreement upon a catastrophic policy; under such conditions, moreover, it is often much easier to agree on abstract or operational goals (e.g., "raising the standard of living," "increase net per-capita product by two per cent annually") than on policies, there being no background of shared experience to serve as a basis for consensus on policy. Lest the reader reach the conclusion that these comments apply only to new development countries, let him consider military policy, where decisions agreed

---

[4] In his "Policy Analysis," *ibid.*, Lindblom explicitly recognizes that his analysis applies to the United States and other "stable, well-established, deeply rooted democracies" (p. 30). But he fails to pursue this limitation and does not realize that there is today no country, including the United States, "stable" enough to fit his analysis.

upon by experienced military personnel were rejected, following their dissection by McNamara's "whiz kids."

The formula that "agreement" equals "high quality" is the more dangerous because of its appeal to a value highly regarded in democratic ideology, as attested to by the abundance of "administration by consent" literature. It is, therefore, highly necessary to emphasize that agreement should follow examination of the consequences of policy and not be substituted for it, in all save the most familiar and stable policy areas.

The conclusion is inescapable, therefore, that the "Science of 'Muddling Through'" thesis has limited validity. It may be more valid for a larger number of policy areas in a relatively stable society, such as the United States, than in countries engaged in high-rate directed social change. But even in the United States many of the most critical policy problems involve factors changing at a high rate of speed.

The Impact of "Muddling Through" on Actual Policy Making

Although Lindblom's thesis includes a number of reservations, these are insufficient to alter its main impact as an ideological reinforcement of the pro-inertia and anti-innovation forces prevalent in all human organizations, administrative and policy making.[5] The actual tendency of most organizations is to limit the search for alterna-

[5] Even more dangerous is acceptance of the "incremental change" attitude by social scientists, as it reduces their functions as an innovating social factor. By limiting their suggestions to incremental change, the social scientist also significantly reduces his utility to policy makers, the latter being well aware of incremental alternatives and looking to the social scientist for new ideas. See Yehezkel Dror, "The Barriers Facing Policy Science," 7, *The American Behavioral Scientist*, 3-7 (January, 1964), esp. pp. 4-5.

tives to the minimum; there is little danger in real life then, that administration will become bogged down in exhaustive search for all alternatives and full enumeration of consequences, in order to achieve "rational-comprehensive" policy making. The "rational-comprehensive" model has at least the advantage of stimulating administrators to get a little outside their regular routine, while Lindblom's model justifies a policy of "no effort."

Taken together, the limited validity of the "muddling through" thesis and its inertia-reinforcing implications constitute a very serious weakness. This criterion in no way diminishes Lindblom's pioneering role in pointing out the shortcomings of the "rational-comprehensive" policy making model. This may well prove to be one of his most important contributions, since the counter-model of "muddling through" is itself open to serious doubts. A choice between these two models would be difficult, but, luckily, may be avoided through reliance upon a third model for public policy making.

A Normative Optimum Model for Policy Making

The bases for an optimum model for policy making are the following assumptions: (1) Optimum policy making involves an effort to increase rationality-content, through more explication of goals, extensive search for new alternatives, conscious attempts to elaborate expectations, with an explicit cut off point, and some formulation of decision-criteria. (2) Extrarational processes play a significant role in optimal policy making on complex issues. This is not only unavoidable because of lack of resources and capacity for complete rationality, but in fact, makes a positive contribution to better policy making. Intuitive judgment, holistic impressions derived from immersion in a situation, and creative invention of new alternatives are illustrations of extrarational phases of optimal policy making. The importance of such processes is not only acknowledged by all experienced policy makers but also by some modern research in psychology, for instance the works of Carl Rogers and Michael Polanyi discussing "experience" and "tacit knowledge" as sources of insight and understanding. (3) These extrarational policy making phases can be improved by various means, such as case discussions, sensitivity sessions and "brain storming." Similarly, the rational policy making phases can be improved, for instance, through increasing the input (especially time), increasing the knowledge and qualifications of policy-practitioners, and by setting up special "think" units for the improvement of conceptual analytical tools. (4) Actual policy making in modern states has a tendency to follow precedents, "incremental change," "muddling through," inertia and routine. Compared with the rate of change in the problems faced by policy, in the levels of aspiration, in the aspiration, in the available alternatives, and in knowledge on the policy making process itself (such as decision-techniques and group dynamics) —most contemporary policy making practices lag behind. This can and should be improved.

A reprocessing of both the "comprehensive rationality" and the "successive limited comparison" models in light of these assumptions may result in a normative-optimum model for policy making which includes the following main features:[6]

---

[6] For a detailed discussion of this model, see Yehezkel Dror, *Public Policymaking Reexamined* (Chandler Publishing Co., 1965). Part Two.

—Some clarification of values, objectives, and decision-criteria.
—Identification of alternatives, accompanied by a conscious effort to consider new alternatives (through survey of comparative literature, experience and available theories) and to stimulate creative alternative innovation.
—Preliminary estimation of expected pay-off of various alternatives and decisions whether a strategy of minimal risk or a strategy of innovation is preferable.
—If the first, the "successive limited comparison" model should be followed. If the latter, the next element is establishment of a cut-off for considering possible results of alternative policies and identification of main expected results, relying on available knowledge and intuition.
—The test of the optimum policy is that it is agreed upon by the various analysts after full and frank discussion of stages 1 to 4.
—A conscious effort is made to decide whether the problem is important enough to make analysis more comprehensive.
—Theory and experience, rationality and extrarationality all are relied upon, the composition of the mix depending upon their availability and the nature of the problem.
—Explicit arrangements are made to improve the quality of policy making through systematic learning from experience, stimulation of initiative and creativity, staff development and encouragement of intellectual effort.

The Need Redefined

To state the problem of policy making as a choice between the "rational-comprehensive" and the "successive limited comparison" methods is misleading and dangerous. It is misleading because other policy making models can be devised. It is dangerous because it leads either to an effort to achieve the impossible or to an encouragement of inertia and a continuation of the status quo.

What is needed is a model which fits reality while being directed toward its improvement, and which can in fact be applied to policy making while motivating a maximum effort to arrive at better policies. By all the criteria, the model presented in "The Science of 'Muddling Through'" is inadequate, having limited validity, and constituting a barrier to the improvement of policy making. Its favorable acceptance, the result in part of its many merits, reflects the widespread disposition of administrators and students of public administration to accept the present as a guide to the future, and to regard contemporary practice as a norm for the future.

The broad acceptance of the "muddling through" thesis indicates that inertia and the tendency to "incremental change" are in fact widespread phenomena. This in itself serves to emphasize the need for models of policy making stressing the limits of such an approach and pointing out the needs and possibilities for better policy making. The normative optimum model presented above is only one variation of such a model, many others being feasible.

It is time for administrative science to enter into the area of inquiry, illuminated by Lindblom, and take up the challenge of providing models for policy making instead of devoting time and resources to managerial techniques, on the one hand, and "Grand Theories" on the other. In doing so, the search should be directed at constructing normative models for policy-making which combine realism and idealism. The models should be near enough to reality to serve as feasible guides for action; at the same time, the models should aspire to a higher quality of public policy making and serve as a means to encourage the improvement of reality.[7]

---

[7] For a good illustration of the approach needed in administrative science, see Charles J. Hitch and Roland N. McKean, *The Economics of Defense in the Nuclear Age* (Harvard University Press, 1961).

Contexts for Change and Strategy: A Reply

CHARLES E. LINDBLOM

The two major objections that Yehezkel Dror brings against my model of decision making through "muddling through" are to be taken very seriously. I grant the first objection immediately; the method is unquestionably one of less than universal use-

Charles E. Lindblom, "Contexts for Change and Strategy: A Reply." Reprinted from the *Public Administration Review*, the Journal of the American Society for Public Administration, XXIV, 3 (Sept. 1964) by permission of the publisher.

fulness. I welcome any attempt to specify more precisely than I have done the circumstances in which "muddling through" is a defensible strategy for decision making.

I have, however, further refined and detailed this model, referring to it as the strategy of disjointed incrementalism, in *A Strategy of Decision*.[1] There it is argued that in a political democracy like that of the United States and probably also in a relatively stable dic-

---

[1] David Braybrooke and Charles E. Lindblom (The Free Press of Glencoe, 1963).

tatorship like that of the Soviet Union, public policy decisions are typically of the kind that call for the disjointed incremental approach. Typically, policy decisions meet Dror's three essential conditions for the application of my model: "(1) the results of present policies must be in the main satisfactory to the policy makers . . . ; (2) there must be a high degree of continuity in the nature of the problems; and (3) there must be a high degree of continuity in the available means for dealing with problems." Examples are policy making on taxation, social security, national security, reform of the judiciary, foreign aid, administrative organization, antitrust, auto traffic, zoning, and agriculture price supports, among others.

Dror's second charge—that the strategy "cannot but serve as an ideological reinforcement of the pro-inertia and anti-innovation forces prevalent in all human organizations"—I am skeptical about. To be sure, it is not a charge that can be conclusively refuted; but Braybrooke and I discuss it at some length. Logically speaking, one can make changes in the social structure as rapidly through a sequence of incremental steps as through drastic—hence less frequent—alterations. Psychologically and sociologically speaking, decision makers can sometimes bring themselves to make changes easily and quickly only because the changes are incremental and are not fraught with great risk of error or of political conflict. American society, for example, is a rapidly changing society. One can argue that it can change as fast as it does because it usually avoids big controversies over big changes. To be sure, anyone who proposes to scrap the world and start over again sounds more radical than one who proposes to start from the here-and-now, making only a sequence of modest changes

in the social structure. But through which of these styles of thought does the continuing transformation of American society receive its impetus?

For administrative decisions, I do not agree that "the 'rational-comprehensive' model has at least the applied advantage of stimulating administrators to get a little outside their regular routine, while Lindblom's model justifies a policy of 'no effort.'" Nothing would be more paralyzing to an administrator than to take seriously the prescription of the rational comprehensive model that he make no decision until he canvas all possible alternative ways of reaching well formulated goals, making sure that he has investigated every possible major consequence of each possible alternative. He can only "get a little outside" his regular routine by practicing some strategy that gives him some direction without asking for the impossible. And this is what the strategy does. For the particular component features of the strategy constitute in effect answers to questions that an administrator must face as to what to do in the face of a decision that cannot be comprehensively analyzed or mastered. They constitute an alternative to mere guesswork, intuition, or random analysis.

Nevertheless, I am quite willing to entertain the possibility that in some subtle respects the strategy has effects on the decision maker's attitudes that might dispose him either more or less favorably toward preservation of the status quo than would some alternative strategy for decision making. It is a question, pertinent to any strategy for decision making, that bears even more investigation than Braybrooke and I have given it.

Dror goes on to ask what kind of model of decision making we need. We need a number of them, I would say, because there are a number of decision making methods and strategies in actual use, each of which needs clarification. We do not need "a model" as I understand Dror to suggest; and it is perhaps a defect of his own proposed model that, trying to encompass too many varied aspects of decision making, his propositions become simply a series of discrete observations and prescriptions on decision making which, taken as a group, are not tightly interlocked and which,

taken one by one, are not each generally valid or acceptable. Moreover, Dror asks that a model: (a) "fits reality" while (b) "being directed toward its improvement" and (c) "which can in fact be applied to policy making" while (d) "motivating a maximum effort to arrive at better policies." I doubt whether any reader, on reflecting on these four criteria for a model, will accept them in combination.

HEW Grapples with PPBS

ELIZABETH B. DREW

As interesting as watching what happens to government when confronted with program planning is observing what happens to program planning when confronted with government. In August 1965, President Johnson called a breakfast meeting of his Cabinet officers and informed them that he was ordering a Planning-Programming-Budgeting System (PPBS), which had shown promising results in the Pentagon, installed throughout the rest of the Executive Branch. Inquiring reporters were told by government officials that shortly we could establish the relative pay-offs of, say, building a dam in Florida, or improving Indian schools, or eradicating syphilis. Henry Rowen, formerly of the Pentagon and now president of the Rand Corporation, was installed as Assistant Director of the Budget Bureau, whence he dispatched skilled program planners throughout the nervous and dubious government agencies. Two years and several attempts at

Elizabeth B. Drew, "HEW Grapples with PPBS," *The Public Interest*, **8** (Summer, 1967), 9-24.

PPBS studies later, the most thoughtful practitioners of the art are arriving at a considerably narrower—though probably no less significant—definition of the possible, and of where PPB's most valuable contributions might lie.

How well PPB has worked, agency by agency, has depended more than anything on how seriously the man at the top has taken it, how hard he worked to attract good people to do the job, how much he lent his authority to the adoption of a system of hard analysis. Impartial and informed judges give the Department of Health, Education and Welfare the highest marks. This makes HEW's experience with program planning all the more illuminating. *The Public Interest* has been given an opportunity to examine HEW's first PPB studies. They provide the best and most interesting indicators around of the state of the art.

HEW last year completed four PPB studies: (1) of selected disease control programs—motor vehicle and passenger injury prevention programs, cancer, arthritis, syphilis, and tuberculosis; (2) of "human investment" programs —vocational rehabilitation, adult basic education, work-experience and training, vocational education, and Title I of the Elementary and Secondary Education Act; (3) of possible programs for improving maternal and child health care; and (4) of potentials for improving income maintenance—through social security increases, larger welfare programs, or a negative income tax. These subjects were chosen for the first studies simply because they seemed to be important, and they appeared at the outset to be amenable to some kind of analysis; and these rather arbitrary criteria had to be settled for because of the pressures of time.

Serious discussion between the agencies and the Budget Bureau on the following year's budget begins in the late summer; therefore any agency analysis of its own programs and proposals must be well in hand by then; therefore sophisticated and complicated analysis such as PPB should probably begin late in the preceding year. Yet HEW's program planning operation, under Assistant Secretary William Gorham, was not fully staffed and ready to plunge in until May of 1966. Gorham's staff was forced to select. In fact it selected five areas of study, but the fifth, comparing programs to aid higher education, foundered on an astonishing lack of basic information.

The generally inadequate information on which to base a program-planning study is one of the factors that has led to revised estimates of what PPB can accomplish, at least in the near term. Program planners now also have a heightened appreciation of the unmeasurable, and of the limitations on their ability to establish honest measures of commensurability between programs. And any illusions—sophisticated program planners were less susceptible to these than were outsiders —that PPB would sweep before it

defensive bureaucracies or powerful client groups or cynical politics should be fairly given up by now. Finally, hosts of civil servants will not think better just because a few people think it would be nice if they would. But gearing tighter thinking—which is essentially all PPB is—into the budget system helps, because the budget is power.

A Lack of Information

Those who picture Washington as one mass of files and computers containing more information than they would like will be comforted by the experiences of program-planners in attempting to evaluate on-going programs. Whatever the files and computers do contain, there is precious little in them about how many and whom the programs are reaching, and whether they are doing what they are supposed to do. If the purpose of an adult basic education program is to teach people how to read and write, the Office of Education might reasonably be expected to know how many people thereby actually learned how to read and write, but it does not. The higher education study was delayed because there simply was too little information about who was receiving federal scholarships, or what happened to all those who had been receiving National Defense Education Act loans since 1958. Did they finish college? Did it affect their subsequent careers? No answers. The Public Health Service might be expected to know whether its various health services are in fact making people healthier, but it does not. The study of disease control was to have encompassed more diseases, but so little was known about the effective treatment of alcoholism and heart disease that these components had to be dropped. Those working on the income maintenance study found that the Welfare Administration could not tell them very much about the public assistance caseload—who was on welfare, where did they come from, why were they on it, what they needed in order to get off.

These simple statistical gaps are inexplicable, and in time they should be filled. More difficult to cope with are the quantitative and behavioral factors which must be part of many PPB formulations, yet for which there is no informational basis. The authors of the study on income maintenance, for example, pointed out that they could find no "supportable answers" to the following questions:

> What will be the labor force participation of recipients with an earned income exemption under Public Assistance?
>
> How will the poor react to negative income tax plans? How will the near-poor react?
>
> What type of expenditures will the poor make with increased income?
>
> How will improvements in income affect the educational attainment of children of the poor?

"Although answers to these questions will always contain a speculative element, they can hardly be raised without better data." Obviously, the lack of such data limits the usefulness of any study of proposals for raising the income level of the poor.

The study of disease control was similarly, but somewhat more surprisingly, beset by quandaries about what assumptions could be made. There is not even material, as William Gorham points out, to make a documentable argument that people who receive regular medical attention are healthier than those who do not! It is known that the wealthier are healthier than the poor, but how much this

has to do with doctors, and how much with characteristics of the entire environment, no one can honestly say. There are those who argue that the medical input is a relatively small one. Moreover, doctors do not think quantitatively; the program planners found that their frame of reference of "prevalence" and "probabilities" and "pay-offs" was alien to the medical experts. The disease control paper is, therefore, heavily dependent upon what are at best educated guesses.

Finally, the limits on the information available to the program planners restricted the ability of the studies to shed light on the most effective route to even narrowly defined goals. Having given up on the idea of comparing the relative pay-offs involved in helping the elderly or drop-outs, in curing cancer or improving the teaching of math, HEW's program planners directed their first studies to "sub-objectives" simply defined: saving lives, raising future earnings, improving the health of children. Yet the disease control study can only discuss the relative effectiveness in saving lives of five disease control programs on which there was sufficient information, omitting such prevalent or lethal illnesses as heart and kidney disease, or emphysema. The human investment study is informative so far as it goes, but it goes only as far as HEW's outer walls, excluding information on such relevant programs as Manpower Development and Training, run by the Labor Department, or the Job Corps, run by the Office of Economic Opportunity. (Even if there were inter-departmental PPB, Labor and OEO have not yet gathered data entirely comparable to HEW's.)

Some of the studies are more conscientious than are others about pointing out assumptions which are only guesses. There are, in fact, wide variations in the styles of HEW's PPB papers. To be sure, they are not entries in any literary competition, though their general style level is higher than that of many, many government documents. The paper on human investment is well organized and clearly stated. But others at times reach levels of near-unintelligibility:

The basis for estimating economic benefits is a comparison of the program alternatives to syphilis in an uncontrolled situation, this provides an analyses [sic] of the basic program. This is not a very real alternative since it is unlikely that syphilis will ever become an uncontrolled disease, until it is erradicated [sic] worldwide. (Disease Control)

Some belabor the obvious, are super-repetitive (we shall discuss . . . we are discussing . . . we have just discussed), are littered with references to arcane studies, leave the reader to find the page which explains the chart, and serve up those vague euphemisms at which bureaucrats specialize. My favorite is in a section on family planning, which refers to "teen-age girls and low-income women with three or more children" as "high-risk groups." Finally, and most disconcertingly, some of the figures in the charts on benefit-cost ratios have been afflicted with typographical errors. (HEW has supplied corrected figures for the purpose of this article.)

The Economics of Disease Control

Despite its weaknesses, the disease control study is an interesting example of simple cost-effectiveness techniques applied to a set of programs, resulting in better information about the payoffs of current programs and of selected alternatives, about which programs are ready for broader application and which need more controlled experimentation, and about the rela-

tive pay-offs of programs involving different kinds of diseases—i.e., their commensurability. Thus the relative priority of spending money as between the diseases could be established. For all of its gaps, the study, say its authors, provides "a basis for choice and decision that was unavailable previously."

The first step is to define the objectives of the programs. The purposes of HEW's disease control programs "are aimed at assisting state and community organizations in the development, operation and improvement of activities to prevent disease and injury or to minimize the health effects through better diagnosis and care."

Programs may achieve objectives the following ways:
   a. demonstrate and test the application of scientific advances to patient care,
   b. provide for additional case finding personnel,
   c. provide training for health personnel in patient care, and technical procedures, and
   d. improve the quality and coverage of medical practice.

Because of the limitations of the available data, however, for the purposes of the study the objective was held to be simply the reduction of the number of deaths as a result of the disease or a reduction of its morbidity. The five disease areas included in the study—injury from motor vehicle accidents, cancer, arthritis, syphilis, tuberculosis—are all either diseases that still are health problems although technology exists for effective control, or where technology is in early developmental stages or non-existent.

The technology for effectively controlling tuberculosis and syphilis is available. The technology for effective control of specific cancer sites "has only recently become available and in most cases is still under development." "Arthritis," quoting the study again, "includes a number of specific diseases where knowledge does not exist to permit prevention, control or even effective amelioration of crippling and/or disabling symptoms in a large number of patients. The limited knowledge that is available is not widely disseminated and only a small portion of the estimated 10 to 13 million people suffering from arthritis have access to good quality diagnosis and care. The federal concern here is to assure that more people receive better care," through demonstrative projects, training of physicians and technicians, and developing methods of diagnosis and treatment. The Public Health Service has only begun to concern itself with the problem of motor vehicle injuries. "The magnitude of this problem," the study points out, "would indicate a major interest for all health agencies."

Having established the objectives, the next step is to establish criteria for judging alternative methods of reaching the objectives. The disease control study used two criteria: the cost per death averted, and the benefit-cost ratio.

The cost per death averted is the cost of the program over five years, divided by the number of deaths averted as a result of the program. The cost is an average cost figure. The cost of averting a death from, for example, cervical cancer, could be from under $2,000 to over $7,000; the average cost used for this study was $3,470, arrived at as follows: "Of the 34,000 lives expected to be saved due to the programs through 1972, 30,000 of these have an average cost of about $2,000; 2,300 have an average cost of over $3,500 and 400 have an average cost of over $7,000. While it is possible to add additional lives saved at the lower figure, any significant investment of funds in this program would probably be oriented toward the more expensive cases thus averaging over $7,000."

The second criterion, the benefit-cost ratio, was also used because of the limitations of using the cost per death averted as the sole criterion: it makes no distinction regarding the ages at which the various deaths are averted, and there is no way to rank those diseases which are not primarily killers (arthritis). The benefit-cost ratio is, simply, the amount of dollars invested divided into the dollars saved. The dollars saved are estimated on the basis of dollars "that would have been spent on medical care—doctor's fees, hospital services, drugs, etc.—and indirect savings such as the earnings saved because the patient did not die or was not incapacitated due to illness or injury. The average lifetime earnings for different age groups is related to the age at which death occurs and a calculation of the present value of lost lifetime earnings. For example, if a twenty-seven year old man died this year of one of the diseases, his aggregate earnings would have been estimated at $245,000 had he lived a full life. However, discounting this at 4 percent to the current year, the economic loss is actually closer to $125,000. Included in this analysis are economic losses based on future earnings discounted to present value."

Obviously, this is a rather crude measure of productivity lost, but it is, as the program planners point out, "better than nothing." They also realize that economic loss and death do not encompass all of the damage caused by disease. "Pain and the impact on family relationships are among the more obvious additional items. We do not know how to bring such items into this kind of analysis as yet, but it seems likely that these additional considerations argue in the same direction as the other benefits. . . . We have no reason at this moment to believe that such considerations would have changed the relative preferences among programs."

Auto Injuries

To take a specific example, the study examined eight alternative methods for reducing motor vehicle injury:

1. Driver Licensing—establishing a medical screening program for licensing;
2. Reduce Driver Drinking—to educate people not to drink before driving;
3. Pedestrian Injury—to educate "accident prone" pedestrians how to cross the street;
4. Seat Belt Use—to encourage people to use seat belts;
5. Restraint Devices—to educate people to obtain and use additional safety restraining devices;
6. Motorcycle Injury—to encourage motorcyclists to use helmets and eye shields to avoid fatal injury;
7. Driver Skill Improvement—establishing a nation-wide driver training program;
8. Emergency Medical Services—providing grants to communities to aid in upgrading the quality of training and facilities available to accident victims from the general public, ambulance attendants, and in hospital emergency rooms.

Following is the computation of the benefit-cost ratio and the cost per death averted of these eight programs:

Motor Vehicle Injury Control Alternatives 1968-1972*

Program	PHS[2] Cost[3] ($ millions)	Savings[2] ($ millions)	Cost Ratio Benefit	Deaths Averted	Cost Per Death Averted
Seat Belt Use	$ 2.0	$2,728	1351.4*	22,930	$ 87
Restraint Devices	.6	681	1117.1	5,811	100
Pedestrian Injury	1.1	153	144.3	1,650	600
Motorcyclist Helmets	7.4	413	55.6	2,398	3,000
Reduce Driver Drinking	28.5	613	21.5	5,340	5,300
Improve Driver License	6.1	23	3.8	442	13,800
Emergency Medical Services	721.5[1]	1,726	2.4	16,000	45,000
Driver Skills	750.5	1,287	1.7	8,515	88,000

* Numbers have been rounded to a single decimal point from three decimal points; therefore ratio may not be exact result of dividing column 1 into column 2 as they appear here.
[1] Includes $300 million State matching funds
[2] Public Health Service
[3] Discounted

Obviously, the driver skills improvers took into account that the benefits ment and the emergency medical services programs have the poorest payoffs in terms of both cost-effectiveness —for each dollar invested they yield $2.4 and $1.7 respectively—and in cost per death averted. Yet the policymak- of the emergency medical services pro- gram could eventually reach more than just victims of auto accidents, and therefore deemed it worthy of support despite its low cost-effectiveness ratio.

A major limitation of the findings was that very little is known about the true effectiveness of a program of trying to persuade people to use seat belts, not to drive while drunk, to use other restraining devices. "Although this level of confidence would make one wary about promoting these programs," the study says, "their low cost and high potential benefits would warrant support." These studies also do not take into account possible improvements in the safety features of the cars themselves, if there are any in the next few years. And while we are on the subject of the automobile companies, this study is an interesting contribution to the argument over whether the best route to improved auto safety is through improving drivers or cars.

Cancer

Four cancer site programs of early detection and treatment were studied for their relative effectiveness: uterine cervix, breast, head and neck, and colon-rectum. All four programs were studied at two alternative program levels, A and B.

Cancer Control Alternatives 1968-1972

Program	PHS Costs (millions)[1]	Total Costs (millions)[2]	Savings (millions)[2]	Benefit Cost Ratio	Deaths Averted	Cost Per Death Averted
A—						
Uterine Cervix	$97.8	$155.2	$1,380.0	8.9	44,084	$ 3,520
Breast	17.7	22.5	101.0	4.5	2,936	7,663
Head and Neck	13.2	12.6	10.1	.8	303	41,584
Colon-Rectum	13.3	12.6	6.4	.5	288	43,750
B—						
Uterine Cervix	73.7	118.7	1,071.0	9.0	34,206	3,470
Breast	8.1	10.1	43.7	4.3	1,284	7,866
Head and Neck	8.1	7.8	8.9	1.1	268	29,104
Colon-Rectum	7.7	7.3	3.7	.5	170	42,941

[1] Grant Awards
[2] Discounted

From this, the program planners concluded that, in the case of cervical cancer, program B, with a slightly higher benefit cost ratio should be supported over A (containing higher-cost screening elements), with A recommended as an alternative should more funds become available. The breast cancer program, on the other hand, shows a slightly higher cost-benefit ratio and lower cost per death averted with the more expensive program. "This indicates," say the program planners, "that the higher cost breast cancer control program would have a somewhat higher priority than certain elements of the uterine cervix program." This study also led them to conclude that improved technology for detection of head and neck and colon-rectum cancers should be further developed before their detection program is expanded.

In contrast to these four cancer detection programs, HEW's lung cancer program is a prevention program, trying to persuade people not to smoke, using mass media, school programs, special demonstrations, education of physicians and dentists. (See chart next page.)

Arthritis

Three alternative arthritis programs, with different emphases, were compared:

1. The establishment of 45 centers, and 1,125 clinics; the training of 9,000 physicians

Lung Cancer Alternatives
(Smoking Curb)
(1968-1972)

Program	Program Costs (millions)	Savings (millions)	Benefit Cost Ratio	Deaths Averted	Cost Per Death Averted
A. Current Program	$ 46.9	$268	5.7	7,000	$6,700
B. Current Program + Professional Education	84.9	635	7.5	16,000	5,306
C. Current Program + Mass/Media	76.9	531	6.9	13,500	5,696
D. All Programs	114.9	875	7.6	22,000	5,222
E. Professional Education Alone	38.0	367	9.6	9,000	4,222
F. Mass/Media Alone	30.0	263	8.8	6,500	4,615

and serving 1,287,000 patients in order to make improved diagnostic and care facilities available to more people.

2. The establishment of 9 centers and 180 clinics; the training of 1,800 physicians and serving 243,360 patients in order to demonstrate and evaluate the feasibility of expanding the program.

3. A program involving the establishment of 1,000 clinics, training 1,000 physicians, and serving 936,000 patients to improve the quality of arthritis diagnosis and care.

Since arthritis is not primarily a killer, the benefit-cost ratio is the most pertinent measure. The study showed the following:

Arthritis Program Alternatives
1968-1972

Program	HEW Costs (millions)	Savings[1] (millions)	Benefit Cost	Number Patients	HEW Cost Per Patient Seen
45 centers 1,125 Clinics (12 years)	$225	$10,510	46.7	1,287,000	$175
1,000 Clinics (13 years)	138	7,645	55.4	936,000	147
9 Centers 180 Clinics (7 years)	47	1,985	42.2	243,360	193
9 Centers 180 Clinics (5 years 1968-1972)	37.6	1,489[2]	37.5	229,320	168

[1] Not discounted—indirect savings only
[2] Discounted

From this, the study concluded "that before undertaking a major long term program, a pilot program (alternative 2) should be undertaken to demonstrate and evaluate the program components."

Syphilis and Tuberculosis

Three alternative syphilis programs were examined:

1. The current program, which includes research, a control grant program to states to help provide for epidemiologists to follow up cases. A significant element—a blood screening program—is paid for privately and is associated with pre-marital medical check, blood bank operations, military service medicals, etc. These costs are included in total program costs since they are directly related to control objectives.

2. An intensified epidemiology program which increases program grants but holds research and blood screening at current levels.

3. An eradication program—a research effort, expanded program grants and extension of blood screening to a larger population base and its inclusion in all hospital pre-admission procedures.

The analysis showed:

Syphilis Control Alternatives 1968-1972

Program	PHS Costs (millions)	Total[2] (millions)	Savings[1] (millions)	Benefit Cost Ratio	Prevalence[4] 1972	Deaths Averted[3]	Cost Per Death Averted
Current	$55.0	$179.3	$2,993	16.7	239,850	11,590	$22,252
Epidemiology	58.5	182.8	3,006	16.4	218,569	12,509	20,880
Eradication	80.3	261.6	3,063	11.7	14,890	15,071	22,938

[1] Discounted
[2] Adds private insurance costs for serologic screening
[3] Based on uncontrolled syphilis
[4] 1965—prevalence 600,000

From this it was concluded that "there does not seem to be a significant difference between the current program and that of intensified epidemiology. An increase of $3.5 million PHS costs over the five-year period (6 percent) would lead to a reduction in deaths of 919 (11 percent) and a reduction in prevalence of 21,000 (9 percent). . . . A 45 percent increase in funds results in a reduction in prevalence of better than 85 percent and a similar reduction in annual deaths. The benefits of this five-year effort beyond 1972 can be expected to yield an increasing benefit-cost ratio. Despite the attractiveness of a five-year eradication program, the current program is recommended with selected reinstatement of hospital sero-logical screening and an objective of moving toward syphilis eradication in ten years. The productivity of the current program would be improved—perhaps significantly—with the additional serological screenings. The effect of this component will be tested before an early build-up to an eradication program is supported."

For the last disease covered in the study, tuberculosis, five alternatives were examined:

1. Current program—research, state control program grants, epidemiology support;

2. Accelerated program—research and additional control program grants;

3. Concentrated program—re-

search and a control program targeted for specific geographic areas of population groups with high tuberculosis rates;

4. Prevention program—involving adding isoniazid to bread and flour products.

There are currently about 100,000 active cases of tuberculosis, with an annual death rate of 8,000. The estimated current annual losses from tuberculosis are about $1.1 billion.

The PPB analysis showed the following:

Tuberculosis Alternatives
1968-1972

Program	PHS Control Program (millions)	Savings[1] (millions)	Benefit Cost Ratio	Deaths Averted	Cost Per Death Averted	Preva-lence[2] 1972
Current	$130	$ 573	4.4	5,700	$22,800	80,000
Accelerated	201	1,598	8.0	7,170	28,000	30,000
Concentrated	170	1,093	6.4	7,085	24,000	55,000
Prevention	432	2,214	5.1	7,945	54,000	10,000

[1] Discounted
[2] 1965—prevalence 100,000

Obviously, the most efficient program is the accelerated one, with a payoff of eight, as opposed to 4.4 for the current program, and 6.4 for a concentrated one. Yet "from the standpoint of deaths averted," the analysts concluded, "the accelerated and concentrated programs have no advantage over the current program. However, the accelerated program obviously would be attractive from the standpoint of the possible seventy percent reduction in the prevalence of tuberculosis." The problem with the fourth program is that it is dependent upon acceptance of a program of placing isoniazid in flour products. "The history of fluoridation," the study says, "does not make one sanguine about the prospects for acceptance of a proposal to add a drug to food products." (How much *this* assumption has been studied is not said.) The analysts ended by suggesting that "A reoriented current program—concentration on areas with high tuberculosis incidence—can be expected to improve the benefit projections. Additional analysis and experience should show how

productive this program might be and would indicate if additional modifications are warranted."

Some Conclusions

Having thus examined alternatives within programs, the final step of the disease control study was to measure the impact of all of the disease control programs by their commensurable data components: program costs, savings due to programs, benefit-cost ratio, number of deaths averted, program cost per death averted.

The analysis showed the relationships presented in the table on page 183.

Based on the over-all study, the analysts concluded that "an investment of 20 percent additional funds for 1968-1972 would support those programs which show very favorable benefit-cost ratios and which have good prospects for significant reductions in annual deaths and morbidity from the selected diseases." From the analysis, they then offered a priority ranking for use of the new funds, as follows:

1. Motor vehicle accident and injury prevention programs.
2. Arthritis. ("This disease cripples rather than kills and it may thus appear as less significant a health problem than syphilis or uterine cervix cancer. However, the potential of adding an additional one to five productive years to 13,000,000 arthritics gives strong support to this program.")
3. Uterine cervix cancer control.
4. Lung cancer prevention.
   Breast cancer.
5. Syphilis.
6. Tuberculosis.
7. A further build-up of uterine cervix cancer program, extending the program to additional population groups where the cost of screening and case identification is higher.
8. Syphilis eradication.
9. Further reduction in the prevalence of tuberculosis.

Human Investment

Not all of the studies were so categorical in their conclusions, so willing to travel so far on the fuel of such indefinite data. The experience in attempting to apply PPB to "human investment" programs—programs designed to raise a person's capacity for self-support through education and training, as opposed to simple money transfers—led the program planners

Benefit Cost Data
Selected Disease Control Programs*
($ millions)[3]

Program	1968-1972 HEW Costs[1] (millions)	1968-1972 HEW & Other Direct Costs[2] (millions)	1968-1972 Savings Direct and Indirect[2] (millions)	Benefit Cost Ratio*
	1	2	3	4
Seat Belt Use	$ 2.2	$ 2.0	$2,728	1351.4
Restraint Devices	.7	.6	681	1117.1
Pedestrian Injury	1.1	1.1	153	144.3
Motorcyclist Helmets	8.0	7.4	413	55.6
Arthritis	37.6	35.0	1,489	42.5
Reduce Driver Drinking	31.1	28.5	613	21.5
Syphilis	55.0	179.3[1]	2,993	16.7
Uterine Cervix Cancer	73.7	118.7	1,071	9.0
Lung Cancer	47.0	47.0[1]	268	5.7
Breast Cancer	17.7	22.5	101	4.5
Tuberculosis	130.0	130.0	573	4.4
Driver Licensing	6.6	6.1	23	3.8
Head and Neck Cancer	8.1	7.8	9	1.1
Colon-Rectum Cancer	7.7	7.3	4	.5

* Numbers have been rounded to a single decimal point from three decimal points; therefore ratio may not be exact result of dividing column 2 into column 3 as they appear here.
[1] Not discounted
[2] Discounted
[3] Funding shown used as basis for analysis not necessarily funding to be supported by Administration

to sharply different views of what PPB could and should do. For one thing, the information available was too paltry for definitive statements about the effectiveness of the programs; for another, proceeding even with utmost caution, the program planners arrived at the conclusion that only one of the five programs studied—vocational rehabilitation—is "demonstrably effective."

Benefits were defined to be the increase in earnings which resulted from each of the programs. The vocational rehabilitation program was estimated to have a benefit-cost ratio of twelve or thirteen to one—i.e., every dollar spent on special training for an otherwise unemployable, physically or mentally handicapped person, is likely to produce twelve dollars or $13 in earnings. In the adult basic education program, actual data about earnings were not available; based on the expected increase in the educational level, however, a benefit-cost ratio of 11 to 1 was estimated. Similarly, there were no data on earnings available to arrive at a reliable benefit-cost ratio for the work-experience and training program connected with the welfare program. Instead, a "break-even" analysis was made, which found that a very small increase in earnings would make the program pay for itself. While the program planners concluded that the work-experience program was therefore potentially effective, they also concluded that this would be possible only if the emphasis of the program is shifted more heavily to training. Vocational educational programs (funded under *thirteen* separate legislative authorities), with a benefit-cost ratio of from 1.6 to 1, to 2.9 to 1, it was concluded, have to be thoroughly restructured if they are to be effective. So little was known about Title I of the Elementary and Sec-

ondary Education Act that no benefit-cost ratio was computed, but from what evidence there was the program planners concluded that modest increases in school expenditures using conventional methods in the conventional school setting produced little improvement in student performance.

Some of this of course is not news. The basic idea behind Title I was to insert money into schools with high proportions of poor children, with insistence that the funds be used for other than "conventional methods." Anyone dimly familiar with education programs had to know that vocational education, with its emphasis on agricultural and home economics training, had fallen behind the times. Anyone who looked closely saw that work-experience, to the extent it was busy-work, could not make much serious difference in income-producing capacities. What the PPB process did was simply to fortify these perceptions, and to transmit some important signals to the policy makers.

Because of the political and social commitments inherent in these programs, and the power of some related groups, such as the vocational educators, a finding that only one could clearly be supported as effective does not lead to the conclusion that four should be jettisoned. And because the clientele of the separate programs, particularly in the short-run, are scarcely interchangeable, little can be concluded about the commensurability of the programs. What can be and was concluded was that in the prevailing tight budget situation the only programs that deserved expansion were vocational rehabilitation and adult basic education, and that meanwhile the human investment programs must be improved. Moreover, the knowledge that the *average* pay-off from a widespread vocational education program is low is only marginally helpful; what should be known is which vocational educational approaches yield the best results, and which the poorest. This is where the PPB process will turn next—to *intraprogram* studies of the most effective methods. There will, for example, be a closer examination of various uses of Title I money, in an effort to determine which appear to provide the highest pay-offs.

Another signal the program planners received from this study was that they had to look beyond program-by-program analysis to find the most effective combination of approaches. An unemployed person, for example, might need certain components of both literacy and training programs. A given school child might be best served by a combination of certain Title I and certain vocational education projects.

Finally, more attention will be turned to gathering data which will lead to more telling evaluations. "The process of analyzing and comparing these programs," said the study, "revealed that the information available about their effectiveness was shockingly inadequate. Only very rough judgments about their relative effectiveness could be reached. Information on costs per participant was often unavailable and had to be estimated. Data on the characteristics of participants (even, in some cases, their age and sex) were inadequate. Information on what happened to the participants during and after the program—gains in educational attainment, employment experience, earnings history, and so forth—was extremely limited. Estimates had to be pieced together from a variety of sources. Information about control groups—for example equivalent members of the work force who did and did not receive vocational education—was virtually non-existent. . . ."

Leadership in Administration

PHILIP SELZNICK

Responsible Leadership

As the organization becomes an institution new problems are set for the men who run it. Among these is the need for institutional responsibility, which accounts for much of what we mean by statesmanship.

From a personal standpoint, responsible leadership is a blend of com-

Philip Selznick, "Leadership in Administration," *Leadership in Administration* (New York: Harper & Row, Publishers, Incorporated, 1957), pp. 142-52, with omissions. Reprinted by permission of Harper & Row, Publishers.

mitment, understanding, and determination. These elements bring together the selfhood of the leader and the identity of the institution. This is partly a matter of self-*conception*, for whatever his special background, and however important it may have been in the decision that gave him his office, the responsible leader in a mature institution must transcend his specialism. Self-*knowledge* becomes an understanding not only of the leader's own weaknesses and potentialities but of those qualities in the enterprise itself. And the assumption of command is a self-*summoning* process, yielding the will to know and the will to act in accordance with the requirements of institutional survival and fulfillment.

From a policy standpoint, and that is our primary concern, most of the characteristics of the responsible leader can be summarized under two headings: the avoidance of opportunism and the avoidance of utopianism.

Opportunism is the pursuit of immediate, short-run advantages in a way inadequately controlled by considerations of principle and ultimate consequence. To take advantage of opportunities is to show that one is alive, but institutions no less than persons must look to the long-run effects of present advantage. In speaking of the "long run" we have in mind not time as such but how change affects personal or institutional identity. Such effects are not usually immediately apparent, and therefore we emphasize the lapse of time. But changes in character or identity may occur quite rapidly.

Leadership is irresponsible when it fails to set goals and therefore lets the institution drift. The absence of controlling aims forces decisions to be made in response to immediate pressures. Of course, many large enterprises do drift, yet they survive. The penalties are not always swift, and very often bare survival is possible even though the fullest potentialities of the enterprise are not realized and significant changes in identity do occur.

The setting of institutional *goals* cannot be divorced from the enunciation of governing *principles*. Goal-setting, if it is institutionally meaningful, is framed in the language of character or identity, that is, it tells us what we should "do" in order to become what we want to "be." A decision to produce a new product or enter a new market, though it may set goals, is nevertheless irresponsible if it is not based on an understanding of the company's past and potential character. If the new venture, on analysis, requires a change in distinctive competence, then *that* becomes the new goal. Such a goal is bound up with principles because attaining and conserving a distinctive competence depends on an understanding of what standards are required and how to maintain them. If a grain processing firm moves into the chemical industry, it must learn how to build into its new division the competence to keep pace with rapid technological changes on pain of falling behind in the struggle against obsolescent products and techniques. Because the technique of attaining this is seldom based on explicitly formulated principles, it would be prudent to staff the new division, *especially* at the top, with men drawn from the chemical industry rather than with men drawn from the parent firm and representing its tradition and orientations.

When an enterprise is permitted to drift, making short-run, partial adaptations, the greatest danger lies in uncontrolled effects on organization character. If ultimately there is a complete change, with a new character emerging, those who formed and sustained the organization at the beginning may find that they no longer fit the organization. There is also the likelihood that character will not really be transformed: it will be *attenuated and confused*. Attenuation means that the sought-for distinctive competence becomes vague and abstract, unable to influence deeply the work of staff and operating divisions. This occurs when the formulation of institutional goals is an afterthought, a way of rationalizing activities actually resulting from opportunistic lines of decision. A confused organization character is marked by an unordered and disharmonious mixture of capabilities. The practical result is that the organization cannot perform any task effectively, and this weakens its ability to survive in the face of strong competition.

In addition to sheer drift stemming from the failure to set institutional goals, opportunism also reflects an excessive response to outside pressures. To be sure, leaders must take account of the environment, adapting to its limitations as well as to its opportunities, but we must beware of institutional surrender made in the name of organizational survival. There is a difference between a university president who *takes account* of a state legislature or strong pressure groups and one who permits these forces to determine university policy. The leader's job is to *test* the environment to find out which demands can become truly effective threats, to *change* the environment by finding allies and other sources of external support, and to *gird* his organization by creating the means and the will to withstand attacks.

Here, too, we come back to the problem of maintaining institutional integrity. The ultimate cost of opportunistic adaptation goes beyond capitulation on specific issues. A more serious result is that outside elements may enter the organization and dominate parts of it. When this happens the organization is no longer truly independent, no longer making specific compromises as necessity dictates while retaining its unity and distinctive identity. Rather, it has given over a piece of itself to alien forces, making it possible for them to exercise broader influence on policy. The transformation of compromise or even defeat into partial organizational surrender can sometimes be a conscious measure of last resort, but it also occurs without full awareness on the part of the participants. In our study of the Ten-

nessee Valley Authority, referred to above, just such a phenomenon was observed. A political compromise with local and national agricultural interests was implemented by permitting part of the TVA as an organization to be controlled by those forces, with extensive and unanticipated effects on the role and character of the agency. The avoidance of opportunism is not the avoidance of all compromise; it is the avoidance of compromise that undermines institutional integrity.

Opportunism also displays itself in a narrow self-centeredness, in an effort to exploit other groups for immediate, short-run advantages. If a firm offers a product or service to other firms, expectations of dependability are created, especially in the matter of continuing supply. If supplies are abruptly discontinued, activities that depended upon them will suffer. Hence a firm's reputation for dependability and concern for others becomes a matter of great importance wherever continuing relationships are envisioned. To act as if only a set of impersonal transactions were involved, with no responsibility beyond the strict terms of a contract, creates anxiety in the buyer, threatens to damage *his* reputation for dependability, and in the end weakens both parties.

The responsible leader recognizes the need for stable relations with the community of which his organization is a part, although he must test the environment to see how real that requirement is. A large and enduring enterprise will probably have to contribute to the maintenance of community stability, at least within its own field of action. In industry, this may take the form of participation in trade associations and other devices for self-regulation. The marginal firm, on the other hand, can afford to be irresponsible in dealing with the community because it is less dependent on stable relations with other firms or with a special clientele or labor force. Such firms have also less need of responsibility to themselves as institutions, for they have fewer hostages to fortune. Generally, responsibility to the enterprise and to the community go hand in hand, each increasing as the transition from organization to institution becomes more complete.

If opportunism goes too far in accepting the dictates of a "reality principle," utopianism hopes to avoid hard choices by a flight to abstractions. This too results in irresponsibility, in escape from the true functions of leadership.

. . . [Let us outline some of the sources of utopianism]. One of these is the *overgeneralization of purpose.* Thus "to make a profit" is widely accepted as a statement of business purpose, but this is too general to permit responsible decision-making. Here again, the more marginal the business, that is, the greater its reliance upon quick returns, easy liquidation, and highly flexible tactics, the less need there is for an institutionally responsible and more specific formulation of purpose. Indeed, the very generality of the purpose is congenial to the opportunism of these groups. But when institutional continuity and identity are at stake, a definition of mission is required that will take account of the organization's distinctive character, including present and prospective capabilities, as well as the requirements of playing a desired role in a particular industrial or commercial context.

Utopian wishful-thinking enters when men who purport to be institutional leaders attempt to rely on overgeneralized purposes to guide their decisions. But when guides are unrealistic, yet decisions must be made, more realistic *but uncontrolled* criteria will somehow fill the gap. Immediate exigencies will dominate the actual choices that are made. In this way, the polarities of utopianism and opportunism involve each other.

Another manifestation of utopianism is the hope that the solution of technical problems will solve institutional problems. We have discussed the "retreat to technology" as a way of avoiding responsibility for the multiple ends that must be satisfied if the institution as a whole is to be successful. To be "just a soldier," "just an engineer," or even "just a businessman" is inconsistent with the demands of statesmanship. It is utopian and irresponsible to suppose that a narrow technical logic can be relied on by men who make decisions that, though they originate in technical problems, have larger consequences for the ultimate evolution of the enterprise and its position in the world.

This brand of utopianism is associated with adventurism, a willingness to commit the organization as a whole on the basis of a partial assessment of the situation derived from a particular technological perspective, such as that of the propagandist in foreign affairs or the engineer or designer in industry. Here again the utopian as technologist becomes the victim of opportunism.

Responsible leadership steers a course between utopianism and opportunism. Its responsibility consists in accepting the obligation of giving direction instead of merely ministering to organizational equilibrium; in adapting aspiration to the character of the organization, bearing in mind that what the organization has been will affect what it can be and do; and in transcending bare organizational survival by seeing that specialized decisions do not weaken or confuse the distinctive identity of the enterprise.

Creative Leadership

To the essentially conservative posture of the responsible leader we must add a concern for change and reconstruction. This creative role has two aspects. First, there is what we have called the "institutional embodiment of purpose." Second, creativity is exercised by strategic and tactical planning, that is, analyzing the environment to determine how best to use the existing resources and capabilities of the organization. This essay has not treated the problem of externally oriented strategies. On the other hand, what can be done to establish policy internally depends upon the changing relation between the organization and its environment.

The inbuilding of purpose is a challenge to creativity because it involves transforming men and groups from neutral, technical units into participants who have a peculiar stamp, sensitivity, and commitment. This is ultimately an educational process. It has been well said that the effective leader must know the meaning and master the techniques of the educator. As in the larger community, education is more than narrow technical training; though it does not shrink from indoctrination, it also teaches men to think for themselves. The leader as educator requires an ability to interpret the role and character of the enterprise, to perceive and develop models for thought and behavior, and to find modes of communication that will inculcate general rather than merely partial perspectives.

The main practical import of this effort is that *policy will gain spontaneous and reasoned support*. Desired ends and means are sustained and furthered, not through continuous command, but as a free expression of truly accepted principles. This presumes that at least the core participants combine loyalty to the enterprise with a sensitive awareness of the principles by which it is guided. Loyalty by itself is not enough, just as blind patriotism is insufficient. There must also be an ability to sense when a course of action threatens institutional integrity.

To be sure, this ideal of rational, free-willed consent is virtually impossible to achieve in organizations that have narrow, practical aims and whose main problem is the disciplined harnessing of human energy to achieve those aims. But such organizations, just because of this narrowness, are but meagerly institutionalized and have correspondingly little need for executive statesmanship. The creativity we speak of here is particularly necessary—and peculiarly possible—where, as discussed earlier, the transition from organization to institution is in process or has occurred.

To create an institution we rely on many techniques for infusing day-to-day behavior with long-run meaning and purpose. One of the most important of these techniques is the elaboration of socially integrating myths. These are efforts to state, in the language of uplift and idealism, what is distinctive about the aims and methods of the enterprise. Successful institutions are usually able to fill in the formula, "What we are proud of around here is. . . ." Sometimes, a fairly explicit institutional philosophy is worked out; more often, a sense of mission is communicated in more indirect but no less significant ways. The assignment of high prestige to certain activities will itself help to create a myth, especially if buttressed by occasional explicit statements. The specific ways of projecting a myth are as various as communication itself. For creative leadership, it is not the communication of a myth that counts; rather, creativity depends on having the will and the insight to see the necessity of the myth, to discover a successful formulation, and above all to create the organizational conditions that will sustain the ideals expressed.

Successful myths are never merely cynical or manipulative, even though they may be put forward self-consciously to further the chances of stability or survival. If a state university develops a concept of "service to the community" as its central ideal, as against more remote academic aspirations, this may have its origins in a sense of insecurity, but it will not be innocent in application. To be effective, the projected myth cannot be restricted to holiday speeches or to testimony before legislative committees. It will inevitably color many aspects of university policy, affecting standards of admission, orientations of research, and the scope of the curriculum. The compulsion to embody the myth in practice has a dual source, reflecting inner needs and outer demands. Externally, those who can enforce demands upon the institution will not be content with empty verbal statements. They will expect conformity and the myth itself will provide a powerful lever to that end.

The executive acts out the myth for reasons of self-expression, but also for quite practical administrative reasons. He requires *some* integrating aid to the making of many diverse day-to-day decisions, and the myth helps to fulfill that need. Sharp discrepancies between theory and practice threaten his own authority in the eyes of subordinates; conformity to the myth will lessen "trouble" with outside groups. Not least important, he can hope that the myth will contribute to a unified sense of mission and thereby to the harmony of the whole. If the administrator is primarily dedicated to maintaining a smooth-running machine, and only weakly committed to substantive aims, these advantages will seem particularly appealing.

In the end, however, whatever their source, myths are institution builders. Making the myth effective willy-nilly entrenches particular objectives and capabilities, although these may not be the ones that initially inspired the sponsors of the enterprise. Myth-making may have roots in a sensed need to improve efficiency and morale; but its main office is to help create an integrated social organism. . . .

Toward a Keynesian Theory of Social Process

AMITAI ETZIONI

The Limited Capacity to Manage

Societies were once viewed as natural entities, which we find untampered with (like a tribe in a jungle enclave) and which change their character (let us say from an agrarian to an industrial economy) without any one man or group of men having planned the change. Recently, we have come to view society as more open to deliberate reconstruction, and its processes as subject to guidance. In the area of economics, the application of Keynesian theory is widely believed to have provided the tools which allow us to avoid mass unemployment, deep depressions, and run-away inflations.

Over the last twenty years, our collective ambition has risen. We decided to change, by design and in accord with guidelines laid down nationally, the relations between the races. Similarly, the President committed his administration to a drive aimed at eradicating poverty. We face numerous other problems which afflict the society, seeking to introduce whatever changes are necessary to reduce crime and drug addiction, to make the highways safe, to de-pollute the air and the water, and so forth. *But the sad truth is that we do not know how to guide societal changes in the desired directions,* and hence ten and fifteen years after various programs have been initiated, many of the problems we set out to solve will still be with us. Fourteen years have already passed since the Supreme Court ruling on desegregation of the schools, and most of them are not desegregated. While the anti-poverty drive is only four years old, most observers are now much more pessimistic about its chances for success than they were in 1964. The carnage on the highways continues at full speed and pollution experts inform us that unless very special new efforts will be made, environmental pollution will increase rather than be reduced. Obviously, we have not yet acquired the art of societal management.

Other societies are not scoring much better; most do worse than we or, if better, had a much easier task in the beginning. Thus, comparatively small, socially homogeneous, inward looking, Scandinavian countries, with few international commitments, tend to manage their own affairs quite well, although in Sweden the housing shortage is monumental; drug abuse is on the rise; and it took the Swedes 22 years to implement a change requiring cars to be driven on the right hand side of the road. Israel, one of the most effectively run societies, set out in 1949 to absorb a number of immigrants equal to the size of its population; it is unclear at this point who will absorb whom—Israel the immigrants, or the immigrants will impose their Middle Eastern traits on Western modernized Israel. Totalitarian societies, though willing to make tremendous economic and human sacrifices to advance the changes that their governments favor, failed in realizing their prime goals of abolishing the state, religion, the class structure, or the profit motive. Fifteen and ten years ago, underdeveloped countries were formulating master plans for their modernization. Fewer than one out of ten were implemented even in part. In short, while there are significant differences in the complexity of problems various societies face, in their respective capacity to handle them, and in the specific kinds of deficiencies their governing processes show, all societies have yet to learn to manage their affairs more effectively, to the extent they wish to engage in such management. In the following pages, we ask first what additional capacities are necessary, and then—What is it all for? What values will the effectively managed society seek to advance?

Societal Cybernetics

Progress in social science over the recent years allows us, I hold, to now develop a Keynesian theory of *societal* processes, i.e., a theory of the factors that limit our capacity to manage and the conditions which will allow us to improve our guiding capacity. It must be noted that having a theory, however valid, is only the first step toward its effective use. At least a generation lapsed after Keynes published his seminal book before it became the basis for societal steerage. Hopefully the application will be shorter this time around.

I spent the last eight years recording and to a degree developing such a theory of societal guidance. While it took me seven hundred pages to outline its major features (*The Active Society*, Free Press, 1968), I can here only indicate roughly what such a conception is like. In doing so I draw on an analogue from cybernetics.

Cybernetics orginally was primarily the study of steering of groups of machines, the study of how they are guided to work jointly to realize goals which the cybernetic overlayer favors. Cybernetics is most developed in mechanical and electrical systems. It assumes here (1) one or more centers that issue signals to the units which do the work (the command post); (2) communication lines which lead from the center(s) to the working units, carrying the instructions for what is to be done, and "feedback" lines which carry information and responses from the subject units to the center (in short, two way communication). (3) While many cybernetic models omit the conception of power, we see it as a main factor: if the steering units cannot back up their signals with rewards or sanctions, they will frequently be disregarded (i.e., the command post must be stronger than those who carry out its instructions). (4) A further subtlety is to distinguish, within the command centers, between sub-units which absorb and analyze the incoming information and those which make decisions (i.e., between knowledge makers and policy makers).

When all these elements are available and function effectively, that is, communication lines are well "hooked-up" and not overloaded, information and decision-making units have free access to each other, etc., we have an effective *control* system. Some engineers and managers think that a social system, be it of a corporation or of a society, can also be run this way. The government is viewed as the cybernatorial overlayer of society. The White House, Congress, state capitols and city halls provide the command positions. Universities, research institutes, experts on the government's staff, and "think-tanks"—the knowledge makers. The civil service, press, radio, and television—the two way communication lines. As we see it, when a cybernetic model is applied to a social system, one must take into account that for both ethical and practical reasons, the citizens cannot be coerced to follow "signals" unless those, at least to a significant extent, are responsive to their values and interests. If the citizens are forced, the system both violates their rights and generates increasing levels of resistance which become a major reason why the society is unable to manage its affairs effectively, whether these be collectivization of the farms or abolishing alcoholism. Effective *societal* cybernetics requires that the downward flow of control signals (from the government to the people) be accompanied by effective upward (from the people to the government) and lateral (among citizens) flows of signals, which express the citizens' values and needs. We refer to these upward and lateral flows, which take the form of votes, letters to Congressmen, petitions, and so forth, as *consensus-building*, and to the combination of control and consensus-building (the societal cybernatorial mechanisms) as *societal guidance*.

The Elements of Societal Guidance

The differences between active and passive societies, between those more and those less able to handle their problems, are best studied by examining one cybernatorial factor at a time, although effective guidance requires their combination.

Knowledge-units: When we examine the amount of funds, the size of manpower and the extent of expertise devoted to collecting and processing of knowledge as compared to other activities (e.g., production of goods and services) we gain an impression of how "knowledgeable" a particular society, government, or federal agency is. Doing so we are immediately struck with one reason societies often score poorly in their self-management: they spend relatively very little on knowledge and much more on "doing." And, most of the funds that go into the production of knowledge are earmarked for the natural sciences, i.e., for the study of the non-social environment. When societies deal with poverty, riots, and urban problems, they often have little knowledge, and even incorrect knowledge, about what the underlying factors are. For instance, the American society has followed for more than four decades a highly punitive policy against the users of marijuana. But the assumptions on which this policy is based, that the weed is damaging or that it leads its users to the consumption of other, clearly debilitating drugs, have yet to be demonstrated. Experts now urge reducing the relief rolls by sending the 900,000 mothers to work, urging that their children be left in day-care centers. Nobody has established yet if the resulting psychological problems this will create for the young children will not create more social costs and human misery than the system seeks to remove. Blue ribbon commissions are appointed to study other issues, but these tend to be composed of prestigious citizens, not experts, who can

dedicate only a small part of their time to studying the issue at hand. The President's Commission on Civil Disorder completed its work in about seven months. But its members held full time jobs "on the side" including such as the mayorality of New York City or the top position of the United Steel Workers. No wonder the members could devote only a few days to the study of the causes and cures of riots. The situation in the relevant professions is not much better: most social scientists' work is not policy-oriented and not readily accessible to key decision-makers. Prestige and promotions go to those who work on esoteric subjects; applied research is frowned upon. Few corporations would open an overseas branch on the basis of so little and amateurish a study as was invested before several major national programs were launched. One example is Project Apollo; the key staff work was done over one weekend in Spring 1961.

The knowledge that is available to experts must be communicated to societal decision-makers, before it can be effectively utilized. Even in corporations, the planning as well as research and development units often have a hard time gaining the ear of the key executives. In society, the social distance between the research centers, where many of the best experts work, and Washington, D.C. (let alone city hall and the state capitol) is often vast. "Burned-out" scientists, academic statesmen and operators frequently further narrow the passage. Those federal agencies which have their own "think-tanks," e.g., RAND for the Air Force, tend to do better in terms of their respective goals, which shows the importance of systematic "input" of information and analysis to policy makers. Obvious? Yes. Usually done? Not adequately.

Decision-making: The decision-making strategies which the "cybernetic centers" explicitly or implicitly follow affect the quality of the societal efforts more than is often realized. Anglo-Saxon societies are inclined to be "pragmatic," to "muddle through," making one small decision at a time; they abhor longer-run and encompassing planning. This approach is quite effective when the environment is relatively stable and the system is basically sound. Then, minor revisions do quite nicely. But when basic turnabouts are required, something more than "tokenism," they have a harder time adapting. The way the war in Vietnam was escalated, small step by small step, following neither a "dove" nor a "hawk" policy, and it seems without genuine attempts at *basic* change of policy, is a typical case in point.

Totalitarian societies often err in the opposite direction. They tend to assume a much greater capacity to control the society from one center, over more matters, and for a longer period of time than they are actually capable of. Thus, they overplan and often launch major projects, "Great Leaps," only to be forced to scale them down or recast them at tremendous economic and human cost.

It would be tempting to state that the most effective decision-making strategy is a happy medium, between democratic under-planning and totalitarian over-planning. It seems more precise to suggest that the capacity of both democratic and totalitarian societies to make encompassing and anticipatory decisions is rising with the improvements that have been occurring rapidly since about 1955 in the technology of communication, knowledge storing and retrieval, computation, and research. That is, we are rapidly gaining *tools* of societal guidance which were not available before. While no

society can effectively manage the many matters which totalitarian states attempt to control, we have now the capacity for more societal policy-making and guidance than democracies assumed—quite correctly until recently —is feasible.

In addition, it may be said that to some degree each society has the decision-making pattern it deserves. Decision-making strategies are not chosen in a vacuum but partially reflect the political structure of the society. Democratic societies tend toward "muddling through" because there is no powerful central authority—even in the presidency—that can impose a master plan, even if this were desirable otherwise. The policies formulated are the outcome of the pushing and pulling of a large variety of interest groups, civic groups, political parties, and varying trends in public opinion. Under these circumstances, straight sailing seems difficult; zig-zagging is the natural course. Totalitarian societies are more able to follow one course but also much more likely to run roughshod over the feelings and interests of most of their constituencies. A "middling" policy-making—one more encompassing and "deep" than democratic decision-making, but also much more humane than totalitarian decision-making—requires not only new technologies of communication and control but also the proper power constellation in society.

Power: All societies may be fruitfully viewed as compositions of groupings (e.g., classes, regions, ethnic groups) that differ in the share of the societal assets and power they command. (In our society, obviously farmhands, Southerners [white and black] and Spanish-Americans tend to have a smaller proportion of power than their share of the population.) The distribution of power in any one society significantly affects its capacity to treat its problems and to change its structure and course, if necessary. It is useful to consider the distribution of power from two viewpoints: between the members of the society and the government (the cybernetic overlay) and among the members of the society.

The government, and more broadly the state, may overpower the society. This occurs when the state bureaucracies either themselves checkmate most other power centers (e.g., as in contemporary Egypt) or—more commonly—do so in conjunction with some other organization (the Party, in Communist China). On the other hand, the state may be overpowered by the society, fragmented the way society frequently is. This has occurred in highly feudalistic societies (e.g., ninth-century France) and continues to occur in contemporary tribal societies (such as Nigeria).

When the state is overpowering, societal guidance tends to be unresponsive to most members' needs and values (as in Stalin's Russia); when it is overpowered, the major societal cybernetic overlayer is knocked out and the society drifts (as is the case in many underdeveloped countries). Only a tense balance between society and state, each one guarding its autonomy, is able to sustain a relatively responsive and active societal guidance. Democracy itself requires such a power constellation: *state power*—to limit conflicts among member-groupings (such as classes and races) to nonviolent give and take, and to prevent the overpowering of some member grouping(s) by others; *autonomous power* of the citizens—to maintain the capacity to change the government, i.e., those in power, those who guide the state if they cease to be responsive

to the plurality of the citizens. Democracy, it follows, is more fully realized the fewer the power differences among the member groupings. As the needs of no member have a superior claim over those of any other, the only way to assure that a society will be responsive to the membership-at-large is to give all members as similar as feasible a handle over its guidance mechanisms. This means that not just the right to vote, but the socio-economic and educational prerequisites for its effective use, must be extended to all citizens before a democracy is fully operational.

To illustrate the effect of power relations on societal guidance, the special features of the war on poverty deserve our attention. The 89th Congress was unusually liberal, due to the anti-Goldwater landslide of 1964, which elected Democrats and liberals where traditionally Republicans and conservatives were chosen. This, plus heavy pressure from the President, made for passage through Congress of an anti-poverty bill. Its implementation was to rely heavily on 1,050 Community Action boards, set up to be the recipients of anti-poverty funds and to manage their programs with "maximum feasible participation of the poor." Leaving aside the question whether this was a wise approach from the viewpoint of the needs of the poor, it surely did not fit the existing power structure, because it by-passed both city hall and the established welfare agencies. In 1966, a fair number of liberals were defeated, less than 3% of the eligible poor voted in elections to the Community Action boards, and by the end of 1967, the anti-poverty program was being restructured so as to bring it under control of the local authorities. Similar points could be made with reference to bussing of school children, attempts to control smoking, or to help the farmhands. A social program needs political backing; if this cannot be marshalled, the program will sooner or later be modified or blocked.

The power relations among the groupings which make up a society shift over time due to a large variety of processes, including technological changes, the spread of education, and a rise in the level of self-organization of some previously less organized groups (e.g., Negro-Americans). As power relations change, new programs become feasible, and old ones are undermined. In other cases, new coalitions are formed; for instance, federal aid to education was initiated when a way was found to answer some of the needs of both public *and* parochial schools.

Consensus Building

Fortunately, societal guidance is propelled not only by power but also by genuine moral commitments of the citizens. People are motivated not only by self-interest but also by their conceptions of national pride, social justice, and freedom. Thus, American subscription to foreign aid, the United Nations, or civil rights can be explained at best in part by the power of their advocates. They also appeal to values such as humanity, peace, and justice—in short to values which many citizens hold. Now, there is less than full agreement among the people of any country with regard to the values to which they subscribe or the ways they believe those can be advanced. Nor are such positions unchangeable. A program's chances to be successful are higher, assuming a given level of power backing, the more it is in line with the values of the majority of the citizens (or succeeds in gaining their

endorsement, if initially the policy conflicted with their values). The idea that the United States may participate in World War I and II was at first (in 1914 and 1939 respectively) quite unpopular with many citizens; by 1917 and 1941, though, a clear majority favored involvement. This contrasts with the war in Vietnam, which was not preceded by such a consensus-building drive nor, indeed, a declaration of war.

Active for What?

Assuming a society developed more effective cybernatorial systems—better knowledge, more effective decision making, higher degree of power balancing for its programs and more consensus to endorse them—which values would it promote and what kind of society would it be?

Social philosophers have tried, at least since the days of Plato's academy and the biblical prophets, to answer these questions, to depict the Good Society. The resulting Utopias make appealing reading but also frequently leave the reader with an acute sense of frustration and sense of deep irrelevancy; these Utopias obviously cannot be realized.

The Utopias also assume that the philosopher or social scientist can speak for man, either divine or establish what his values and needs are, and set them forth in the form of an ordered platform. As I see it, such a task is both presumptious in the extreme (the philosopher plays king if not God) and unlikely to succeed.

The values a society effectively manages will have to be those *its* citizens will seek to advance. A Keynesian theory of societal processes informs the citizenry where to turn to get more of the values, more fully, more rapidly realized—not what their values ought to be. Actually, only as society becomes more active, both in pursuing its goals and in providing for all its citizens opportunities for true and full participation, will many of the members and society itself discover what the deeper wishes are.

Our answer, if you wish, is "procedural"; we point to ways man may be more in command of societal processes and less subject to their blind fluctuations, rather than spell out where precisely he will guide the processes once he is more fully in command. That, by the way, is entailed in the traditional conception of democracy: the best way for citizens to choose their government and to make it realize their values. True, an active society will advance several key values, without which it cannot be active, e.g., broad participation of as many citizens as possible in its political life. This, in turn, requires free and informed citizenry, and at least a measure of economic well-being so that the struggle for survival will not absorb all their energies. And, such a society will promote other key values, e.g., broad effective participation in politics will advance social justice. But all this put together provides only for a rather "basic" Utopia; the rest will have to be filled in, by the members, acting jointly, making society more responsive to *their* needs and values.

The Corporation: How Much Power? What Scope?

CARL KAYSEN

The proposition that a group of giant business corporations, few in number but awesome in aggregate size, embodies a significant and troublesome concentration of power is the cliché which serves this volume as a foundation stone. I propose here to analyze this proposition, both to trace out what I consider its valid content to be, and to reflect briefly on its possible implications for social action. Let me anticipate my conclusion on the first point by saying that its familiarity is no argument against its truth.

The power of any actor on the social stage I define as the scope of significant choice open to him. Accord-

Reprinted by permission of the publishers from Edward S. Mason, editor, *The Corporation in Modern Society* (Cambridge, Mass.: Harvard University Press, copyright 1959 by the President and Fellows of Harvard College), pp. 85-105.

ingly, his power over others is the scope of his choices which affect them significantly. Our fundamental proposition thus asserts that a few large corporations exert significant power over others; indeed, as we shall see, over the whole of society with respect to many choices, and over large segments of it with respect to others. It is worth noting that this sense of "power" is not that in which we speak of the "power" of a waterfall or a fusion reaction, or any other transformation in a fully deterministic system; rather it is appropriate to a social system in which we see human actors, individually or in organized groups, as facing alternative courses of action, the choice among which is not fully determined without reference to the actors themselves.

We usually demonstrate the concentration of power in a small number of large corporate enterprises by showing what part of various total magnitudes for the whole economy the largest enterprises account for. The statistics are indeed impressive: I shall list a few of the more striking.[1]

1) There are currently some 4.5 million business enterprises in the United States. More than half of these are small, unincorporated firms in retail trade and service. Corporations formed only 13 per cent of the total number; 95 per cent of the unincorporated firms had fewer than twenty employees.

---

[1] The sources for the figures quoted are listed in order below.

Total business population: 1956, 4.3 million; 1954, 4.2 million, whence my current estimate. See U.S. Department of Commerce, Bureau of the Census, *Statistical Abstract of the United States 1957* (Washington, D.C., 1957), p. 482.

Corporate share and size distribution: U.S. Department of Commerce, Office of Business Economics, *Survey of Current Business* (April, 1955); figures refer to January 1, 1952, for share, and January 1, 1947, for size distribution. If anything, the figures understate the numerical preponderance of small unincorporated enterprises today.

The census figures refer to 1954. See U.S. Department of Commerce, Bureau of the Census, *Company Statistics 1954*, Bulletin CS-1 (Washington, D.C., 1958).

Asset holding of large corporations: U.S. Treasury, Internal Revenue Service, *Statistics of Income, Part 2, 1955* (Washington, D.C., 1958), Table 5, pp. 41 ff.

Research and Development Expenditures: U.S. National Science Foundation, *Science and Engineering in American Industry* (Washington, D.C., 1956).

Defense Contracts: "100 Companies and Affiliates Listed According to Net Value of Military Prime Contract Awards, July 1950-June 1956." Department of Defense, Office of Assistant Secretary of Defense (Supply and Logistics), mimeo release dated 10 April 1957.

For a fuller but slightly dated discussion, see M. A. Adelman, "The Measurement of Industrial Concentration," *The Review of Economics and Statistics*, 23 (1951), 269-96, reprinted in *Readings in Industrial Organization and Public Policy*, ed. R. B. Heflebower and G. W. Stocking (Homewood, Ill., 1958).

2) A recent census survey covered all the firms in manufacturing, mining, retail and wholesale trade, and certain service industries: in total some 2.8 million. These firms employed just under 30 million persons. The 28 giant firms with 50,000 or more employees—just 0.001 per cent of the total number—accounted for about 10 per cent of the total employment. The 438 firms with 5000 or more employees (including the 28 giants) accounted for 28 per cent of the total. In manufacturing, where large corporations are characteristically more important than in the other sectors covered, 263,000 firms reported just over 17 million employees: 23 giants with 50,000 or more employees reported 15 per cent of the total, 361 with 5000 or more, just under 40 per cent.

3) The most recent compilation of the corporation income-tax returns showed 525,000 active nonfinancial corporations reporting a total of $413 billion of assets. The 202 corporations in the largest size class—each with assets of $250 million or more—owned 40 per cent of this total.

4) The last survey of the National Science Foundation reported some 15,500 firms having research and development laboratories. The largest 7 among them employed 20 per cent of the total number of technical and scientific personnel in the whole group, and accounted for 26 per cent of the total expenditures on research and development. The largest 44, all those with 25,000 or more employees in total, accounted for 45 per cent of the total number of technicians and scientists, and more than 50 per cent of the total expenditures.

5) The one hundred companies that received the largest defense contracts over the period July 1950-June 1956 received nearly two thirds of the total

value of all defense contracts during the period. The largest ten contractors accounted for just short of one third of the total value of all contracts. These were General Motors, General Electric, American Telephone and Telegraph, and seven large aircraft manufacturers.

Large corporations are not of the same importance in all sectors of the economy.[2] In agriculture they are of no importance; in service, trade, and construction, proprietorships and partnerships and small corporations that are essentially similar in all but legal form predominate. Conversely, activity in the utility, transportation, mining, manufacturing, and financial sectors is overwhelmingly the activity of corporations, and predominantly that of corporate giants. The share of total business accounted for by corporations in these sectors ranged from 85 per cent for finance to 100 per cent of utilities; by contrast it was between 50 and 60 per cent for trade and construction, less than 30 per cent in service, and less than 10 per cent in agriculture. The five sectors in which large corporations predominate produced 51 per cent of the total national income, and 57 per cent of the privately-produced national income. Moreover, the strategic importance of these sectors as compared with trade and service—the largest part of the small-business part of the economy—is greater than their contribution to national income would indicate. The relative share of giant corporations in these sectors was larger than in the economy as a whole. The corporate income-tax returns for 1955 showed the relative importance of the largest corporations, as in the accompanying table.

Many more figures similar to these could be added to the list. They show clearly that a few large corporations are of overwhelmingly disproportionate importance in our economy, and

[2] The figures on the relative importance of corporations come from R. A. Gordon, *Business Leadership in the Large Corporation* (Washington, D.C., 1946), p. 14, and Appendix A. These figures refer to 1939; no more recent ones are available and they almost certainly understate the relative importance of corporations. The shares of the sectors in national income are calculated from the figures for national income by industrial origin for 1956 given in *Statistical Abstract of the U.S. 1957*, p. 300. The share of large corporations in asset holdings of all corporations are from the *Statistics of Income, Part 2, 1955*, Table 5, pp. 41 ff.

The Relative Share of Giant Corporations in Various Sectors of the United States Economy

Sector	ALL CORPORATIONS		CORPORATIONS WITH ASSETS OF $250 MILLION OR MORE	
	Number (thousands)	Assets (billions of dollars)	Number	Proportion of assets of all corporations (percentage)
Manufacturing	124.2	201.4	97	42
Mining*	9.7	13.3	5(19)	17(32)
Public utilities	4.8	62.9	56	72
Transportation	21.9	43.5	30	61
Finance	214.6	474.9	218	46

* The figures in parentheses show the number and share of corporations with assets of $100 million or more, since the number of mining corporations in the largest size class is so small.

especially in certain key sectors of it. Whatever aspect of their economic activity we measure—employment, investment, research and development, military supply—we see the same situation. Moreover, it is one which has been stable over a period of time. The best evidence—though far from complete—is that the degree of concentration has varied little for the three or four decades before 1947; more recent material has not yet been analyzed. Further, the group of leading firms has had a fairly stable membership and turnover within it is, if anything, declining.[3] We are thus examining a persistent situation, rather than a rapidly changing one, and one which we can expect to continue into the future.

Disproportionate share alone, however, is not a valid basis for inferring power as I have defined it. In addition, we must consider the range of choice with respect to significant decisions open to the managers of the large corporation. The disproportionate share of the sun in the total mass of our solar system would not justify the ascription to it of "power" over the planets, since in the fully-determinate gravitational system the sun has no choice among alternative paths of motion which would change the configuration of the whole system. Though the relative weight of the sun is great, its range of choice is nil, and it is the product of the two, so to speak, which measures "power." It is to an examination of the managers' range of choice that we now turn.

Our economy is organized on a de-centralized, competitive basis. Each business firm, seeking higher profit by providing more efficiently what consumers want, is faced by the competition of others, seeking the same goal through the same means. Coordination and guidance of these activities is the function of the system of markets and prices. These form the information network that tells each manager what is and what is not currently profitable, and, in turn, registers the effects of each business decision, of changes in consumers' tastes, and the availability and efficiency of productive factors. Ideally, in a system of competitive markets, the signals would indicate only one possible course for any particular manager consistent with profitability. Nor would this depend on the degree to which the manager was committed to the goal of profit-maximization; margins between costs and prices would be so narrow as to make bankruptcy the alternative to "correct" choices. In practice, of course, no real firm functions in markets operating with the sureness, swiftness, and freedom from frictions that would eliminate the discretion of management entirely and make the firm merely an instrument which registered the forces of the market. But firms operating in highly competitive markets are closely constrained by market pressures, and the range of economic decision consistent with survival and success that is open to them is narrow.

By contrast, there exist much less competitive markets in which firms are insulated from these compulsions and the range of discretionary choice in management decisions is correspondingly widened. There is a wide variety of situations which can confer such market power on firms. In practice, the most important is large size relative to the market: the situation in which a few large firms

[3] See Adelman: "The Measurement of Industrial Concentration," S. Friedland, "Turnover and Growth of the Largest Industrial Firms, 1906-1950," *Review of Economics and Statistics* (February, 1957), and J. F. Weston, *The Role of Mergers in the Growth of Large Firms* (Los Angeles, 1953).

account for all or nearly all of the supply. Large size relative to the market is associated with large absolute size of firm. Other reasons, including barriers to the entry of new firms into the market provided by product differentiation and advertising, by patents, by control over scarce raw materials, or by collusive action of existing firms, or by government limitation of competition, are also significant, but they are of less importance than the oligopolistic market structure common in those sectors of the economy that are dominated by large firms.

In manufacturing, nearly two-thirds of the identifiable markets, accounting for about 60 per cent of the value of manufacturing output, showed significant elements of oligopoly; they were especially important in the durable-goods and capital-equipment fields. In mining, the proportion of identifiable markets with oligopolistic structures was much higher, but since the largest mining industry—bituminous coal—is unconcentrated, these accounted for less than 25 per cent of total mineral output. Public utilities, transportation, and finance are all subject to more or less direct government regulation, of more or less effectiveness. But the underlying market structures in these areas are either monopolistic, as in electric and gas utilities and telephone communication, or oligopolistic, as in transportation and finance.[4] Thus, typically, the large corporation in which we are interested operates in a situation in which the constraints imposed by market forces are loose, and the

scope for managerial choice is considerable. It is this scope combined with the large relative weight of the giant corporation that defines its economic power; it is substantially on its economic power that other kinds of power depend.

The powerful firm can use its power primarily to increase its profit over what it could earn in a competitive market: the traditional economic view of the drawback of market power has been the achievement of monopoly profit by the restriction of supply. But it need not do so. While the firm in the highly competitive market is constrained to seek after maximum profits, because the alternative is insufficient profit to insure survival, the firm in the less competitive market can choose whether to seek maximum profit or to be satisfied with some "acceptable" return and to seek other goals. Further, the firm in a competitive market must attend more closely to immediate problems, and leave the long future to take care of itself; while the firm with considerable market power necessarily has a longer time-horizon, and takes into account consequences of its decisions reaching further into the future. This in turn increases the range of choice open to it, for the future is uncertain, and no single "correct" reading of it is possible. Many courses of action may be consistent with reasonable expectations of the future course of events. The more dominant the position of any particular firm in a single market, the further into the future will it see the consequences of its own choices as significant, and correspondingly, the wider will be its range of significant choice. The width of choice and the uncertainty of consequences combine to rob the notion of maximum profit of its simplicity; at the minimum of complexity, the firm must be viewed as seeking some combina-

[4] These estimates are taken from Carl Kaysen and D. F. Turner, "Antitrust Policy, an Economic and Legal Analysis" (to be published by Harvard University Press, Cambridge, Mass.). See chap. ii and the appendices. The figures are based on data for 1954 for manufacturing, and on scattered years for other industries.

tion of anticipated return and possible variation, at the same time perhaps safeguarding itself against too much variation. But even this is too simple. In the absence of the constraints of a competitive market, the firm may seek a variety of goals: "satisfactory" profits, an "adequate" rate of growth, a "safe" share of the market, "good" labor relations, "good" public relations, and so forth, and no particular combination need adequately describe the behavior of all large firms with significant market power.

The large corporations with which we are here concerned characteristically operate many plants and sell and buy in many markets. Their power in some markets can be used to reinforce their power in others; their large absolute size, and the pool of capital at their command, adds something to their power in any particular market which is not explained simply by the structure of that market. In the extreme, the operations of the firm in a particular market can be completely or almost completely insensitive to its economic fortunes in that market, and thus the range of choice of decisions with respect to it may be widened far beyond that possible to any firm confined within its boundaries. Absolute size has to a certain extent the same effect in respect to the operations of any particular short time-period: the impact of likely short-period losses or failures may bulk insufficiently large to form a significant constraint on action.

We have spoken so far of the powers of choice of the corporation and the management interchangeably. By and large, this is justified. Corporate management is typically—in the reaches of business we are examining —an autonomous center of decision, organizing the affairs of the corpora- tion and choosing its own successors. While stockholders are significant as part of the environment in which management operates, they exercise little or no power of choice themselves. The views of stockholders, as reflected in their willingness to hold or their desire to dispose of the corporation's stock, are certainly taken into account by management, but only as one of a number of elements which condition their decisions. The ideology of corporate management which describes them as one among a number of client groups whose interests are the concern of management—labor, consumers, and the "public" forming the others—is in this particular realistic.

How does the giant corporation manifest its power? Most directly, in economic terms, the noteworthy dimensions of choice open to it include prices and price-cost relations, investment, location, research and innovation, and product character and selling effort. Management choice in each of these dimensions has significance for the particular markets in which the firm operates, and with respect to some of them, may have broader significance for the economy as a whole.

Prices and price-cost relations, in turn, show at least four important aspects. First is the classic question of the general level of prices in relation to costs: are profits excessive? Second, and perhaps more important, is the effect of margins on the level of costs themselves. Where the pressure of competition does not force prices down to costs, costs themselves have a tendency to rise: internal managerial checks alone cannot overcome the tendency to be satisfied with costs when the over-all level of profit is satisfactory. Third, there is the problem of interrelations among margins on related products: does the price of a

Chevrolet bear the same relation to its costs as the price of a Cadillac, or is there a tendency to earn more in the long run on resources converted into the one than into the other? This form of distortion of price-cost relations is common in the multiproduct firm, and can coexist with a modest average profit margin. Finally, there are the interrelations, both directly within a single firm and indirectly through labor and product markets, of prices and wages. Where price increases are the response to wage increases which in turn respond to price increases, the pricing policy of a firm or group of firms can be an inflationary factor of some importance. This has been the case in the steel industry in the postwar period.[5] A related problem is the behavior of prices in the face of declining demand. When a group of firms can raise prices relative to wages although unused capacity is large and increasing, they make a contribution to aggregate instability, in this case in a deflationary rather than an inflationary direction. Here again the steel industry provides a recent example.

The investment decisions of large firms are of primary importance in determining the rates of growth of particular industries, and where the roles of these industries in the economy is a strategic one, their impact may be much wider. Again we may point to the steel industry. Overpessimism about expansion in the early postwar period contributed to the continuing bottleneck in steel that was apparent until the 1957 recession. In the twen-

ties, the slowness with which aluminum capacity was expanded led to recurrent shortages in that market. The speed, or slowness, with which investment in nuclear-fueled electric power generation is now going forward, even with the aid of considerable government subsidy, is again the product of the decisions of a relatively small number of major power producers. This is not to argue that the pace chosen is the wrong one, but simply to indicate a choice of possible broad significance, lying in large part in the hands of a few corporate managements.

A particular kind of investment decision, the consequences of which may reach far into the future and beyond the specific firm or industry involved, is the decision about location. Where new plants are placed both in regional terms and in relation to existing centers of population affects the balance of regional development and the character of urban and suburban growth. Characteristically, it is the large multiplant enterprise which has the widest set of alternatives from among which to choose in making this decision; smaller firms are tied closely to their existing geographic centers.

Even more far reaching are the choices of large enterprises in respect to innovation. Decisions as to the technical areas which will be systematically explored by research and development divisions and decisions as to what scientific and technical novelties will be translated into new products and new processes and tried out for economic viability have very deep effects. Ultimately, the whole material fabric of society, the structure of occupations, the geographic distribution of economic activity and population are all profoundly affected by the pattern of technical change. Not all sig-

---

[5] See Otto Eckstein, "Inflation, the Wage-Price Spiral, and Economic Growth," *The Relationship of Prices to Economic Stability and Growth*, papers submitted by panelists appearing before the Joint Economic Committee, 85 Cong., 2 Sess. (Washington, D.C., March 1958).

nificant technical change springs from the activities of organized research and development departments, but they do appear to be of increasing importance. And the disproportionate share of a few large corporations in this sphere is greater than in any other. Here again, I am not arguing that the decisions now taken on these matters are necessarily inferior to those which would result from some different distribution of decision-making power, but only pointing to the locus of an important power of choice.

It is worth remarking, on a lower level of generality, that the concentration of the power of choice with respect to new products and new models of old products in a few hands has a significance which is enhanced by the large role which producers' initiative plays in determining consumers' choices in our economy. Whether the extent and character of advertising and selling in our economy is something idiosyncratically American, or simply a product of the high average level of income combined with its relatively equal distribution, it is clear that the importance of these institutions adds to the importance of the producers' power of choice in respect to product change and new products. Further, selling and advertising are likewise relatively highly concentrated, and both the pervasiveness of "sales talk" in the media of communication and the relatively large amounts of its income our rich society spends on all kinds of durable goods give decisions in the sphere of product character and selling techniques a wide impact.

The significance of the economic choices that are made by the powerful large firm can be summed up in terms of their effects on the achievement of four basic economic goals: efficiency, stability, progressiveness, and equity.

Economic efficiency means producing the most of what consumers want with available supplies of resources. It involves not only the idea of technical efficiency—for example, performing any particular technical operation with the cheapest combination of inputs required for a unit of output—but the more subtle idea of not producing less of any one particular good in relation to others, and conversely, more of another, than consumers' desires indicate. In more concrete terms, whenever one particular good is priced high in relation to its costs, while another one is priced low, then too much of the second and too little of the first tends to be produced in relation to consumers' demands. When the price-cost margin on a product remains high over a period of time, this is an indication of economic inefficiency. So is continued price discrimination, in the sense in which we defined it above. In addition, of course, the lack of competitive pressure on margins may lead to inefficiency in the simpler sense as well: not producing the actual goods with the minimum amount of resources possible. The exercise of market power thus leads frequently to economic inefficiency.

Stability of output and employment at high levels, and, perhaps a little less important, of price levels, is an economic goal which is generally given great weight. The exercise of pricing discretion can contribute to destabilizing forces both in upswings and downswings of activity. As we argued before, there are examples of wage-price spirals in which a significant upward push on wage levels in general, and thus on price levels, is exercised by particular pricing decisions. The maintenance of margins in the face of declining demand is less clear and striking in its effects, but it probably makes a net contribution to further destabilization in comparison with some moderate decline. On the other hand, it is clear that stable prices and wages are far more desirable than continuous declines in both in the face of declining aggregate demand; and thus the choice typically made by the powerful firm may be less than the best but considerably better than the worst possible one.

When we come to test the economic decisions of the large firm against the standard of progressiveness, we find that we can say little that is unequivocal. That large firms spend heavily on research and development is clear. That some industries in which the application of improved techniques and growth of output of new products is spectacular are industries—such as chemicals, oil, electronics—dominated by large firms is also clear. But when we try to look deeper, obscurity replaces clarity. Is the present degree of dominance of large firms a necessary condition of the amount of progress experienced, or even a sufficient condition? Are larger firms more effective, per dollar of expenditures, in producing new ideas and new methods than smaller ones are, and over what size range is this true? Should corporations spend on research and development much more or much less than they now spend? Should the incentives of the market be allowed more or less control than they now have of the whole chain of sequential and interrelated processes from the first observation of a new natural phenomenon or the first conception of a new scientific idea to the introduction into the market of a new product or the application on the production line of a new technology? These are all questions to which well-informed and competent students do not give the same answer, if indeed they give any. However, it is enough for our present purpose to say that there are specific examples of the importance for technical progress of competition, and particularly of the kind of competition represented by new and small firms that are not heavily committed to present products and processes, in sufficient number to cast doubt on the universal correctness of the judgments of powerful dominant firms.[6] While we cannot assert that these judgments are likely to be always wrong, we also cannot say that they need no corrective. When technical change can take the spectacularly wasteful forms that it has achieved recently in the automobile industry, in which new products, introduced at considerable production and marketing expense, are not cheaper to produce, cheaper to operate, nor more durable than those they supplant, and their increase in serviceability, functional efficiency, or even aesthetic appeal is at best debatable, it is hard to deny that "progress" and "free choice in the marketplace" both become phrases of rather dubious content. All the potential gain in productive efficiency in the automobile industry over the last decade, and probably more, has gone into "more" product rather than into cost savings and price reductions. This result is the product of decisions of a small number of managements—perhaps only one—and it underlines the appropriateness of raising the question of whether there is not too much power in the hands of those responsible for the choice.

The standard of equity is at least as slippery as that of progressiveness, al-

6 See R. Maclaurin, *Innovation and Invention in the Radio Industry* (New York, 1949); A. A. Bright, Jr., *The Electric Lamp Industry* (New York, 1949); C. Kaysen, *United States v. United Shoe Machinery Co.* (Cambridge, Mass., 1956); J. Jewkes *et al.*, *The Sources of Invention* (London, 1958).

though for different reasons. While the importance of equity in the sense of a fair distribution of the income of society as a goal is undeniable, equity itself is not measurable by any economic standard. We have long since abandoned reliance on the notion that the reward of the marketplace is necessarily a "fair" reward, even when the market functions effectively and competitively. Indeed, some of our interferences with the functioning of markets are justified on equity grounds, reflecting our social dissatisfaction with the income distribution resulting from the unchecked operation of the market. But, although little exists in the way of comprehensive standards of equity which command wide acceptance, certain specific judgments are possible. "Excessive" property incomes are suspect: high profits based on monopoly power are widely subject to criticism. Where market power is translated into sustained high profits, the result can be described as inequitable as well as inefficient. Further, where management decision translates a portion of the high profits into high salaries, bonuses, stock options, and generous pension plans for itself, the imputation of unfairness is strengthened. These are recorded as views that command fairly wide agreement, not as economically inevitable conclusions nor necessary moral judgments. It may be that the equally high incomes of crooners and .400 hitters are logically open to as much criticism; in fact, however, they are not so much criticized.

Any discussion of equity moves rapidly from an economic to what is essentially a political view, since equity is ultimately a value problem whose social resolution is of the essence of politics. When we make this move, a new order of equity problems connected with the power of the large firm appears. This is the problem of the relation between the large enterprise and the host of small satellite enterprises which become its dependents. These may be customers bound to it by a variety of contractual relations, such as the service stations bound to the major oil companies who are their suppliers (and frequently their landlords and bankers as well), or the automobile dealers connected with the manufacturers by franchise arrangements. Or they may be customers without explicit contractual ties, yet nonetheless dependent on the maintenance of "customary" relations with large suppliers of their essential raw material, as has been the case with small fabricators of aluminum and steel products, whose business destinies have been controlled by the informal rationing schemes of the primary producers in the frequent shortage periods of the postwar decade. Or they may be small suppliers of large firms: canners packing for the private brands of the large chain grocers, furniture or clothing manufacturers producing for the chain department stores and mail-order houses, subcontractors producing for the major military suppliers. In any case, these small firms are typically wholly dependent on their larger partners. It is worth noting that this dependence may be consistent with a fairly competitive situation in the major product market of the large purchaser, or even the over-all selling market of the large supplier, provided the particular submarket in which the transactions between large and small firm occur is segmented enough to make it costly and risky for the small firm to seek new sources or outlets.

All these relations present a double problem. First, is the treatment which the dependent firms experience "fair" in the concrete: Have there been cancellations of dealers' franchises by major automobile manufacturers for no cause, or, worse, in order to transfer them to firms in which company executives had an interest? Have aluminum companies "favored" their own fabricating operations at the expense of independent fabricators during periods of short supply?[7] Second, and more fundamental, is what might be called the procedural aspect of the problem. Whether unfair treatment by large firms of their small clients abounds, or is so rare as to be written off as the vagary of a few executives, the question of whether it is appropriate for the large firm to possess what amounts to life-and-death powers over other business remains.

And the same question arises more broadly than in respect to the patron-client relations of large firms and their dependent small suppliers and customers. All of the areas of decision in which powerful managements have wide scope for choice, with effects reaching far into the economy, that we discussed above raise the same question. Not the concrete consequences of choice measured against the economic standards of efficiency, stability, progressiveness, and equity, but the power and scope of choice itself is the problem. This view of the problem may appear somewhat abstract, and even be dismissed as a piece of academic fussiness: if the outcomes are in themselves not objectionable, why should we concern ourselves with the process of decision which

led to them; and, if they are, why not address ourselves to improving them directly? But so to argue ignores the point that choice of economic goals is itself a value choice, and thus a political one; and that direct concern with the loci of power and constraints on its use may legitimately rank in importance as political goals with the attainment of desired economic values. If the regime of competition and the arguments of *laissez-faire* ever commended themselves widely, it has been primarily on political rather than economic grounds. The replacement of the all-too-visible hand of the state by the invisible hand of the marketplace, which guided each to act for the common good while pursuing his own interests and aims without an overt show of constraint, was what attracted general ideological support to the liberal cause. The elegance of the optimum allocation of resources which Walras and Pareto saw in the ideal competitive economy by contrast has remained a concept of importance only to the most academic economist. When the invisible hand of the competitive market is, in turn, displaced to a significant extent by the increasingly visible hand of powerful corporate management, the question *Quo warranto?* is bound to arise, whatever decisions are in fact made. And the fact is that the power of corporate management is, in the political sense, irresponsible power, answerable ultimately only to itself. No matter how earnestly management strives to "balance" interests in making its decisions —interests of stockholders, of employees, of customers, of the "general public," as well as the institutional interests of the enterprise—it is ultimately its own conception of these interests and their desirable relations that rules. When the exercise of choice is strongly constrained by competitive

---

[7] See, on automobiles, the *Hearings* on Automobile Marketing Practices before the Interstate and Foreign Commerce Committee of the Senate, 84 Cong., 2 Sess. On aluminum, see the *Hearings* before Subcommittee No. 3 of the Select Committee on Small Business, House of Representatives, 84 Cong., 1 Sess. (1956) and the *Hearings* before the same Subcommittee, 85 Cong., 1 and 2 Sess. (1958).

forces, and the power of decision of any particular management is narrow and proportioned to the immediate economic needs of the enterprise, the political question of the warrant of management authority and its proper scope does not arise. When, as we have argued, the scope of choice is great and the consequences reach widely into the economy and far into the future, the problem of the authority and responsibility of the choosers is bound to become pressing.

The market power which large absolute and relative size gives to the giant corporation is the basis not only of economic power but also of considerable political and social power of a broader sort. Some of the political power of large business is of course the product of group action to defend group interests and, in this sense, presents no problems peculiar to large business, except perhaps the problem of the large availability of funds and certain nonpurchasable resources of specialized talent and prestige in support of its interest. That we pay, in the form of percentage depletion, an outrageous subsidy to the oil and gas business (which goes to many small producers as well as to the giant integrated oil firms) is a phenomenon of no different order than that we pay nearly equally outrageous ones to farmers. On the other hand, it is money rather than votes which supports the one, and votes rather than money which support the other; and the latter situation is, as the former is not, in accord with our professed political morality. More special to the position of the large firm is the power in both domestic and foreign affairs which the large oil companies have by virtue of their special positions as concessionaires—frequently on a monopoly basis in a particular country—in exploiting the oil of the Middle East and the Caribbean. Here the large firms exercise quasi-sovereign powers, have large influence on certain aspects of the foreign policy of the United States and the Atlantic Alliance, and operate in a way which is neither that of public government nor that of private business. While the oil companies are the most spectacular examples of the involvement of strong American companies with weak foreign governments in areas which are important to national policy, they are not the only ones, and other examples could be cited.

Perhaps the most pervasive influence of big business on national politics lies in the tone of the mass media. Both because of the influence of advertising—itself heavily concentrated in the largest firms, and the big-business character of many publishing and broadcasting enterprises, the political tone of the media is far from reflecting even approximately the distribution of attitudes and opinions in the society as a whole. But an influence may be pervasive without thereby being powerful, and the importance of this state of affairs is open to argument.

It is when we step down from the level of national politics to the state and local levels that the political power of the large corporation is seen in truer perspective. The large national-market firm has available to it the promise of locating in a particular area or expanding its operations there, the threat of moving or contracting its operations as potent bargaining points in its dealings with local and even state political leaders. The branch manager of the company whose plant is the largest employer in a town or the vice-president of the firm proposing to build a plant which will become the largest employer in a small state treats with local government not as a citizen but as a quasi-sovereign power. Taxes, zoning laws, roads, and the like become matters of negotiations as much as matters of legislation. Even large industrial states and metropolitan cities may face similar problems: the largest three employers in Michigan account for probably a quarter of the state's industrial employment; in Detroit the proportion is more nearly a third. At this level, the corporation's scope of choice, its financial staying power, its independence of significant local forces are all sources of strength in dealing with the characteristically weak governments at the local and often at the state levels.

The broader social power which the high executives of large corporations exercise—in part in their own positions, in part in their representative capacity as "business leaders"—is more difficult to define and certainly less definite than the kind of political power and economic power discussed above. Yet it is no less important, and to the extent that it is linked to the economic power of the large firm—a point to which I return immediately below—no less relevant to our discussion. One aspect of this broad power to which we have already referred is the position that corporate management occupies as taste setter or style leader for the society as a whole. Business influence on taste ranges from the direct effects through the design of material goods to the indirect and more subtle effects of the style of language and thought purveyed through the mass media—the school of style at which all of us are in attendance every day. Further, these same business leaders are dominant social models in our society: their achievements and their values are to a large extent the type of the excellent, especially for those strata of society from which leaders in most endeavors are drawn.

This, more shortly stated, is the familiar proposition that we are a business society, and that the giant corporation is the "characteristic," if not the statistically typical, institution of our society, and, in turn, the social role of high executives is that appropriate to leading men in the leading institution.

How much is this kind of social power, as well as the political power discussed above, connected with the market power of giant firms? Is it simply a consequence of their economic power, or does it depend on deeper elements in our social structure? These are questions to which any firm answer is difficult, in part because they can be interpreted to mean many different things. To assert that any diminution in the underlying power of large firms in the markets in which they operate would lead to a corresponding decrease in their social and political power appears unwarranted; so does the assertion that universally competitive markets would end the social and political power of business. But there are important connections. Part of the power of the business leaders comes from the size of the enterprises they operate and the number of people they influence directly as employees, suppliers, customers; absolute size, in turn, is highly correlated with relative size and market power. Freedom in spending money is connected with both absolute size, and the security of income which market power provides. The initiative in the complex processes of taste formation might shift away from smaller and more competitive businesses toward other institutions to a substantial extent; and the ability of firms to spend large resources on shaping demand would be lessened by reductions in their market power. Thus diminution of the economic power of large firms would have a more-than-trivial effect on their power in other spheres, even if we cannot state firmly the law that relates them.

The reasons for concern about the social and political power of business are also worth consideration, since they are not obviously the same as those which the concentrated economic power of large corporations raise. There are two aspects of this question which appear worth distinguishing. The first is the already-mentioned point of the irresponsibility of business power. Its exercise with respect to choices which are themselves far from the matters of meeting the material needs of society that are the primary tasks of business further emphasizes this point. The process of selection of business leaders may be adaptive with respect to their performance of the economic function of business; there is no reason to expect that it should be with respect to the exercise of power in other realms. In short, why should we entrust to the judgment of business leaders decisions of this kind, when we have neither a mechanism for ratifying or rejecting their judgments and them, nor any reason to believe them particularly suited to make these judgments? Second, we can go further than merely to raise the question of whether the training and selection of business leaders qualifies them to make the kinds of decisions and exercise the kinds of power we have discussed. In some quite important respects, it is clear that business values and business attitudes are dysfunctional in meeting our national needs. This is true both with respect to the many problems which we face in our international relations, and with respect to important domestic problems as well. If we look on our economic relations with the underdeveloped nations, especially those of Asia and Africa, as primarily tasks of business firms to be met through the market under the stimulus of market incentives, supported to some extent by special subsidies, it appears unlikely that we will succeed in achieving our political and security goals. If our attitudes toward other governments are heavily colored by ideological evaluations of the kind of economic organization they favor, from the standpoint of our own business ideology, our world problems will be made no easier. And in the domestic sphere, there is a range of problems from education to metropolitan organization and urban renewal which cannot be dealt with adequately if viewed in business perspectives and under business values.

We can sum up these points by saying that the position of big businesses and their leaders contributes significantly to our being a "business society." Do we want to be? Can we afford to be?

These rhetorical questions indicate clearly enough my own view on whether or not we should try to limit or control the power of large corporate enterprise. The crucial question, however, is whether such power can be limited or controlled. Broadly, there are three alternative possibilities. The first is limitation of business power through promoting more competitive markets; the second is broader control of business power by agencies external to business; the third, institutionalization within the firm of responsibility for the exercise of power. Traditionally, we have purported to place major reliance on the first of these alternatives, in the shape of antitrust policy, without in practice pushing very hard any effort to restrict market power to the maximum feasible extent. I have argued elsewhere that it is in fact possible to move much further than we have in this direction, without either significant loss in the over-all effectiveness of business performance or the erection of an elaborate apparatus of control.[8] While this, in my judgment, remains the most desirable path of policy, I do not in fact consider it the one which we will tend to follow. To embark on a determined policy of the reduction of business size and growth in order to limit market power requires a commitment of faith in the desirability of the outcome and the feasibility of the process which I think is not widespread. What I consider more likely is some mixture of the second and third types of control. Business itself has argued vehemently that a corporate revolution is now in process, which has resulted in a redirection of business goals and conscious assumption of responsibility in broad social spheres. This theme has been put forward by academic writers as well.[9] To whatever extent such a "revolution" has taken place, it does not meet the need for the institutionalization of responsibility which the continued exercise of wide power demands. It is not sufficient for the business leaders to announce that they are thinking hard and wrestling earnestly with their wide responsibilities, if, in fact, the power of unreviewed and unchecked decision remains with them, and they remain a small, self-selecting group.[10] Some of the more sophisticated accounts of the revolutionary transformation of business identify business as a "profession" in the honorific sense, and imply that professional standards can be relied on as a sufficient social control over the exercise of business power, as society does rely on them to control the exercise of the considerable powers of doctors and lawyers. This is a ramifying problem which we cannot here explore; it is sufficient to remark that there is, at least as yet, neither visible mechanism of uniform training to inculcate, nor visible organization to maintain and enforce, such standards; and, further, that even if business decisions in the business sphere could be "professionalized" and subject to the control of a guild apparatus, it seems less easy to expect that the same would be true of the exercise of business power in the social and political spheres.

Some likely directions of development of explicit control can be seen in the kinds of actions which now provoke Congressional inquiry, and the suggestions which flow from such inquiries. Concern with the wage-price spiral has led to Congressional investigation of "administered prices" and to suggestions that proposed price and wage changes in certain industries be reviewed by a public body before becoming effective. A combination of the increase of direct regulation of some of the economic choices of powerful firms with an increase in public criticism, and perhaps even institutionalized public discussion of the choices which are not explicitly controlled, appears probable. Such a program will, in effect, do by a formal mechanism and systematically what is currently being done in a somewhat haphazard way by Congressional investigation. On the whole, it is this which has been the active front. The

[8] See Kaysen and Turner, "Antitrust Policy."

[9] A. A. Berle, Jr., *The Twentieth Century Capitalist Revolution* (New York, 1954); A. D. H. Kaplan, *Big Enterprise in a Competitive System* (Washington, D.C., 1954), and A. D. H. Kaplan, J. Dirlam, and R. Lanzilloti, *The Pricing Policy of Big Business* (Washington, D.C., 1958).

[10] See E. S. Mason, "The Apologetics of Managerialism," *Journal of Business, University of Chicago*, **31** (1958), 1.

development of mechanisms which will change the internal organization of the corporation, and define more closely and represent more presently the interests to which corporate management should respond and the goals toward which they should strive is yet to begin, if it is to come at all.

Some Long-Range Implications of Computer Technology for Human Behavior in Organizations

DONALD N. MICHAEL

In 1962, I wrote:

Computers are especially useful for dealing with social situations that pertain to people in the mass, such as traffic-control, financial transactions, mass-demand consumer goods, allocation of resources, etc. They are so useful in these areas that they undoubtedly will help to seduce planners into inventing a society with goals that can be dealt with in the mass rather than in terms of the individual. In fact, the whole trend toward cybernation can be seen as an effort to remove the variabilities in man's on-the-job behavior and off-the-job needs which, because of their nonstatistical nature, complicate production and consumption. Thus, somewhere along the line, the idea of the individual may be completely swallowed up in statistics. The planner and those he plans for may become divorced from one another, and the alienation of the individual from his government and individual from individual within government may grow ever greater.[1]

That was four years ago. Today I should like to speculate further on the possible implications for human behavior in organizations in the light of

D. N. Michael, "Some Long-Range Implications of Computer Technology for Human Behavior Organizations," *The American Behavioral Scientist*, **9** (April, 1966), 29-35.

[1] *Cybernation: The Silent Conquest* (Santa Barbara, Calif.: Center for the Study of Democratic Institutions, 1962).

the computer's capabilities and in the perspective of the needs of tomorrow's society and its individual members.

I will argue here that a combination of circumstances—for example, the size of our population, the complexity of the social welfare programs needed to operate a technologically-based society effectively and felicitously, the increasing availability of powerful and esoteric techniques for planning and implementing these programs, and an insufficiency of highly skilled professionals to do all that needs to be done—will push and pull us toward an increasingly rationalized society in which the computer plays a powerful role.

I will also argue that a variety of behavioral pressures—chiefly the inability of institutions to change as fast as their role in society requires, plus the need to give meaning to the roles of many professionals whose average ability is displaceable by computers—will encourage the persistence and proliferation of nonrationalized patterns of behavior.

I don't think these counterpressures will result in a stalemate. Rather, there will be an increasing separation between operating missions, life styles, and social roles for those institutions and individuals involved in rationalized activities compared to those involved in nonrationalized ones. Just how wide this bifurcation will become remains to be seen.

By "rationalization" I refer to those

activities and attitudes which are applied to the systematic implementation of efficiency and effectiveness. The computer, by virtue of its ability to manipulate enormous amounts of data and to simulate the behavior of complex human and material systems, becomes the core component conceptually and organizationally, as well as materially, in modern rationalization methods. Here I shall speak more of rationalization than of computers because its techniques and associated attitudes extend, in principle, beyond the computer. In fact, the true application of rationalization would include the deliberate introduction of opportunities for the operation and display of the extrarational, the whimsical, the ineffable. In some cases today, those conducting highly rationalized activities using the understanding provided by the behavioral sciences, recognize these factors as significant for efficiency, and doubtless others will do so in the future. But the emphasis will often be on "cold" logic, partly because the decision makers will be ignorant of or indifferent to the role of the extralogical, partly because the actual significance of the extralogical may be unknown in the particular program, and partly because a particular situation may, in fact, require that cold logic be given the highest priority.

However, one way or another, in enough important situations to make the trend significant for our expectations and understanding of coming developments, the computer will necessarily be the core and dominant guide to rationalized processes. Increasingly, the attempted solutions to social problems will be statistical solutions, partly because the aggregate needs of large societies lend themselves to statistical solutions and partly because the techniques for defining as well as solving those problems depend so much on the statistical methods and "world views" of the social technicians and their computers. This is very important—the people who will be turned to for advice in *defining* what the problem is as well as how it can be *solved*, will be those who because of their techniques will define the problem as a statistical problem. Already planners and administrators are tending to place undue emphasis on—that is, coming to value most—those aspects of reality which the computer can deal with just because the computer can do so. The individual—the point off the curve—becomes an annoyance.

In what follows, then, it is the implications of rationalization for human behavior which we will explore, recognizing that for the vast most part the computer will be the basis of and the opportunity for this increased rationalization.

In order to appreciate the context in which problems and opportunities for individual growth and organizational process will present themselves, it is necessary to keep in mind some circumstances which will both push and pull this society toward increasing rationalization.

Of the many factors which will influence the use of computers, certain demographic characteristics of this country over the next two decades will be overriding. We expect around 235 million people in the United States by 1975, about 250 million by 1980, and a world population of 4 billion by 1977. Over the next decade the number of women between the ages twenty and twenty-nine—prime child-bearing age—will increase from 12.1 million to 18 million. There will be 7 million more families in 1970 than in 1964. About half the population will be twenty or under by 1975, and during the same period the number of those over sixty-five will increase almost 20 per cent. This is based on the unlikely assumption that no major medical developments will increase the length of life for more people. According to President Johnson in his recent message on housing and urban development, by 1980 approximately 30 million more people will be living in metropolitan areas than in 1960. Our cities will be merging into a megalopolis stretching from Norfolk to Bangor, from Minneapolis to St. Louis, from San Francisco to Santa Barbara. Even our present concept of a "city" will alter significantly as physical mobility becomes ever greater, communications ever more accessible, and new developments and towns sprawl feverishly over the countryside in answer to the implacable demand for new dwellings for the growing population.

These numbers, transformed into potential demands on the society, point to a second factor pushing us in the direction of greater rationalization: greater complexity among the conditions with which the society will have to deal. Eliminating poverty is one such condition; appropriate education for high rates of occupational change and increasing amounts of leisure time is another, the multiple problems of environmental pollution, traffic, water resources, crime control, and tax bases, which will increasingly plague those cities now fusing into megalopoli, represent still others. All these problems will overlap and interact on a scale of mutual influence which has never before confronted those trying to sense the areas of problems and opportunities for the public welfare or for the private sectors of the economy. Extraordinarily powerful conceptual methods will be necessary to cope with such complexity.

A third factor has to do with the sheer scale of the efforts involved in coping with tomorrow's problems and in taking advantage of tomorrow's opportunities. Small efforts and hesitant programs simply won't do. Supporting the evolution of emerging nations will require enormously expanded programs operating over many years. Smaller wars, such as in Korea or Viet Nam, will be a continuing drain on resources. Space and oceanography will consume huge material and skilled human resources, as will the city building and rebuilding necessary for coping with our growing population. While estimates vary, it is probable that we will have to introduce 30 million *new* dwelling units over the next thirty-five years. Almost any socially worthwhile program will take unprecedentedly large investments in humans and hardware, to say nothing of dollars.

A fourth factor, and a relatively radical consideration for Americans, will be a growing requirement for long-time planning. We don't expect to get to the moon by 1970 by ad libbing that program from day to day. Nor did we build the Polaris submarine system on a hit-or-miss basis. Similarly, it will become increasingly apparent that planning an education system adequate for the future will mean research on learning, teacher selection, preparation, and so on, which will have to be initiated years before it is applied in the classroom. City building will require that plans be worked out so the city can evolve systematically over one to two decades. So too with large-scale oceanographic programs aimed at developing an undersea farming or colonizing capability. So too with packaging long-range developmental programs for emerging nations. But such programs cannot be turned on and off easily. Too much material and psychological and political commitment is involved. Research, development, and capital investment programs are built into everything from congressional "porkbarrels" to university empires, and the subsequent interlocking of vested interests produces a supporting inertia of commitment of formidable proportions. Hence, in some parts of public and private institutions, there will be greater need for and application of powerful rationalized methods for initially assigning program priorities, for evaluating program progress, and for terminating or modifying programs when they no longer merit high priority.

A fifth factor encouraging rationalization will be the persisting shortage of qualified professionals and managers. We don't turn out many of these—mainly because we don't know how. We will, of course, make increasing attempts to mass produce excellence and wisdom but if we do succeed it won't be in the next decade or so, and it won't be on a scale commensurate with the increasing demand for first-rate minds to guide our ever more complex society. Even now we are short of top-flight professionals and managers to the point of jeopardizing, or at least inhibiting, the full growth of socially desirable programs. Therefore, we can expect organizations to develop more careful selection of the problems to which the experts apply their skills and more careful organization of activities to insure that these skills are efficiently used.

The conservation of the highly skilled will encourage rationalization in another way, one which will have novel effects on organizational arrangements: There will be increasingly extensive use of technicians and subprofessionals to do the nonessential work of the professional. We have the precursors of this type of occupation with the teacher's aide and the laboratory technician. The aide will be used along with the computer to lighten the enormous burdens of many professionals, especially at the higher levels. To develop such aide roles will require a careful breakdown of the essentials and nonessentials of skills and procedures within the professional task. As a result, what the professional does and how he or she does it will become a more precise and more rationalized activity with an increasingly rationalized state of mind associated with it.

In addition to these pushes toward rationalization, there will be strong pulls in that direction. In the first place, we can expect very substantial increases in the knowledge needed to understand and manipulate society and to alter its institutions. Without the enormous abilities of the computer there would probably be only modest improvements over the next couple of decades in the ability of the social sciences to predict and control behavior, but I believe the computer will change this. On the one hand, the computer provides the social scientist with the means for combining in complex models as many variables as he wants in order to simulate the behavior of men and institutions. In the past it has always been argued that, aside from conceptual limitations, the behavioral scientist simply couldn't deal with as many variables as were important in understanding and predicting human behavior. Now he can. Of course, he will be limited to those variables which can be logically manipulated, which leaves out a lot of human behavior. But it includes a great deal too. Then he can test these models against conditions representing "real life." For, on the other hand, the computer provides a unique capacity for collecting and processing enormous amounts of data about the state of individuals and society today—not ten years ago, not five years ago, but today. Thus the behavioral scientist not only can know the state of society *now* to the extent it is represented by these data, but he can use them to test and refine his theoretical models.

Already the computer has impressively improved our ability to describe the way men analyze and solve certain types of problems. It has substantially increased our ability to predict how various populations with specific background characteristics will deal with conflicting information on political issues. And it has complicated election day ethics by predicting the outcome on the basis of East Coast votes before West Coast voting is finished. It also provides the technology for teaching four- and five-year-olds to read.

With such expanded knowledge we can expect institutions to arrange their missions and approaches to take advantage of the potent methods available. In fact, we are already familiar with the use of computerized data for student and personnel screening and assignment, and in defense department strategic planning and weapons systems research and development. In the second place, our society emphasizes technology and science as the most efficacious means for solving problems. This belief, combined with the proliferation of scientists and technologists newly turned out by our universities, presages an increasingly influential role for these people. Since society and its leadership are eager for their contributions to hardware development and to information useful for policy planning and implementation, we can expect more of them in decision-making and policy-planning positions in government and industry. And in those positions we can expect that their temperamental tendencies

and trained capacities, as well as trained incapacities, will result in greater emphasis on and attraction to rationalized procedures for dealing with the issues society poses.

In the third place, there are now many frustrated decision makers and policy planners deflected from using their potentially rationalized approaches to these issues. Others in the system refuse to give them the information they need, using the privileged information they possess to block planners and decision makers higher up. And still others in the system are able to redirect programs and to obscure the results because those in planning and policy have inadequate means for discovering or verifying what has happened "out there" or "down the line." Naturally, planning and policy people will be attracted to institutional arrangements which would remove these impediments to systematic planning and its systematic implementation. Rationalization and particularly the vast capacities of the computers used as data banks to store, compare, and process information will be more and more attractive to those whose farsighted plans are now blocked by shortsighted, indifferent, or contrary human beings with other less inclusive plans to implement. This will give further impetus to the trend toward centralized decision making, planning, and operations management—for the resources needed to bypass present barriers are the same ones which can be more effectively used by centralized planning personnel to reach out, through their computers and related techniques, into the working environment and obtain from them much better data than ever before available for planning, for managing, and for evaluation.

What, then, are some implications of increased rationalization for the management role from the top of the hierarchy, where the major decisions and plans are made, to the bottom, where they are carried out (recognizing, of course, that plans and policies have, to some extent, been generated by middle-management actions as well)? The implications will vary in degree and impact in different types of institutions at different levels. I will not differentiate carefully here: Our present understanding of these trends probably doesn't merit precise analysis.

Those who have analyzed management in relation to computer-using systems concur that the quality of management in government or industry will change and that those doing the tasks of management will need more flexibility, imagination, and fundamental intelligence than is now usually required. This will be so because organizations will be far less dependent on men to do routine decision-making tasks which require little originality, imagination, or high levels of intelligence. There is every reason to believe that over the next twenty years computers will come to have a fairly substantial capability for doing routine kinds of "thinking" of the sort which new preoccupies middle management. Some of you are familiar with the comments on these matters of Levitt and Whisler from the *Harvard Business Review*. Let me quote Paul Ginberg of General Electric:

Future development of electronic computers gives promise of providing to humans a capability to effectively cope with vastly more complex problems than currently can be solved. When this capability has been achieved, a single manager or decision-maker will be responsible for tasks that today require delegation among many individuals. Fewer decisions will be required since more complex problems imply formulations that encompass many more actions. The tendency

will be to centralize the control within the political and economic organizations. This will be accomplished by a reduction in the number of echelons existing within an organization and also at any given level fewer components of equal rank will be required to effectively carry on the activities assigned to that echelon. As a result of these changes, fewer managers will be making decisions that control the actions of more individuals than we see today. The checks and balances on the decision-maker will be reduced, since he is then a member of a group with fewer total members to criticize and restrain his actions. Subordinate individuals in an organization who are directly affected by the decisions rendered will be in a weaker position than they are today. Their ability to detect and counter undesirable actions will be reduced, since they will *not* have an increased ability afforded by the computers to understand the more complex problems comprehended by centralized management.

One thing seems clear, whatever the manager's tasks, organizations which are cybernated will not require as many managers per organization as they do now. It need hardly be added that many of those who are presently specialized clerks and repositories of information (and this includes those executives who have been useful chiefly as "live" data banks) will be eliminated as duplication of information storage is eliminated and as individual offices lose their own specialized and restricted data processing and information storage systems. Also, outlying branches of institutions will need fewer clerks, data processors, and information retrievers; their small computers will tie into the central one, making it possible for data to be processed automatically and returned speedily by teletype from the central computer.

Whereas government and industry presently deal with lessened employment needs in the white- and blue-collar echelons (chiefly by waiting for the natural attrition of turnover), this is not so likely to be a plausible solution to reduction in management and other middle-level professional personnel, such as the middle-level engineer whose tasks are being performed increasingly by computers. Such jobs do not "turn over" as quickly or as regularly as nonprofessional ones; presently, much of the psychological and financial security of these positions is tied closely to the particular company involved. Thus, persons employed at these levels will have to be deliberately and explicitly fired. Furthermore, firings will not always be "across the board"—although in some cases a "percentage reduction" in a division of, say, a given type of engineer, will be the procedure. This means that managers may have to single out for firing persons with whom they have worked closely. Clearly, this will produce much emotional stress on those who do the firing. Moreover, if this is a frequent enough pattern, it's likely to engender anticipatory hostility and certainly a cynical sense of "replaceability" in those who work for the higher echelons and who sense themselves as potential victims of rationalization.

Some organizations may begin to recruit management for their hard-nosed ability to fire their fellow workers when firing is needed. Others may choose to make themselves attractive to the public and to ease their own consciences by deliberately eschewing such practices, inventing instead featherbedding methods for holding on to their middle-level professionals or at least cushioning the transition. Indeed, it may well be that over the next two decades a major task for those who do make the grade in management will be to figure out acceptable forms of featherbedding for their less successful associates. After all, this is not a new experience in our society; we are not surprised at men being "kicked upstairs" or having positions "invented" for them. Another approach that will undoubtedly receive much attention will be the attempt to reorganize the tasks of management so that those partial tasks which can't be done by computers can be transformed into full-time roles for live middle-level managers and engineers. Top management will also have to invent new ways of giving middle management some kind of involvement in the organization as those functions which they used to perform and which used to provide this sense of involvement become depersonalized through rationalization.

Certainly a hard-nosed approach to terminating the jobs of middle-level professionals is not going to encourage loyalty to the organization. Lacking loyalty and security, many of those who now work overtime in an effort to further enmesh themselves in the higher echelons of the organization may find the ends not worth the effort. Moreover, as the average school provides a better quality of education for their children, and as living conditions across the nation homogenize, the incentives to stay with a given organization will also decrease. It is likely, then, that at least in industry we can expect increasing mobility among middle-level personnel who, additionally motivated by the knowledge that at any time they may become the victims of rationalization, coolly and cynically seek out the best possibilities for themselves.

It may well be that later in the next two decades this country will find it is gaining a new supply of aggressive middle-level professionals who are not so security oriented as those of the last few decades, and who harbor the aggression—perhaps the hostility—and certainly the drive to take risks and push hard in this kind of environment. Here I am speaking of the products of the antipoverty programs, those who will come out of the slums still harboring many of the dog-eat-dog values of childhood, and moreover, guilt-ridden at their separation from and rejection of their uneducated parents. This will be a latter-day version of the syndrome of the American-born second generation, who dealt with guilt and hostility toward their immigrant parents through hard-driving, ulcer-producing ambitions.

Developing basic techniques in and keeping up with the technology of rationalization will require that decision makers and policy planners continue their education throughout their managerial careers. This pressure for learning and relearning is already beginning, and it is quite likely that men in midcareer will find themselves increasingly useless to their organizations unless they can keep up. At present, reeducation in midcareer is a new experience for most professionals, including managers. And evidently for many it is an emotionally difficult experience. To all the other insecurities of upper-middle-class life is now added the threat of being dispossessed from it because of failure to pass the new tests for professional advancement, tests which reflect on one's own intellectual abilities. The tension will be shared by the families of those confronted with the new requirement. In this tension and its resolution lie new challenges for the family, especially for the status-conscious, heavily indebted families of surburbia.

Since management people with training in quantitative techniques will be in ever greater demand, top management will look covetously at research and engineering groups as a source of talent. Such creative people may not make better policy planners and decision makers than others with similar quantitative technique experience, but top management may think they will, and indeed, some of those in R & D may aspire to the higher status of top management roles. In the past, a major reward for innovation and competence has been to move the person into a managerial position. Thus, competing skill needs as between management and R & D will be exacerbated.

Because management will be a highly competitive, intellectual, and political activity, with a high proportion of washouts, young people will be less inclined to move into this field unless they feel quite sure they have the special talents needed, and top management will be less inclined to send its junior people for further training unless it is fairly certain that they will measure up to the next requirements. Since these requirements will be changing rapidly during this time and demanding more and more facility and expertise in management, there will be a premium on aptitude testing techniques.

We should expect, then, an efflorescence of and improvement in selection techniques and, as these things usually go, they will be applicable to the rest of the laboring force as well. This means that with the growing sophistication of testing techniques for predicting aptitudes and success and their growing application, there will be a lessening sense in the individual of the feeling that one can make of the world what one wishes. In other words, we are in for a modern form of Calvinism in which the evidences of foreordainment will not be found in the Bible but in the psychological test. Such a reduction in the individual's sense of potency and ability to make his own way in the world will inevitably produce profound changes in values about the individual and freedom.

I've said enough already to suggest that there will be strong counterpressures to those pushing for greater rationalization. An explication of these counterpressures will help us foresee other trends in organizational processes which are intimately related to the existence of the computer because these pressures will tend to counteract the enlarged utilization of the computer.

Describing a major source of opposition, the Prentice-Hall *Report on Business* says: "there is . . . little doubt that computer installations are severely resisted at the management level by groups who fear a shift in the balance of power at a management level. This in fact has taken place in many installations."[2] Conventional administrative and political styles will persist in many places—or at least fight very strong rear-guard actions— because some of those threatened by the new demands of greater rationalization are strong members of existing institutional power hierarchies. It is one thing to fire workers with whom one neither identifies as a person nor shares power. It's another thing to fire —or be able to fire—a colleague who but for the grace of God might be you or who has the power leverage to resist.

Three consequences follow: Management, anticipating internal strife at its own level, will often delay this painful reorganization by going slowly in the use of computers; or management may push ahead but, as suggested earlier, go to great efforts to make featherbeds for its peers; or various parts of management may act to sabotage those computer-based activities which threaten it. Thus, in many organizations we can expect a variety of efforts intended to contain the pressures to rationalize. How long they can hold out will depend on how successful their more computerized competition is at doing what the foot-draggers are supposed to be accomplishing—whether it's making profits or monitoring a government-sponsored re-education program. Of course, higher levels of rationalization won't always lead to more effective actions; the results might be quite the contrary when logic-based techniques are imposed in Procrustean fashion on activities better realized through the operation of the extra-rational. But doubtless there are many activities which will be done better through imaginative application of the computer, and in these cases the long-run consequence will be to demolish the obfuscators and foot-draggers. The process will be uneven, however, and during the next couple of decades we can expect to see many embattled and successful holdout organizations, or parts of organizations, whose special appeal for those working in them will be their "old-fashioned" and "more human" approach. Speaking of his own organization, one executive put it this way: "We examined the possibilities of putting in computers, and even though we knew they could help us do a better job, we decided not to go ahead because they would cause drastic human dislocations."[3]

A second counterpressure results from the complexity of the issues to be dealt with combined with the effectiveness and ubiquitousness of "public information" or public relations definers of "reality." These sources of selected and slanted information will make it possible to present an image of rationalization even when the "facts" may come closer to business-as-usual disor-

[2] *Report on Business*, December 16, 1961; Sec. 2, p. 17.

[3] "Computers: How They're Remaking Companies," *Business Week*, Special Report, February 29, 1964.

ganization, if not chaos. The "war on poverty" is a precursor of this sort of pseudo or semi-rationalized activity. It appears much more rationalized than it is in fact. This is not to say there is no effort to rationalize the program; at some levels, especially near the top, the effort is very real. But as the program diffuses into the operational areas, it becomes much more subject to political patronage, empire building, emotional and operational vested interests, and so on. The "systems approach" at the Federal level often gives way to local pushing and shoving, which is publically cloaked as "refining programs and procedures," or "encouraging local participation." Sometimes it is but often it most definitely is not. It may be that eventually the program will become rationalized down as well as up the line, but for reasons we shall discuss later it and future social welfare programs like it may not become rationalized very far. This leads to a third pressure militating against rationalization. Increasingly, this society will have to find a meaningful role for all the average professionals mass-produced by an essentially uninspired, although improved, educational system. For the fulsome use of the computer is, as we have seen, already displacing the mediocre manager and engineer, programmed learning could displace the mediocre teacher, and so on. We could stop their displacement by thwarting the trends toward rationalization but, as pointed [out] earlier, this is unlikely except on a voluntary basis and often there will be very real and pressing needs for rationalization which would make its inhibition very dangerous to the national welfare as well as to the viability of competing organizations. An alternative to deliberately proscribing rationalization in order to preserve professionals' jobs would be to invent and pay for new roles for the displaced and the unhired, which, at the same time, would facilitate the conduct of social welfare programs. If the programs were properly designed, even the use of average talents would make them more effective than past efforts in the social welfare field. Temporarily, at least, their contribution would be a meaningful one.

Paying well for mediocre service, of course, has its analogue in that this affluent society pays very well for mediocre material goods. But a true precedent exists on a grand scale already: The government pays for enormous amounts of mediocre research and development, either directly through grants and contracts or indirectly through the tax privileges it offers foundations and other nonprofit organizations. It is generally conceded that much of what now passes for scientific and technological research is trivial and second rate. In the words of the late Norbert Wiener: "I am rather skeptical about crash projects, and a great deal of the apparent science explosion comes from the use of many people who are labeled and popularly understood as scientists in this mass work that comes in crash projects. . . . So I say that one of the needs of science at the present is to keep the monkeys away from the typewriters."[4]

But research does keep many average physical scientists and engineers pleasantly and affluently busy, and it supports a huge infrastructure of managers, project and program review committees, proposal writers, and public information manufacturers. What is more, a review of the parallel and overlapping social welfare research and demonstration programs of the various

---

[4] Norbert Wiener, "Intellectual Honesty and the Contemporary Scientist," in *The American Behavioral Scientist*, November, 1964, p. 16.

government agencies clearly demonstrates that there can't possibly be enough first-class people to do the work, and that the activated and proposed studies and actions are at best only vaguely related to any systematic set of concepts or goals. There are exceptions, of course, and there will be more over time. But using the vast and growing army of average-ability professionals in government, industry, universities, and private agencies in such ways that they can retain their self-respect and remain affluent consumers of our increasing productivity will require the establishment and persistence of operationally sloppy social welfare programs. In this sense, the poverty programs, for example, becomes an end in itself rather than a means to another end. It is a splendid device not only to alleviate unemployment-based poverty from the bottom, but to prevent it from creeping up the skilled scale. Of course, it will take highly rationalized activities at some levels to insure that such poorly rationalized activities fulfill their purpose at a supportable social and economic cost.

Both the resistances and the counteractions to rationalization will encourage behavior different not so much in kind as in degree from the past. In some quarters, there will be more emphasis on and more appeal in face-to-face relationships and intimate self-enlarging experiences. These are the means par excellence of avoiding or compensating for the depersonalized existence of highly rationalized operations. They are also the means for finding a dignified role not potentially replaceable by a machine. That is, not replaceable as long as the sucess of the face-to-face relationship is not measured primarily in terms of profit making or efficiency. Finally, it is a means

for throwing a monkey wrench into rationalized machinery, for face-to-face relationships always have the potential for placing on the system demands which cannot be met statistically or even "logically."

The most evident expression of this last counterresponse to rationalized systems is the social protest-type activity, such as the Berkeley demonstrations, sit-ins, and other nonviolent devices for disrupting the system. Bending punchcards and overloading the mayor's switchboard so he can't get calls in or out are other actual examples. We can expect more inventions of protest behavior as a way to give personal meaning in a world too big and too complex to find other ways of identifying with its larger trends and circumstances.

However, protest and other face-to-face activities, such as teaching and Peace Corps involvements, will themselves have a tendency to become rationalized. Using these resources efficiently and effectively will impose its own demands for organization and structure. But again, the interstices of these programs and projects will be able to harbor many unrationalized souls and activities. Those who find their roles being transformed into highly rationalized ones will either capitulate or spin off new activities rich in human turmoil and confusion. And so on.

This process is not new, of course, but will show itself with new intensity, I think, as efforts increase to rationalize many areas which now run sloppily, untroubled by up-to-date knowledge about their impact—or lack of it— and unconcerned with planning a decade or more ahead.

A second form of reaction to greater rationalization, for those affluent enough, will be more self-indulgence— or self-social welfare, if you will. People will "owe it to themselves" to get back to themselves and closer to others, to get out of the computerized world of work and into the immediate world of direct experience. Look at all the indulgent attention we are giving the poor to help them lead the good life. Novelty and sensation seeking will be pursued on an expanding scale as will be more deliberate and systematic efforts to enlarge one's "sense of self."

In addition to the proliferation of already familiar ways of getting more "kicks" and culture out of living, a less familiar method seems to be an excellent bet for widespread popularity. I refer to psychedelic, or hallucinogenic, or experience-widening chemicals. Now prohibited by the government except for licensed research, these agents are nevertheless being used quietly by all sorts of people, many of them sober and sensible, enthralled with the intensity of immediate aesthetic and emotional experience available in this way. The toxicity level of these agents seems to be remarkably small for most people. They are nonhabit forming and could be produced very cheaply. They may provide a splendid counterbalance to the constraints of highly computerized, systematized work environments, thereby allowing some the best of both worlds, much as the drudgery and privation of the medieval peasant was made more bearable by the vision of heaven and the splendor of the Church. Legally or illegally, I expect these chemical agents to be in wider use in the years ahead.

Finally, let me draw your attention to another existential factor of exceeding importance, one which vastly complicates the whole issue of when the computer will be used and when it will not. There is no reason to suppose that during the next couple of decades our understanding of the human condition will be so broad and deep or the versatility of the computer so great that we will be able to make wise and sufficient decisions solely by using computers and related techniques. On the other hand, there is every reason to believe that we will have a far deeper and broader understanding of the human condition as a result of the capabilities of the computer.

New knowledge and technologies will be available to decision makers and policy planners as a basis for the increasingly potent manipulation of man and his environment. At the same time, the complexity of the issues dealt with, plus greater clarity about what is known regarding the issue, will confront these social "movers" with the humanistic necessity of making decisions and plans which transcend in their content and consequences those included in a purely rationalized approach to the situation.

The challenge we face is that of somehow developing wise men who understand the limits of human knowledge and have the integrity and courage to withstand the great pressures to value most about the society those aspects of it which can be comprehended and dealt with within the compass of the computer and rationalized activities.

Furthermore, the public (whatever that means) will be an inadequate arbiter; for the problems will be too complex and the techniques for defining and coping with them too esoteric for even the college graduate to know which policy most meets his own long-run interests. The general situation is illustrated by a statement by Harry Schwartz of the *New York Times*:

. . . the public seems happily content with little or no knowledge in situations where adequate explanation must rest directly upon the concepts and techniques of mathematics. It is as if there were a tacit agreement between those who direct this country's mass media and the rest of us; they will not offer, and we will not demand, anything to do with serious mathematics. There are exceptions, of course, but these are rare.[5]

In all, top leadership in many organizations will find that while the computer relieves them of minor burdens, it will enormously increase the demands on them to wrestle with the moral and ethical consequences of the policies they choose and implement. In the past, the executive has been able to avoid facing many of these consequences by claiming he had too little knowledge about the real world or too little control over it to feel very much responsibility for the consequences of his feeble attempts to deal with that essentially unknown and powerful environment. With the new

[5] The *New York Times*, Book Review Section, February 21, 1965.

tools at his command, he will be able to use this "out" less and less. The implication is clear to me: The top-level manager and decision-making professional will have to seek intensively for wisdom all his life. Of course, he will have to be a perpetual student of the techniques of rationalized decision making, but even more, a student of the humanities. If he is not wise—if he is unthinking or single-minded in his application of the computer—he will fail eventually and our society too will fail under such leadership. But providing wise men in the numbers and at the rate needed is a challenge whose outlines we can see only dimly. Our desperate task is to transform this vague appreciation into wise men. We should have begun yesterday. It is by no means clear that we can provide them in time. Nor is it clear that we cannot. But we must do much more than just hope.

The Bogey of Automation

DANIEL BELL

In discussing automation, it may be useful to keep in mind an old Jewish saying: *For example is no proof.* Often the argument about automation is carried on by citing spectacular examples —such as new control equipment, sensing devices and the like—rather than focusing where it should be focussed, on the aggregate effects of automation on the economy as a whole. In other words, even though many jobs have been eliminated in particular industries (e.g., printing or coal mining)

the question remains whether the present phase of automation really poses new and wholly unprecedented problems for the economy.

In the past year there has arisen a new "school," the Ad Hoc Committee on the Triple Revolution, which has argued three propositions: 1) That automation—or, to use Donald Michael's phrase, Cybernation—represents a radical break from previous kinds of mechanization *in its economic effects*; 2) That the pace of technological change in recent years has been accelerating; and 3) That the immediate, visible consequences of the first two propositions are demonstrated by the continuing high level of unemployment which, this year for the first time since

1957, has dipped below the 5 per cent mark.

In this essay, I shall argue that the first proposition is false; that the second proposition is unprovable and, if one narrows the idea of technological change to the specific measure of an increase in the rate of productivity, probably false as well; and that unemployment is and remains a serious problem, but *not* because of automation.

The Ad Hoc Committee has made its claims in sweeping terms:

A new era of production has begun. . . . Cybernation is already reorganizing the economic and social system to meet its own needs . . . As machines take over production from men, they absorb an increasing proportion of resources, while the men who are displaced become dependent on minimal and unrelated government measures—unemployment insurance, social security, welfare payments.

Donald Michael, in his book *The Next Generation*, predicts that "in the next ten to twenty years cybernation will disrupt the whole labor market, from executives to menials." The basis for these conclusions is the idea of a revolution "brought about by the combination of the computer and the automated self-regulating machine." In short, what is "new" is not simply additional mechanization but the threat that computers will take over much of the work of production throughout the economy.

The difficulty with this reasoning is that it is based on speculation, not fact. As Charles Silberman pointed out in the January 1965 *Fortune*, "ten years after computers started coming into use, *no fully automated process exists for any major industry in the U.S. Nor is there any prospect for the immediate future*" (his italics). Furthermore, when the Department of Labor recently made a study of the probable effects of automation during the coming decade, it found that there was no likelihood of "computerization" in sixteen of the country's thirty-six largest industries. Of the remaining twenty, six would be able to use computers, but only in their offices. Only fourteen of the thirty-six industries could possibly use computers to control production itself; and of these, eight are industries like petroleum refining and electric power, which are already highly mechanized. In all, the thirty-six industries studied account for almost half of civilian employment. Thus the prospect that the entire manufacturing economy will be run by computers employing only a handful of workers remains in the realm of science fiction.

The same can be said, I'm afraid, about the view expressed in much recent writing to the effect that we live in a new era of "accelerated pace of technological change" (a theme of John Diebold's book); for the startling thing is that not only do we lack any precise measurement of technological change, we lack even a definition of the phenomenon that is presumably being described. What do we mean by "technology"? Is it machinery and equipment? If so, how do we establish an aggregate measure of such things as computers, tools and dies, drop forges, and the like? One measure could be the monetary value of a piece of capital equipment, but a moment's reflection would show how useless this is for measuring technological change. The cost of a large road-building bulldozer, for example, may rise because of oligopolistic market power, thus causing artificial inflation, or new equipment may be of a "capital-savings" type, which has largely been the case since 1957. Thus any effort to measure technological change by the growth in the monetary value of a nation's stock of capital goods would be misleading.

Is the narrowing of time intervals between the discovery of a new invention and its industrial application a measure of technological change? We are told by Gerard Piel and others that such time intervals are shrinking, and the transistor is often cited as a case in point. But one often forgets the inventions which have failed, so far, to pay off: In 1946-47 it was widely predicted that cheap atomic energy would transform our energy output; but now, almost twenty years later, atomic energy is barely becoming competitive with other energy sources like coal.

The most useful view is the one taken by economists, which maintains that technological change is change that increases the efficiency of a given set of productive forces; it is, to put it crudely, a change that gives you more production for less work. But how is efficiency to be measured in the economy, or in a particular industry? The most common measure we have is the year-by-year changes in the output per man-hour. This is the measure of what economists call "productivity."[1] It is arrived at by dividing the market value of the goods and services produced during a given year (in the economy as a whole or in a particular industry) by the numbers of man-hours it took to produce them. Productivity so defined is obviously a gross measure. It in no way identifies whether increased efficiency has been brought about by new machinery or by a better-skilled labor force, or even by a speed-up of work done on the job. Still, if we are to learn whether technological change has been vastly accelerated in recent years, this is the only consistent measurement we have.

What, then, do the productivity figures show? In the period between 1909-47, output per man-hour in the total private economy increased an average 2 per cent a year. Since the end of the war, the rise in productivity has averaged 3 per cent a year, an increase of 50 per cent. But a closer look gives us a far different picture, for the most spectacular gain in productivity— 5.7 per cent from 1947 to 1959—was not in industry but in agriculture. It was caused not by "automation" but by the fact that "excess" workers or disguised unemployed were drawn off the farms by higher paying factory jobs during and after the war.

In manufacturing the figures fail to show such startling change. Here output per man-hour in the postwar period has increased on the average by only 2.5 per cent a year. Therefore, if we go by the only measure we have, gross as it is, it would appear that there is little evidence for the proposition that the rate of technological change is accelerating rapidly. There seems to be some slow upward movement in the rate of change, the result of a healthier and better-educated labor force, new organizational techniques, and new technology. But the growth of technology today does not appear to create problems very different from those that have consistently faced the economy over the last sixty years.

What, then, of unemployment? A high rate has persisted for eight years

---

[1] Productivity is the measure of the efficiency of a given set of economic factors, and is not to be confused with the gross national product which is the total monetary value of goods and services. The increase in productivity in the economy is different from the increase in national product, and the two are not always linked. One can have increases in productivity in the economy while the gross national product is decreasing —usually because firms will strive to reduce costs and increase efficiency when business take a downturn.

now, and is decreasing only at a snail's pace. If "automation" is not the cause, what is?

The general explanation should be fairly obvious: the economy has failed to grow as rapidly as the national rate of productivity, plus the increase in the labor force. If the output per man hour of a labor force of 70 million workers rises by 3 per cent each year, the economy must add two million jobs a year merely to keep pace with the increase in efficiency. Furthermore, we may expect that between now and 1970 the labor force itself will grow by about one and a half million people a year owing to the World War II baby boom. It is now estimated that the national product must increase by 4.5 per cent annually during the next five years simply to prevent unemployment from increasing. Yet the economy has been able to attain this rate of growth in only three of the last eight years.

The underlying reasons for this failure are not hard to find. We have inherited a staggering deficit from the deflationary economic policies put into effect during the Eisenhower years. Between 1947 and 1957, the gross national product increased at a rate of 3.8 per cent a year. From 1957 to 1962, however, it sagged to 3.1 per cent while the labor forces swelled at an annual rate of 800,000. During these five years unemployment increased by an average of 200,000 annually. The problem was not the elimination of jobs by automation but the failure of the economy to grow sufficiently during the Eisenhower administration.

Since then, during the Kennedy-Johnson years, there has been some improvement: the number of jobs increased by 1.5 million in 1963 and 1964. But the labor force itself grew by 1.2 million, and thus total unemployment declined by only 290,000. Recent economic growth has not been rapid enough to make up for the deficits of the previous period.

We have been talking, it should be emphasized, about the economy as a whole. The problem of economic expansion, however, provides the basic clue to the differing effects of change on those industries which have become outmoded for technological or social reasons. In the 1950s, jobs declined in the textile industry, not because of automation but because young people, marrying earlier, spent more of their incomes on homes and furnishings than on clothes. In the coal industry, hundreds of thousands of jobs were lost as the competition of natural gas and oil reduced the demand for coal. Union economists claim that in 1963 the automobile industry produced as many cars as it did in 1955, with 17 per cent fewer workers. But this would only prove that the productivity in the auto industry was increasing at the same rate as in American industry generally. (In fact productivity in the auto industry is considerably higher than the average but this is offset by the tremendous profits made by the major companies.) The important fact is that until two years ago the output of the auto industry was not growing—given the state of the American highways we were better off for that—and under these conditions high productivity could only result in a shrinking labor force. In the last year the number of jobs in Detroit has grown and unemployment is lower than the national average. Clearly an industry has to expand in order to absorb increases in productivity if employment in that industry is to remain stable or to grow.

Some examples may help to make this point clear. During the past few years no industry has made greater use of automation than the federal government, which has had to handle an extraordinary amount of "data processing." But when the Civil Service Commission undertook a survey of 1,325,000 employees in ten federal agencies it found that over a period of three years only 1,628 had been displaced from their jobs by computers; and of these, 77 per cent were reassigned at the same level, while no more than 2 per cent actually lost their jobs. Automation was relatively harmless in this case because the federal government is a rapidly expanding industry. Similarly, the recent, and long overdue, introduction of electronic equipment in banks probably will not throw many employees out of work, because banking—like the telephone industry, another example of large-scale automation—is still growing. True, there will now be fewer *additional* jobs in these industries than before automation. But this after all is how the standard of living rises—higher productivity allows industry to handle more work at less cost. If it were not for the dial system, the telephone industry would now require the services of every female in the United States.

Still, we all know that the effects of increased productivity in some industries can be cruel. In the printing industry, an entire craft is faced with extinction as typewriter-linked computers replace linotype machines. But where there is effective collective bargaining, the rate of technological displacement can be adjusted to the retirement pattern of the labor force in that industry, and a man's job can be safeguarded as long as he is willing and able to work. (In the New York newspaper dispute, the publishers were willing to grant this attrition principle, but the union insisted that the present *level* of jobs be permanently maintained.)

It is important to locate the problem accurately, for some of the popular arguments about "automation" are dangerously misleading. It is frequently claimed, for example, that the causes of unemployment are "structural": changes in technology are allegedly becoming so drastic that the unskilled and poorly educated will *never* be able to find jobs of any kind. According to this view, unemployment can be eliminated by retraining workers and launching a wholesale educational effort to upgrade the incompetent and the poor, or simply by giving them an income without work. The argument is that technology is making man redundant.

We find curious alignments among those who make "structuralist" arguments of this kind. On the one hand, there are conservative writers and officials of the Federal Reserve Board who oppose government "interference" in the economy and vast public spending. They fasten on the automation issue in order to attack Keynesian fiscal and monetary policies. For if the problem of unemployment can be traced simply to a lack of manpower training, rather than a failure of demand, there is no need to engage in deficit financing to solve. Just retrain the unemployed.

On the other hand, the contingent represented by such writers as Robert Theobold of the Ad Hoc Committee on the Triple Revolution, the economist Ben Seligman, and others further to the left do not believe that the American economy can solve the unemployment problem by Keynesian methods. They find in "automation" proof that a crisis is brewing which can only be solved by drastic changes in the system.

It should be obvious that efforts to improve manpower training and the education of the poor are worthwhile, to say the least. But few of the leading academic economists such as Paul Samuelson and Robert Solow of M.I.T. and James Tobin of Yale believe that these measures can bring about full employment nor do they agree that structural changes have made full employment an unattainable goal. They argue that unemployment is high not because automation has put the unskilled and the badly educated out of work, but because the aggregate demand for labor has been weak—again, the economy has not grown fast enough. As one economist recently put it: Does anyone believe that if the United States got into a war like the Korean War we would still have unemployment? The answer is quite clear: more spending would create jobs for all who wanted them. And much of the current concern about manpower retraining might vanish, too; the experiences of World War II and the Korean War showed that when there is a demand for labor, industry goes to great lengths to adapt work to existing skills; or it develops rapid training programs of its own. And this is what happened in Detroit today where the new demand for autos has reduced "structural" unemployment.[2]

---

[2] This is, of course, an ad hominem way of dismissing the argument, but it is supported by a careful analysis of the structuralist hypothesis by Robert M. Solow of M.I.T. in his 1964 Wicksell lectures, *The Nature and Source of Unemployment in the United States*. Professor Solow has meticulously demonstrated, for example, that there was *no increase in regional variation* of unemployment between 1950 and 1960. Nor have the proportions of unemployment between occupations (from managerial to unskilled) and *between industries* varied over the past ten years. Yet according to the structuralist hypothesis, some regions should have been more affected than others; and the unskilled should have borne a more than proportional increase in the rates of unemployment. The evidence that, over the decade, there has been no increase in regional variation, or in the pro-

The question, then, is how to stimulate expansion in the economy. The administration, of course, has argued that a sufficiently large tax cut would increase aggregate demand and employment. And in fact the experience of the past year indicates that the tax cut has had a positive economic effect. But as Leon Keyserling, among others, has cogently argued, the tax cut is socially ineffective because it often puts money in the hands of groups who spend it in ways that are of little benefit to the economy as a whole. It has, for example, sometimes made extra sums available to corporations which have used the money for investment abroad—thus compounding the balance-of-payments problem—rather than increasing the purchasing power of low-income groups.

Keyserling, and other liberal economists have insisted that economic expansion will come about more readily, and various social needs would be served best, by direct government spending in areas such as housing, urban transport, medical care, and education. This argument seems to me convincing.

But it has been extraordinarily difficult to get the government to undertake programs of this kind. Those of the Johnson administration are a step in the right direction but are hardly more than a beginning. It has recently been estimated, for example, that to achieve even the modest goals set by the Eisenhower Commission for adequate national health, education, urban development, transport etc. by 1975 will cost more than $1,130 billion.[3] This is about $150 billion more

---

portions of joblessness between groups, would indicate support for the "aggregate demand" thesis I am arguing here.

[3] In *The Dollar Costs of National Goals*. The National Planning Association, Washington, D.C.

than the estimated total gross national product itself if we grow at the rate of four per cent a year during the coming decade. In fact it will require a net growth rate of economy as it is now organized. These facts make all the more absurd the claims of the Ad Hoc Committee that technology is making manpower redundant. With so many needs to be filled, we must have a rise in productivity that will require not only increased automation but the full employment of the entire labor force. Meanwhile, the specters of automation can only distract us from the really difficult political and economic problems that lie ahead.

Annotated Bibliography

Recent Books on Automation

Manpower Report of the President
1965 (U.S. Government Printing Office, $1.75)
This is the third of the annual reports now required by Congress. The three reports together provide a comprehensive picture of the manpower resources of the country. The 1963 report is still the most useful, in that it supplies basic data on productivity and future manpower needs. The 1965 report concentrates on retraining and development.

Unemployment in the United States
by Robert M. Solow.
(Almquist & Wiksell, Stockholm)
A 51-page essay which is the most meticulous analysis of the "structuralist" hypothesis about unemployment that I know of.

Men Without Work: The Economics of Unemployment
edited by Stanley Lebergott.
(Prentice-Hall, 1964, paper $1.95, cloth $4.95)
An excellent compendium that brings together the conflicting views on the automation issue, plus material on characteristics of the unemployed, and training programs here and abroad.

Automation and Technological Change
edited by John T. Dunlop.
(Prentice-Hall, 1962, paper $1.95, cloth $3.95)
An American Assembly volume which usefully parallels the Lebergott collection in concentrating on the consequences of automation for businesses, for collective bargaining, and for changes in society.

The New Improved American
by Bernard Asbell.
(McGraw-Hill, 1965, $5)
Hailing the potential of automation, Asbell argues that coming changes will require a complete overhaul of our educational system. His descriptions of the inadequacy of American education are telling, and his proposals for necessary reforms are provocative. Yet as Asbell asserts, it is doubtful whether the reasons for such reforms lie in the needs of the new technology.

Beyond Automation:
Managerial Problems of an
Exploding Technology
by John Diebold.
(McGraw-Hill, $7.50)
A hortatory volume, collecting Mr. Diebold's legislative statements and public addresses over the past several years; with such statements (under the heading of "A Program for Action") as: "The State of New York should conduct and sponsor detailed studies of the human and economic consequences of automation within the state," 216 overblown pages for $7.50? A disgrace.

The Automation Hysteria
by George Terborgh.
(Machinery and Allied Products Institute, $4)
Despite the flamboyant title and somewhat strident tone, this book by an economist who, a generation ago, challenged the Alvin Hansen thesis of economic stagnation, is a useful compilation of evidence on the economic effects of automation so far. By concentrating however on refuting the "alarmists" one is left with the bewildering sense that automation presents no problem at all.

The Next Generation
by Donald N. Michael.
(Random House, $4.95)
An effort to identify the kinds of social changes and problems which the country may face in the next twenty years, the

book suffers from a skimpiness (e.g., twelve significant technological areas are covered in twenty pages) which reduces its use for any serious student of the problem.

Bureaucracy and Its Clientele—A Case Study

ELIHU KATZ   S. N. EISENSTADT

Theory and Research on Bureaucratization

In the broadest sense, the theoretical problem here deals with the conditions affecting the degree of bureaucratization of an organization, specifically of the bureaucrat-client relationship. We are interested in the factors that make for varying degrees of bureaucratization as well as the factors (presumably the same ones) that influence the direction of organizational change. Indeed, in the writings of Max Weber and Robert Michels the problem of organizational change is essentially identical with the theme of bureaucratization.[1] If

Elihu Katz and S. N. Eisenstadt, "Bureaucracy and its Clientele—A Case Study," *Administrative Science Quarterly*, **5**, 253-271, with minor omissions.

---

[1] Max Weber, "The Presuppositions and Causes of Bureaucracy," in Robert K. Merton, Ailsa P. Gray, Barbara Hockey, and Hanan Selvin, eds., *Reader in Bureaucracy* (Glencoe, Ill.: The Free Press, 1952), pp. 60-68. Of course, Weber was also concerned with the role of internal factors making for a greater degree of bureaucratization in the organization, a notable example being his discussion of "The Routinization of Charisma," which tends to develop when a group faces the problem of leadership succession, *ibid.*, pp. 92-100. This also gives a brief statement of Robert Michels' argument (*ibid.*, pp. 88-92), as does his *Political Parties* (Glencoe, Ill.: The Free Press, 1949).

the classical sociological writings were concerned with bureaucratization, the later writings have devoted themselves to the problems of overbureaucratization. Thus, discussions of deviations from the ideal-type bureaucracy outlined by Weber focused on overbureaucratization as a threat to the attainment of the very goals for which the organizations were established. The leading character in these discussions, the official who converts means into ends, has been frequently described both in literary and scientific publications. The same is true for the accompanying manifestations of exaggerated hierarchy and red tape.[2]

Recently, however, with the beginning of empirical research on organizational behavior, these assumptions about the unidirectional evolution of organizations have been put into broader perspectives. Thus, recent empirical research seems to suggest that (1) the trend toward total bureaucratization of organizations may sometimes be averted;[3] (2) actual bureau-

---

[2] The best known of these essays is probably Robert K. Merton, "Bureaucratic Structure and Personality," in Merton, *et al.*, *op. cit.*, pp. 361-71.

[3] Seymour M. Lipset, Martin A. Trow, and James S. Coleman, *Union Democracy* (Glencoe, Ill.: The Free Press, 1956), try to specify the conditions that contribute, in at least one case, to the maintenance of trade-union democracy rather than oligarchic bureaucracy.

cracies are compounded of nonbureaucratic elements also;[4] (3) bureaucracies, once established, are by no means
unchanging;[5] and (4) when changes
do take place, they are not always in
the direction of greater bureaucratization and formalism.[6]

Factors Affecting Bureaucratization in the Official-Client Relationship

The literature provides a number of
suggestions concerning the factors affecting bureaucratization in general.
Weber's emphasis has already been
noted.[7] Succession is another familiar
example. When a new director takes

over from a predecessor, he has little
choice but to insist on relatively
greater formal relations, to demand
adherence to the appointed channels
of communication, and the like.[8] Another factor is monopolization. When
an organization has a monopoly on
certain goods or services (as most public bureaucracies have, of course),
there is little chance of effective protest on the part of the client and no
possibility of recourse to a competitor;
under such conditions, bureaucrats
may permit themselves an attitude of
detachment and ritualistic formalism
vis-à-vis their clients.[9]

The reverse of each of these influences should be associated with a
lesser degree of bureaucratization.
Thus, a smaller organization or one
which suffers a reduction in size ought
to be less bureaucratic. So should an
organization that is aware that its
clients have a choice between it and a
competitor.

Each of these factors, of course, has its
impact on the official-client or the superior-subordinate relationships.[10] But
there are other factors worth singling
out for their specific impact on these
relationships. It is well known, for example, that soldiers in combat relate
to others and to their officers in a
much less bureaucratic way than they
do behind the front lines or in peacetime.[11] Closely related findings emerge
from a study of the informal social
organization that superseded the formal organization of a naval unit on a

---

[4] This, of course, refers to the dominant
trend of present-day research, which has been
concerned with the existence and the functions of informal social relations in the context of formal organization. But more important for our present purpose is the incipient
concern for informal aspects of relationships
between bureaucrats and the public. See, for
example, Morris Janowitz, Deil Wright, and
William Delaney, *Public Administration and
the Public* (Ann Arbor, Mich.: Institute of
Public Administration, University of Michigan
Press, 1958); Edwin J. Thomas, "Role Conceptions and Organizational Size," *American
Sociological Review,* **24** (1959), 30-37;
George F. Lombard, *Behavior in a Selling
Group* (Cambridge, Mass.: Harvard University Press, 1955). For a recent critique of
the assumption that the several elements of
Weber's ideal-type bureaucracy are necessarily
intercorrelated, see Stanley H. Udy, Jr., " 'Bureaucracy' and 'Rationality' in Weber's Or-
ganization Theory," *American Sociological
Review,* **24** (1959), 792-95.

[5] See Peter M. Blau, *The Dynamics of
Bureaucracy* (Chicago: Chicago University
Press), especially Chapter III.

[6] See Ralph H. Turner, "The Navy Disbursing Officer as a Bureaucrat," in Merton,
et al., op. cit., pp. 372-79. Also compare
Blau, *loc. cit.,* for an example of the way in
which variations in supervisory practice affected the extent to which employment
agency officials used racial bias vis-à-vis their
clients.

[7] Max Weber, "The Presuppositions and
Causes of Bureaucracy," in Merton, *et al., op.
cit.,* pp. 60-68.

[8] Alvin W. Gouldner, *Patterns of Industrial
Bureaucracy* (Glencoe, Ill.: The Free Press,
1954), pp. 59-101.

[9] Merton, *et al., op. cit.,* p. 369.

[10] For a discussion of the effect of size, see
Thomas, *loc. cit.*

[11] Samuel A. Stouffer, *et al., The American
Soldier: Combat and Its Aftermath* (Prince-
ton, N.J.: Social Science Research Council,
Special Committee, 1949-1950), p. 100.

tiny, unpopulated Pacific island.[12] Similarly, workers on the night shift were treated differently by their supervisors than were day-shift employees,[13] just as, in Gouldner's study, workers in the mine successfully resisted greater bureaucratization while office workers in the same company did not.[14] The common elements in these situations would seem to be the relative danger or unusualness of the task, the relative isolation from social contacts outside the organization, and relative independence from the immediate presence of upper echelons in the hierarchy. One suspects that certain of these factors would also be appropriate to cases such as Diamond's study of the debureaucratization of a quasi-military group by early American settlers organized as the Virginia Company.[15]

As a final example of debureaucratization, Turner's study of the navy disbursing officer during wartime will serve particularly well.[16] Turner indicated several factors that influenced these officers to depart from the orientation prescribed by the rule book to establish more diffuse relations with some of their clients and to show favoritism. First, many clients of the disbursing officer were his superiors in rank and, consequently, his superiors in other role relationships. Secondly, he found it advantageous to help others who could reciprocate, such as the mess officer. This dependence, in part a function of his isolation from other social contacts, was embedded in a more general interdependence

created by the war.[17] Finally, client and bureaucrat were dependent on each other because, especially during the war, the higher authorities who were to be consulted in case of doubt were both physically and psychologically distant.

This dependence of clients and officials on each other appears as a key factor in the other cases as well, and for much the same reasons.[18] The danger, the isolation, the aborted hierarchy of combat, the night shift, the mine, the Virginia Company, and the naval unit on the Pacific island made men dependent upon each other over and above the specific relations defined for them by their formal organizations. The attempt to enforce ordinary peacetime or daytime relations under such circumstances—that is, the attempt to behave in the accepted bureaucratic manner, or even more, to be overbureaucratic—is what apparently leads to desertion (where one is able to leave) or to mutiny (where one cannot).

Role Impingement as a Characterization of Bureaucratization and Debureaucratization

The notion of dependence may be viewed sociologically as a special case of the impingement of other role relationships on a given bureaucratic relationship. In Turner's study, for example, the observed debureaucratization could be considered a product of the regularized contacts in other roles that existed between the disbursing officer and his clients. Moreover, if

[12] Charles H. Page, "Bureaucracy's Other Face," *Social Forces*, **25** (1946), 89-91.

[13] Lipset, *et al.*, *op. cit.*, p. 139.

[14] Gouldner, *op. cit.*, pp. 105-54.

[15] Sigmund Diamond, "From Organization to Society: Virginia in the 17th Century," *American Journal of Sociology*, **63** (1958), 588-94.

[16] Turner, *loc. cit.*

[17] For example, Turner omits the interdependence based on the common danger.

[18] Note again that we are using "bureaucrat-client" in a generic sense, implying superordinate-subordinate relations (such as in combat, the mine, the Virginia Company) as well.

debureaucratization may be characterized in terms of the impingement of nonbureaucratic roles on bureaucratic ones, then overbureaucratization may be characterized as either the formalistic segregation of a bureaucratic relationship from all other role relations (even relevant ones) or, in its totalitarian form, as the imposition of the bureaucratic relationship on relations outside the scope of the bureaucracy. The bureaucratic ritualist would be an example of one who arbitrarily views all extrabureaucratic roles as irrelevant to the conduct of his office, while the totalitarian bureaucrat "takes his authority home," as, for example, the sergeant bullying his men off duty.

In effect, overbureaucratization and debureaucratization represent a disturbance in the relationship between an organization and its environment that is not envisioned by the classical model of bureaucracy. This model envisages the roles of both bureaucrat and client as segregated to some extent from their other roles; their roles are "specific" to the interaction setting and in this bureaucratic setting it is irrelevant, for example, that both bureaucrat and client belong to the same political club. However, even in the ideal-type bureaucracy a role is not completely independent of other roles; some outside roles clearly may be, or must be, considered. If an old man, obviously unable to wait his turn in a long queue, is given special attention by a clerk, this is not a case of an irrelevant role relationship being allowed incorrectly to impinge on the bureaucrat-client relationship. In general, the classic model of bureaucracy requires only that the bureaucratic organization not be directly dependent on external factors for its manpower, its resources, or its motivation for carrying out its organizational task. If an organization relies directly upon any one segment of the population for financing, or for political protection, these sources of support will clearly receive particularistic attention in the dispensation of the organization's services. It is such direct dependence that mechanisms such as boards of trustees, budget bureaus, and the like try to avert by insulating bureaucratic organizations from their sources of support. What is true for the organization as a whole is true for its members as well. If a bureaucrat receives direct rewards from outside the organization in addition to, or instead of, his rewards from within, obviously his independence of action as a bureaucrat is thereby reduced.[19]

Clearly, then, there is a very delicate balance—varying from organization to organization—between the specific roles defined as relevant to relations within the bureaucracy and those outside roles defined as irrelevant. Note the parallel to our notion of role impingement in Gouldner's concept of "latent identity."[20]

Israeli Officials and New Immigrants

Increasingly, in recent years, the contact between immigrants and the new societies to which they have come is mediated by professionals and bureaucrats. The customs agent, the so-

[19] To cite a familiar example, a civil servant looking to a political party for rewards for his performance in his role as civil servant may do so because he is a political appointee, because he is ideologically committed to his party, or for other reasons.
[20] After developing this analysis of role impingement, we encountered Gouldner's concept and noted its close similarity. . . . Others who have employed analytic concepts similar to the concept of role impingement are Lloyd Fallers, *Bantu Bureaucracy* (Cambridge: Heffer and Heffer, 1957); Frank Jones, *The Infantry Recruit: A Sociological Analysis of Socialization in the Canadian Army*, unpublished doctoral dissertation, Harvard, 1956; Thomas, *loc. cit.*

cial worker, the policeman, the public health nurse, the housing administrator, and the like constitute the immigrants' main connections with the community to which they come, and it is these officials who provide aid and advice, which in earlier migrations were obtained more informally or not at all. This change is characteristic not only of the reception of immigrants in present-day Israel but also of the reception of Puerto Ricans and Southern Negroes in New York and Chicago, and of other immigrant groups in the areas receiving them.[21] This change is in part a consequence of the greater bureaucratization of these areas in the last generation and in part a consequence of the theory and practice of the welfare state which, adapting itself to the immigrant, proffers many social services unknown to the immigrant of an earlier generation. In Israel, this change is also a consequence of the different pattern of motivation and different demographic composition of present-day immigrants compared with the "pioneer" immigrants of the turn of the century.[22]

The remainder of this chapter is devoted to a preliminary discussion of some of the problems arising out of the contact between immigrants to Israel and the officials with whom they deal, viewed against the theoretical considerations set forth in the first part of this chapter. The kind of immigrant with whom we are particularly concerned comes from non-Western countries (such as Yemen, Morocco, Iraq, and so on), where he is likely to have had little or no contact with formal organizations.

The question to which we now turn is why so many of the official-client relations observed seemed to be moving in the direction of lesser bureaucratization. We do not mean to imply that Israeli organizations prior to the influx of the non-Western immigrants were close approximations of the Weberian ideal-type, for the small size of the country and the common struggle made for wide networks of interpersonal relations embracing officials and clients alike. The pioneering and egalitarian ideologies frowned on status differentiation, differential distribution of rewards, as well as on formalities of all sorts. Not least important, political parties exerted considerable influence on appointments to and conduct of the public bureaucracies.

As we have already said, the mere increase in organizational size and responsibility might have been expected to result in increased bureaucratization of relations between official and client, between supervisor and worker, and so forth. To this rapid increase in numbers add the divergence of cultural background between the majority of recent immigrants coming from non-Western countries and the European bureaucrats dealing with them, and one would certainly expect an increase in bureaucratic formalism.[23]

Yet our preliminary observations indicate that this is not the case. We have, of course, found some evidence of increasing bureaucratization as a response to the influx of new immi-

---

[21] A review, by Nathan Glazer, of several recent books treating Puerto Rican migration makes this point; see "New York's Puerto Ricans," *Commentary*, 26 (1958), pp. 469-78.

[22] See S. N. Eisenstadt, *The Absorption of Immigrants* (Glencoe, Ill.: The Free Press, 1955), pp. 64-8, 172 ff., "The Framework of Bureaucratic Absorption."

[23] In 1948, at the time of the establishment of the state of Israel, persons born in Africa and Asia constituted 15 per cent of the population; five years later, in 1953, they constituted 38 per cent of the population. See Moshe Sicron, *Immigration to Israel: 1948-1953* (Jerusalem: Central Bureau of Statistics, 1957), pp. 43-50.

grants. Thus, in one cooperative organization, for example, the hierarchy became sharply elongated. Previously any member was able to reach the highest official of the organization rather directly and informally, nor was it particularly important whether he brought his problem to one or another of the top officials. Now, the same organization has developed a strict chain of command and a new immigrant with a problem must proceed strictly through the established channels and talk only to the relevant official. Yet, even in this organization, as far as the actual interaction between official and client is concerned, there is evidence of considerable debureaucratization.

Repeatedly, however, we have found in institutions as diverse as health clinics and bus companies widespread evidence of debureaucratization in the relationship between officials and new immigrants. We have found cases where the official has assigned himself a greater number of tasks vis-à-vis his clients than those assigned him by his organization. We find considerable evidence of the growth of personal relationships between officials and new immigrants. We have even found cases where the official becomes the leader of a kind of "social movement" composed of new immigrants, thus completely reversing the expected trend which is supposed to lead from movements to bureaucracy. A major key to this unanticipated phenomenon is the notion of dependence we have developed, which takes quite a different form at this point. We shall try to describe what we think we have found, and, in part, we shall do this in terms of case studies. In one case, officials assumed a teaching role vis-à-vis their clients. In another, officials departed from their prescribed role as agents of socialization in certain pat-

terned ways. In the third case, officials became the leaders of an incipient social movement.

Bureaucrats as Teachers: Dependence on the Client's Performance of His Role

The most characteristic form of debureaucratization in the relationship between bureaucrats and new immigrants in Israel is the assumption by the bureaucrat of the role of teacher along with (or at the expense of) his other functions. Consider, for example, the bus driver who gets out of the bus to teach the idea of a queue—"first come, first served"—an idea which is new to many of his new immigrant passengers. Similarly, the nurse at the well-baby clinic may be seen teaching women, informally, which of their needs are appropriate to the health services and which should be taken to other organizations. Or, the manager of the government-subsidized grocery in the new immigrant settlement may take the initiative and go into homes to teach housewives how to prepare certain foods with which they have had no previous experience.

In all these examples, the bureaucrat takes the time and effort to teach a client something about his (the bureaucrat's) expectations concerning how the client role is to be played. In other words, the bureaucrat teaches the client how to be a client so that he (the bureaucrat) can go on being a bureaucrat. This, it seems to us, is a form of dependence, but one which we have not considered so far; it is dependence on the client to act in a way which makes it possible for the bureaucrat to do his job.

In other words, it is expected by the bureaucrat and the bureaucracy that the client will bring with him to the bureaucratic context certain knowledge of expected roles from "outside," even though he may have had no previous contact with this particular bureaucracy. In Western society, for example, one is prepared for one's first encounter with a customs inspector by virtue of one's single-purpose relationships with other officials, tradesmen, and the like. When this preparation is lacking, the bureaucrat himself, in the examples cited, added a dimension— teaching—to his relationship with the client. And this change is an example of debureaucratization both because it adds another role to the specifically prescribed one and because the quality of interaction in the teacher-student relationship necessarily impinges on the more formal bureaucrat-client relationship. Yet these are the very elements which are officially alien to the ideal-type bureaucracy.[24] What is more, as we shall presently see, the teaching relationship may bring further debureaucratization, although conceivably it may simply permit the bureaucrat to perform his role as originally prescribed.

Consider the case of the bus driver. Introductory texts in sociology like to cite the driver-passenger relationship as an example of a purely instrumental, secondary relationship. Neither party matters to the other as an individual. One would not expect the bus driver to modify his behavior vis-à-vis new immigrants or anybody else, yet our preliminary observations seem to indicate that he does. Like other bureaucrats who come into contact with new immigrants, the bus driver tends to assume a teaching role, too. Besides trying to teach the idea of queuing, bus drivers were observed trying to per-

suade immigrant passengers that the cost of a ride on one bus was the same as the cost on the bus that had just gone by, or that the driver did not personally profit from each fare he collected, or that the decision for the bus to leave the terminal was not his. The consequences of the formal organization of a bus company that are understood by client and bureaucrat in modern society are simply not "obvious" to the non-Western immigrant. . . .

It is important to note, however, that an official's dependence on the client to perform his role is probably of a different order from the kinds of dependence we discussed in the other examples reviewed in the first part of this chapter. In the earlier examples, the client actually had power over the bureaucrat—he could affect his wellbeing both as a member of the bureaucratic organization and as an individual. Thus, the clients of the disbursing officer were his superiors in other relationships, or the men in combat or in the mine could withdraw their reciprocal protection of their superior. In the present instance, however, the passenger has power over the driver in very much the same sense that a baby has power to disrupt the family schedule, and clearly this creates dependence of quite a different order.[25]

---

[24] This would be particularly true when a bureaucrat's aim is to bring his client to want the bureaucrat's services; thus, this might be more true of a storekeeper than a nurse, and more true of a nurse than a bus driver.

[25] Replying to a query whether the "dependency" of the child does not sometimes confer power equal to or superior to that of the person on whom dependency exists, Parsons distinguishes between power defined as "relative importance in carrying out the functional performance of the system" and as the "ability to cause trouble by threatening to disrupt the system." In this latter sense, "the child, and other persons or groups in dependent positions have considerable 'power.'" See Talcott Parsons and Robert F. Bales, *Family, Socialization and Interaction Process* (Glencoe, Ill.: The Free Press, 1955), p. 46, n. 18. It is this second type of power which concerns us at this point.

Bureaucrats as Socializing Agents

The process of a bureaucrat stepping outside his role to teach a new immigrant how to act his role as client is highly reminiscent of the processes of socialization and social control as analyzed by Parsons.[26] In the socialization of the child, or in the process of psychotherapy, the socializing agent steps out of his place in the larger social system and assumes a role in the "deviant" subsystem. Thus, the mother is a member of the inclusive family system consisting of father, mother, and children. To bring a new child into this more inclusive system, she must use her role in the earlier mother-child subsystem and selectively reward the child for obedience and disobedience to the new expectations of the inclusive system while at the same time providing a basis of support for the child in his effort to learn the new role. At times, however, the mother may fail as socializing agent, because she herself prefers to remain in the "deviant" subsystem and, ignoring the father and the rest of the family, acts to "keep the child for herself."

The parallel seems striking to us. The assumption of a teaching role by the bureaucrat and the "personalizing" of the bureaucrat-client relationship seems to function for the process of immigrant socialization as does the behavior of the socializing agent vis-à-vis the child. One of the objects of our empirical study will be to determine whether this kind of bureaucratic behavior (whatever its dysfunctions for the organizational routine) contributes more to the adaptation of the new immigrant than the unbending bureaucrat-client relationship.

Even more striking, perhaps, is the parallel to the kind of mother who "keeps the child for herself." Thus, a bureaucrat who has assumed a teaching role may fail to bring the new immigrant client to play the role expected of him by the bureaucracy and may, instead, remain a member of the "deviant" subsystem. This possibility is most conspicuous perhaps in the case of the village instructors who are assigned to each new settlement of immigrants. These instructors are part of a regional Settlement Authority which, in turn, is part of a nationwide Settlement Department. Sometimes, instead of mediating between the new immigrants and the authorities, the instructor becomes so much a part of his village community that his major effort is devoted to "representing" the interests of his clients vis-à-vis the authorities.

The village instructor typically lives among his clients and is potentially available all day long. His job, as compared with the bus driver's, is a highly diffuse one and includes teaching the settlers, who were semiskilled craftsmen or peddlers, to be farmers, co-operators (as this is understood in the *moshav*),[27] and Israelis. In this case debureaucratization is manifested not merely in the establishment of informal relations, but rather in the surrendering of part of the bureaucrat's commitment to his bureaucracy in favor of acceptance of a role in the system which he is expected to change.

Of course, this is only one of the ways that the instructor—given his highly diffuse and flexible role—can

---

[26] *Ibid.*, Chapter II.

[27] See S. N. Eisenstadt, "Sociological Aspects of the Economic Adaptation of Oriental Immigrants in Israel: A Case Study of Modernization," *Economic Development and Cultural Change*, 4 (1958), 269-78; Alex Weingrod, *From the Millah to the Moshav: Culture Contact and Change in a New-Immigrant Village in Israel*, unpublished doctoral dissertation, University of Chicago, 1959.

shape his relations with his clients. Some instructors, obviously, take quite the opposite position. The control of the resources necessary for the very existence of their clients permits them to move in the direction of overbureaucratization. They may interfere in matters—religious observance, for example—which ought properly to be outside their (very broad) spheres of influence.

An even more complicating factor is that the instructor, apart from his bureaucratic role, is often eager to make his clients full-fledged members of the nationwide small-holders cooperative movement or even of his political party, and to have them identify with its ideology, participate in its activities, and so on. Among the instructors who play this double role—which is by no means always considered illegitimate by the upper echelon of the Settlement Authority—many tend to view the various aspects of their bureaucratic role of training immigrants in agriculture and administration as a means to the end of full citizenship. This goal, for the ideologically oriented Israeli, implies the assumption of political and ideological commitments. Such instructors aim at making their clients members of a solidary movement of which they themselves are a part. This subsidiary aim makes the instructor even more dependent on the settlers. They may easily threaten not to participate in the movement unless the instructor provides them with various benefits and allocations for which he is the intermediary, though these may not be their due. In response the instructor may either move in the direction of debureaucratization and succumb to these demands, or he may attempt to use his bureaucratic position to force the clients to assume the political and ideological roles he envisages for them.

Bureaucrats as Leaders

A bureaucrat serving as "representative" or as "organizer" of his clients is by no means the extreme example of the kind of debureaucratization which may result from the bureaucrat's assumption of the role of socializing agent. Sometimes bureaucrats become charismatic leaders of groups of their clients.

Consider, for example, the case of several nurses employed at a well-baby clinic in a relatively segregated immigrants' "transitional community" within one of the major cities. In this setting the nurse—like the village instructor—is expected to be a teacher and to establish the kind of relationship required for successful teaching. Thus, along with the curative and preventive medicine practiced in such clinics, she must teach the women how to care for themselves and for their children in the particular manner prescribed by the modern scientific and philosophical orientation of the well-baby clinic. The authority of the nurses observed, however, extended beyond these rather broadly defined functions. They became generalized counselors and the clinic soon took on the air of a kind of social center where women gathered to greet each other, to gossip, and to move within the orbit of the nurses.

Some of the nurses had become preoccupied with the position of women in non-Western families. Apparently, this particular problem had first attracted attention as a result of the frequently negative reactions of their clients' husbands to one or another of the practices recommended by the clinic. Having thus become sensitized to the subordinate role of their clients within their families, the nurses added the reconciliation of family conflict to their counseling efforts, and, in fact, some of the nurses considered it part of their job to teach women their "rights" vis-à-vis their husbands. In several instances we have even heard nurses recommending divorce to their clients! Step by step, then, these nurses seem to have moved out from their broad but relatively well-defined functions (which include teaching) to assume an even broader teaching and counseling role and, in some instances, to leadership of a kind of "suffragette" movement among their clients. In such cases, the leader does not appear averse to illustrating her message with reference to her own private life or that of her friends. And to the extent that they follow, the clients look to their leaders for active support and guidance, and for a share in the consequences of their behavior.

The leadership role, as played by the bureaucrat, represents a considerable degree of debureaucratization. It represents, in part, exchange of the authority vested in the bureaucratic office for the "voluntary" loyalty of clients; that is, such leadership exists not only by virtue of an "appointment" but by virtue of being "chosen" by followers as well. To that extent, the bureaucrat must submit himself to the authority, and to some of the norms, of his followers. Moreover, he has considerably extended the sphere of his influence from the specific tasks assigned to him to the wider, more diffuse, tasks inherent in the leadership role.

The Party Cadre

FRANZ SCHURMANN

The Cadre Concept and Its Development

Before we continue the discussion of the organizational development of the Chinese Communist party, something must be said about the cadres. The word "cadre" has by now become so common in the Western literature on Communist China that it is usually taken for granted. Yet the real significance of the cadre concept is not always fully understood.[1]

Franz Schurmann, "The Party Cadre," *Ideology and Organization in Communist China* (Berkeley: University of California Press, 1966), pp. 162-172.

[1] For a discussion of cadres based on Soviet conceptions, see Philip Selznick, *The Organizational Weapon, A Study of Bolshevik Strategy and Tactics* (New York, Toronto, Lon-

Strictly speaking, a cadre (or *kanpu* in Chinese) is someone who holds a formal leadership position in an organization. A Party secretary is a Party cadre; a military officer is a military cadre; an official is a government cadre; and so on. However, the cadre concept is so fundamental to Chinese Communist organizational thinking that it has acquired connotations far beyond its basic meaning. Colloquially, the word cadre generally refers to Party members who exercise leadership roles. It is also used to designate a leadership style. A cadre is a leader who is supposed to lead in a certain way. The ideal cadre is supposed to

don, 1952), pp. 18-20. Selznick uses the term "deployable personnel" to characterize the Soviet conception of the cadre. As is evident from our discussion, this collectivist conception is different from the individualist conception of the Chinese Communists.

act as a combat leader, in intimate relationship with his followers, yet always responsive to higher policy.

Every cadre in Communist China has a specific rank. Tables of cadre rank (*pienchih*) exist for every unit of organization. These tables are essentially similar to the *nomenklatura* in the Soviet Union.[2] They are the basis for salary payments and promotions. When cadres are transferred from one unit to another, the basis for promotion and transfer is the table of cadre-ranking.[3] In the strictly formal sense, the Chinese Communist cadre is similar to his Soviet counterpart. However, there are important differences in leadership style.[4] The following pages will briefly discuss the evolution of the cadre concept in Communist China.

Lenin ended his *What Is to Be Done* with a prediction that "the real vanguard of the most revolutionary class" would now emerge and lead the revolution. From the beginning, the Chinese Communist party never doubted that it was the vanguard of the Chinese revolution. During the first fifteen years of the history of Chinese communism, the vanguard emerged, but there were struggles as to who was the true vanguard. A new approach began during the Yenan period. It was now thought that the vanguard must not simply "emerge," but must be created, trained, and "cultivated." As a result, the Chinese Communists developed a continuing concern, in theory and practice, with the problem of leadership. The central concept in this new approach was that of the cadre.

During the Yenan period the Chinese Communists began to think systematically about cadres. The word was widely used in Chinese Communist literature before that time, but without discussion of what was meant by it. Even in some of Mao's writings during the early years of the Yenan period, discussions of the cadre concept and cadre policy are still phrased in generalities.[5] By the late 1930's, however, discussion of the cadre concept becomes more precise. Liu Shao-ch'i, in particular, began to write widely on the subject. Mao Tse-tung, in his "Position of the Chinese Communist Party in the National Struggle," dated October 1938, devotes a whole section to "cadre policy." Mao starts off by saying that "without many leadership cadres possessing both ability and virtue, our Party cannot fulfill its historical tasks." The phrase "ability and virtue" is simply an earlier version of the later "red and expert"; the idea,

---

[2] The *nomenklatura* is kept highly secret in the Soviet Union. Thanks to the Smolensk documents, we have some idea of how the *nomenklatura* operates in the Soviet Union; see Merle Fainsod, *Smolensk under Soviet Rule* (Cambridge, Mass., 1958), pp. 64-5. We have no comparable documents for Communist China.

[3] The difficulty in obtaining information on the Chinese Communist *nomenklatura* is indicated by the fact that even Taiwan intelligence publications have little to report on the subject. The most complete treatment I have yet seen is *Kungfei jenshih Koshih chih yenchiu* (Taipei, 1957), particularly pp. 190 ff.

[4] The Russians use the word *cadre* to designate the men of the vanguard, but mostly in its collective sense. The Russian use is true to its etymology and the way it is understood in the West. The Japanese introduced the word into the Far East, and it soon found its way into the Chinese language. At first, the Chinese Communists understood the word *kanpu* in its collective sense, but in time it changed from a collective to an individual connotation—the Chinese Communist *kanpu* became an individual leader.

[5] See, for example, Mao Tse-tung, "Fight for the Participation of the Masses in the Unified Struggle against Japan," *Selected Works* (Chinese edition), I, 267-68; the report is dated May 7, 1937.

at least in form, may have been borrowed from one of Stalin's speeches.[6] Mao continues that, though many cadres have arisen, more are needed; the systematic training of large numbers of cadres is the major task of the Party. In his call for more recruitment of non-Party cadres, Mao says that use must be made of "the great amount of [leadership] talent that exists outside of the Party."

Mao then proceeds to state his criteria of a good cadre: "[He is one who can] resolutely carry out the Party line, submit to Party discipline, be in close contact with the masses, have the ability to work independently, be willing to act 'positively,' and who does not seek private advantage." Mao ascribed to his enemy Chang Kuo-t'ao a wrong cadre policy: he "recruited his private party, organized factions, and finally rebelled against the Party."

If cadres had to have the right attitudes toward the masses, the top leaders also had to have proper attitudes to the cadres. Mao listed three requisites for the attitudes of top leaders toward their cadres: understanding them as persons; using them; and protecting them. To do this requires giving them directives, as well as allowing them to assume responsibility and develop their own "creativity." Their level of consciousness must be raised through education. And they must be constantly investigated in their work, "their successes praised and their errors corrected." Merely to investigate after an infraction has been committed is wrong. If they have committed errors, the correct method to be used is "persuasion." But against those who have committed serious errors, and "who do not accept guid-

ance," the methods of "struggle" are to be employed. Patience and not hastiness in using "struggle" is required. Lastly, the top leaders must take into consideration the difficulties that the cadres face: sickness, living conditions, and family problems.

Mao described the ideal cadre, in effect, as a combat leader fighting in a context of guerrilla war. The distinction that Mao still made between cadres and leaders disappeared later, and the term came to be used to describe leaders in general. Top leaders were later simply called "leadership cadres," *lingtao kanpu*. The conception of the cadre as a combat leader was not ideally suited to the tasks of civil administration that faced the Chinese Communists after 1949. What was needed then were men to take over the administrative and managerial positions in civil society. Since these were labeled cadre positions, the term cadre, from 1949 on, began to acquire another connotation, namely that of institutional leadership. Yet at the same time, organizational leaders were expected to behave in the manner of combat leaders. Here was a new kind of "official" that was quite unfamiliar to the Chinese. The perplexity of the ordinary Chinese was reflected in a confused definition of the word cadre given in a New Phrases Dictionary published in Shanghai in 1951. Although all publishing houses were put under state control, the new ideology had obviously not yet completely penetrated the minds of the editors. In 1951, the dictionary gave the following definition of the word: "Cadres are all kinds of leadership core cadres in revolutionary brigades. . . . The cadre is not an ordinary person, *laopaihsing*, nor is he a so-called worker in a government bureau. He is different from the usual employees in bureaus, as well as fighters in [military] units.

---

[6] See Stalin's speech to graduates of the Red Army academies delivered on May 4, 1935 (*Problems of Leninism* [Moscow, 1954], pp. 657-62).

[Cadre] means one who has a certain degree of political awareness and is responsible for certain political tasks."[7]

Needless to say, the "definition" is not only confused, but meaningless. However, by 1954, a revised edition of the same dictionary came up with a more precise definition: "Cadre: generally speaking, it means a worker in a state institution. Persons who work in state institutions or a department of production, capable of unifying and leading the masses to carry out Party and government policies and directives, to implement duties and programs promptly under the leadership of the Party and higher-level government institutions are cadres."

Yet, at the same time, the cadre "must possess revolutionary character and revolutionary working manner, be capable of cementing ties with the masses and taking the lead actively. In other words, he must be capable of being the tutor of the masses and in turn being the pupil of the masses."

These two parts of the definition give the essential meaning of the word cadre, as stated at the beginning of this section. On the one hand, the cadre is someone who holds formal position of leadership in an organizational unit. On the other hand, he is to have the leadership style of a combat leader. He is to be both expert and red.

Sociologists distinguish between institutional and personal leadership, with the implication that they are mutually exclusive.[8] Leadership based on "expertise," in the Chinese Communist sense, means leadership exercised through some organizational office or role; in this sense, it may be spoken of as institutional. By contrast, the Chinese Communists regard cadre leadership as basically personal, in the sense of a combat leader directing his troops in battle. The Chinese Communists, by now, regard red and expert as at least somewhat contradictory. To put it in concrete terms, it is difficult for a person to act like a cadre in organizational office. Like everything else in Communist China, the cadre concept appears to have a basic contradiction built into it. This aspect of the cadre concept has made for the different connotations of the word at various times. During the early 1950's, when the Chinese Communists were emulating the Soviets, the "expert" aspect was most prominent. However, toward the latter part of the 1950's, the "red" aspect came to the fore. During the early 1950's, the institutional aspects of leadership were stressed, but during the later 1950's, the personal-leadership aspects.

A cadre is thus a leader. In the chapter on management, we shall discuss some other leadership styles that may be seen as alternatives to that of the cadre. There we distinguish four different styles: traditional bureaucrats, modern bureaucrats, managers, and cadres. Here we shall merely state some of these differences to make clear the nature of the particular leadership style.

Cadres and managers differ from both kinds of bureaucrats in their basic orientation to the world. Bu-

---

[7] *Hsin mingtz'u tz'utien* (Shanghai, 1951), p. 5079*b*.

[8] Though the sociological terminology is not standard, the basic ideas run along similar lines. Institutional leadership derives from the formal position held—from the position invested with authority. Personal leadership derives from the voluntary acceptance of command on the basis of personal characteristics.

Reinhard Bendix, in this sense, distinguishes between leadership and authority. For a summary of some of current views on leadership, see Amitai Etzioni, *A Comparative Analysis of Complex Organizations* (Glencoe, Ill., 1961), pp. 115-16.

reaucrats strive for routinization, for the creation of stable predictable environments. Cadres and managers live in a changing world and accept change as the norm. Traditional bureaucrats differ from their modern counterparts in the selection of means to achieve institutional routinization: Traditional bureaucrats try to achieve this through the creation of networks of mutual involvement, by human solidarity as expressed in webs of personal relationships. The Weberian modern bureaucrat, however, tries to create and maintain a system of rational and legal rules—he sees things in technical rather than human terms; he prefers the solidarity of formal rational organization—"organic" solidarity as Durkheim would say. The traditional bureaucrat sees only "mechanical" solidarity as reliable; bonds of personal friendship and trust hold institutions together. The traditional bureaucrat, given his orientation to human beings, sees the need for values, for an ethos, for religion. The modern bureaucrat is concerned with norms, rules which compel certain modes of behavior.

Cadres differ from managers in similar ways. Though they both see themselves as living in a world of change, challenge, and insecurity, they differ as to the means through which organizational goals and solidarity can be achieved. The manager thinks in terms of techniques, both technological and organizational; he prefers rational organization, for he has the confidence that he can manipulate it and use it to achieve his own ends; he likes rules because he knows he can bend them to his will, to enforce compliance from his workers. The cadre, however, is a leader who thinks in terms of human solidarity. He knows how to "solidarize" men so that goals can be achieved; he can manipulate their thoughts and sentiments; he operates,

not with ethos but with ideology; he strives for a different kind of mechanical solidarity, namely that of the combat team.

During the past decade and a half in China, the "reds" and the "experts" have competed for leadership over economic affairs. Whereas the "experts" have advocated managerial styles of leadership, the "reds" have advocated cadre leadership. However, during the Yenan period, the cadre's opponent was not the manager but the traditional bureaucrat. During the revolutionary terror of the civil-war period, local officials were attacked as severely as the landed gentry. The traditional bureaucrat who wanted harmony and sought to maintain the status quo was regarded as the opposite of the red cadre who saw struggle as the means to change the status quo and create a new society. Yet, despite the great differences that separate the two, they both think primarily in terms of human rather than technical solidarity. This similarity accounts for the endemic Chinese Communist fear that the cadre, particularly when he reaches middle age and acquires status, may degenerate into a traditional bureaucrat.

Sources of Recruitment

During the first years after 1949, it seemed for a time that the Chinese Communists were deviating from the policy, developed during the Yenan period, of recruiting combat cadres. The need for men of skill forced them to recruit from sections of the population that did not promise to furnish large numbers of revolutionary cadres. As we have pointed out in the introduction, successful revolutionary movements often recruit from existing elites in order to find organizational leaders. The Kuomintang did this when it seized power in the middle 1920's. Although there was little left of China's traditional elites in 1949, one group existed from which men could be recruited: the intellectuals.

Late in 1952, An Tzu-wen, chief of the Orgburo of the Central Committee, reported on "cadre work" in the Chinese People's Republic over the preceding three years.[9] Given his dual involvement in organizational problems both of Party and Government, An Tzu-wen was directly concerned with basic policy-making on organizational questions. He began by listing the quantitative successes scored in cadre-recruitment policy. On October 1, 1949, exclusive of military cadres, there were 720,000 cadres in the country. By September 20, 1952, the number had risen to 2,750,000. Most new cadres were recruited from below, and comprised three elements: worker and peasant "positive elements" (that is, activists) who had emerged "from the various movements and struggles"; students graduating from higher schools and middle-level specialized schools, who were assigned tasks in national construction; and a number of "old intelligentsia" recruited "from society" and trained as cadres.

Significantly, An Tzu-wen did not mention the Party as a source of cadre recruitment. In mid-1951, there were 2,700,000 Party members in the army, state agencies, factories, mines, and schools. In mid-1953, there were 1,200,000 Party members in the army.[10] Assuming that Party membership in

the army in mid-1951 was around the one-million mark, this means that there were only around 1,700,000 Party members in the nonrural civil sector. Many of these were probably ordinary people without leadership positions in organization. It is clear that the new rulers in Peking were looking far beyond the Party to find men to staff the new positions. An Tzu-wen cited three important sources of recruitment. First, the "positivists" who gushed up from the movements; most of these were working-class people with more "virtue" than "ability"; we know that many workers were rapidly promoted to supervisory positions in factories, but probably only a few of them were given complex administrative positions. Second, the students, undoubtedly a much more promising source of recruitment; most of them had been sympathetic to the Communists, even though they were usually not involved in the illegal Party organizations of the cities; these were the "new intellectuals." Third, the "old intelligentsia": The new regime preferred young to old intellectuals, but, as An Tzu-wen indicated, the older ones were needed as well.

The Communists were in a dilemma at this point. The party was overwhelmingly composed of peasants on the day of the "Liberation." The new policy called for a halt in indiscriminate recruitment, a raising of standards, a lengthened probationary period, and expulsion of unusable peasant elements. Moreover, workers were the main target of recruitment, since their class position was "correct." Too many intellectuals were of bourgeois origin. This meant that a corps of non-Party cadres of workers began to join the Party rapidly.

At the same time, non-Party intellectuals began to move into administrative and managerial positions. If

---

[9] An Tzu-wen, *Chunghua jenmin kunghokuo san-nien-lai ti kanpu kungtso* (Peking, 1952). An Tzu-wen is a Hunanese with training in the Soviet Union. He once was Mao Tse-tung's private secretary. He has been involved in personnel and control work in both Party and government since 1949. As of late 1960, he was the chief of the Orgburo of the Central Committee.

[10] *Jenmin jihpao*, July 1, 1951 and 1953.

the Chinese Communists had simply changed their recruitment policy and allowed all the new intellectual cadres to come into the Party, the Party would probably have soon turned into an elite club, resembling the Soviet Communist party under Stalin, or into a new version of the Kuomintang. But Mao and Liu had not built up the Party so laboriously during the Yenan period to see it swamped by intellectuals, no matter how sympathetic to the new order.

The solution, for the moment, was to recruit and train intellectuals. More cadres had to be trained, for China faced urgent economic tasks. The only way to do it was to intensify the program of higher education. An Tzu-wen stated flatly that the chief training ground for cadres are the "regular schools." During the preceding three years, 66,000 students had been graduated from universities and assigned government jobs. Most of them went into the field of economic construction. In the summer of 1951, of 15,749 graduates, 15,643 had been assigned jobs by the government. In the summer of 1952, of 27,000 graduates, 16,000 had been assigned to the economic sector, and of these 12,000 directly to production units. In addition to the regular schools, national and provincial ministries set up special training classes. But An Tzu-wen also spoke as a Party man when he points out that "people's revolutionary universities" have been set up to train political cadres. The system of "people's universities" began to emerge as an *alter ego* of the regular educational system. Peking has its People's University and it has Peking University. All China has this parallelism in the educational system. The Party schools are supposed to give the political cadres some liberal education. They learn a little of everything from sci-ence to literature, all within the context of heavy political indoctrination. Most students are from workers and peasant families. The difficulty in this early period was that the Party schools had just recently been set up, whereas the older schools had a solid tradition.

The leadership was unhappy about having to rely so heavily on the intelligentsia. An Tzu-wen complained that many cadres, particularly those recruited from the old intelligentsia, still suffered from "employee viewpoints, pure-technique viewpoints, and tendencies not to be concerned with politics." They have no confidence, he said, in the positive elements that have "gushed forth" from the movements; they dislike the young "superior" cadres, they insist on "qualification and seniority" as criteria for promotion, develop vested interests, obstruct the promotion of new cadres, insist on vertical rule, stress "culture and technique," disregard the merits of the man, and, lastly, have no interest in cadre-training programs. All this, he felt, impedes the promotion of deserving cadres, particularly those of worker and peasant origin.

These "wrong attitudes" were exactly those that later were attributed to bureaucrats in the *Sufan* and other movements. But here these attitudes were implicitly attributed to the intellectuals. The traditional bureaucracy was recruited from the country's literati, and it was not surprising that even under the Communists the educated moved back into the bureaucracy. Unless stern measures were taken, An Tzu-wen said, the intellectual non-Party cadres would sooner or later turn back into traditional bureaucrats; they must either be transformed into true cadres or be replaced.

The recruitment problems discussed by An Tzu-wen were to remain during the subsequent years. He identified the

Graduates from Higher Schools (in thousands)		
	Universities and higher	Middle and
Year	technical schools	technical schools
1949	21	72
1950	18	75
1951	19	57
1952	32	68
1953	48	118
1954	47	169
1955	55	235
1956	63	174
1957	56	146
1958	72	191
1959	70	n.a.
1960	135	n.a.
1961	162	n.a.

SOURCE: *Weita ti shih-nien* (Peking, 1959), p. 172; and *Shin-Chugoku Nenkan* (Tokyo, 1965), p. 382.

Number of Engineers and Technicians (in thousands)	
Year	Number
1952	164
1953	210
1954	262
1955	344
1956	449
1957	496
1958	618

SOURCE: *Weita ti shih-nien* (Peking, 1959), p. 163.

two major sources of recruitment for cadre position: the masses, that is, workers and peasants; and the intellectuals. This is a concrete social example of the red and expert problem. On the one hand, the regime needed trained men to fill positions of institutional leadership; the only possible source for such individuals was the body of intellectuals trained in the country's higher schools. On the other hand, the regime needed political men to lead the masses in the great drives for its social and economic development. The only possible source for the red cadres were the working masses themselves. The regime needed the professionals to fill the staff positions in industry, administration, and schools; and at the same time, it needed the red cadres to fill the important positions of line leadership.

As a result of this red and expert contradiction, and the recruitment policies that derived from it, a bifurcation of elites occurred in the country. The political elite consists of the red cadres, the social elite of the intellectuals. The former derive their status from political power based on ideol-

ogy, the latter from social prestige, based on education. So far, there is no evidence of a single "new class," in Milovan Djilas' sense. The attempt to combine the two elites during the Great Leap Forward did not succeed. Mao's complaint, in his 1957 speech on contradictions, that the intellectuals had not yet fully accepted socialism, still appears to hold true today. This does not mean that the intellectuals are disloyal, but rather that, like all professionals, they are more motivated by self-interest than by commitment to collectivity. On the other hand, the attempt to raise the red cadres to the same intellectual level as the "good students" from bourgeois families has not fully succeeded. One girl I interviewed in Hong Kong explained why so many of China's brightest students still came from bourgeois families: education begins in the family, long before the child enters primary school. The environment in worker and peasant families clearly is not so conducive for preparing the child intellectually as that of urban bourgeois families.

From a sociological point of view, the red and expert contradiction is the most important in China today. It reflects not only the bifurcation of elites, but the gulf between a modern coastal sector and a backward inland sector. It also reflects the contradiction inherent in the cadre concept. We have argued that the cadre is supposed to be both an institutional and a personal leader. The former demands expertise, the latter ideology. One can imagine the tension this must produce in individual cadres. Worker-peasant cadres are constantly worried about their level of education, whereas intellectual cadres are worried about their ideological stance. Reinhard Bendix has argued that contradictory expectations can produce rational behavior in individuals. This indeed may be one of the positive results of the contradictory nature of the cadre concept.

Research Chronicle: Studying High Schools

JAMES S. COLEMAN

I shall describe at some length the intellectual developments that led to my research on the adolescent society and its impact on my subsequent intellectual development and further research. I do this, not because I feel that the mechanics of carrying out research once designed are unimportant, but because I feel that the most difficult matters to communicate in science and scholarship, and yet the most crucial, are the linkages that lead from ideas to research, to new ideas, and on to further research. If a student can obtain a feeling for the movement from ideas to research—a realization that his deepest concerns about society can become the basis for his research—then he need see no dichotomy between these two. If he can come to see, in turn, that the research, grounded in these deep concerns, is his principal means of refining and developing them, then he will hardly settle for their separation. . . .

I felt it was possible to isolate parts of American society that were nearly enough self-contained social systems

From "Research Chronicle: The Adolescent Society" by James S. Coleman in *Sociologists at Work* edited by Philip E. Hammond, © 1964 by Basic Books, Inc., Publishers, New York.

to sustain full-fledged status systems. Yet an important attribute of adult life in Western society is its role segmentation. This means that there is an interlinking of many subsystems except in the smallest communities, and it is hard to define the boundaries of an adult's relevant status-giving environment. It means also that if an adult does not find his self-esteem in one of his roles, he may focus energies on another, so that any social system as delimited for research purposes is likely to have been psychically abandoned by those of its members who were not rewarded by it. Any effect of the social system's rewards on the psychological states of its members was thus likely to be attenuated. This is far less true among children in school, whose relevant social environment is still small and whose freedom to choose their own activities is far more limited. . . .

The Problem of the Study as Proposed

As outlined in the 1955 and 1956 proposals, the study was to measure three classes of variables: the "social climate" of the school, the determinants of the social climate, and its consequences for adolescents subject to it. The term "social climate," rather than more precise terminology, was a compromise to give the proposal's readers a heuristic sense of what the study was about. Throughout the research, it turned out to be a particularly appropriate term for communicating the general intent of the study to nonsociologists, most of whom remembered that the "social climate" that existed in their high schools differed from that which they faced in later life. In more precise terms, this means two attributes of the adolescent status system: the amount of pluralism in the status structure (that is, how many different paths to informal status there were) and the degree to which the paths to status were in accord with educational goals, independent of them, or antagonistic to them. The pluralism derived from my basic interests; the pro-anti school dimension was included because of its importance for education.

The rather simple view of the structure of status systems as pluralistic or monolithic was elaborated in my ideas at that time, but even more as the study progressed. For example, pluralism can arise through the existence of separate subcultures, each holding one value as important, or without subcultures, where all members of the system hold several values to be equally important. I shall return to this point in discussing the substantive ideas that developed from the study.

The focus on status systems instead of a total "social climate" was justified on the grounds that status systems are patterns of reward established in a social system, and it is such reward patterns that shape the activities and aspirations of the system's members. This implies a lack of interest in such other aspects of the social climate as the customs (the particular styles of clothes or the special linguistic terms)

or the mores (the levels of sexual morality). I was not concerned with how free the sexual restraints were, though I was concerned with how much time and attention were devoted to sociosexual pursuits and their relation to the patterns of reward.

The determinants of the "climate" that I felt such a study could examine consisted of two: attributes of the community and attributes of the school and staff. The consequences included, particularly, the questions of deepest concern to me. Would a pluralistic system allow more persons to have high self-esteem? Would the level of over-all achievement be higher? Would adolescents in such a system find it easier to hold to their personal tastes when they differed from others? Would they be less constrained in occupational choice? In addition, there were questions concerning the consequence of value-conflict between adolescents and staff: Would such conflict reduce the correlation between ability and scholastic achievement by pulling adolescents' attention in other directions? Would it carry over and generate negative attitudes toward the community as well as toward the occupational role of teacher?

The Methodology of the Study as Proposed

In essence, what I wanted was to use survey techniques of data collection and analysis to do something new —to study the functioning of a social system. We had bordered on this in the ITU[1] study, and some of the research mentioned earlier had begun to use group characteristics to analyze the effects of social environments on

[1] See S. M. Lipset, M. Trow, and J. S. Coleman, *Union Democracy* (Glencoe: The Free Press, 1956).

individuals, but I wanted to do more than any of these studies did. I wanted to take the social system rather than the individual as the unit of analysis.

Parenthetically, this has led to comments on the study, as it turned out, from a number of colleagues to the effect that I had no dependent variable. I think this will be a characteristic of such studies; in contrast to most social research, they will have no single dependent variable. The difference is analogous to the difference between (1) finding the coefficients of a regression equation to account for the variance in a dependent variable and (2) finding the coefficients of a system of simultaneous equations which link together a number of variables. It is quite obvious that the latter research will appear less focused than the former, for it attempts to lay out the structure of relations in a system rather than to explain the variance in a single variable.

I was far from completely successful in this aim to study ten social systems by survey methods, but it should be clear that this was my aim. I did not plan to relate one characteristic of an individual to another characteristic of that individual, and the study did not do so. The statistical analysis at nearly all points classified persons according to their position within the social system of the high school (as members of the leading crowd, as persons who were outside but wanted in, as persons whom other adolescents wanted to be like or be friends with, as best students, or best athletes) and related *these* characteristics to attributes of their background, to their activities, their aspirations, their achievement, and their attitudes. As a consequence, the units of analysis were roles and statuses in the social system, not individuals—and the statements that could be made from the analysis

were statements about the system, inferred from the status accorded to particular roles, the kinds of persons who were found in these roles, the self-esteem held by people in particular roles, their attitudes and activities.

The methodological difficulties in testing our ideas in the ITU study with a single case and my more ambitious aim here, to use survey techniques to study the functioning of a social system, led me to look toward a design in which many social systems would be studied comparatively or a few would be studied through a combination of internal analysis of each system and comparative analysis of the several systems. The study developed into the latter, though it could easily have been the former if chance had ruled thus. As the first proposal was written, in the early spring of 1955, the research involved the use of a large number of schools associated with a Columbia University Teachers College self-study group of schools.[2]

This methodological question (see *Union Democracy*, pp. 478-480, for a discussion) has yet to be solved satisfactorily. There are many advantages to an intensive single-case analysis which in effect examines the working parts of the system. Yet many of our data-collection and statistical-analysis methods are designed to show a static cross section in time, and so long as they are thus a comparative analysis of several systems (in my case, schools) is more easily carried out. A caveat to this may be made where it is pos-

---

[2] That proposal was never accepted. Neither the Ford Fund for Advancement of Education nor the Carnegie Corporation was interested, and since these were the principal sources of funds for such research at that time, the plans for the research had to be set aside. The spring and summer of that year I spent with Herbert Menzel in analysis of the study of doctors introducing new drugs.

sible, as in the present research, to study roles and statuses in the system statistically. By sampling roles rather than individuals and using roles as the units of analysis, as was done in this research, it becomes possible to infer something about the functioning of the system. If that were not possible, the present research would have failed completely, for the number of schools was too small for a statistical analysis based wholly on the school as the unit.

It is painfully evident to anyone who attempts to study a social system that our quantitative research techniques are in their infancy. For, by sensitive observation and description (as exemplified, say, by William Foote Whyte's *Street Corner Society*),[3] we can trace the functioning of a social system. Yet, when we attempt to carry out quantitative research in such a system, we find ourselves stymied. We shift from a sensitive examination of events, in which intimate sequence in time suggests causal relations between events, to a crude measurement of "characteristics" and a comparative cross-sectional analysis that relates one characteristic to another. That is, when we shift from qualitative reporting to quantitative analysis, we change our very mode of inference.

In qualitative description, we report a stream of action in which the interlinking of events suggests how the system functions. An example from *The Adolescent Society* illustrates this, though such reporting was rarely done.

[How do you get in the top clique?] Well, I'll tell you, like when I came over here, I had played football over at. . . . I was pretty well known by all the kids before I came over. And when I came there was . . . always picking on kids. He hit this little kid one day, and

I told him that if I ever saw him do anything to another little kid that I'd bust him. So one day down in the locker he slammed this kid against the locker, so I went over and hit him a couple of times, knocked him down. And a lot of the kids liked me for doing that, and I got on the good side of two or three teachers.

In order to carry out quantitative analysis, we must collect a number of such systems (in this case, high-school student bodies) and then carry out a comparison to show the interrelation of characteristics. The stream of action is gone, and the whole character of the analysis changes.

Is it not possible to combine quantitative research with the study of a single system? I will offer some suggestions toward an answer near the end of this paper, but for the present it is sufficient to say we cannot do it now.[4]

The design of the present study can be seen as stemming directly from the methodological statement in the Appendix to *Union Democracy*. The discussion of characteristics at different levels of a social system shaped the plans for data analysis, and the discussion there, stating the pros and cons of single-case and comparative analysis, led to the compromise—using ten schools rather than one or many and using a two-wave panel (to capture some of the system's dynamics) instead of either continuous observation or a single cross section.

The methodological design, then, was to consist of questionnaires at two points in time (initially to be a year apart, but, as it turned out, at the beginning and end of the school year). Because the research was to depend

---

[3] William F. Whyte, *Street Corner Society* (Chicago, Ill.: The University of Chicago Press, 1943).

[4] Beginnings in this direction are made by Roger Barker and his associates. See *Big School-Small School* (Palo Alto, Calif.: Stanford University Press, 1963).

on internal analysis, and since it was impossible to sample roles and structures in a loosely structured system, the total student body was included. Because determinants of the social systems were to be looked for in the community and the staff of the school, questionnaires were to be mailed to the parents, and teachers were to be interviewed. (The design showed a lack of realism at this point, for the number of teachers could be estimated even at that point to be around five hundred, and to interview so many persons is no small research project in itself. Instead, the research depended on questionnaires from teachers in the schools.) . . .

In the first few weeks of school in the fall of 1957, we administered the questionnaires in each school, using one day at the school for administration. (In this fall quarter I was not teaching, having taught the preceding summer.) Questionnaires were administered in English classes (from 40 minutes to 56 minutes in length) by our own staff. It was emphasized that no one other than our staff would ever see their responses. This and the fact that the questionnaire rather quickly moved into areas that interested them very much (who their friends were, who was the most popular with the opposite sex, who was in the leading crowd) appeared to establish a frame of reference in which they were not answering as *students* but as *adolescents*. If this had not been so, I expect we should have obtained stereotyped responses such as adolescents often give to teachers.

The remaining details of the field work and initial processing of data I will compress into a few points.

(1) Teachers' questionnaires were distributed, filled out, and mailed directly to us by teachers.

(2) Parents' questionnaires were mailed, using addresses obtained from school files, and returned to us by mail.

(3) The large task of copying students' records, including absences, grades, rank in class, and scores on standardized achievement tests, was facilitated by a fortunate circumstance: two undergraduates from Antioch came to the National Opinion Research Center, were sent to us, and after short training in coding were sent to the schools. At each, they spent several days coding this information.

(4) In May of 1958, we returned to the schools for one day and administered spring questionnaires. In each school, we carried out recorded interviews with a small sample of seniors, again using them as informants about the status system, as we had done in the group interviews during the pretests.

(5) The coding, punching, and cleaning of cards was done by a temporary staff made up principally of graduate students.[5] This occupied most of the academic year 1957-1958 and part of the summer of 1958. For carefully precoded, standardized questionnaires such as we had, this is an unconscionably long time (even taking into account the sociometic data, which had to be coded from lists of names); but as long as research like this is a one-shot affair, using amateur

---

[5] We debated at several points whether to do the study, or some parts of it, within NORC where I had an appointment and had worked on another project. The additional overhead that would have been necessary beyond that already taken by the university led us to decide against it. This made for few additional problems, but only because Kurt Jonassohn, as assistant project director, was extremely efficient and meticulous in supervising coding, key-punching, and initial runs. Nevertheless, the whole of the academic year 1957-1958 was occupied by the mechanical details of getting the data ready to analyze.

personnel for the mechanical details, it will likely remain this.[6]

During the late summer and fall of 1958, analysis was begun in some detail. At that time, Univac I had been installed at the University of Chicago, and we determined to carry out on it much of the sociometric analysis (as well as calculations of correlations among scores such as grades, IQ, and achievement tests and percentaging of ordinary tabulations). In retrospect, the difficulty of programing in machine language and the entrapment that occurs to one when he begins to program meant that a large portion of my own time was wholly wasted.[7]

. . . A curious disorientation at the early stages of data analysis has accompanied all but the simplest research projects I have been engaged in; yet here it was much greater than before or since. In retrospect, it is evident that there is one fundamental cause, and that cause itself had several sources. The cause was that I simply did not know how to carry out the analysis. This, in turn, was partly due to the fact that initially none of the variables at the level of the school was turning out right. Wholly prior to any attempt to measure the pluralism of

the different status systems, we had to measure the importance of different status dimensions taken separately; but, depending on what measure was used, the rank order of the schools, especially in the middle ranks, shifted greatly. In an attempt to get confirmation through consistency among different grades in school, from 9 to 12, we found wild fluctuations from grade to grade in several of the small schools. We had hoped to find wider variation in the schools than we did find; the resulting low variation meant that the schools could not be ranked precisely on the importance of different dimensions. Also, there was the continuing puzzle of the most upper-middle-class school, in which scholastic achievement had from the start appeared to be valued little in the adolescent community, with social activities and sports valued highly. Why should this school, of all schools, appear so consistently low in its adolescents' evaluation of scholastic achievement?

But going beyond the measurement of separate dimensions of status in the schools, we needed to obtain two derivative measures: the pluralism of the status system and the consistency of its values with those of the staff. Though we had not measured the staff's values with enough sensitivity to obtain variations in their adherence to scholastic success as a standard, we could nevertheless approximate the value-consistency measure simply by a measure of the importance of scholastic achievement to the students. Thus, a partially satisfactory measure could be obtained for this variable.

But the status pluralism became extremely difficult. For one thing, a totally unsuspected variable arose to confound the whole issue of pluralism. The pluralism hypotheses implicitly assumed that the dimensions of status were alike in other respects, but in

---

[6] Research organizations with which I am familiar, NORC and BASR, are little better, since they, too, operate with amateur personnel gathered for temporary work. In my experience, it is only in the IBM machine work, the upper administrative levels, and interviewing that the research organization provides professional aid for the academic researcher—though these elements are themselves important.

[7] The programs did do nearly all we hoped, but the cost in my time was extremely great. On the other hand, it was this experience as much as any other that led me to realize how remarkably suited a digital computer is for statistical analysis of social systems, in contrast to the usual IBM card machines. This has led me much further into the development of methods for studying social systems with computers.

these schools they were not. Most confounding was the difference in ascriptiveness of the different systems: in four schools, status was far more dependent on family background than in the other six. Furthermore, this tendency toward ascribed status was not unrelated to the importance of various other avenues for status. In particular, the importance of scholastic achievement proved to be correlated with the importance of family background.

A second important difference among the dimensions of status was in their source: in some cases, such as athletics, the source appeared largely to be in the solidarity-producing functions the activity performed for the adolescent community itself; in some cases, such as cars, clothes, or good looks, it appeared to lie in the power of the attribute relative to the opposite sex; in others, such as scholastic success, it lay in the direct rewards provided to the successful by the staff; in still others, it lay in the autonomy and freedom from adults the activity implies. A general difference between status-giving attributes or activities was their relation to the two surrounding institutions: the school with its staff, rules, rewards, and so forth and the adult society, with its rules, rewards, and so forth. Some status-giving activities were sponsored by the surrounding institution; others were in reaction to it.

This variation split the problem wide open; unless these other attributes of the status dimensions were held constant, the sources and effects of pluralism could hardly be examined. Yet, whatever pluralism there was in these systems was highly related to the content of the important status attributes.

The embarrassing question is why this point did not come up until that late stage of the research. In the very selection of the schools, this should have been evident at the outset. The reason it was not was that we were very pleased to find small social systems with *different* status systems, and we wanted to make certain that the differences were as great as possible within the limits of the population of schools. We therefore neglected problems that would arise in our study of pluralism.

Thus, the research was stymied, when it came to the analysis, by problems that should have been apparent in the design. Corrections might have been made at the outset. If, for example, a large sample of schools had been studied less intensively, the problem could have been by-passed by holding constant the content of the status systems (and the size of the school) when examining the sources and effects of pluralism. The stymie in this case did not mean it was impossible to study the sources and effects of pluralism, however. Other ways were found of doing so, but this will be discussed later.

The design of the research also helped bring about this disorientation in another way. The hypotheses were stated in such a way that they required statistical comparisons between different status systems but there were only ten schools. The research was designed to do both comparative analysis among the schools and internal anlysis of each school. The methodology of the former was quite clear, but that of the latter was less so. What I mean by internal analysis stemmed from the ITU study: translating hypotheses that related to the organization as a whole into subhypotheses, at least one of which could be tested within the organization. Thus, by comparison of the political behavior of large and small locals within the ITU, we were able to test statements about the importance of large autonomous locals as sources of opposition.

Within these schools, there was far less substructure by which such internal comparisions could be made.[8] Thus, I was disoriented by literally not knowing how to carry out the analysis. Only very slowly did a different mode of internal analysis of the system develop: the analysis of roles. In these informally structured social systems there were no a priori designations of roles, so we had, first, to locate the occupants of various roles. We did this from the nominations made by adolescents in the questionnaires. The roles thus determined were:

Members of Leading Crowd

Role Models $\begin{cases} \text{someone to be like} \\ \text{someone to be friends with} \end{cases}$

Those with Many Friends
Girls that Boys Would Most Like to Date
Boys that Girls Would Most Like to Date[9]
Best Students
Best Athletes (boys)
Best Dressed (girls)
Most Popular with Opposite Sex (as seen by own sex)

Then slowly, and without our really being aware of it, *the analysis became almost wholly an analysis of roles*, as an examination of the book will indicate. But because we were still thinking in terms of comparisons of social units (as the ITU study compared shops or locals), it was done slowly and painfully and far less well than it might now be done. Throughout the whole analysis, we maintained the fiction that the principal mode of analysis was that of comparison between schools, while, in fact, coordinate with this we were carrying out an analysis of roles and statuses within the system. Such an analysis of roles is not well formulated in the literature, and I shall attempt later in the paper to describe it. . . .

Thus, I think that part of the disorientation I experienced was a result of finding a disjunction between the narrow framework of hypotheses that I had specified about status systems and the dominant processes that were affecting these status systems. The disorientation lifted only when I wrote Chapter 1 of the report (and of the book), which, by setting the frame of reference of the book as the development of an adolescent subculture in industrial society, provided the focus of the book. Thus, the book as it stands is not an examination of the hypotheses of the research about sources and consequences of status pluralism. Instead, it is an examination of the structure of status systems in high schools and the various sources and consequences of the status system.

Is such a transformation a good thing or a bad one in research like this? From one point of view, it is certainly bad, for the problem as posed is shunted aside and partly lost. From other points of view, however, it may be quite good. Instead of forcing the social system under study to give answers to a set of narrowly defined questions (as specific hypotheses must be), it may be better to give the system more freedom, posing only very broad questions—in this case, questions about the sources and consequences of adolescent status systems— rather than hypotheses about the sources and consequences of one attribute of the status system—its pluralism. For if, in studying a social system, one abstracts from it only those ele-

---

[8] All but one had four grades, which were to some degree separate social systems, and, in retrospect, the analysis would have been greatly aided by treating each grade as a unit. This would have given 39 cases for boys and 35 cases for girls, rather than 10 and 9.

[9] This role and that of the girls (above) were not used in the analysis, though they were measured.

ments important to him, he may inexplicably find that his results are weak, inconclusive, and inconsistent wholly because he neglects those processes dominant in the system.

Yet it is important to recognize that the research did remain rather highly focused. It carried out no analysis of individuals, only of these social systems; and it attempted not to describe in full richness the functioning of these systems but only to examine the values that arose within them and the related dimensions of status.

In any case, the shift from my hypotheses to more general problems of these status systems occasioned some part of this disorientation experienced in the analysis. At the same time, the shift brought on some real excitement, for the processes that were shaping status systems in the adolescent community were extremely interesting. Important changes in the total structure of society appeared to be having an impact here, with the weakening of family, the interposition of educational institutions to interrupt generational continuity, the rise of a separate subculture based on age. In addition, a remarkably great disparity was growing: the increasing social sophistication of the young and the freedom and resources to choose their leisure pursuits, combined with a longer and longer period of financial and occupational dependence. I felt I had happened onto some of the most important social changes of the period and, equally important, social changes which could have a powerful impact on the viability of educational institutions.

It should be clear, of course, that the research did not *test* whether these broad changes were occurring in society. Some of the research results appeared to indicate the existence of these changes, but to test such problems requires a different—and difficult—research design. Instead, the research took these points as premises—premises that provided a frame of reference for the research results and helped bring consistency into them.

Thus, these interests and excitements came to supplant those with which the study began. They were forced into the open by the three papers I mentioned above, and at the conclusion of the third there was enough organization of ideas to generate the structure for the book. Chapter 2 had been written before this time, as had parts of Chapter 3; Johnstone had written the section on use of mass media, and many of the tabulations later used in various chapters had been made. Then, after this reorientation was explicit, the other chapters were analyzed and written in about the order of appearance in the book. This analysis and writing, during the months of July and August 1959, were probably the most extended period of intensive, uninterrupted, intellectual concentration I have sustained—a period of complete asceticism. My family was in Baltimore; I was staying in a room at International House in Chicago, and my only contact with the outside was telephone calls to a machine operator and daily meetings with the girl drawing charts and typing chapters.

This appeared, both at the time and in retrospect, to be a very disorderly way of carrying out research analysis. Is it? Could not the book have been far better if the analysis had proceeded in a more orderly fashion? Certainly this intensive period would have been impossible, had not many of the tabulations already been done, had not most of the mechanical problems already been disposed of.

It may be, however, that such a period is necessary, not in order to carry out analysis, but in order to carry out synthesis. The synthesis necessary in any coherent research is often neglected in our examination of research activity. We can teach methods of analysis; yet any extensive research of the sort that results in a book requires something equally important: an organization or synthesis which provides the essential structure into which the pieces of analysis fit.

Such synthesis is perhaps better done, as it was in the ITU study, over a longer period and as the result of extended discussions between the authors over a period of time.[10] Yet the whole problem of how it is best done and what the interplay between analysis and synthesis should be is an open one. . . .

The Methodological Consequences of the Research

The methodological consequences of this research for my subsequent work have been of several sorts. One is what was termed above "role analysis." Analysis of social units based on survey data has ordinarily been conceived in terms of what has been variously called contextual analysis, structural-effects analysis, or compositional-effects analysis. In such analysis, a dependent variable is explained in terms of two (or sometimes more) independent variables: a variable characterizing the individual and a variable characterizing the group, ordinarily the aggregate of the individual independent variable. But most of the analysis in *The Adolescent Society* is not of this sort. It first identified roles and then carried

out much of the analysis as an internal analysis of roles. By identifying certain positions of high status (members of the leading crowd, the role models, and those with many friends) and seeing what kinds of persons arrived at those positions, it was possible to learn both about the value systems in the school and about the impact of the external social structure. For example, persons characterized by other roles (best students, best athletes) were examined to see how often they were in positions of status, and from this analysis of the relation between roles one could infer the status and power that derived from various activities in the school. Persons were characterized in terms of their background and examined to see how they appeared differentially in positions of status, thus showing the penetration of ascriptive background factors into the status system of the school.

Again, it was possible to examine some of the effects of the system directly by such analysis of roles through scrutinizing the attitudes held and the activities engaged in by those in positions of status. As one example, the strong psychological impact of the system was apparent in the far more positive self-images held by those with high status and in the differentially positive images held by those in various roles (best student, leader in activities, most popular). The differential attitudes of those in the role of athlete toward the role of athlete and of those in the role of best student toward the role of best student showed the impact of the system on the values of students.

It was still the case that much comparison among schools was necessary, but this comparative analysis was based on the role analysis discussed above. For example, the relative status of athletes and scholars differed from

---

10 Equally important in that research was the fact that the synthesis was already far more fully developed by Lipset at the beginning. The research did not drastically modify the original focus but elaborated and confirmed it.

school to school, and that difference was used to characterize the value difference between the schools.

It would be valuable to have an explicit methodology of such role analysis, for it seems that much can be learned about the functioning of a social system in this way. What can be learned differs radically, according to whether roles are filled through popular consent (as in this research), by authoritative appointment, or by other attributes. Where the roles are filled by popular consent, for example, their occupants may be studied to infer the values of the members of the system. In any case, there seems to be a field waiting for definitive methodological treatment. The most exciting point in such methodology is its intimate connection with sociological substance. For it is clear that if analysis of a social system is to proceed very far, it must discard the study of individuals qua individuals and let attributes of the system such as roles, norms, activities, values, and statuses constitute the very units of analysis.

Computer Techniques and Dynamic Synthesis

The research, and the experience with computers it entailed, convinced me that it was possible to analyze social structures with computers in ways that had never been possible without them. This conviction led to an extensive research project in the use of computers for the analysis of social systems. The research is beginning to bear fruit, but it is still more nearly a promissory note than an accomplished fact. Although several partial analyses have been carried out, progress has not met my hopes. I believe the reason is that such an analysis of a functioning system requires techniques totally different from our usual statistical analysis. In order to carry out the analysis, some parts of the structure must be modeled; there must be a more intimate mixture of analysis and synthesis than occurs in our old techniques. Yet I suspect that when we come to have these methods well developed, the old ones, in which the analysis is done by machine tabulations and the synthesis according to a vague and unreliable model in the researcher's head, will show their crudity.

It is likely that the requirements of studying a social system and the possibilities afforded by a computer will begin to influence radically even the kind of data collected. Let me return for a moment to the mention that was made earlier of the stream of behavior and how it is lost when we turn to quantitative analysis of a social system. What seems to occur is this: the roles, institutions, and other parts of the system are identified, and then an account of the stream of behavior that flows among them is given, mostly through example of concrete cases drawn from observation to interview. This has both structure and dynamics that are missing from most quantitative analyses of social units based on survey data. A good role analysis of the sort described above puts into the analysis the necessary structure. But it still lacks much of the process which constitutes the functioning of the system.

One means of reintroducing the processes of the system or organization is through system simulation based on data rather different from data we usually collect in quantitative analysis. Suppose that we first identified the major roles and role relations in the system, sampled these, and then obtained data on the types of response made by a person in a given role when faced with a given situation. This might be done quite precisely or quite loosely, but the important point is that the result would be an inventory of contingent responses for each role. These results then become the critical set of data necessary for synthesizing a model of the system; in ways we conceive only vaguely now, it becomes possible to pose questions about the system's functioning—questions that cannot be answered now either by our quantitative analyses of systems or by qualitative ones. Such work must at present be stated in very tentative form, but it indicates the direction of ideas first set off by the disorientation that this research produced. . . .

Organizational Measurement and Its Bearing on the Study of College Environments

ALLEN H. BARTON

Classifying organizational measures

Empirical studies of organizations have consisted largely of two types: qualitative case studies and surveys of organization members. The qualitative studies tend to be limited to descriptive data on single organizations; the surveys have usually been limited to one organization and to one status group within the organization—normally the lowest status level, the workers, students, or rank-and-file members. In recent years the qualitative studies have become more analytical and aimed at discovering generic relationships and processes; the cumulation of such analytically focused case studies provides one source for systematic comparative analysis of organizations. The quantitative studies have also progressed. Some have ingeniously employed the records of individual and organizational behavior kept by the organizations themselves to provide quantitative evidence of relationships, processes, and trends. Others have expanded the sampling survey to cover several or even hundreds of organizational units, and in some cases to cover two or more status groups within each unit.

The development of comparative studies creates a need for classification and measurement of organizations as such. The measurement of organizational characteristics is in a very primitive state compared with the measurement of individual attributes. This paper presents a collection of examples of organizational measurements, drawn from empirical studies, and examines certain features of them. The term measurement is used here in a broad sense to cover all systematic classificatory procedures, ranging from simple two-way classifications (like "having close supervision versus general supervision") to numerical counts and scores which can be treated as continuous variables (size, productivity, per cent of members satisfied). The studies examined cover a wide variety of institutions: factories, colleges, prisons, political parties, military units, unions, hospitals, churches, women's clubs, courts, newspapers, schools, and so on.

There are three ways in which measurements of organizational characteristics can be distinguished: by the sub-

Allen H. Barton, "Organizational Measurement and Its Bearing on the Study of College Environments," *Organizational Measurement and Its Bearing on the Study of College Environments* (New York: College Entrance Examination Board, 1961), pp. 1-41.

stantive attribute measured, by the formal structure of the measure, and by the source of the data.

A simple *substantive* classification of what is measured may be the best starting point. We may distinguish three external characteristics of organizations:

Inputs: The kind of personnel recruited, the economic resources available, the physical facilities.

Outputs: The physical production, effects on people, or other services and consequences of organizational activity.

Environment: The characteristics of the community in which the organization belongs, or its relations with the public or with other organizations.

We may also distinguish three main types of "internal characteristics," each of which has important subdivisions:

Social structure (formal and informal relationships within the organization): Formal authority structure, power structure, communication and job contact structure, informal social relationship, division of labor and departmentalization, and size.

Attitudes (broadly defined to include values, norms, perceptions, satisfaction, and similar individual states of mind): Organizational goals and values, norms concerning organizational roles, perceptions of organizational characteristics, and satisfaction with role or with organization.

Activities: Individual role behavior, collective activities, and administrative devices.

This sixfold classification of substantive attributes of organizations, with its further subcategories, is not intended as a basis for a theory of organizations; rather it seems useful because similar problems may arise in measurement of attributes classified under a given heading. In the long run, of course, the development of

measurement and the development of theory support one another.

The formal aspect of measurements which is most significant for organizational measures is the relation of the units from which the basic data are gathered and those which are characterized by the eventual measurement. Concrete organizations consist of individuals; of interacting pairs; of intermediate units such as work groups, departments, and local branches; and of certain collective facilities such as buildings, budgets, bank accounts, rule books, traditions, and symbols. Measurements of organizational properties may be derived from basic data gathered at any level of the components of the organization. The main distinctions which we will make are:

Additive measures: Based on simple addition or averaging of attributes of individual organization members. Thus a school whose pupils have mainly high IQ's can be said to have a "high average IQ"; a ship, most of whose crewmen are happy, is a "happy ship."

Distributional measures: Based on the distribution of individual member characteristics but not corresponding to individual properties in the same direct manner as the additive measures. Measures of the *homogeneity* or *variation* of groups of individuals do not correspond to any property possessed by an individual; the same applies to measures of *correlation* between individual attributes in a group. These properties emerge only at the group level.

Relational pattern measures: Based on relationships of pairs of individuals within the group. These are often called "sociometric measurements" of group properties, and include the ratio of in-group friendships to those where one pair is outside the group; the average frequency of interaction between group members; and more complex patterns of relationship such as clique structure or the "shape" of communication nets.

Integral measures: Based on organizational attributes which are not derived from data on individual members, but from the programs, outputs, or possessions of the organization as a whole.

Contextual measures: Based on data on larger units of which the organization is a member, such as the community or the national organization of which it is a part; or on the relationship of the organization being studied with other organizations in its environment.[1]

We will also consider the source of the basic data which are measured. The main types of sources follow.

Institutional Records: These may take the form either of raw files, records of decisions, transcripts of meetings, lists of rules, and so forth, or of already prepared statistics. In some cases the data are found in generally published sources such as directories or government reports; in other cases it must be sought in the organization's files. Most organizations keep voluminous records, although they seldom have prepared precisely those statistics which the researcher would like.

Direct observations: These include "field notes" by the researcher or his agents describing events in the organization; checklists of objects or activities which the observer is to look for; systematic schemes for coding observed activities, like the Bales Interaction Process Analysis; and "ratings" of organization properties to be made by the observer on the basis of his interpretation of what he observes.

Informant reports: These are descriptions, systematic checklists, or ratings which are obtained by the researcher from small numbers of people already familiar with the organization. People who belong to an organization or have dealings with it generally know a good deal about it, although they may be subject to serious bias in some matters. They are able to tell us about past events we cannot observe. Interviews, papers written at the reseacher's request, and letters to the researcher giving requested information are all ways of tapping this special knowledge. We include here only information gathered from relatively few, selected informants, not that obtained by mass questionnaires. People in certain positions may have unusually good information—not only the leaders but specialists and "old-timers."

Reports of samples of members: This technique involves asking large numbers of participants to give descriptions or ratings of the organization and its members, through the use of standardized interviews or questionnaires. Their reports are analyzed quantitatively, to tell us the characteristics of the organization *as perceived* by aggregates of members.

Surveys of individual attitudes and behavior: In this technique we survey individuals concerning their own attitudes or behavior; they are reporting not on the organization in general but on themselves. These *self-reports* are obtained systematically from large numbers of members, and analyzed quantitatively to produce measures for the whole group or organization.

These different sources are of different value depending on what properties we are trying to measure. If we want to know whether a college has any fraternities, it is rather foolish to

---

[1] These distinctions are discussed systematically and with many examples in a paper by Paul F. Lazarsfeld and Herbert Menzel, "On the Relation between Individual and Collective Properties," in Amitai Etzioni, ed., *Complex Organizations: A Sociological Reader,* (New York: Holt, Rinehart, and Winston, 1961), pp. 422-441. In that paper a somewhat different terminology is used.

ask several hundred students this on a questionnaire; probably any one of them could tell us accurately, and if we want to be sure there are officials who could tell us immediately in response to a phone call, letter, or visit. The college catalogue or prospectus usually reports this fact, and there are even published directories which are reasonably accurate on this point. On the other hand, if we want to know whether the students are interested in philosophy, we might look at statistics of course enrollments, we might count attendance at public lectures, or we might ask a sample of them to report how interested they were and what they have done which expresses their interest.

What follows is a collection of examples of the empirical measurement of organizational characteristics. The examples are classified according to the substantive attribute measured; within substantive types we group examples according to the formal structure of the measures—additive, emergent, relational-pattern, or integral. For each empirical measure we try to show which type of data-gathering technique was used.

To add interest and show how such measurements are used in the analysis of actual studies, we generally give a table or report a relationship between the measurement being considered and other organizational variables. This paper is not intended as a summary of empirically supported *propositions* about organizations, nor does it

go seriously into the question of how organizational studies analyze their data. Our focus here is on measurement, and the presentation of relationships is simply intended to give a better feel for their actual use.

The relationships which we use as examples are almost without exception relationships between two organizational characteristics; they are on the level of organizational units. It should be pointed out however that there is another very significant use of organizational characteristics; that is, as "conditioning factors" in the study of relationships among characteristics of individuals. Such tables typically take an original relationship among two individual characteristics, and present it separately for those respondents who are in different organizational contexts. Thus Lazarsfeld and Thielens take their initial finding that older professors are less permissive toward radical political groups, and see whether it holds in all attitude climates, even very liberal ones. They classify colleges by the proportion of professors who are permissive, and within each category present the average permissiveness score for each age group. The permissiveness scores (on a scale ranging from zero to four) appear to fall off somewhere less among the older group where the attitude climate is strongly permissive, as seen in Table 1.[2]

[2] Paul F. Lazarsfeld and Wagner Thielens, Jr., *The Academic Mind* (Glencoe, Ill.: The Free Press, 1958), p. 249.

TABLE 1   Average level of individual permissiveness toward radical groups according to professors' age at three groups of colleges

| | AGE OF PROFESSORS | | |
Permissiveness level at colleges	40 or younger[a]	41 to 50	51 or older
High (60% or more of professors clearly permissive)	3.13[347]	2.98[146]	2.76[136]
Medium (40% to 50%)	2.81[290]	2.49[177]	2.13[194]
Low (0% to 39%)	1.90[245]	1.54[151]	1.46[159]

[a] Smaller size figures indicate total number of professors on which average scores are based.

From the viewpoint of the psychology of political opinions, this is the most significant way to present the result. On the other hand the student of organizations could use the same data in a different way. He could formulate the notion of "age-grading" of opinions as an attribute of organizations; and convert the three-variable "contextual" table into a two-variable table which would show that "age-grading" was less in highly permissive schools than in less permissive schools:

A number of our examples will have this dual quality of representing an organizational condition influencing the correlation of two individual attributes, on the one hand; and a relationship of two organizational characteristics, one of them having the form of a correlation of individual attributes, on the other.

The presentation of such a classified roster of examples as this can only be a first step toward the drawing of methodological conclusions. We will not prescribe the best way for measuring various aspects of organizations nor give any comprehensive set of directives for researchers to follow. It is hoped, however, that by our assembling a large number of actual examples and exploring their formal features, researchers will be alerted to a wide range of possibilities in the measurement of organizational characteristics, and will have a clearer conception of the formal nature of their measurements.

TABLE 2   "Age-grading" of professors' opinions in three groups of colleges

Permissiveness level	Difference between average permissiveness score of youngest and oldest professors
High	+.37
Medium	+.68
Low	+.44

Measures of Input

Human Inputs

Many important consequences flow from the kind of people who are recruited by an organization. This organizational attribute is most directly measured by taking *averages* or *rates* of the individual members' attributes. For instance, a study of forty-three school systems explored the relation of staff characteristics to acceptance of educational innovations.[3] Questionnaires were secured from all teachers in each of the forty-three systems; the systems were then characterized by the per cent of teachers who had five or more years of professional training; who had 150 books in their personal library; who had traveled abroad; and so on. These staff characteristics were correlated with a score based on counting up how many educational innovations were practiced in the schools, the "adaptability scale."

It appears from these data that the innovative school systems have more cultured and widely traveled teachers, as well as teachers with more professional training and teaching experience. Perhaps these measures could be combined into indices of cosmopolitanism and of professionalism. Buley also shows that the higher the per pupil expenditures of the school system, the more cosmopolitan and professional the staff and the more innovative the school (Table 3).

A multivariate analysis of these characteristics would be the next step in understanding their operation. We would like to know whether the high expenditures are related to innovativeness only to the extent that they

---

3 Hilton C. Buley, *Personnel Characteristics and Staff Patterns Associated with the Quality of Education* (unpublished Ed.D. project, Teachers College, Columbia University, 1947).

create a high-quality staff or whether the staff quality is merely an inessential by-product. Can a high-quality staff create an innovative school even without high per pupil expenditures, or are they both necessary conditions? Unfortunately this type of analysis was not carried out.

Studies of voluntary organizations pay great attention to the composition of the membership, perhaps because their survival rests on individualistic motivations of their members. Thus a study of 100 local units of a national civic association (the League of Women Voters) classified the locals by the average educational level of their members, as revealed in a sample survey of the membership. A

TABLE 3   Relation of staff characteristics to adaptability of school systems

Proportion of teachers in system who:	Correlation with adaptability of system
Own over 150 books	.55
Have traveled abroad	.57
Have traveled over 500 miles from home in year	.59
Have five or more years of professional training	.58
Are not of local origin	.38
Saw five or more plays in last year	.16
Have less than 10 years teaching experience	—.48

high educational level of membership was found to be positively related to various measures of organizational effectiveness.[4] A survey of 177 women's organizations in a New England city classified them by the religious and ethnic composition of their membership, as reported by their officers in

response to a questionnaire.[5] This was shown to be related to their social prestige as organizations according to judges' ratings; the highest prestige organizations were exclusively Old-American Protestant, and Catholic organizations appeared mainly in the lower-prestige levels. . . .

A special aspect of input measures is the study of the social origins of leadership groups. This has been most widely practiced in studies of national governments, political party leadership, and legislature.[6] But it has also been used to characterize school boards[7] and college trustees.[8] One well-known study used existing records and biographical sources to measure the educational composition of boards of trustees of twenty universities from 1860 to 1930, disclosing a marked increase in the proportion of businessmen, bankers, and lawyers at the expense of other groups.[9] Unfortunately, these studies seldom proceed beyond *describing* the input to elite positions; they do not *correlate* the nature of the elite with other organizational attributes.

For some problems the *variance* within the human input is a significant characteristic. A large body of research on school problems deals with

[4] Robert Kahn, Arnold Tannenbaum, Robert Weiss, et al., A Study of the League of Women Voters of the United States, 5 mimeo (Ann Arbor: Survey Research Center, University of Michigan, 1956).

[5] Mhyra S. Minnis, "Cleavage in Women's Organizations," American Sociological Review, 18 (1953), 47-53.

[6] H. D. Lasswell, D. Lerner, and C. E. Rothwell, The Comparative Study of Elites: An Introduction and Bibliography (Stanford, Calif.: Hoover Institute, Stanford University, 1952); Donald R. Matthews, The Social Background of Political Decision-Makers (Garden City, New York: Doubleday, 1954).

[7] Neal Gross, Ward S. Mason, and Alexander W. McEachern, Explorations in Role Analysis (New York: Wiley, 1958), pp. 190, 204-05.

[8] N. P. Beck, Men Who Control Our Universities (New York: King's Crown Press, 1947).

[9] Earl McGrath, "The Control of Higher Education in America," Educational Record, 17 (1936), 259-72.

the question of whether individual classes should have a narrow or wide range of ability.[10] Differences in the range of abilities of the student body is a major characteristic of high schools with consequences for the program, the informal social relations, and the effect on students; colleges likewise may be "highly selective" or possessed of a wide range of students. The study of women's clubs in one city mentioned earlier classified the membership as to whether it was homogeneous or mixed in terms of religion (relying in this case on estimates of the officers rather than a membership survey); only twenty-four per cent of the clubs were religiously mixed if Protestants are considered as a single group.[11] The mixed clubs appeared mainly at the upper-middle levels of organizational prestige; the very high and very low-prestige organizations were almost all homogeneous. A study of one hundred school systems measured the religious homogeneity of the school boards in terms of the Catholic/non-Catholic split, and found it related to homogeneity regarding their role prescriptions for the school superintendent.[12] On the other hand a study of local chapters of the National Foundation for Infantile Paralysis measured membership homogeneity of 37 chapters and found it *unrelated* to various measures of performance.[13]

Economic Inputs

No less important than the human resources are the economic resources of an organization. Most economic input variables must be considered *in-tegral characteristics* of the organization. We can readily find the total budget or assets of most organizations from official records; we do not have to add up some figures characterizing each member. This is because in the modern societies with which we are concerned the market mechanism eliminates particularistic relationships as a basis of an organization acquiring resources, replacing them with generalized "purchasing power" which can be treated as an object in itself.

Economic resources are generally found correlated with quality of human inputs, with activities, and with outputs. As we have seen from the school studies, the expenditure per student was closely related to the quality of the staff and to the amount of innovation in educational practices.[14] Total capital has been found highly related to the survival chances of retail firms;[15] to the output of colleges;[16] income per staff member of hospitals to the proportion of internships which are filled.[17] Occasionally economic inputs have unexpected relationships. A study of change in voluntary associations over time found that income and wealth of the association can continue to grow even after its membership goes into decline.[18] A study of the pro-

---

[10] Ruth B. Ekstrom, *Experimental Studies of Homogeneous Grouping* (Princeton: Educational Testing Service, 1959).

[11] Minnis, *op. cit.*

[12] Gross *et al.*, *op. cit.*, pp. 186-87.

[13] David Sills, *The Volunteers* (Glencoe, Ill.: The Free Press, 1958).

[14] Buley, *op. cit.*

[15] F. S. Chapin, *Contemporary American Institutions* (New York: Harper & Bros., 1935), Ch. V.

[16] R. H. Knapp and H. B. Goodrich, *Origins of American Scientists* (Chicago: University of Chicago Press, 1952); John D. Russell and Floyd W. Reeves, *Finance*, Vol. 7 of *The Evaluation of Higher Institutions* (North Central Association of Colleges and Secondary Schools, 1936).

[17] R. Christie, "Classification of Hospitals" (Unpublished report, Bureau of Applied Social Research, Columbia University, 1959).

[18] John E. Tsouderos, "Organizational Change in Terms of a Series of Selected Variables," *American Sociological Review*, **20** (1955), 206-10.

duction of scientists found, as expected, that the proportion of graduates becoming scientists was higher for colleges with more able entering students, and for colleges with higher cost of attendance.[19] But when the human input factor was held constant, the high-cost colleges were *less* productive than medium and low-cost colleges (Table 4).

TABLE 4   Production of scientists by liberal arts colleges as related to cost of attendance

Minimum annual cost	Adjusted productivity index[a]	Number of colleges
$250-430	4.2	16
$430-530	4.9	18
$550-860	3.6	16

[a] Quality of entering students was held constant.

Physical Facilities

It is often important to measure the physical facilities of an organization as a measure of its capacity to do its job or as indicators of other organizational factors. These facilities are also *integral characteristics*, attributed to the organization as a whole, as are the economic factors. A study of hospitals uses a score based on the presence or absence of twenty-four facilities or items of equipment as a possible indicator of quality.[20] The basic information was published in a professional journal for hospital administrators. The number of books in the college library is reported in the published directory; it can be used as a very rough indicator of college quality.[21] School studies score such items as the presence of encyclopedias in classrooms, the existence of art materials, whether there is a class library

shelf—these items being observed and noted on a checklist.[22] Factories have been classified by their technological processes into those using traditional skilled-craft techniques versus modern mass-production methods. One study found that the more modern the plant's technology, the larger the percentage of managerial staff who were recruited from college rather than from the plant's own workers.[23] Physical arrangements in housing projects,[24] machine layout in factories,[25] and campus or dormitory layout.[26] have all been studied as influences on informal social contacts of organization members.

We have distinguished among human, economic, and physical inputs, but it is possible to combine items of each of these types into summary indices of resources. The "quality index" for colleges of Lazarsfeld and Thielens was based on the size of the library (physical input), the proportion of Ph.D. degree holders on the faculty (human input), the annual budget per student and the tuition fees (economic inputs), along with an output indicator: the production of scholars receiving the Ph.D. degree or graduate

---

[19] Knapp and Goodrich, *op. cit.*

[20] Christie, *op. cit.*

[21] Lazarsfeld and Thielens, *op. cit.*, pp. 411-14.

[22] Paul R. Mort and Francis G. Cornell, *American Schools in Transition* (New York: Bureau of Publications, Teachers College, Columbia University, 1937); Francis S. Cillie, *Centralization or Decentralization?* (New York: Bureau of Publications, Teachers College, Columbia University, 1940).

[23] Robert C. Stone, "Factory Organization and Vertical Mobility," *American Sociological Review*, **18** (1953), 28-35.

[24] William H. Form, "Stratification in Low and Middle Income Housing Areas," *Journal of Social Issues*, **7** (1951), No. 1 and 2, "Social Policy and Social Research in Housing," 109-31.

[25] Charles R. Walker and Robert H. Guest, *The Man on the Assembly Line* (Cambridge: Harvard University Press, 1952).

[26] Leon Festinger, *et al.*, *Social Pressures in Informal Groups* (New York: Harper & Bros., 1950).

fellowship. This combining of an output measure with input measures made sense in this case because they were not trying to relate "quality" to academic output, but to the frequency of outside attack and the response of administration and faculty to it. Their general finding was that schools with more economic, human, and physical resources were more frequently subject to outside attack than poorer schools, but that the administration of such schools was more often active in protecting faculty rights.[27]

Measures of Output

The output of an organization naturally varies with its purposes. Some organizations produce physical commodities, some perform services, some try to influence the public, some try to change people's attitudes or abilities, and some essentially make decisions for the society or other collective units. Organizations may of course have diverse consequences for different groups —a business firm may be rated by investors in terms of its "output" of profits, by engineers in terms of its physical input-output ratios, by public relations men in terms of its ability to make people like it, by workers in terms of job satisfactions. As we shall see, the indicators of output range over all possible formal types.

Physical Output Measures

Physical output of work groups is relatively easily measured as long as comparable products are being made. A large literature of industrial studies tries to find the causes of differences in physical output between comparable groups. Where all members of a work group do the same thing—wiring re-

lays or sewing pajamas—the total output is an *aggregate* of the individual outputs. On the other hand, an assembly-line process combines the output of each member into a single end product, for instance, an automobile; the hourly output of automobiles from an assembly line is an *integral characteristic* of the work group.

The productivity of research organizations is sometimes treated like that of factories, and measured in terms of the number of papers published.[28] If we reject the idea of measuring research output "by the pound," we may weight each paper by the frequency with which it is quoted by other writers in the field,[29] or by some expert judgment of each. This then approaches our next type of output measure, which is a rating of quality of performance of services. The same applies to educational institutions: a count of number of graduates or number of Ph.D.'s awarded is a "physical output" count for an organization engaged in "processing" people.

Measures of Service Performance

Research organizations are perhaps better conceived as organizations performing a rather complex set of services. The difficulty of directly measuring services tends to force researchers to use *ratings* by competent judges as the basis of measurement.[30] A Massachusetts Institute of Technology study of 42 research groups used ratings of

[27] Lazarsfeld and Thielens, *op. cit.*, Chap. 7.

[28] L. Meltzer, "Scientific Productivity in Organization Settings," *Journal of Social Issues*, **12** (1956), 32-40.

[29] H. W. Peter, "Human Factors in Research Administration," in R. Likert and S. P. Hayes, *Some Applications of Behavioral Research* (Paris: UNESCO, 1957), pp. 128-32.

[30] D. C. Pelz, "Some Factors Related to Performance in a Research Organization," *Administrative Science Quarterly*, **1** (1956), 310-25.

groups by superiors, by the other groups, and by their own members to assess productivity.[31]

"The uniformly high rating which all research groups give themselves shows the difficulty of getting good estimates of performance from the groups themselves. . . . In fact the leaders of low-performance groups tend to rate their groups even higher than do the members."

The researchers faced with this lack of correspondence among three sources of ratings decided, reasonably enough, that the two "outside" ratings, by superiors and by other groups, were more likely to be valid, and "self-evaluation" was treated as a separate psychological variable. The productivity rating by the outsiders was positively related to both the amount of job-oriented interaction and personal friendship; but it declined with the length of time the group had been together.

Studies of military units in training could use some direct physical measurement of task performance, like number of hits on target. However the total "services" rendered by military groups are likewise quite complex, and ratings by trained observers are usually employed. A study of small scout squads in the army put the squads through 12 simulated battlefield situations, taking six hours.[32] They were watched by observers who rated their performance; the rating in this case was not a single, over-all rating but was broken down into a large number of "segmental ratings," through the use of a standardized rating form; the over-all score was built up from a weighted sum of these. This perform-

ance score was correlated with an index of group cohesion, determined by sociometric data on informal social relations among squad members. The result was a definite relationship, as shown by Table 5. . . .

TABLE 5   **Military performance as related to group cohesion for 12 scout squads**

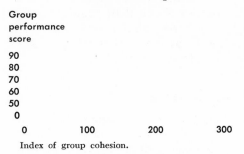

Group performance score

90			
80			
70			
60			
50			
0			
0	100	200	300

Index of group cohesion.

Measures of Effect on the Public

The difficulties of measuring the output of organizations which aim at influencing public attitudes and behavior is notorious.[33] Occasionally large-scale field experiments have been used in which public response was measured by comparing sales increases or attitude changes in response to particular campaigns. An unusually extensive measurement of the public-relations output of organizational units is found in a study of the League of Women Voters.[34] By sampling surveys of the general public in twenty-two communities, it was possible to determine the extent to which the organization had conveyed certain information about its purposes and program to the sector of the public which it was trying to reach. As a minimum indicator of perform-

---

[31] Peter, op. cit., p. 135.

[32] Daniel M. Goodacre III, "The Use of a Sociometric Test as a Predictor of Combat Unit Effectiveness," Sociometry, 14 (1951), 148-52.

[33] Paul Wasserman, Measurement and Evaluation of Organizational Performance (Ithaca, New York: Graduate School of Business and Public Administration, Cornell University, 1959).

[34] Kahn, Tannenbaum, and Weiss, op. cit.

ance in this area they used the per cent of women who had heard of the organization at all. This was correlated with various internal characteristics of the local organization, such as the power structure as rated by the members (Table 6).

TABLE 6 Public-influence output as related to power structure in 22 local units of a civic association

Relative power of membership versus officers	Per cent of public who had heard of organization
Low	40%
Medium	50%
High	64%

A recent study measured the effectiveness of precinct political workers in terms of votes obtained in an election.[35] To do this it was necessary to hold constant the "input" of people the precinct worker had to deal with. The three social factors which correlated most highly with party choice were the proportion of "old" versus "new" immigrant nationalities, the rental level, and the proportion of home owners. By a regression equation it was possible to account for eighty per cent of the variation in party choice among precincts. The deviations of actual vote from the vote expected on the basis of population characteristics formed a measure of the output of the political organization. This was shown to be related to such plausible factors as the number of people the local committeeman talked to on an average day, the proportion of local voters knowing his name (another measure of "public effect"), and whether the committeeman was employed by the local gov-

ernment. These correlates were measured by data from surveys; the basic output data were all derived from official records—voting statistics and census data.

Measures of Effect on Members

A broad class of organizations is designed to produce effects on people who are brought into the organization to be trained, treated, or indoctrinated —schools, prisons, hospitals, churches, and training units within all kinds of organizations. Students of "correctional institutions" have long reported their effectiveness (or ineffectiveness) as measured by the proportion who fail to be corrected. Hospitals use certain rates of death, recoveries, or infectious complications to rate themselves, taking into consideration variations in their intake. Churches have more difficult problems in defining the effects which they intend to produce, aside from mere institutional growth or survival.

The most extensive development of measurement of effects on members is found in educational institutions. A whole specialty of "human bookkeeping" has developed, using standardized measures of changes in individual performance. This is done mainly for internal control purposes, but it also makes possible comparative studies between institutions wherever the same measures are used. The field of educational measurements is too vast to examine systematically here; we will only note a few major types of measurements which have been used in interinstitutional comparisons. An early example was the attempt to use vocabulary scores of students as a measure of school effectiveness; this was of course quite misleading as long as the initial vocabulary and the effect of continuing outside influences was not con-

[35] Phillips Cutright and Peter H. Rossi, "Grass Roots Politics and the Vote," *American Sociological Review*, 23 (1958), 171-79.

trolled.[36] The problem of different starting points was taken into account in a study of the effect of college education on general knowledge through the use of a long-term panel method with tests before and after college.[37] Colleges were found to vary enormously in the amount of gain they produced in humanities, social science, and natural science information; there were even some institutions where the students appeared to know less in these areas when they left than when they arrived.

More recently, efforts have been made to develop individual measures of a generalized "critical thinking ability" in order to compare this output for different types of colleges and programs. A comparative study of eight colleges measured this output by a before-and-after study of students over one or two years, and suggested a number of institutional characteristics as possibly related to it. These are discussed in Section 6b, Measures of "Collective" Activities.[38]

The influence of colleges on nonintellectual factors such as attitudes and values has been very extensively, if not entirely adequately, studied. (These studies have been summarized by Jacob,[39] and criticized by Barton.) Very broad and long-term effects were considered in a survey which obtained data from graduates of various types of colleges and programs, including their occupational distribution, average income, rate of community and political participation, attitudes on social issues, and reading habits.[40] . . .

Another form of long-run measure of educational output is the occupational distribution of graduates, or the rate going into certain professions. The "productivity of scientists" of colleges has been elaborately studied.[41] A more recent study measures "output" of a wider range of scholarly professionals.[42] These measures of specific outputs cannot of course be used for an overall evaluation of the institution; Knapp and Goodrich point out, for instance, that the low production of scientists in some older eastern liberal arts colleges is in part due to their greater "production" of lawyers, diplomats, business executives, and so forth.

All these measures of "human outputs" are based on *aggregating* individual performances, but unlike the studies of industrial productivity, they are concerned particularly with what members do or are capable of doing after they leave the organization as indications of the organization's effect in training, curing, or indoctrinating.

A sore point in research on educational institutions has been the measurement of the "quality" of schools. A National Education Association pamphlet summarizing research on the relationship between cost and qual-

[36] F. G. Bonser, L. H. Burch and M. R. Turner, "Vocabulary Tests as Measures of School Efficiency," *School and Society*, 2 (1915), 713-18.

[37] W. S. Learned and B. D. Wood, *The Student and His Knowledge* (New York: Carnegie Foundation for the Advancement of Teaching, Bulletin 29, 1938).

[38] L. B. Mayhew and P. L. Dressel, *General Education: Explorations in Evaluation* (Washington: American Council on Education, 1954).

[39] Phillip Jacob, *Changing Values in College* (New York: Harper & Bros., 1957).

[40] Patricia Salter West, "The College Graduate in American Society" (unpublished Ph.D. dissertation, Department of Sociology, Columbia University, 1951); Ernest Havemann and Patricia Salter West, *They Went to College: The College Graduate in America Today* (New York: Harcourt, Brace & Co., 1952).

[41] Knapp and Goodrich, *op. cit.*

[42] R. H. Knapp and J. J. Greenbaum, *The Younger American Scholar: His Collegiate Origins* (Chicago: University of Chicago Press, 1953).

ity contains an enlightening discussion of the varying indicators which may be used and their difficulties.[43] It distinguishes three kinds of measures: "Quality as teaching personnel, facilities, and amount of schooling." "Quality as scores on achievement tests." "Quality as emphasis on fundamental objectives and sound procedures."

In our terms, the first of these are measures of input; the second, of output; and the third, a combination of *attitudes* concerning organizational goals and *activities* engaged in by organization members and the organization as a whole.

Of the input measures, the authors note:

"This type of evidence is of some value. Its weakness is in the assumption that enough trained teachers, more teaching facilities, and more time spent in school result in better educational returns. This may be true. But it is not proved by this kind of evidence, for actual educational results are not measured."

Turning to attempts to measure "actual educational results," the authors note that researchers generally restrict themselves to achievement tests:

"The assumption here is that the ability to score high on tests is quality in education. . . . Low achievement in the basic educational skills and fundamental fields of knowledge, providing proper account is taken of such factors as the learning capacity of those tested, might indicate lack of quality in an area of major educational purpose."

Two kinds of difficulties are noted. The first is that proper account may

not be taken of the learning capacity of the student input, and of the effects of continuing stimuli outside the school from family and neighborhood. The second is more serious:

"These critics remind us that test results may not reflect ability to apply knowledge and skills in later life, and that results measurable by tests represent but a small part of what a pupil should know in school."

This is partly the old quarrel over what the goals of the school should be—just how "small" a part of its output is represented by "basic educational skills and fundamental fields of knowledge." It also involves a question of whether achievement tests adequately predict the long-run educational results even within these fields. Finally, the criticism suggests that the long-term intellectual and nonintellectual results may not be "measurable by tests" at all.

This brings us to the third type of measure:

"A third type of research on the cost-quality relationship in education seeks to go beyond quantitative data on personnel and facilities or test scores as measures of quality. . . . This third type of study assumes that to test the inner essence of educational quality one must go into a school system and carefully observe what is going on there. What are the purposes of the school program? What are the teachers teaching, and how are they teaching it? . . . . Are such fundamental ends as the development of individual pupil initiative and the ability to think, consciously and effectively pursued?

"Accordingly, trained observers using a check list of many items go into a school system and into individual classrooms to observe the extent to which such fundamental educational objectives and procedures are found."

---

[43] National Education Association, Committee on Tax Education and School Finance, *Does Better Education Cost More?* (Washington, D.C.: National Education Association, 1959), pp. 8-11.

This approach, like the first one, involves certain assumptions:

"Among the shortcomings of this approach to quality education are that it is somewhat subjective, that its reliability depends upon the degree of training of the observers, and that it assumes that excellent learning situations, as defined by qualified persons, result in quality educational returns."

It appears from this remark that the "inner essence" of educational quality is after all the "returns"—the effects produced on the students. However, the difficulty in objectively measuring these effects, especially when educational goals are defined in terms of broad and long-range outcomes, has induced educators to fall back on the observation of staff activities and attitudes which experts *believe* will produce the desired output. The formulation of an expert judgment on the quality of a school's procedures is made more reliable (if not more valid) by breaking it down into a large number of independent observations. The measure of quality which results, remains based on expert opinion rather than on direct measurement of output.

Reliance on this form of codified professional opinion has been intensified by the fear that use of restricted and crude measures of output would permit outsiders to strait-jacket educational progress toward new goals. However this procedure involves the contrary danger that a well-codified, quantified system of expert rating will be confused with an objective measure of educational output, permitting a "mutual admiration society" method of rating of educational institutions by educators.[44] (Something like this happened in the assessment of the "output" of psychoanalysis by psychoanalysts.) This replaces output measurement with a form of "social validation" of the institution's performance —the oldest and most traditional of all forms of evaluation. Eventually, the problem of measuring complex and long-term effects must be faced if we are scientifically to validate the professional opinions, and find out the educational consequences of various inputs, activities, and organizational goals. There will also have to be a clarification of the value judgments of different effects which go into the notion of "quality." In the end it may be possible to construct a multi-dimensional measure of effects, to which different groups can apply their own sets of evaluative weights.

One of the most significant efforts to measure a wide range of outcomes over a relatively long run was made by the eight-year study of graduates of "progressive" schools who attended college.[45] While there is argument over the extent to which one can generalize from this group of graduates (they were rather highly selected within their own schools, and all were going to college), the study utilized a very ingenious set of measures of both academic and nonacademic performance over the college years. It is significant that this effort at objective measurement of output was produced by progressive educators at the high school level in response to the "traditionalist" criticisms of college administrators; in the relations between institutions dominated by different ideologies, mere social validation would not work.

---

[44] I. L. Kandel, *American Education in the Twentieth Century* (Cambridge: Harvard University Press, 1957), pp. 97, 135-37.

[45] Wilford M. Aikin, *The Story of the Eight-Year Study* (New York: Harper, 1942); Eugene R. Smith, Ralph W. Tyler, *et al.*, *Appraising and Recording Student Progress* (New York: Harper & Bros., 1942).

Measures of Decisions as Output

There are some specialized organizations or parts of organizations whose chief output consists of decisions; for example, legislatures, courts, administrative agencies, top management units. Measurement of this kind of output presents special problems of classification and measurement. Studies of the courts have focused on the sheer volume of cases handled, since the problem of backlog and delay has been so prominent. The University of Chicago Law School researchers have shown that part of the difference between court systems which are up to date in their calendars and those which have long delays is accounted for by the amount of time spent on the bench by the judges—an obvious enough point but one which required careful analysis of official records and statistics to verify.[46] The measurement of court output by number of cases is rather like measuring research groups output by number of papers; it assumes that the average *quality* of justice or truth, respectively, does not vary between the organizations so compared.

In studying the decisions produced by juries, the University of Chicago group developed ingenious methods of data-collection and experimental comparison.[47] In one study, judges recorded the decisions of juries in actual cases, along with descriptive information about the cases. At the same time they were asked how they themselves would have decided the cases if they had been trying them without a jury.

Thus each case was decided twice, once by a jury and once—hypothetically—by the judge, after both had listened to the identical trial. Some sharp differences between judge and jury "decisions" were noted; judges, for instance, would have convicted twice as many defendants in criminal cases as the juries actually did. Whether judge's or jury's output of decisions is "better" is not stated, but a major difference in *type* of output is clearly indicated.

Another technique employed was to assemble groups of actual jurors who were awaiting call to hear cases, and have them deliberate on cases presented through a tape-recorded re-enactment. In this manner the same case could be "experimentally" decided by many juries, and the decisions of juries differently composed or instructed could be compared. The group decisions were by no means predictable from the majority or mean of individual opinions at the start of deliberations; they were the product of highly complex group processes, although influenced on the average by certain input or procedural factors. The application of the technique of "experimental decision-making" to other types of organization offers a highly flexible means of studying the "output" of individual decision-makers or decision-making organizations in response to various assumed situations, under various organizational conditions.

Environmental Variables

By environmental variables we mean characteristics of the larger social units in which the organization is located—community, region, industry, and so forth; or information on the *relationships* between the organization and its

---

[46] Hans Zeisel, Harry Kalven, Jr., and Bernard Buchholz, *Delay in the Court* (Boston: Little, Brown & Co., 1959).

[47] Jury Project: Forthcoming volumes by Harry Kalven, Fred Strodtbeck, Hans Zeisel, and others, of the University of Chicago Law School.

environment—its "public relations," its "interorganizational relations," and perhaps its relations with other units or levels within some larger-scale organization of which it is a part.

Community or Regional Contexts

A study of local chapters of the National Foundation for Infantile Paralysis used organizational and official records to measure two salient features of the environment of local chapters: the polio rate of the county (a measure of the need for the organization's services), and the income level of the county (a measure of available community resources). It was found

TABLE 7 **Per cent of polio chapters raising over 34¢ per capita**

Median family income of county	POLIO INCIDENCE RATE OF COUNTY[a]		
	High	Medium	Low
High	75%$_{253}$	57%$_{384}$	54%$_{83}$
Medium	64%$_{484}$	35%$_{793}$	25%$_{298}$
Low	29%$_{51}$	4%$_{406}$	3%$_{318}$

[a] Smaller size figures indicate total number of counties on which percentages are based.

that the local chapter's organizational achievement in fund-raising, as measured by per capita contributions, was strongly influenced by both of these environmental features, as seen in Table 7.[48]

In a study of local unions, the relevant context was the region, which was described by its degree of unionization. The locals themselves were classified by their degree of militancy as revealed in their voting on referenda concerning union policies. Working entirely with available institutional statistics, the investigator was able to find strong evidence for the proposition that union members in less or-

ganized industries are more militant.[49]

There is a large body of studies of local school systems which relate school system attributes to community characteristics. From available census and other governmental data it is possible to measure the educational level, taxable wealth, per cent foreign-born, population density, occupational distribution, population growth, and economic trends of a community; some of the factors are assumed to be related to the values of the community members, and some to their resources. It was found that the wealth and the educational level of the local population were the factors most highly related to a measure of educational innovation, as well as to school expenditures, training of school staff, and other organizational features.[50] Public attitudes toward modern educational practices, measured by surveys of parents, were also found to be related to the practices used in the schools. However it was not clear from the analysis whether they exerted any independent effect when community background factors were held constant, or indeed whether they were not the product of the school system practices.

For colleges, the importance of community and regional contexts is presumably less striking since they typically draw students, resources, and boards of control from a wider area and a more limited segment of the public. Yet these factors should be worth investigating. The growth of local community colleges may create

---

49 K. J. W. Alexander, "Membership Participation in a Printing Trade Union," *Sociological Review*, **2** (1954), 161.

50 Paul R. Mort and Francis G. Cornell, *American Schools in Transition* (New York: Bureau of Publications, Teachers College, Columbia University, 1941); Donald Ross (ed.), *Administration for Adaptability* (New York: Institute of Administrative Research, Teachers College, Columbia University, 1958).

op. cit., p. 194.

izational measurement

a class of institutions much more subject to these local influences,[51] while
the degree of discrepancy between the
personnel of a high-quality college and
the surrounding community may have
its own special effect on campus life.
A study of regional effects made in
the early 1930's related attitude toward
the Negro to years in college, for
northern college students at Ohio
State University, southern college students at the University of Alabama,
and students of northern origin attending a southern college (see Table
8).

TABLE 8   **Mean score on scale of
attitude toward Negro[a]**

Year in college	Northern students in northern colleges	Northern students in southern colleges	Southern students in southern colleges
Freshman	6.4	6.2	5.0
Sophomore	6.7	5.8	4.9
Junior and senior	6.8	5.2	5.0

[a] Scale ranged from 1 (least favorable) to 11
(most favorable).

The results suggest that college attendance in the North may have had
some liberalizing influence on students
of northern origin, but that the southern colleges had no such influence on
its students; and that going to college
in the south effectively changed the
attitudes of students of northern origin to conform to the southern norm.
How much of this effect derived from
the faculty and the program, how
much from contact with fellow students, and how much from general
contact with the population and institutions off the campus was not distinguishable.[52]

[51] David Riesman, *Constraint and Variety
in American Education* (New York: Doubleday, 1958), pp. 135-36.
[52] V. M. Sims and J. R. Patrick, "Attitude
Toward the Negro of Northern and Southern
College Students," *Journal of Social Psychology*, 7 (1936), 192-204.

Public Relations

Public relations refers to the attitudes and beliefs of the community or
regional public toward the organization, as distinct from their sociological
attributes or their opinions in general.
In spite of the enormous amount of
attention (and money) devoted to
public relations, there is very little
empirical data on the relationship of
public opinion about an organization
to other organizational characteristics.
There is much common sense support
for the notion that an organization
will do better in a friendly rather than
a hostile environment, but community power structures and decision processes are complicated and do not usually reflect public opinion, as known
through surveys, in any direct way.

One study which has tried to correlate public opinion of organizations
with other organizational characteristics is a study of eight industrial firms
and the five local unions which represented their workers in a midwestern
city.[53] The study produced a number
of results which were not entirely obvious. Generally the public liked companies and unions which the workers
liked. Public approval was much less
closely related to management's satisfaction with its labor relations, and it
was downright negatively related to
management's satisfaction with the
union. This suggests that either the
workers are communicating their opinions effectively to other community
members by informal contacts, or that
the community in general has the
same impressions and is using the
same standards to evaluate organiza-

[53] W. E. Chalmers, M. K. Chandler, L. L.
McQuitty, R. Stagner, D. E. Wray, and M.
Durber, *Labor-Management Relations in Il-
lini City*, 2, "Studies in Comparative Analysis" (Champaign, Illinois: Institute of Labor and Industrial Relations, Univerity of
Illinois, 1954).

tions as do the workers. It also suggests that management tends to like weak and ineffectual unions, and that their standards for judging labor relations differ widely from the public's and the workers'. . . .

Interorganizational Relations

An important part of the environment of local school systems are other local organizations which may be favorable and give support, or may be indifferent or hostile. This has been measured *as perceived* by local school officials through use of a checklist of local organizations.[54] Another study of 100 local school systems secured the superintendent's perception of the demands of eighteen different groups, including both organizations, categories of the public, and specific role partners, in regard to four policy problems.[55]

The study of one hundred locals of the League of Women Voters measured the degree of conflict with other community organizations as reported by members of the Boards of Directors in response to a survey. The amount of such conflict proved to be *positively* related to organizational effectiveness as rated by informed judges including national and state leaders.[56]

Unions and business firms have a special form of pair relationship which has been much studied on a case basis, and on which systematic comparative and even correlational studies are coming to be available. We have earlier given a table showing the correlation between labor-management relations as viewed by each side and public approval of the union and company,

based on eight company-union pairs in one city.[57] A study of four union locals in another city suggests that the degree of union conflict with the company, as measured by ratings of informed officials, is positively related to the members' loyalty to the union, measured by an attitude survey.[58] There have also been attempts to correlate union-management conflict with characteristics of their community or industrial environment.[59]

A recent study of organizations in the health field has attempted directly to obtain data on the entire matrix of interorganizational relations of health organizations within one community. The findings take the form of "sociometric" matrices showing the amount of communication, referrals, joint activities, and transfer of resources between different types of organizations.[60] This type of data makes it possible to characterize organizations by the same kinds of sociometric indices as those developed for relational analysis of individuals. The temporary National Economic Committee reports of the 1930's are another instance in which interorganizational relationships were studied.[61] Elaborate "sociograms" of interlocking directorates and other

[54] R. P. Gallagher, *Some Relationships of Symbiotic Groups to Adaptability in Public Schools* (unpublished Ed.D. project, Teachers College, Columbia University, 1947).

[55] Gross, *et al., op. cit.*, Chaps. 15, 16.

[56] Kahn, Tannenbaum, and Weiss, *op. cit.*

[57] Chalmers, *et al., op. cit.*

[58] Arnold S. Tannenbaum, "Control Structure and Union Functions," *American Journal of Sociology,* 61 (1956), 536-45.

[59] Clark Kerr and Abraham Siegel, "The Interindustry Propensity to Strike: An International Comparison," in A. Kornhauser, R. Rubin, and A. M. Ross (eds.), *Industrial Conflict* (New York: McGraw-Hill, 1954), pp. 189-212.

[60] Sol Levine and Paul E. White, "Exchange as a Conceptual Framework for the Study of Inter-organizational Relationships" (unpublished report, Harvard School of Public Health, 1960).

[61] Temporary National Economic Committee, *The Distribution of Ownership in the 200 Largest Non-Financial Corporations,* Monograph 29 (Washington, D.C.: U.S. Government Printing Office, 1940).

relationships among corporations were presented; however there was no systematic attempt to relate this descriptive data to other behavior of the corporations.

Measures of the relationships between educational institutions and other organizations—the flow of communications, resources, and influence, and the existence of "interlocking directorates" with business, labor, religious, and governmental organizations—would provide a most interesting set of data. There is little systematic measurement of these relational factors in the literature on colleges, in spite of the enormous amount of speculation and argument over such issues as "business control." Beck obtained information from published directories and biographies of the extent to which college trustees were also directors of corporations, and McGrath showed the declining proportion of ministers and the rise of businessmen membership on college boards of control from 1860 to 1930. However, there are no correlations of the extent of businessman or religious influence so measured with other attributes.

In a qualitative study of the problem in a few private East Coast universities, Baltzell maintains that there is a direct relationship between control of colleges by the leaders of "upper-class" financial and industrial organizations and the type of social organizations which exist for the students:

"It is the purpose of this chapter to show how the private secondary school . . . and certain fashionable eastern universities serve the sociological function of differentiating the upper classes in America from the rest of the population. In other words, in addition to their manifest and most important function, that of providing an education, these private educational institutions serve the latent function of acculturating the members of the younger generation, especially those not quite to the manor born, into an upper-class style of life."[62]

Precisely because the college or university selects so many students who are not destined for the upper class, this requires the creation of "an intricate system of exclusive clubs . . . to insulate the members of the upper class from the rest of the students . . . ." These clubs and fraternities are created and supported by outside, upper-class business and financial interest groups through their representation on boards of control and their ability to grant or withhold financial support, in Baltzell's view. He notes of the University of Pennsylvania that "most of the benefactors and trustees of the university discussed above belonged to one or another of these four original fraternities." As a test case in the power of these outside economic interests he refers to the defeat of Woodrow Wilson's attempt to abolish Princeton's eating clubs and set up a "house" plan (such as that later created, with "upper-class" support, at Harvard). Baltzell's examples are drawn from the world of the old eastern universities and the old eastern upper class; similar principles may apply to the maintenance of fraternities in colleges and state universities in other parts of the country by more localized elite groups.

One of the few pieces of quantitative data on the relation between sources of economic support and other college attributes is found in a study by the North Central Association which aimed to validate criteria for accreditation. Budgetary data were obtained from colleges concerning the

[62] E. D. Baltzell, *Philadelphia Gentlemen* (Glencoe, Ill.: The Free Press, 1958), Ch. 12, p. 293.

breakdown of income between student fees, endowment, taxation, "continuing gifts and grants," and borrowing.

These forms of support were then correlated with indices of student performance, faculty quality, and administration quality. Interestingly enough the "stable" factor of endowment was less favorable for quality than the "unstable" factor of student fees. Reliance on "continuing gifts and grants" and on borrowing were negatively related to quality.[63]

Larger Organizational Context and Relationships

We have been considering all kinds of organizational units which may be studied comparatively as objects of measurement; this has included work groups within a factory, small army and air force units, government agencies, and research groups within industry, as well as formally independent organizations. For any such subordinate unit within a larger organization, the characteristics of that larger organizational setting are of the highest importance.

Thus a research project can be located within an academic, governmental, or business organization. Research workers in these three settings report quite different patterns of pressure and support from their superiors, as shown in Table 9.[64]

Besides classifying the "part" by attributes of the whole to which it belongs, we may classify it by information on the actual *relationships* between part and whole.

The study of 100 League of Women Voters locals included measures of the relationship of each local to the national organization in terms of degree of conflict. The investigators

		CONDITIONS REPORTED BY ORGANIZATION'S RESEARCHERS	
Type of organization	Papers count	Have high freedom	Have $10,000 plus in funds
Academic institution	86%	90%	38%
Government agency	83	71	67
Business firm	39	50	84

TABLE 9   Conditions of research in different organizational settings

found that conflict with higher levels was related to relatively poor performance, at least as measured by a rating scale which included opinions of the higher level officers.[65]

A quite extensive set of measures was used to describe relationships between local Jewish Centers and their national organization. The national officials regularly recorded all contacts between the national office and the local centers on a standard form, which included the means of contact (telephone, letter, visit), who initiated the contact, and what the subject matter was. Unfortunately this information was not used analytically but only for over-all description; it might have shown interesting correlations with attributes of the local centers, including their conception of the proper functions and authority of the national organization, about which there was long-standing controversy.[66]

One of the simplest versions of the organizational context variable is whether in fact the unit studied is part of a larger organization or independent. Newspapers can be classified as independent or part of a chain or local monopoly. There are trend studies of the share of the newspaper market

---

63 Russell and Reeves, *op. cit.*
64 Meltzer, *op. cit.*

65 Kahn, Tannenbaum, and Weiss, *op. cit.*
66 Oscar I. Janowsky, *The JWB Survey* (New York: The Dial Press, 1949).

held by independents and chains over time.[67] One study compared the content of the press in cities with two independent dailies with that where both papers were owned by one company and found very little difference.[68]

Thirty-two "community" school systems were compared, of which 16 were in independent suburban towns, and 16 were in informally defined "neighborhood communities" within New York City, and thus controlled by one centralized Board of Education. The general population characteristics were matched, so as to isolate the effects of independence versus centralized control on local schools. A large number of relationships were found, as seen in Table 10.[69]

The locally controlled schools were more flexible in a number of ways; the schools which were part of the New York City system excelled in bureau-

TABLE 10   School practices in 16 independent and 16 centrally controlled school systems

School practices	Independent schools	Centrally controlled schools
Movable classroom furniture used	11	0
Teacher experimentation encouraged by superintendency	12	6
Course of study developed cooperatively by local teachers	14	2
Adequate provision for vocational education	6	16
Provision for pupils with special disabilities	8	16
Adequate tenure provisions	2	16
Total schools studied	16	16

[67] Alfred McClung Lee, The Daily Newspaper in America (New York: The Macmillan Company, 1947).

[68] Stanley Bigman, "Rivals in Conformity," Journalism Quarterly, 25 (1948), 127-31.

[69] Cillie, op. cit.

cratic virtues like tenure, pensions, and presence of highly specialized services.

For colleges the question of organizational setting takes the form of the "type of control" over the college whether it is under the state government, a church body, or under independent auspices. "Control" as indicated in the standard directories is a deceptively simple attribute. Colleges are traditionally classified as publicly controlled, church controlled, and privately controlled. The Catholic colleges are most clearly described by this means, in that their administrators are invariably members of the authority structure of the Catholic Church. However, the closer student of church affairs would be interested in many further details and would deny any "monolithic" hierarchical control system. The locus of control of Protestant "church-related" colleges is much more ambiguous. The extent of church representation on the board of trustees, and whether the president must be a minister of the church, are not generally stated in the published catalogues and directories.

Lazarsfeld and Thielens tried to create a measure of church control using those indicators which were available in the published sources: whether *any* church representation is required on the board, and whether chapel attendance or courses in religion are compulsory. The latter two are of course measures of the program of activities of the institution, which are presumed to be *consequences* of strong church control.[70]

The distinction between those colleges controlled by governments and those which are independent of government control is somewhat more

[70] Larzarsfeld and Thielens, op. cit., pp. 407-09.

clear-cut. The trustees of publicly controlled colleges are generally elective
or appointed by the political authorities; in either case they are closely tied
to the dominant political organizations
in the state. However most states have
legal devices and long-established customs for leaving a certain autonomy
in the hands of the state college and
university administrators and faculties.
It might be possible to construct some
measure of the *degree* of political control over "public" institutions.

Even the crude classification of control as public, private nonsectarian,
Protestant, and Catholic shows significant relationships with other organizational characteristics. As shown in
Table 11, it was related to the attitude-
climate of the faculty, as measured
on a scale of permissiveness toward
Communist, Socialist, and "radical"
political activities.[71]

Type of control was naturally related quite directly to the relationships between the college and political
leaders. The aspect of these which was
measured was the amount of "pressure
to avoid controversy" from the legislature and local politicians, as shown in
Table 12.[72]

The behavior of the college trustees
under different conditions of political
pressure is markedly different for the
public and private colleges. See Table
13.[73]

In these last examples the measure
of "pressure" is an aggregative measure based on individual perceptions:
the per cent of faculty members who
report pressure from a given source.
It should be noted that this is quite
different from using the proportion
of liberals or of Ph.D.'s among the
faculty to characterize that group;

[71] *Ibid.*, p. 128.
[72] *Ibid.*, p. 181.
[73] *Ibid.*, p. 182.

TABLE 11   Political permissiveness of faculty by type of control and size

Type of control	MEAN PER CENT OF FACULTY WHO ARE "CLEARLY PERMISSIVE"[a]	
	Large institutions	Small institutions
Private	57%[497]	53%[326]
Public	49%[821]	23%[113]
Protestant	—	32%[291][b]
Catholic	12%[93]	3%[115]

[a] Smaller size figures indicate total number of professors on which percentage is based.
[b] Includes 28 respondents from large Protestant institutions.

here we are using them as informants
about the behavior of *other* groups.
The behavior of the politicians would
ideally be measured by interviewing
or observing or analyzing records of
the behavior of the politicians themselves. The professors' perceptions of
their behavior are used only as a
readily available substitute. Such a
measure obviously presents problems;
if pressures are really present, why
doesn't everyone report them? Is a college where 50 per cent report pressures under "twice as much pressure"
as one where only 25 per cent report
them? Perhaps they just have better
internal communications. The assumptions underlying the use of such "rates
of perception of others' behavior" need
to be closely examined.

Social Structure Variables

We now come to variables characterizing the inner workings of the organization. The term "social structure"
actually covers a wide range of attributes, which will be considered in
turn.

Formal Authority Structure

Some gross aspects of the formal authority structure can be indicated by
simple *rates*. The degree of bureau-

TABLE 12	Level of pressure from politicians on public and private colleges	
Degree of pressure reported[a]	Per cent of public colleges under various degrees of pressure	Per cent of private colleges under various degrees of pressure
Low	29%	57%
Medium	32	18
High	39	25
	100%31	100%28

[a] Here colleges were classified as under low pressure if less than 20 per cent of the respondents report increased pressure; medium if 20 to 39 per cent report pressure; high if 40 per cent or more report it.

TABLE 13	Trustee behavior under low and high political pressure at public and private colleges[a]			
	PUBLIC COLLEGES		PRIVATE COLLEGES	
Trustee pressure on administration	Political pressure high	Political pressure low	Political pressure high	Political pressure low
High	11	1	6	4
Low	5	14	6	12
Total colleges	16	15	12	16

[a] Dividing line between high and low is 20 per cent of faculty reporting pressure for privately controlled colleges, but 30 per cent for public colleges.

cratization of schools has been measured by the proportion of total personnel in administrative jobs;[74] that of voluntary organizations by the proportion of paid staff to volunteers.[75] Speculation about the growth of bureaucracy in business firms is abundant, but actual data over time are scarce. Haire presents a staff/line ratio over time on several cases, and concludes that:

"In the early years, while the line grows linearly, the staff grows by some exponential function (though no single one seems to describe the curve well). Later, in another period of growth, they grow at quite similar rates."[76]

The over-all closeness of supervision in a plant might be indicated by the average length of time a worker can go without intervention by his supervisor.[77]

Another aspect of the formal authority structure is the average span of control of all officers, or of officers at each given level.[78] The basic data for such a measure is a simple question, observation, or count from the formal organization chart, of the number of people to whom each official is supposed to give orders routinely. This is a kind of average based on counting *relationships* of a certain type in which an individual is engaged, or is supposed to be engaged. If we make our count simply from the formal organization chart or the book of rules, we are not characterizing people by what they actually do but by what the formal rules say they should do. We are aggregating data on "formally defined statuses" which may represent no more than the ideas of some long-dead writer or chartmaker; if we aggregated data based on the actual people oc-

74 Frederick W. Terrien and Donald L. Mills, "The Effect of Changing Size Upon the Internal Structure of Organizations," *American Sociological Review*, 20 (1955), 11-13.

75 Sills, *op. cit.*, pp. 70, 204-06.

76 Mason Haire, "Biological Models and Empirical Histories of the Growth of Organizations," in Mason Haire (ed.), *Modern Organization Theory* (New York: Wiley, 1959), Ch. 10, esp. p. 292.

77 Elliot Jaques, *The Measurement of Responsibility* (Cambridge: Harvard University Press, 1956).

78 James G. March and Herbert A Simon, *Organizations* (New York: John Wiley & Sons, 1958); William M. Evan, "Indices of the Hierarchical Structure of Industrial Organizations," paper delivered at Fourth World Congress of Sociology, Stresa, Italy, 1959; J. C. Worthy, "Organizational Structure and Employee Morale," *American Sociological Review*, 15 (1950), 169-79; Lyndall F. Urwick, "The Manager's Span of Control," *Harvard Business Review*, 34 (1956), 39-97.

cupying these formal statuses the results might be quite different. These two kinds of aggregative measures should be clearly distinguished: those based on actual people and their behavior or beliefs; and those based on written rules or charts, or on the testimony of people who simply assume that the formal rules are followed. The term "formal" in our category of authority structure has a somewhat ambiguous meaning—on the one hand implying what has been formalized in written rules, on the other implying what the participants consider *legitimate*, which may differ from the written rules because of ignorance, differences in interpretation, or because an orally transmitted revision has supplanted the written rules which are now considered "dead" and legitimately ignored. Both of these notions of formal authority are distinct from the question of who holds actual power or influence.

A type of "count" based not on individuals and their relationships but on *integral characteristics* of the formal organization, either indicated in written materials or testified to by participants, is the *number of levels* of authority. More complex characterizations of the formal structure of who can legitimately give orders to whom arise if we consider the possibility that lines of authority may not be simple. The old Taylor notion of having several foremen over each work group, each giving orders within a limited functional area is an example of such a complex authority structure. Such structures can always be represented by matrices with all organization members listed along the two sides, and entries in the cells representing answers to the question, "Does A have the right to give orders to B?" This may be specified both by frequency: "Does he have this power routinely or

only exceptionally?"; and by subject-matter—for example, "on topic X?", "on topic Y?". The Taylor notion assumes that the actions of subordinates can be separated analytically into those relevant to different topics, which are to be controlled by different foremen. A count indicating the *diffuseness* of authority could be made by going through a checklist of the items on which orders can legitimately be given. In a "total institution" the officials can tell their subordinates not only how to do their jobs but what to eat, what to wear, when to go to bed and when to get up, and so on.[79] The notion of "close" versus "general" supervision is measurable in terms of the number of aspects of job activities which are observed and regulated by the superior. A measure indicating the degree to which an organization has a "complex authority structure" as compared with a simple "line organization" could be based on an average of the number of people entitled to give orders to each organization member. In the pure line organization this would be just one; in the "functional" organization it might be several. Unfortunately there are few examples in which actual measurements have been made of these formal organizational characteristics; comparative studies usually limit themselves to qualitative characterizations of them.

A case study of a national health organization informally compared it with other large voluntary associations and suggested that the official decentralization of authority over spending the funds raised was a major factor in maintaining the vitality of the local units and avoiding bureaucratic devia-

---

[79] Erving Goffman, *On the Characteristics of Total Institutions* (Proceedings of Symposium on Preventive and Social Psychiatry, Washington, D.C.: Walter Reed Army Institute of Research, April 1957).

tions from the official goals.[80] More formal measures of the effects of centralization-decentralization have been used in studies of school systems.[81]

A well-known experiment in industrial sociology manipulated the degree of centralization of formal authority in several units within a business firm by changing the rules and giving new training to the first and second-line supervisors. In two offices the supervisors were given training in how to delegate and decentralize; in two similar offices the supervisors were trained to exercise closer supervision over subordinates. Effects were measured both for productivity and for job satisfaction. Over a year's time the more centralized offices had higher production, but lower worker satisfaction.[82]

A series of surveys by the American Association of University Professors has tried to measure the formal authority of the faculty in college and university government.[83] A long checklist of powers and organizational forms was filled out by the informants in each of several hundred colleges; it included such items as whether the faculty was consulted in various appointments and in various budget matters, whether there was an academic senate, whether there was definite plan for exchange of opinion with the trustees, and so on. A crude scale of "faculty self-government" was created by giving numerical weights to various possible answers to each question, and the results were compared for a group of 173 institutions surveyed both in 1939 and 1953 (Table 14).

Such a repeated study of the same units could of course give rise to turnover tables, showing the extent to

TABLE 14   Faculty authority in 173 colleges

Faculty self-government index	DISTRIBUTION OF COLLEGES		
	1939	1953	Change
0-4	38.7%	17.3%	—21.4%
5-9	31.8	32.4	+ .6
10-14	16.8	31.8	+15.0
15-28	12.7	18.5	+ 5.8
Total	100.0%	100.0%	

which there had been both gains and losses, and the extent of gradual versus drastic shift in scale position. By dividing the sample in terms of information on possible causes or conditioners of organizational change, one might be able to trace the influence of such factors on faculty self-government in college. This would have represented the first panel analysis of organizations as subjects.

Influence Structure

By influence structure we mean who actually determines what goes on in an organization; this need not correspond to the formal authority structure. The purest determinant of influence would be to observe whose desires prevail in a series of conflicts. A fairly close approximation of this method is found in a study of eight industrial firms in a midwestern community.[84] The influence of the union was rated by the researchers, on the basis of both formal documents and interviews with participants, within each of 12 problem areas such as hiring and firing, grievance procedures, setting piece rates, efficiency and tech-

---

[80] Sills, *op. cit.,* pp. 44-6, 72-5.
[81] Cillie, *op. cit.*
[82] Nancy Morse and E. Reimer, "The Experimental Change of a Major Organizational Variable," *Journal of Abnormal and Social Psychology,* **52** (1955), 120-29.
[83] American Association of University Professors, "The Place and Function of Faculties in College and University Government," *A.A.U.P. Bulletin,* **41** (1955), 62-81.

[84] Chalmers, *et al., op. cit.*

nical change, and so on. All eight plants were ranked by combining these into a single index of union influence, and the researchers tried (within the limits of their eight cases) to assess the effects of union influence. One highly plausible finding was that union influence correlated −.57 with management satisfaction with labor-management relations, while it correlated +.64 with union leader satisfaction. . . .

If we want to go beyond perceptions and ratings of influence to measure "the thing itself," we enter a very complex area. The basic concept of influence refers to the ability to make things happen in social groups according to our wishes. It is a *causal* concept, and the logic is thus that of an experiment: if A is more influential than B, the following type of observations will be made: when A wants X to occur and B wants Y, then X tends to occur; if A wants Y to occur and B wants X, then Y tends to occur. The *amount* of influence is measured relatively for different individuals or subgroups, by seeing what happens when their wishes are in opposition; the result is a rank-order.

The attempt is sometimes made to treat influence not as a causal concept, which implies a time-dimension, but as a simple *correlation* concept. This has been done in studying influence within legislative bodies.[85] If the individual Senator's vote is highly correlated with the decision of the Senate as a whole, over a series of issues, he is assumed to be influential. However this does not distinguish the influential leader from the perennial bandwagon follower. What would be required is information on each Senator's *initial* position on the issue, to get at the time-order of personal desires and ultimate group decision. Even so we could not distinguish between Senators who actually went around and influenced others, and those who were simply very perceptive as to what the majority would ultimately decide; to compare influence requires *conflict situations* in which the two Senators were initially on opposite sides.

The Lipset study of the printers' union employs objective historical data to support the characterization of that union as highly democratic—that is, as one in which the influence of the members relative to the officers is high.[86]

Among the indicators given are the frequency with which the incumbent administration is turned out of office in elections,[87] and the frequency with which administration-backed referenda on changes in union rules or officers' salaries have been defeated.[88] The implicit comparison is with most other unions where such conflicts have not existed or where the membership does not succeed in defeating the incumbent officers. There is some question to be raised here: granted that there is conflict between administration policies and member interests, the success of the members in defeating the administration is a measure of membership influence. It is, however, conceivable that an administration might so well represent member interests that such conflicts do not arise; the history of duration in office and success in passage of referenda would then look

---

[85] D. MacRae and H. D. Price, "Scale Positions and Power in the Senate," *Behavioral Science*, 4 (1959), 212-18; Robert A. Dahl, "The Concept of Power," *Behavioral Science*, 3 (1957) 201-15.

[86] Seymour Martin Lipset, Martin A. Trow, and James S. Coleman, *Union Democracy* (Glencoe, Ill.: The Free Press, 1956).

[87] *Ibid.*, pp. 4, 46.

[88] *Ibid.*, pp. 53-60.

like that of a thoroughly authoritarian union. One would have to look into the content of administration policies and of member desires or interests to tell whether we had a "satisfied democracy" or a successfully repressive dictatorship. The Stalinist contention that socialist societies need no opposition parties is based on the claim that their governments are guaranteed to produce the former situation.

The measures of influence which we have described are often referred to as measures of power. It seems more useful to restrict the concept of power to one source of influence: control over sanctions. By sanctions we mean rewards and punishments, either formally built into the organization or informally controlled. A wealthy member of an organization may have power based on his ability to give or withhold financial support; a member who holds public office may have power based on his ability to use his official discretion (or to abuse his authority) to reward or punish other members; a prestigeful member may have power based on his ability to give or withhold prestigeful association with himself; an attractive woman may have power based on giving or withholding her favors. Influence is more than power, to the extent that *persuasion* enters in. The member of a group who can present facts or arouse value-laden sentiments in such a way as to influence the other members' own judgments can exert influence without using power.

Communication and Job
Contact Structure

The communication structure of organizations has been studied in various ways, both directly by asking about or observing the flow of information, and indirectly by seeing who has what

information. The study of one hundred local civic organizations found that where the members had more power, the officers rated themselves as more highly informed about the members' wishes, and actually attended more discussion group meetings.[89] A case study of organizational change within a prison observed that increased communications between the rehabilitation staff and the administration led to a change in the power position of the guard staff and of the inmate elite of "fixers."[90]

A quantitative measure of frequency of communications was used in the study of two Air Force wings.[91] Despite the fact that the formal authority structure was identical, it was found that in Wing B the assistant to the director of materials played a major role in the communications structure, while his opposite number in Wing A did not. Communications frequency was measured by work-contact questionnaires and from contact diaries kept by the major executives during a sample week. In the wing where he had a higher communications frequency and scope, this assistant was rated as having considerably more "say about how the wing gets its work done," on a questionnaire of all higher officers. Furthermore, in Wing B the maintenance officers generally occupied a higher position of communications and power. The author's qualitative observations as to the consequences were:

"In Wing A the director of opera-

---

[89] Kahn, Tannenbaum, and Weiss, *op. cit.*
[90] Richard H. McCleery, *Policy Change in Prison Management* (East Lansing: Governmental Research Bureau, Michigan State University, 1957).
[91] James D. Thompson, "Authority and Power in 'Identical' Organizations," *American Journal of Sociology*, **62** (1956), 290-301.

tions dominated maintenance executives . . . . On several occasions he planned major operations on the basis of his own inadequate estimates of maintenance capabilities and later, to the general confusion, was forced to change his plans. The director of material was handicapped, in staff meetings, by the fact that he had to transact business with operations executives without the help of his chief assistant, the maintenance control officer, whose position gave him detailed information about maintenance schedules and capacities . . . .

"In Wing B the directors of operations and material worked more closely together, checking on each other's needs and capacities at several stages of their planning."

In this Air Force study we see the use of both power ratings and direct measures of communications frequency between individuals and status groups, along with a qualitative characterization of effectiveness of output; if more than two cases of "identical" organization had been available, statistical measures of the relationships among these variables could have been used.

The basic form of measures of communication in organizations is that of a who-to-whom matrix. Such a matrix gives us scores of individual frequencies of originating or receiving communications; as in the Air Force study, organizations can then be classified by whether a given status-position or status-group has a high or low communications score. It is also possible to derive indices from the matrix as a whole as well as from its marginal totals. Consider for instance the data in Table 15 which was produced by a hospital study which asked nurses, technicians, and attendants how often they discussed each of eight topics

with members of their own or other hierarchical or functional groups.[92]

Such a matrix sums up numerical estimates made for the researcher by the respondent; it would also be possible to have asked directly about each pair relationship in the organization and then had the researcher do the addition from the raw data. In any case once we have such a matrix we have a measure of the mean communications on the topics covered between any two status groups, as well as within each. Summary measures could be made by comparing within-status to between-status communications; this would tell us how "status-centric" an organization was. We could also compare the separate matrices for each of the eight topics of discussion, and see which were more status-centric than others. These are all examples of what we have called *relational pattern* measurements.

TABLE 15   Amount of discussion between members of hospital status groups

MEAN NUMBER OF TOPICS DISCUSSED WITH GROUP MEMBERS

Groups reporting discussions[a]	Doctors	Nurses	Technicians	Attendants
Nurses	4.5	6.4	5.0	4.5
Technicians	3.5	5.0	6.1	5.2
Attendants	3.2	4.0	5.6	6.1

[a] Question not asked of doctors.

Pace and Stern have developed a 300-item College Characteristics Index by which student or faculty samples can report on various aspects of the college. In their own analysis the items have been classified in terms of Henry Murray's list of personality needs—achievement, aggression, nurturance,

---

[92] Elliot G. Mishler and Asher Tropp, "Status Interaction in a Psychiatric Hospital," *Human Relations*, 9 (1956), 187-203.

play, and so forth. Student needs are to be measured by a personality test (the Activities Index), while the extent to which the college provides resources for meeting these needs is measured by the College Characteristics Index.

It is quite possible however to reclassify the items according to *sociological* categories and construct our own indices from them. For example, in the College Characteristics Index we find several items which ask for respondent ratings of faculty-student contact:[93]

"The professors seem to have little time for conversation with students."

"Faculty members seldom visit informally with students in dormitories or residences."

"Faculty members and administrators will see students only during their regularly scheduled office hours."

"The professors really talk *with* the students, not just *at* them."

From seven such items we can form a crude index of faculty-student contact by adding up the per cent who indicate that there is considerable contact. From Pace and Stern's pretest data on five colleges the following results can be computed using our index (Table 16).

A measure based on an actual count of relational data for all pairs within an organization is what we have termed a relational pattern measure. Where we have measures based on respondent *ratings* of the general level of communications between two status groups as a whole, as in the college study above, we have what might be called "*perceived* relational patterns." The hospital study lies somewhere between

in that each respondent was asked about the frequency of *his own* contact with all members of another status group.

TABLE 16   Faculty-student contact at five colleges

College	MEAN PER CENT PERCEIVING CONTACTS[a]	
	Student respondents	Faculty respondents
Midwestern state college	37$_{100}$	(No data)
Private eastern men's college	50$_{100}$	67$_{20}$
Private university	41$_{68}$	47$_{11}$
Municipal college	23$_{111}$	31$_{15}$
University of Chicago	65$_{44}$	62$_{25}$

[a] Smaller size figures indicate total number of respondents on which percentages are based.

Informal Social Relationships

By informal social relations we mean contacts other than those strictly required by the job—friendly conversations, going out together after work, going out of one's way to help someone else, liking or disliking fellow members. There is a large literature on the effects of informal groups on formal organizations, starting with the Western Electric study.[94] In discussing measures of output we gave the findings of a study of military performance of twelve scout squads as related to their informal "group cohesion."[95] By group cohesion in this study was simply meant the frequency with which members of a six-man squad *chose other members* as desirable partners for a set of nine activities, minus the frequency of rejecting other members as undesirable partners, on a sociometric questionnaire. Questions took the form:

93 Robert C. Pace and George G. Stern, A *Criterion Study of College Environment* (Syracuse: Syracuse University Research Institute, Psychological Research Center, 1958); Robert C. Pace, "Five College Environments," *College Board Review*, 41, 24-8.

94 J. J. Roethlisberger and W. J. Dickson, *Management and the Worker* (Cambridge: Harvard University Press, 1939).
95 Goodacre, *op. cit.*

"If you were going on pass what man (or men) would you *want* to go on pass with and what man (or men) would you *not want* to go with?"

"During an attack what man (or men) would you *choose* to share a foxhole with and what man (or men) would you *not* choose to share a foxhole with?"

Like communications questions, those on informal social relations basically take the form of a who-to-whom matrix, and from these matrices various *relational pattern indices* can be derived. And as before we may skip over the basic relational questions and ask the respondents for various kinds of ratings of their own or their group's *over-all* relationships with others in the organization. Thus members of the League of Women Voters were asked:

"Are there groups or persons with whom you do not associate but with whom you would especially like to be friendly?"

The proportion of members in each local league who report the existence of such "social distance" is negatively related to the effectiveness of the local organization, as rated by outside judges.[96] Another question asked for members' *perceptions* of the existence of cliques:

"Are there any groups of persons who tend to stick together within your [local unit]?"

The locals were characterized by the per cent of members who reported such cliques; this was also negatively related to effectiveness. Furthermore, the proportion of local officers who reported being members of such a group had a still higher negative relation to effectiveness.

Another type of interpersonal relationship measured by member percep-

tions was the degree of conflict within and between various strata of the local unit; surprisingly enough this seemed generally to be positively related to member participation (Table 17).

The application of sociometric methods to studies of colleges was pioneered by Newcomb, who found that the influence of Bennington on its students' attitudes was related to their degree of social integration in the student body.[97] Girls who manifested on entrance the liberal values to which the faculty and dominant students were committed were more likely to become popular; likewise girls who became popular tended to become more liberal. There can be little doubt that the informal social life of a college campus can be powerful in supporting or opposing the activities of the teaching staff.

A general rating of the type of informal social relations present at college can be constructed out of a number of items on the College Characteristics Index.[98] The items include such statements as:

"It's not hard to get into a game of bridge, tennis, golf, and so forth, even for a novice."

"Most of the students form lasting friendships here."

TABLE 17   Correlation of various types of conflict with member activity in 100 local leagues

Type of conflict	Correlation with member activity
Member versus member	.35
Member versus board	.27
Member versus president	.10
Board member versus board member	.13
Board versus president	.13

[97] Theodore M. Newcomb, *Personality and Social Change* (New York: Dryden Press, 1957).

[98] Pace and Stern, *op. cit.*

[96] Kahn, Tannenbaum, and Weiss, *op. cit.*

"Students spend a lot of time at the snack bars, taverns, and in one another's rooms."

"The student who wants privacy and time for personal care has a hard time here."

"A student can be pretty lonely here if he doesn't happen to hit the right social group."

The mean per cent of students answering these questions favorably to high level of social relations was as follows at five colleges (Table 18).

TABLE 18   Index of Social Relations Among Students of Five Colleges

College	Mean per cent of students reporting high level of social relations[a]
Midwestern state college	72%[100]
Private eastern men's college	65[100]
Private university	68[68]
Municipal college	58[111]
University of Chicago	48[44]

[a] Smaller size figures indicate total number of students on which percentage is based.

A study of the printers' union in New York City asked each member a series of questions, both general and specific, about informal social relations within the occupation group:[99]

"How often would you say you spend time with other printers off the job?"

"Do you ever visit any other printers you know in their homes or do any printers ever come to your home?"

"With whom do you actually spend more of your free time—other printers or those outside the trade?"

"Would you think of your three closest friends—it doesn't matter whether or not they are printers. Now, just tell me their first names so we don't get them mixed up. (Asked of

each friend): What is his occupation?"

This set of items was scored to form an index of social relations with other printers. In the study this index was computed only for individuals, since there was no comparative data on other unions. It could be shown that the printers who were more involved in informal social relations in the "occupational community" were more involved in union government,[100] and gained more information about union political issues over the course of the union election campaign.[101] The analysts believed that the amount of informal social relations among printers was considerably higher than that of most other working-class occupations, and that this helped explain the greater participation and institutionalized democracy within the printers' union. An adequate test of this comparative hypothesis would require computing a general measure of informal social relations for the printers and a number of other unions, and relating it to a measure of democracy.[102]

Division of Labor and Departmentalization

The division of labor, like the formal authority structure, can be considered an aspect of the organization's rules or organization chart. The official job specifications, if such exist, can be analyzed, and at least for organizations carrying on similar processes the relative scope of jobs can be measured by the number of activity categories covered by each job. Thus in one automobile plant we might be able to say that the average worker's job covers twice as many activity categories as that of the average worker in another such plant. It has been suggested, on

[99] Lipset, et al., op. cit., p. 437.

[100] Ibid., pp. 72-5, 94-7.
[101] Ibid., pp. 84-9.
[102] Ibid., pp. 425-27.

the basis of industrial morale studies conducted by a large corporation, that too fine a division of labor results both in lowered worker morale and in overstrain on the managers who must coordinate the divided activities.[103] The narrow span of control used in many industrial organizations is said to result from the fine division of labor and the need for continual detailed coordination which follows from that. Unfortunately, the detailed findings of the studies on which these conclusions were based are not published. French industrial sociologists have developed the notion of "job reintegration"; this could be measured not only for individual jobs but for the organization as a whole.[104]

Another formal-rule aspect is the way in which jobs are combined into departments or similar groupings. Organizations may have many specialized "service departments" each dealing with many "line departments"; or they may have "integrated departments", each containing its required service personnel. There has been little research on this topic. Qualitative studies of bureaucratic agencies report that the division of the staff into many specialized departments tends to create a

divergence of interests, attitudes, and policies.[105]

The problem of academic specialization and departmentalizations has been discussed in the literature on "general education" in the colleges. Mayhew and Dressel, in a qualitative study of organizational features which distinguish colleges which had a large influence on student social attitudes from those which had little influence, suggest that the presence of a general education staff with its own identity is important.[106] Where general education courses are taught by representatives of specialized departments, their effectiveness appears to be less. Gusfield, in another qualitative paper, suggests that the problem of staffing general education programs is related to the weakness of general education "departments" as compared with traditional specialized departments in providing job security and professional advancement.[107] . . .

---

[103] Worthy, *op. cit.*

[104] Georges Friedmann, *Ou va le Travail Humain* (Paris, 1950).

[105] Philip Selznick, *TVA and the Grass Roots* (Berkeley: University of California Press, 1953); March and Simon, *op. cit.*, p. 42.

[106] Mayhew and Dressel, *op. cit.*, pp. 345-46.

[107] Joseph R. Gusfield, "General Education as a Career: A Sociological Analysis," *Journal of General Education*, **10** (1957), pp. 37-48.